Hacking Windows® XP

Hacking Windows® XP

Steve Sinchak

WILEY

Wiley Publishing, Inc.

Hacking Windows® XP

Published by
Wiley Publishing, Inc.
10475 Crosspoint Boulevard
Indianapolis, IN 46256
www.wiley.com

Copyright © 2004 by Steve Sinchak

Published by Wiley Publishing, Inc., Indianapolis, Indiana

ISBN: 0-7645-6929-5

Manufactured in the United States of America

10 9 8 7 6 5 4

About the Author

Steve Sinchak is an entrepreneur that has started several technology-related businesses and is currently running a Web development firm known as SSMGi that owns and operates several Web sites. As president of the small company, he is responsible for financial, as well as technical, aspects of the business, such as application programming and infrastructure design and maintenance.

Steve has been working with computers for more than 10 years. Starting with a desktop which had a 286-based processor, 1MB of RAM, and was running DOS & Windows 3.1, he taught himself how to make his computer run faster on the outdated hardware. Driven by curiosity to customize Windows and make it run faster, he spent countless hours researching and experimenting with the inner workings and features of Windows. His primary claim-to-fame in this subject matter is as the creator of TweakXP.com, the number-one site for tweaking Windows XP. What started out as an idea for a new Web site that combined his interest in tweaking Windows and Web programming has grown into a massive database of tweaks and tips for Windows XP that attracts more than 3 million visitors a year.

Currently, Steve is a senior at Marquette University in Milwaukee, WI, studying management IT and computer science. He splits his spare time between classes, running his businesses, and spending time with his family and friends.

Credits

Executive Editor
Chris Webb

Development Editor
Scott Amerman

Production Editor
Gabrielle Nabi

Technical Editors
Greg Guntle
Wiley-Dreamtech India Pvt. Ltd.

Copy Editor
TechBooks

Editorial Manager
Kathryn A. Malm

Vice President & Executive Group Publisher
Richard Swadley

Vice President and Executive Publisher
Bob Ipsen

Vice President and Publisher
Joseph B. Wikert

Executive Editorial Director
Mary Bednarek

Project Coordinator
Erin Smith

Permissions Editor
Laura Moss

Media Development Specialist
Kit Malone

Proofreading and Indexing
TechBooks Production Services

Cover Image
Anthony Bunyan

This book is dedicated to my parents Larry and Mary Jo, my brothers Jason and David, my sisters Jackie and Kimberly, and my girlfriend Emily.

Acknowledgments

Writing this book while juggling classes and my business was often pretty difficult. Almost all of my free time for the last four months has been consumed by writing, leaving very little time for my girlfriend and friends. First, I would like to thank my girlfriend, Emily, for her love, support, understanding, and help when things got really tight. Thank you so much. You mean the world to me.

I'd also like to thank everyone in my family for the love, support, and motivation that they have always shown me. Dad, thanks for bringing home that old IBM AT from work many years ago. Who would have thought it could start something that would lead me to eventually write a book? Mom, thank you for your constant motivation and love throughout all of the challenges in my life.

I'd like to thank my close friends, Paul and Tom. Although they made writing this book very difficult at times, with their constant distractions, I wouldn't want it any other way. Going to Miller Time pub with you two to take breaks from writing was priceless.

Next, I'd like to thank everyone at Wiley for their work on this book. Chris Webb, thanks for giving me this opportunity and for your suggestions in the early stages. Scott Amerman, thank you very much for your help and suggestions with writing the chapters. Thank you for turning me into an author.

Everyone at TweakXP.com also deserves a big thank you—especially Allan Grossman, the forum administrator of the TweakXP.com support forums. Thank you very much for helping me with the site and for turning the forum into one of the best support forums for Windows XP. I would also like to thank all of the forum moderators, news posters, active members, and daily visitors. You have all played an essential role in the success of TweakXP.com. Thank you very much!

Contents at a Glance

Contents

Part III: Securing Your System   277

Chapter 12: Protecting Your Computer from Intruders 279

Chapter 13: Fighting Spam, Spyware, and Viruses 303

Chapter 14: Protecting Your Privacy 315

Introduction

Windows XP is a great operating system. It is faster and more secure than any other version of Windows. However, for some, it is not fast and secure enough. By picking up this book, you have started a three-part journey that will guide you through all of the steps of customizing, optimizing for performance, and securing Windows XP. I am not talking about minor little tweaks; this book is going to show you how to conduct major surgery on your Windows XP box.

Visually, Windows XP is superior to all other Windows versions. No other version of Windows has ever looked this good. So how could you make it look better? Customize it! Impress your friends and refresh your dull desktop with a cool new look. I am going to show you how to completely change the way Windows XP looks during all stages of its operation.

Performance-wise, Windows XP has made great advances. However, for some computer users of older hardware, running Windows XP can be like trying to pull a 100-foot yacht behind a tiny import car. Although Windows XP will not bust your CPU quite so much as a yacht would, it can slow down the operation of your computer because there are so many new features. To help you out, I am going to show you how to get the new features under control; I'll also tell you about some tricks that I have found to speed up the operation of Windows XP. If you already have the V12 4 x 4 of computers, and you have no problem pulling the 100-foot yacht, then you will still benefit from the performance tips.

Windows XP is a lot more secure than prior Windows operating systems. However, as we all know from recent history, it has not been doing very well. This book is going to show you how to use some of the new features of Windows XP Service Pack 2, as well as many other cool security tips, to make Windows XP much securer. Congratulations on starting your journey. Your computer will be in better shape than ever in no time!

About This Book

This book is the result of several years of research into the subject of the Windows operating system. It is a more polished and portable companion to the author's Web site, TweakXP.com, which is located at www.TweakXP.com. Most of the information contained in this book is completely new content that was never before published on TweakXP.com.

This book is meant to be read from start to finish in order. However, it was also written so that it can be used as a reference manual of different hacks. Feel free to skip around if you do not want to take the full journey of customizing, optimizing, and securing Windows XP.

Assumptions

This book is aimed at the intermediate to advanced Windows XP user. If you are a beginner computer user, then this book may not be for you. If you understand the basic operations of Windows XP, then dive right in.

You will need access to a computer running Windows XP Professional or Windows XP Home to perform the hacks listed in this book. Attempting to use the information in this book on any other version of Windows may result in a headache.

How This Book Is Organized

In this book, you will find 14 chapters spread across three parts. Each part covers a different theme, and each chapter is broken down into sections supporting the chapter's topic. The first two parts are laid out in logical operating system event order, such as boot, logon, and interface. The third part is laid out in order of steps.

Part I: Customizing Your Computer

Chapter 1 will start off by customizing the very first part of Windows XP that you see, the boot screen, and will finish up by customizing the logon screen. Then, Chapter 2 will pick up where Chapter 1 left off and will cover how to customize the Start menu and the new Start panel. Chapter 3 will cover customizing your desktop, and Chapter 4 will discuss how to use themes and visual styles as well as how to create your own. To wrap up customizing Windows XP, Chapters 5 and 6 will cover how to customize Windows Explorer and other methods to enhance the Windows Interface using cool special effects.

Part II: Increasing Your Computer's Performance

Chapter 7 will kick off Part II by covering methods that analyze your computer to find possible bottlenecks. Then, Chapter 8 will pick up by speeding up the boot time. Chapter 9 is dedicated to reducing the sign-on time and Chapter 10 will show you how to increase system responsiveness by adjusting many hidden settings. To wrap up Part II, Chapter 11 will cover hacks that speed up the loading time and execution time applications and will also cover how to speed up your network and Internet connection.

Part III: Securing Your Computer

Chapter 12 will mark the beginning of Part III by covering how to protect your computer from intruders. It will show how to analyze your computer's level of vulnerability, as well as how to use firewalls. It also gives you several security tips on how to make Windows XP rock-solid. Chapter 13 will cover how to make Windows XP more secure against SPAM and Spyware and viruses. Finally, Chapter 14 will wrap up *Hacking Windows XP* by discussing ways to protect your privacy by removing recorded user information from various parts of the operating system.

Conventions Used in This Book

In this book, you will find several notification icons—Caution, Tip, and On the CD—that point out important information. Here's what the three types of icons look like:

 Provides valuable information that will help you avoid a disaster.

 A brief tip that will provide help or other useful information.

 Refers you to links, files, and software that are on the companion CD in the back of the book.

Hacking Precautions

Although all of the hacks and tips mentioned in this book have been tested, if a step is accidentally missed or a typo made, your computer could experience severe problems. To make sure that your computer is protected, I highly recommend that you use the Windows XP system restore feature.

Windows XP system restore is a great program that monitors all of the changes to your computer. If you make a change to the system registry as one of the hacks in this book requires you to do, you can always undo the change by reverting to an earlier system restore point. By default, Windows XP creates a restore point once per day. But if you are making a lot of changes to your computer, it is a good idea to create a restore point before every computer modification. The following two sections will show you how to use system restore to create a restore point, and how to restore your computer to an earlier checkpoint.

Creating a System Restore restore point

1. Click the Start button, expand All Programs, Accessories, and System Tools, and select System Restore.

2. When System Restore loads, select Create a Restore Point and click Next.

3. Type in a short description for the checkpoint in the box and click Create.

4. Once the restore point is created, just hit Close.

Restoring your computer to an earlier restore point

1. Click the Start button, expand All Programs, Accessories, and System Tools, and select System Restore.

2. When System Restore loads, select Restore My Computer To An Earlier Time and click Next.

3. Browse through the calendar and select the restore point that you want your computer to revert to and click Next.

4. The Confirm Restore Point Selection screen will be displayed. Click Next to proceed. Keep in mind that you may lose any files that were created when you revert to an earlier restore point. Make backup copies of important documents and files on a floppy or network drive of important documents just in case.

Once you click Next, your computer will reboot and revert to the earlier restore point.

Customizing
Your System

Customizing the Look of the Startup

Windows XP has a great new look, but after a while, the new look can get old. With the help of some cool tools and tricks, you can change many parts of Windows XP.

This chapter will guide you through customizing two parts of your computer, the boot screen and the Welcome/logon screen. You will learn how to replace the boring boot screen with premade screens and even how to make some of your own.

Then, this chapter will move on to customizing the second part of your computer startup, the Welcome/logon screen. This screen can be customized in several ways, such as selecting to use the new Welcome screen or the old Windows 2000 style logon screen. Also, there are a handful of different hacks that will help you customize each screen and make it look even better. Would you like to replace the Welcome screen with a screen you made yourself? You will also learn how to replace the Welcome screen and how to make one of your own.

Customizing the Windows XP Boot Screen

Every time I turn on my computer, I am forced to stare at the boring Windows XP boot screen. Although, I must admit, I found the moving blue bars very amusing at first, after a few months, I became bored and wanted something different. Although changing the boot screen is not a feature that the Windows XP team at Microsoft has built into Windows, doing so is still possible.

Changing the boot screen

The image that is displayed during the boot is hidden away in a system file called `ntoskrnl.exe`. This system file is loaded during the system boot and is what displays the boot image and animation.

When users first started to make their own boot screens, they would use resource hacking tools to hack into the file and replace the old Windows XP bitmap image file with one that they made. Then, they would swap the old system file with the hacked version of the system file so that the new boot screen would be displayed.

The majority of users do not start off by making their own boot screen. Instead, they download one that someone else made from the Web. Unfortunately, the only way to distribute a boot screen is to share the system file that the author has hacked from his or her system. This method of distributing boot screens works for some people, but it may cause serious problems for the majority of users.

The problems of changing the boot screen

If you download a hacked system file with a new boot screen and replace the old file on your computer, after you restart, you may find that your computer will not start and will give you a nice error message. "C:\Windows\System32\ntoskrnl.exe is missing or corrupt." Missing or corrupt? Uh-oh. This is the most common problem that users experience when trying to change their boot screen using the file swap technique.

Users that get this message, or any similar error message, are receiving it because they replaced their system file with a file that is not compatible with their version of Windows XP.

Windows XP was released in many different languages for different parts of the world. Each language version of XP has a slightly different version of code. Additionally, Microsoft continuously releases software update patches to update the code of the system files such as the monthly security updates and almost yearly service packs. All of these factors result in several different versions of the boot screen system file floating around on the Web.

You could find a boot screen file that was made from a hacked system file from the German version of Windows XP. Or more commonly, you could find a boot screen that was made from a hacked file from the original version of Windows XP. When you try to install that boot screen on a computer that, for example, has Service Pack 2 installed on the English version of XP, you will have problems.

Windows XP will only work with a specific version of the system file that contains the boot screen. This arrangement complicates the change of the boot screen with the common file swap technique. It will do so because users will have difficulty telling on what version of Windows XP a particular boot screen that is distributed on the Web will work.

Users have to be aware of more than just the version problem. Because you are downloading a hacked version of a critical system file that is executed during the boot sequence, you could possibly download a version that someone modified and in which he or she put some variation of malicious code that could harm your computer. Read the next section to find out how to change your boot screen safely.

How to safely change your boot screen

Check out the following ways to change your boot screen by using special tools that will allow you to do it safely.

Several different boot-screen-changing programs are available on the Web. Some of these programs are shareware and others are freeware. I have used them all. Not all of them have been user-friendly, and some of them have been an out-and-out pain. The one I prefer to use is BootSkin by Stardock, which also happens to be free. This program is by far the easiest and safest one to use to change the boot screen. Instead of replacing the system file, it just installs a special driver that skins the boot. This arrangement does not impact system performance and is a nice alternative to having to deal with system files.

 You can get a copy of this cool app from the companion CD in the Chapter 1 folder or on the Web at www.bootskin.com.

The BootSkin app is a great piece of software, but it does not do everything. Currently, it does not allow you to use the thousands of boot screens already made that are posted all over the Web. It will only allow you to run boot screens that were made especially for the program. True, hundreds of boot screens are available for this application, but *thousands* of hacked system files are out there.

Because of this limitation, I have decided to show you all how to convert these hacked system file boot screens into safe BootSkin files. But first, let's get started using the app.

Using BootSkin to change your boot screen

Once you have the BootSkin application installed, start it up by using the link in the Start menu under WinCustomize and perform the following steps:

1. Once you have the application running, changing the boot screen is very simple. Just navigate through the list of boot screens by using the scrollbar arrows, as shown in Figure 1-1.

2. Once you find the boot screen that you like, click the item and then click the Preview button to see a full-screen animated preview of what the boot screen will look like.

3. Click a button on the mouse again to exit the full-screen preview. If you like the boot screen, then click the Apply button. That's it!

Once you reboot, your new boot screen will be displayed every time. If you would like to change your boot screen back to the default Windows XP boot screen, reopen the BootSkin program and select the default system boot screen from the top of the list; click Apply.

Where to get more boot screens for BootSkin

Want more boot screens that will work with BootSkin? The following are two sites where you can find more skins that are already compatible with the program.

- **Win Customize:** www.wincustomize.com/skins.asp?library=32
- **Skinbase:** www.skinbase.org/section.php?sections=BootSkin

FIGURE **1-1: Stardock's BootSkin browsing through the available screens installed on the computer. This figure includes some boot screens that were downloaded and installed as shown in the next section.**

Another advantage of using the Bootskin app, besides the safety it provides, is the small size of the skin files. Instead of having to download a hacked system file that can be quite large, BootSkin files are a fraction of that size.

Once you have downloaded the boot screens that ...you want, Just... double-click them and they should automatically be loaded into the BootSkin program and be available for selection if the file has the .bootskin file extension. If that is not the case, then you will have to do a little work to get the file into the right format. Some boot skins that you will find from other sites such as Skinbase could be in a ZIP archive. A BootSkin file is just a ZIP archive that was renamed. To make ZIP archive skins work, just rename the .zip to .BootSkin and you will be able to import the skin by double-clicking the file. Once you have clicked the BootSkin file, it should show up in the list and you will be able to select it as your boot screen.

How to convert boot screens to work with BootSkin

Because BootSkin will only allow you to use boot screens that are in the BootSkin format, if you would like to use all of the boot screens that are floating around the Web, you will need to convert them into the BootSkin format. Doing so will involve a lot of steps, but after a short while you will be flying through them in no time.

First, I recommend that you browse around the Web and download some boot screens. Following is a list of a few good sites from which to get boot screens:

- *ThemeXP*: `www.themexp.org/view.php?type=boot`
- *Belchfire*: `www.belchfire.net/showgallery-8.html`
- *XP Theme*: `www.xptheme.info/resources_view.cfm/hurl/restype_id=4/`
- *EZ Skins*: `www.ezskins.com/product.phtml?xpBootScreens`

Make sure that when you download the screens you save them all in one place. I made a folder on my desktop called Boot Screens in which to store mine.

Now that you have some boot screens downloaded on your computer, you are ready to start converting them to use with BootSkin. Follow these steps to get started:

1. First, extract the image files from the boot files you downloaded. You could do this with a resource hacking tool, but then you would have to worry about converting the image with an image editing program with the special boot color palette; this is just not the easiest way. Instead, I recommend you use a program that was originally designed to change the boot screens to extract the image files. It is a free application called LogonUI & Boot Randomizer by User XP.

You can copy this file from the Chapter 1 folder on the companion CD. Or, you can download a copy of LogonUI & Boot Randomizer from `www.belchfire.net/~userxp/indexlbr.htm`.

This app is loaded with features, but you will only need the image extraction feature.

The LogonUI & Boot Randomizer application has the capability to change the boot screen with any existing hacked system file boot screen. However, I do not recommend you use it for that purpose because of problems that I have experienced using the program and because I do not like the fact that it patches the kernel system file. Because of that, every time you apply a new system update that modifies your kernel system file, you will have to download a new version of the application so that it will work with the new kernel file and will not automatically revert your system file to the older version.

2. Now that you have the file for the app extracted and ready to use, launch the app by double-clicking `LogonUIBootRandomizer.exe`. The first time you run this application, it will want you to set it up so that it can change your boot screen. If you see the multiboot screen, click OK, as that is your only option. Then when the NTFS Detected screen, as shown in Figure 1-2, appears, click the Close button.

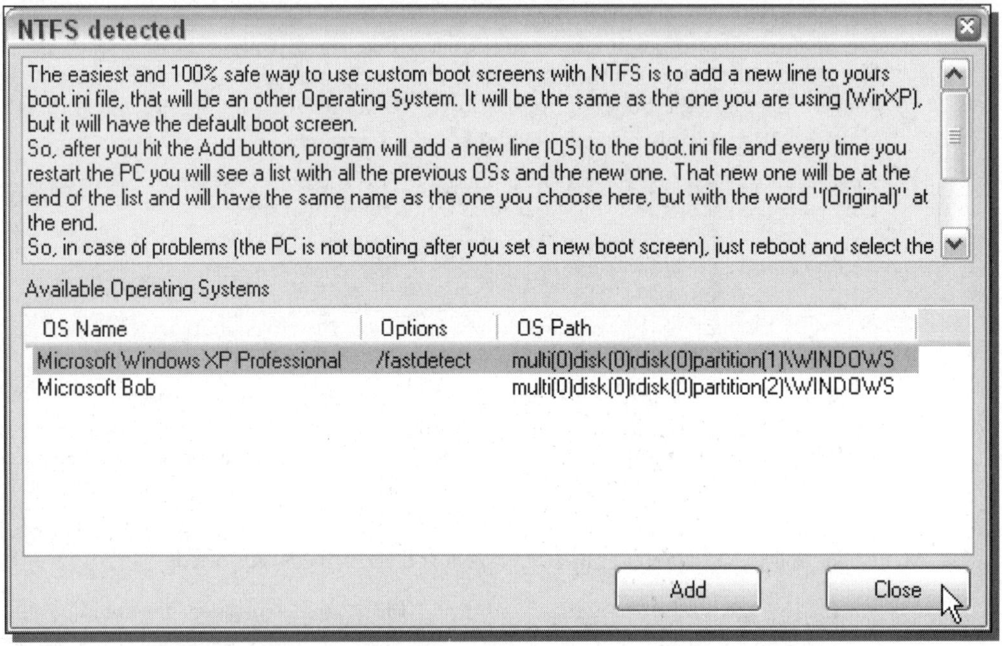

NTFS detected

The easiest and 100% safe way to use custom boot screens with NTFS is to add a new line to yours boot.ini file, that will be an other Operating System. It will be the same as the one you are using (WinXP), but it will have the default boot screen.
So, after you hit the Add button, program will add a new line (OS) to the boot.ini file and every time you restart the PC you will see a list with all the previous OSs and the new one. That new one will be at the end of the list and will have the same name as the one you choose here, but with the word "(Original)" at the end.
So, in case of problems (the PC is not booting after you set a new boot screen), just reboot and select the

Available Operating Systems

OS Name	Options	OS Path
Microsoft Windows XP Professional	/fastdetect	multi(0)disk(0)rdisk(0)partition(1)\WINDOWS
Microsoft Bob		multi(0)disk(0)rdisk(0)partition(2)\WINDOWS

Add   Close

FIGURE 1-2: LogonUI NTFS Detected screen, which asks you to add another line to the boot.ini file so that your system will be set up for LogonUI to change your boot screens.

Tip   If you get an error the first time that you run LogonUI saying that the comctl32.ocx component cannot be found, download this file from the following URL, or any other site, and put it in the same folder as your application: www.belchfire.net/~userxp/comctl32.zip

3. Next, you may be prompted with a third configuration screen if you are running Windows XP Service Pack 1. The screen will say that it has detected Service Pack 1 installed and wants to know if you want LogonUI to work with older (nonService Pack 1) boot skins. Click Yes on this screen. When the application has started up, you are going to see the final configuration screen asking you where the folders on your computer are for your boot screens. This step is important, as you will need to specify the folder on your computer to where you download all of the boot screens. Click the three dotted button on the right of the text boxes (. . .) to specify the path easily. Click OK, when you are done. You are now finished with the LogonUI app.

4. If you still see the configuration screen, click OK once more. Now you should see a list of your boot screens in the upper-left window. Click one of the screens to see a preview, as shown in Figure 1-3. If you receive a message asking if you want it to locate the progress bar automatically, click OK, wait a few seconds, and you will then see a preview.

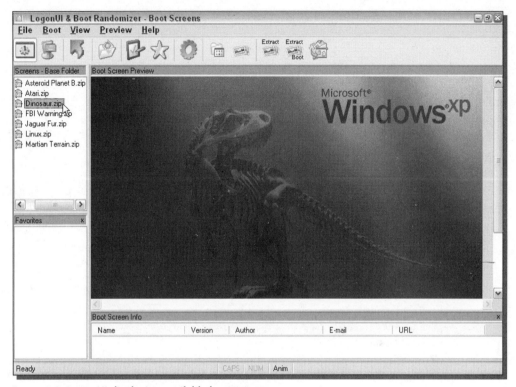

FIGURE **1-3: LogonUI displaying available boot screens.**

5. Select the boot screen from the list that you want to convert so that it shows up in the preview area. Then, right-click the Preview of the boot screen, and select See Bitmaps in File, as shown in Figure 1-4.

6. The background of your screen will go gray and you will see some numbers in it. Each of the numbers in the box represents an image file stored in this system file. Click number 1, and you will see a preview of the image. Then click the Save button and the Save Picture dialog box will show up, as shown in Figure 1-5.

7. At this point, you will want to change the file format to a bitmap. This can be done by clicking the Format drop-down box and selecting .bmp from the list because Stardock's BootSkin app can only read bmp files.

8. Next, you should change the location and name of the file to a new folder named after the name of the boot skin so that identifying and finding the image file will be easier later. It is best to place this folder inside of a master boot skins folder such as my boot screens folder I mentioned earlier to keep things organized and simplify the conversion process. You can do so by clicking the button with three dots on the bottom of the dialog box. Once you get the file name and folder set, click the Save button.

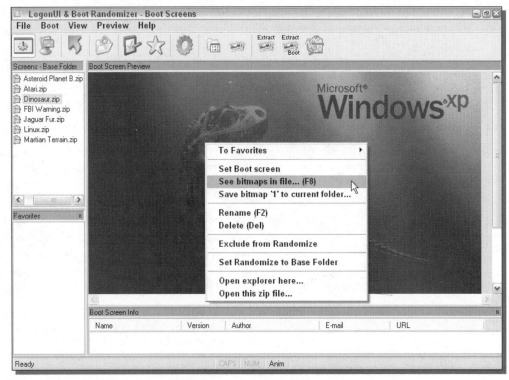

FIGURE 1-4: LogonUI See Bitmaps in File pop-up menu.

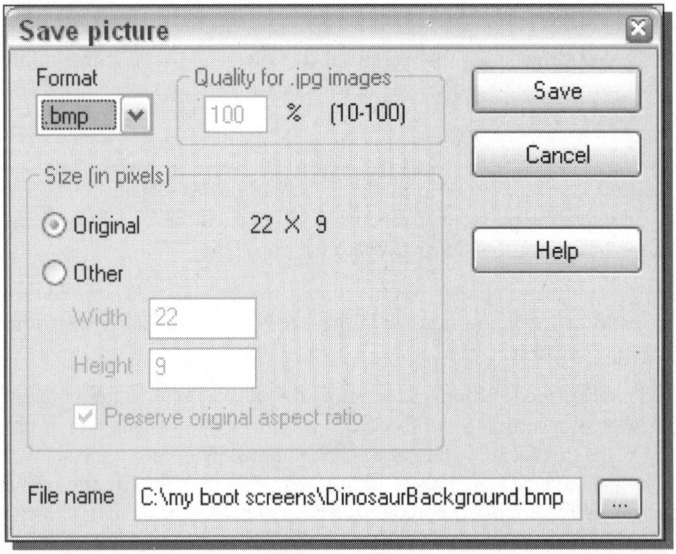

FIGURE 1-5: Save Picture dialog box.

9. Now, you are almost finished with the extraction portion of converting the boot screen. If the boot screen that you are converting also has a progress bar (the active bar moving left to right on the screen), then you have to do one more step. (If the boot screen does not have a progress bar, skip to the next step.) After you have clicked the Save button in the last step, return to the screen that shows all of the different numbers for the different bitmaps stored inside the file. The progress bar is stored in bitmap number 4. Select the number 4 item from the list and click the Save button. Then repeat step 8 to save the bitmap file.

10. You are now finished with the LogonUI app portion of the conversion and are getting close to completion. The next step is to create a BootSkin configuration file. The format of the configuration file is simple, as shown in Figure 1-6.

 A copy of a configuration file called BootSkin.ini is in the Chapter 1 folder on the companion CD-ROM at the back of the book. I recommend that you use this file as a guide when making your own configuration file.

Open up a copy of Notepad from the Accessories menu in the Start panel to create your own configuration file. The first line of the file should contain [BootSkin] to indicate that this is a configuration file to the BootSkin application. Type in **Type=0** in the

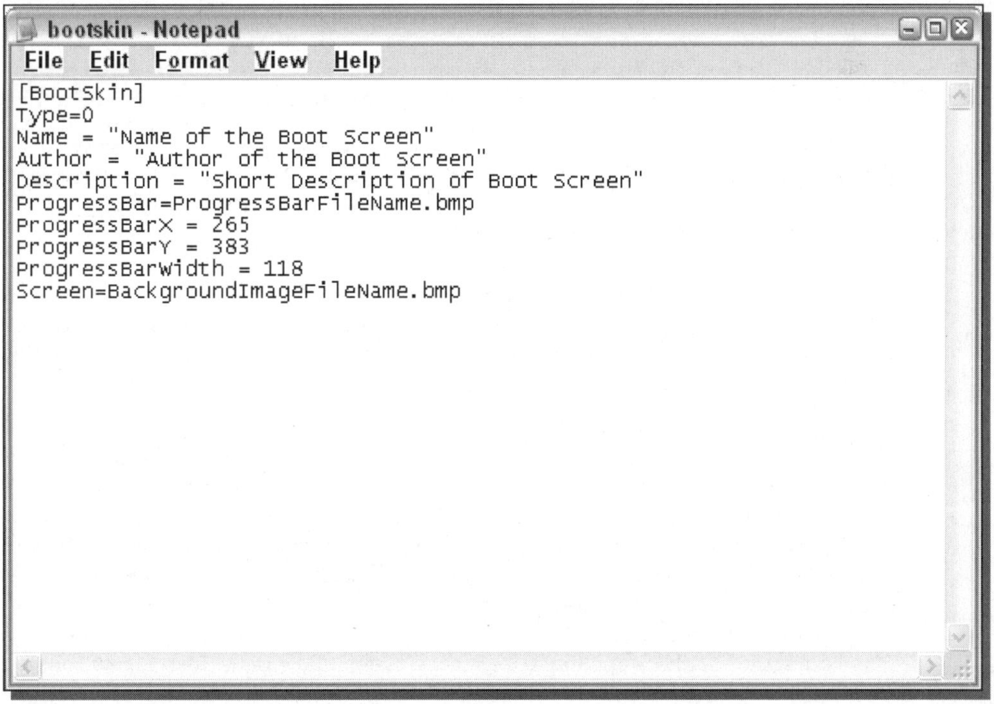

```
bootskin - Notepad
File  Edit  Format  View  Help
[BootSkin]
Type=0
Name = "Name of the Boot Screen"
Author = "Author of the Boot Screen"
Description = "Short Description of Boot Screen"
ProgressBar=ProgressBarFileName.bmp
ProgressBarX = 265
ProgressBarY = 383
ProgressBarWidth = 118
Screen=BackgroundImageFileName.bmp
```

FIGURE 1-6: A BootSkin boot screen configuration file.

second line to tell BootSkin what type of screen this is. Next, you will need to include some identification information in the file. Type **Name="Name of your screen"** on the next line. Do the same for author and description, as shown in Figure 1-6. Now you will have to specify which bitmaps you want to use for the progress bar. Type in **ProgressBar=ImageName.bmp.** Next, you will have to specify where the progress bar will be displayed because BootSkin makes it possible to display the progress bar anywhere on the screen. The location of the progress bar will be determined by the coordinates that you enter in the configuration file. Type in **ProgressX=265** and **ProgressY=383** on the next two lines. Feel free to replace 265 and 383 with any numbers you like. Keep in mind that the resolution of the boot screen is 640 × 480, which limits the maximum x value to 640 and the y value to 480. The width/length of the progress bar must also be specified. Type in **ProgressBarWidth=118** to do this. If the boot screen that you are converting does not have a progress bar, then just omit the four lines involving the progress bar. The last part of the configuration file is where you specify what you want the background image to be. Type in **Screen=BackgroundImage.bmp** to set this. When you are finished typing in all of the configuration data, save the configuration file in the folder that you named and extracted all of the bitmaps to in step 8.

11. The last step of the process is to copy your newly created files to the BootSkin skin directory. If you installed BootSkin to the default location, it is located at c:\Program Files\Stardock\WinCustomize\BootSkin\skins\. Create a new folder in this directory that is the same as the name that you entered in the configuration file in the last step. Then, copy the two image files (one if you have no progress bar) and the bootskin.ini file to this folder. The next time you start up BootSkin, you should see your new boot screen.

Although performing these steps might seem (and be) a little time-consuming at first, once you have converted a boot screen, any conversions thereafter should take you a minute or less.

As mentioned previously, the process I just described to change your boot screen is the safest possible way to do so. You will not have to get caught up in the mess of looking for compatible boot screens for your version of Windows and you also will not be limited to any number of available boot screens if you use my conversion tips.

Making your own boot screens for BootSkin

Now that you know how to convert boot screens, making your own boot screen will be a snap. The most difficult part of the process would be creating your image file. To get started, you first need to know the basics.

If you have not already noticed, boot screens are a 640 × 480 resolution image. These images are limited to only 16 colors (4 bits). This limitation makes the ability to create a cool-looking screen a little difficult. The help of a nice graphics converter utility makes the image look much better when you have to convert it to only 16 colors. A good utility that I use is the free version of Stardock's Skin Studio. This is a program that was designed to make Visual styles for their Windows Blinds application, but it also has a good graphics converter that was made especially for BootSkin within it. Download a copy of this utility from www.stardock.com/products/skinstudio/downloads.asp. Once you have it downloaded and installed, you can start the application from the Object Desktop folder in the Start menu. Follow these steps to convert your images:

1. The first time that you run Stardock's SkinStudio, you will be greeted with a registration screen. If you do not want to register, just click the Register Later option and the program will load. Now that you have Stardock's SkinStudio started, you will want to click the Close button on the Welcome screen that asks you what you want to do, because what you want to do is not listed there.

2. Next, click the Tools menu bar item and expand BootSkin and then select Prepare Image.

3. This will bring up the Boot Screen Image Prepare window. Click the Browse button and select the image that you want to convert on your computer.

4. Then, you will see a preview of your image converted by a method known as dithering. This process allows the image to look better by using the same technique that newspapers use to print color and photographs on paper. Most newspapers are printed with only three colors. Dithering makes it possible for the massive newspaper presses to print an image that appears to include thousands of colors from only three basic colors. How is this possible? It is all a trick with your eyes. All images in a newspaper are made up of thousands of tiny dots. Each of the dots is one of the three printing colors. The placement of the dots and combination of one or more colors is what gives the illusion of color. For example, if you want to print something in a color such as orange, then print a grid of red and yellow dots next to each other. There are various methods to dither the image built-in so that you can play around and see which one makes your image look best using the drop-down box next to the dither image check box, as shown in Figure 1-7.

5. Once you have the image looking the best that you can get it, just click the Save button and you are set!

If you do not want to use the boot screen preparer and do not know how to use Adobe Photoshop or any other robust image editor, I suggest you visit the Belchfire.net Web site that automatically converts and resizes background photos for you: http://server1.belch fire.net/Inno_Resize/. Just click the Browse button and select your image file, then click the Convert button, and sit back for a few minutes and your converted image should come up eventually. I have found that the site does not work well with files other than bitmaps, so it might be a good idea to convert your image to a bitmap first and then let the converter resize the image and decrease the colors automatically.

If you would like to make your computer's boot screen more attractive and alive, an animated progress bar is for you. To add a moving progress bar to your boot screen, just make a bitmap image that is saved in 16 colors that has a resolution of 22 x 9 pixels . Don't worry about trying to animate it; that small image will be moved around automatically by the program displaying the screen.

Once you have your image files in 16 colors and at the right sizes, just create a new folder in the BootSkin skin folder (C:\Program Files\Stardock\WinCustomize\BootSkin\ skins) and copy in your image files. Then create a quick bootskin.ini file for your boot screen from the sample file in the Chapter 1 folder on the companion CD and you are finished.

Load up BootSkin to preview your new skin and, if it looks good, you are ready to roll. If you reboot to see your new boot screen in action and you notice that the boot screen does not show

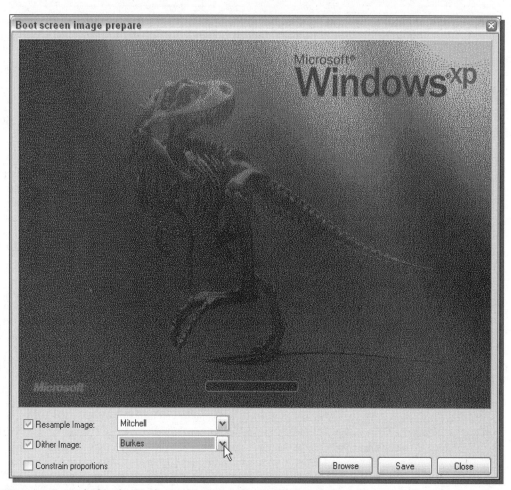

FIGURE **1-7**: Stardock's Skin Studio Boot image preparer, showing the dithering methods available to make your image look its best when converted to 16 colors.

up correctly or at all, the problem may be caused by the bitmap file being in a format other than 16-colors/4-bit options available. Make sure that your file is converted correctly and is saved in only 16 colors. With the correct configurations in place, everything should work properly.

Customizing the Logon Screen

Windows XP has introduced a great new way to log on to your computer, known as the Welcome screen. The new Welcome screen provides a refined method to log on compared to the old boring Windows 2000 logon screen. Not only does the new screen look good, but users can now see all of the users set up on the machine and can easily log on by clicking the user's name.

This Welcome screen has provided a nice alternative to the old logon method, but some people just don't like change and want the old logon method back. If you are one of the users that wants to say goodbye to the Welcome screen, then this section will not only help you get it back, but it also will show you some neat tricks to make it a little more visually appealing. If you thought the new logon screen is cool, you will love this next section about making the Welcome screen even cooler.

Working with the Welcome screen

The Welcome screen is one of the most versatile parts of the whole operating system. It is possible to customize the heck out of this screen. You can completely change the way it looks, the locations of all of the buttons and images, and much more. You can even restrict what is displayed on it. The Welcome screen is great for users that want to customize their boxes.

Changing a users icon on the Welcome screen

Each user that is set up on your computer can associate an image that appears next to his or her name on the Welcome screen, as shown in Figure 1-8. By default, Windows will randomly

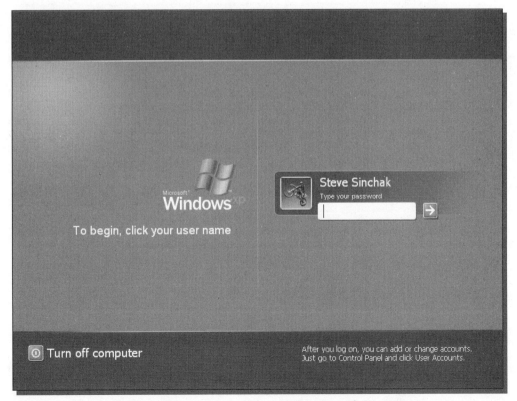

FIGURE 1-8: The new Windows Welcome screen with an image next to the user's name.

select an image for you, but this selection can easily be changed. If you do not like the images that Windows has to offer, you can select any other image.

The process of changing a user's image is very simple. Just perform the following steps and you will have it changed in no time:

1. Open up the user manager by clicking the Start menu and selecting Run. Then type in **nusrmgr.cpl** and click OK. This is a shortcut to User Accounts that will save you time going to Control Panel and then clicking the User Accounts icon.

2. This will start up the New User Accounts Manager. To change a user's picture, just click the user name.

3. Then, click Change My Picture text and you will see a screen with all of the different images that are built into Windows XP.

4. If you see one you like, just select it by clicking it and then click the Change Picture button. If you do not like any of them, click the Browse for More Pictures option, as shown in Figure 1-9.

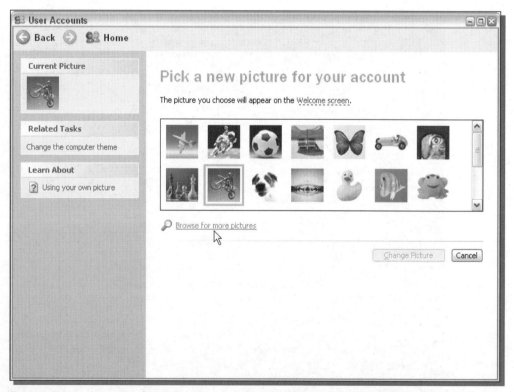

FIGURE 1-9: User Accounts' change image screen showing the option to select additional images for a user's picture.

5. This will pop up a Browse dialog box. Browse though your files and select the image that you want to use, and click Open. Any image that you select will automatically be resized to fit. If you want to make a image that will take up all of the space, the correct aspect ratio is 1 to 1, as the size of the square that is displayed is 48 × 48 pixels.

Now you have changed a user's Welcome screen image and also the image that is displayed in that user's Start panel.

Removing a user from the Welcome screen

One of the unfortunate side effects of the Welcome screen is the listing of all of the user accounts on the computer. What if there is an account that you do not want the whole world to see? Using the same feature that Microsoft uses to hide system accounts from the Welcome screen, you can hide user accounts as well.

Hiding user accounts can be done by a simple hack in the registry. Hidden away in the local system settings is a list of accounts that Microsoft does not want to appear on the Welcome screen. These accounts are primarily system accounts under which different processes that run in the background use to execute.

To hide a user from the Welcome screen, all you have to do is create an entry on the list for the user you want to hide. Follow these steps to find out how to add a user to the list:

1. Click the Start button and select Run, then type **regedit** in the box and click OK.

2. This will start up the system Registry Editor. You are going to want to expand the following keys: HKEY_LOCAL_MACHINE, SOFTWARE, Microsoft, Windows NT, CurrentVersion, Winlogon, SpecialAccounts, and UserList.

3. You should now see the list of the account names, and parts of account names, that the system will look for and will hide. To add a name to the list, just right-click and select New ⇒ DWORD value, as shown in Figure 1-10. A DWORD is a specific data type of an entry in the system registry. In short, the DWORD data type allows an integer value to be stored.

4. When the new key is created, enter in the name of the user's account as the name of the key. Once you have done this, you can close regedit.

After log off and back on or reboot, the user will not be displayed on the Welcome screen. If you ever want to log into the account that you hid from the Welcome screen, just press Ctrl+Alt+Delete on your keyboard once, twice, and you will be able to type in the name of the user under which you want to log in. This way, you can hide an account from your family or friends but can still log into it.

If you ever change your mind and want the account to be displayed on the Welcome screen again, just delete the entry that you made in the list in the System Registry and everything will be back the way it was.

Changing the Welcome screen

The new blue Welcome screen looks great, but after a while, a change would be nice. Also, modifying the Welcome screen is another way you can customize your computer and make it

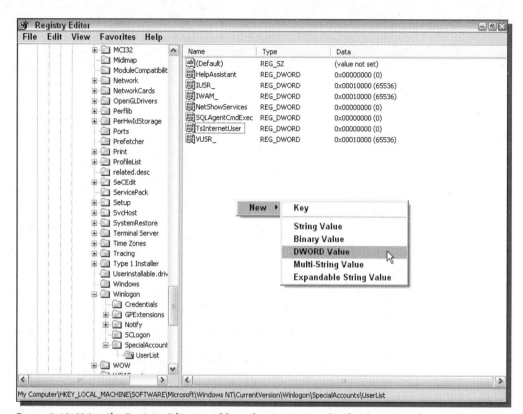

FIGURE 1-10: Using the Registry Editor to add another DWORD value for the name of a user that will be hidden on the Welcome screen.

more unique. You can change the Welcome screen by two different methods using different tools. As with the methods to change the boot screens, there are different advantages to each.

The first way to change the Welcome screen will be a manual approach that may not be the easiest method available but will allow you to use any of the thousands of hacked logon screens on the Web. The other method will be much easier, but it will be limited to only using Welcome screens that were made especially for the program.

Manually changing the Welcome screen

Changing the Welcome screen manually is not as complicated as you would think. A value in the registry needs to be changed to point to the Welcome screen you want to use. Once you do that, you are finished.

To get started, you are going to want to download a few Welcome screens (also referred to as logon screens) from the Web. The following are two sites from which you can download thousands of Welcome screens:

■ *ThemeXP*: www.themexp.org/cat_login.php

■ *Belchfire*: www.belchfire.net/showgallery-6.html

Visit both of these sites and download some different logon screens and then experiment with them. When selecting a boot screen, you need to find one that will look good with your screen's current resolution. If you have a very large monitor (19-inch and greater) and are using a large resolution (1280 × 1024 or greater), you may have difficulty finding Welcome screens that were made for your computer's high resolution. If you are an owner of a large monitor or resolution, the only workaround or solution to the problem would be to create a logon screen of your own or write the author of the screen asking them to release a version for your specific resolution. Additionally, you will need to make sure the Welcome screens are compatible with your computer's operating system version.

Just like the hacked system files for the boot screens, these Welcome screens are just another hacked system file, so you still have to watch out for version conflicts. Although if you accidentally downloaded a Welcome screen that is the wrong version, then you will have a far less serious problem than if you downloaded the wrong version of a boot screen.

You will find that a lot of the Welcome screens that you download do not have a version marked. To find what version you are selecting, just extract the ZIP file or self extracting archive, right-click it, and select Properties. Doing so will bring up the properties, and you will be able to see the version. If the version says 6.0.2600.0, then you have a Welcome screen file from the very first version of XP. On a computer with Windows XP Service Pack 1 installed, the logonui.exe file has a version number of 6.0.2800.1106. If the version is not similar to 6.0.2XXX.X then you may not have downloaded a valid file. In theory, if you replace a file with an earlier version, you might run into some problems.

I replaced my newer Service Pack 1 Welcome screen with a Welcome screen that was made with a system file from the original version of Windows. I did not experience any problems, but I cannot guarantee that if you do the same you also will be problem-free. Also, security fixes or other enhancements might appear in the later version of the code, so if you replace the latest code with old code, you might be missing out on important updates. Experiment with caution and be aware of the risks.

Now that you know what to watch out for, you are ready to start replacing the Welcome screen manually. To do so, follow these steps:

1. Click the Start button and select Run. Then type **regedit** in the box and click the OK button. This will start up the Registry Editor.

2. Expand HKEY_LOCAL_MACHINE, SOFTWARE, Microsoft, Windows NT, CurrentVersion, and lastly Winlogon. Now you will see several different values on the right side of the screen for many different logon properties. The property that we are interested in is named UIHost.

3. The UIHost property specifies the path to the Welcome screen that will be loaded and displayed. Right-click UIHost from the list and select Modify, as shown in Figure 1-11.

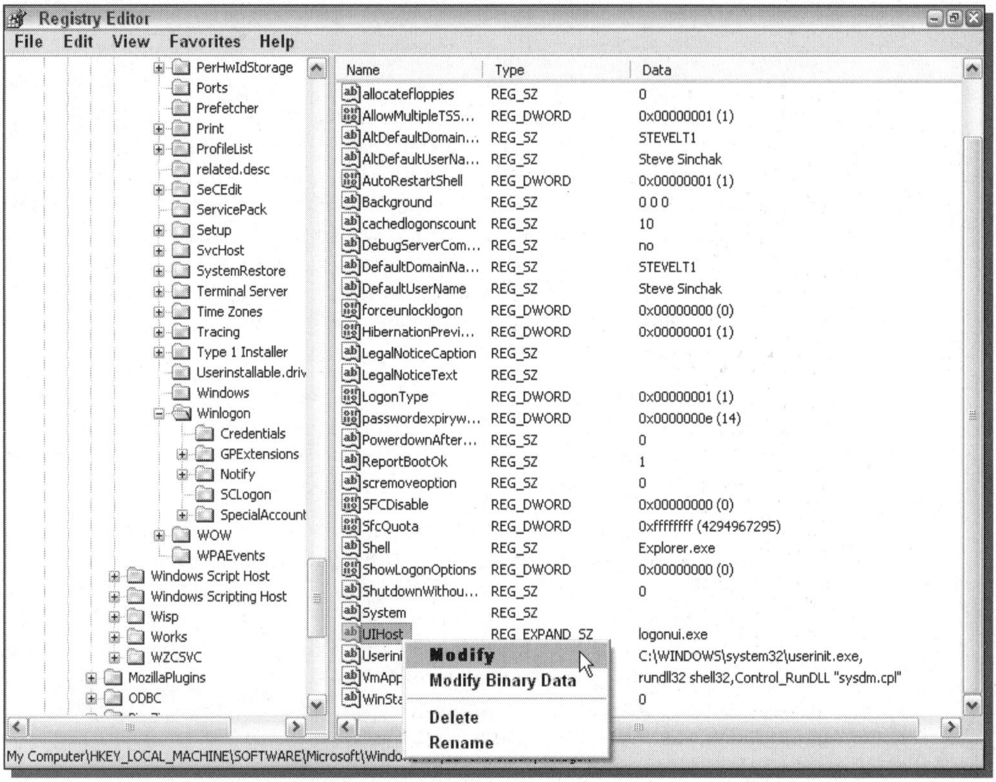

FIGURE 1-11: Registry Editor modifying the UIHost property.

4. Next, just type in the full path to the `logonui.exe` file or whatever you named your new Welcome screen. One thing to keep in mind: avoid storing your Welcome screens in a directory path that has spaces in the names of the directories. I suggest you create a folder on your hard drive called WelcomeScreens. So you will be changing the value of UIHost to `C:\WelcomeScreens\CoolNewLogonUI.exe`.

5. Once you make the change, it will go into effect immediately. If you click the Windows key+L at the same time, this will lock your computer and will bring up the new Welcome screen.

If you ever want to revert to the default Windows XP Welcome screen, just change the UIHost property back to `logonui.exe`. (You may have to change the C to the correct drive letter on which you installed Windows.)

On the CD   To make this process faster, I have included an undo file on the companion CD called `welcome_undo.reg` that will automatically revert to the default Welcome screen.

There must be a better way to change your screen than doing it manually, right? Well, yes and no. A few programs are available on the Web that will automate the editing of the system registry. One of the most popular programs is called Logon Loader, by Daniel Milner. Logon Loader allows you to easily change the Welcome screen by only clicking a few buttons.

Using LogonStudio to change the Welcome screen

LogonStudio is a software app that was developed by Stardock. This application is similar to the BootSkin application, discussed previously, in that it does not modify the system files. Although this method is very simple to use, the Welcome screens must be designed to work with LogonStudio. This is not a big deal, because there are hundreds of Welcome screens that people already made for this program, but users will find that they will not be able to use any of the thousands of Welcome screens made from hacked system files. Depending on what Welcome screen you like, you may or may not be able to use it with this program.

Although you have to give up a little flexibility in the screens that you can use, you will have added safety and ease of use. Because you will not be working with hacked system files, you don't have to worry about getting the correct version and the possible problems that running an older version could cause. Also, using LogonStudio is very easy. You can change your Welcome screen with just a few clicks.

To get started, you will need to download a copy of LogonStudio at Stardock's Web site: `www.stardock.com/products/logonstudio/download.html`. Once you have the app downloaded and installed, most likely you will want to download a cool Welcome screen to use with it. You can download hundreds of Welcome screens from the following sites:

- *WinCustomize*: `www.wincustomize.com/skins.asp?library=26`
- *SkinPlanet*: `www.skinplant.com/library.cfm?lib=5`
- *DeviantArt*: `skins.deviantart.com/windows/xplogon/`
- *Skinbase*: `www.skinbase.org/section.php?sections=logonstudio`

Once you have downloaded a few screens, you can install them by just double-clicking them if they have a `.logonxp` file extension, which will open them up. If the files that you download do not have a `.logonxp` file extension and instead just have a `.zip` file extension, rename the files to `.logonxp` so that you can easily import them into LogonStudio. LogonStudio will then be started automatically and will display the new Welcome screen in the preview box, as shown in Figure 1-12, when the files are double-clicked.

If for some reason the Welcome screen that you download does not have a `.logonxp` file extension, and is just a `.zip` file with a folder containing several bitmap image and configuration files, you can still install the Welcome screen. If you have a Welcome screen that fits that description, then you will just have to manually copy the folder with the Welcome screen files to the LogonStudio folder that is normally located at `C:\ProgramFiles\WinCustomize\LogonStudio`.

FIGURE 1-12: LogonStudio showing new Welcome screen installed.

Tip

When you browse to the LogonStudio folder, you will notice that each Welcome screen has its own folder with the files for the Welcome screen inside. If you ever want to delete a Welcome screen, just delete the folder with the corresponding name.

Changing the Welcome screen with LogonStudio is very easy to do. Just click the name of the screen from the available logons list. A preview will show up in the preview box, and if you like it, click Apply or OK and you are finished.

Depending on your computer setup, you may experience problems when using some Welcome screens with monitors that are set at a large resolution. If you experience a problem like this with a specific Welcome screen, you are out of luck. Try finding a different version of the Welcome screen that was made for higher resolutions. This can be very difficult because resolution data is usually not posted with the Welcome screens.

Tip

If you ever want to revert to the original system Welcome screen, just click the Restore Default XP Logon button and it will uninstall the LogonStudio app and prevent it from taking over the Welcome screen. You will also have to do this if you are using LogonStudio to display a Welcome screen and then want to use a hacked system file Welcome screen. First, you will have to start up

LogonStudio and click the Restore Default button, and then you can edit the registry to point to the new Welcome screen. If you do not click the Restore button in LogonStudio, then you will never see your new hacked system file because LogonStudio will still be active and will automatically replace it.

Creating your own Welcome screen from a hacked system file

When users first started to change their Welcome screen, they used the same approach that was used with the boot screens. Resource-hacking tools such as Resource Hacker were used to replace the bitmaps that are stored inside the `logonui.exe` file. Then, they would adjust the string values within the file with the same tool to change the layout of the screen. Although there are now apps that were built to make Welcome screens easier, I still believe that the best way to create a Welcome screen by hacking your system file is to use Resource Hacker. I have had problems with other tools that attempt to automate the process of hacking the system file resources because the programs will usually only work with one version of the system file. If you have a newer system file than the program was designed to work with, then you won't see the Welcome screen.

As I stated earlier, the best way to create a Welcome screen from a hacked system file is to do it manually using a cool app called Resource Hacker (www.users.on.net/johnson/resourcehacker), written by Angus Johnson. This method will allow you the greatest amount of flexibility because you are not limited to the features of a Welcome screen editor. Although this method is a little complex, it is the best way to create a high-quality and unique Welcome screen.

I am going to show you the basics of how to get started, but I am not going to go into great detail on all of the great things that you can do because there are just too many. Instead, at the end, I will tell you about some great Web sites that I use as references when I want to make a Welcome screen from scratch.

1. The first step is to make a copy of your `logonui.exe` file. This file can be found in the System32 directory inside the Windows directory. The exact path is usually `C:\WINDOWS\system32`. Copy the file to a new folder, maybe your Welcomescreen folder. Also, feel free to rename the file at this time. You can name it anything you want, because when you want to install it, you just have to enter the path and the file name in the registry as you did above when installing a custom hacked system file Welcome screen.

2. Next, you can start editing the bitmaps in the file. To do this, I recommend using Resource Hacker. You can download a copy of Resource Hacker by visiting www.users.on.net/johnson/resourcehacker. Once you get a copy up and running, open up the `logonui` file that you just copied. You can do this by clicking the file menu bar item and selecting the file from your drive.

3. Once the file loads in Resource Hacker, you will see an interface similar to Windows Explorer. You will have four folders: UIFILE, Bitmap, String Table, and Version Info. To get started, expand the Bitmap folder. You will then see several more folders that are numbered. Every numbered folder contains a different image. Expand the numbered folder for a preview of the image that is stored inside it.

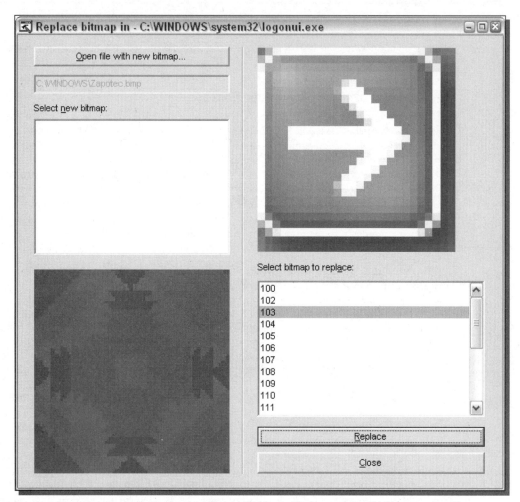

FIGURE **1-13: Using Resource Hacker to replace bitmaps in the logonui.exe Welcome screen file.**

4. Now let's assume that you want to extract one image out of Resource Hacker so that you can modify it using your favorite paint program and then replace the old image with your modified one. To extract an image, make sure that the image you want is selected and displayed in the preview pane and then click the Actions item from the menu and select Save [Bitmap : XXX : XXXX], where the X's are numbers. Once you have an image modified, or if you want to completely replace an existing image, click the Action menu bar item again. Select Replace Bitmap. This will bring up a new screen that will list all of the bitmaps in the file. Click the Open File With New Bitmap button and select the image you want to import. Make sure it is a Windows Bitmap file, as JPEGs and GIFs will not work! Next, scroll through the list, as shown in Figure 1-13, and select the image that you want to replace. Click the Replace button and you are finished.

5. Once you get all of the bitmap images swapped out with ones you made yourself, you can move on to editing some of the strings in the string table folder. This is where all of the font names and text that appear on the Welcome screen is stored. You can edit the text just like using a text editor. Just be careful that you do not accidentally delete a quote from the ends of the strings. Also, do not change the index numbers or you will run into problems. Once you are finished editing a specific string table, just click the Compile Script button and you are finished with the strings.

6. The next part allows you to be really creative but it also can be really complex. The UIFILE folder stores all of the detailed configuration information for the screen. Items such as transparency levels and font sizes are stored here. When you first view the UIFILE 1033 resource, you may not see anything at all. Just scroll down and you will begin to see the script. Just like the string table, when you are finished editing it, click the Compile Script button.

7. The last step is to save your changes to the file by clicking the File menu bar item again and just click Save. Now, you can edit the registry to test out your new screen.

It will probably take you a little while to finally get the screen the way you want it. One site that I use as a reference is called Windows XP Logon Screen Secrets, written by Paul Andrews, which is located at `webpages.charter.net/joolsie/LogonScreens.htm`. This is a great site that will tell you all of the details on how to modify the UIFILE so that you can get the most out of your Welcome screen.

Creating a Welcome screen with LogonStudio

LogonStudio is not only a great program to change your Welcome screen with, but it also is a good program to create it with too. If you do not want to waste a few hours manually perfecting your Welcome screen and do not desire the flexibility the manual approach offers, then using LogonStudio is the app for you.

Creating a Welcome screen with LogonStudio is very simple. Also, you can easily edit Welcome screens that you downloaded by clicking the Edit button from within LogonStudio when you have selected a screen. However, some of the screens will not be able to be edited because significant changes have been made to Logon Studio recently that make some of the earlier Welcome screens incompatible with the editor.

To create a new Welcome screen from scratch, follow these steps:

1. First, if LogonStudio is not already started, start it up from the Start menu's All Programs menu in the WinCustomize folder. Once it is started, click the New button, as shown in Figure 1-14. This will bring up a new window that will ask you for details on the new Welcome screen, such as the name and the author's information. Fill it out, and then click the Create button.

2. Next, the editor will show up and you will see what looks like the default Windows XP Welcome screen. The best way to get started is to just start playing around with different features. When working in the editor, there are two different ways to select an item to work on. You can just click most items, but if you want to get to an item faster, or an item that you cannot click, use the Elements browser. Using the editor is a lot like

FIGURE **1-14: Using LogonStudio to create a new Welcome screen**

programming in Microsoft's Visual Basic. When you click an element, you will see a list of properties appear in the Properties browser.

3. For example, let's assume that you want to change the background color. To do this, you can click the blue background, or you can select the Center Panel from the Elements browser. Once the Center Panel is selected, you will see several properties appear in the Property browser. The ones that you will be interested in working with to change the background color are `Firstcolor` and `Lastcolor`. To change the color, just click the color boxes in the Property browser and select a new color, as shown in Figure 1-15.

4. Working with images is also very easy with the editor. If you want to set a photo or an image you made as the background for the Welcome screen, you can just select the [Bitmap] property of the picture properties item from the Center Panel element browser. Once you select your bitmap and it is displayed, you may want to change how it is displayed such as if it is a pattern and you want it titled or if you want it stretched across the screen. To do that, just click the Style properties drop-down box and select the style you want.

5. Replacing the images for the different buttons is also very easy. Just use your mouse to select the image that you want to change, and then one property, called [Bitmap], will

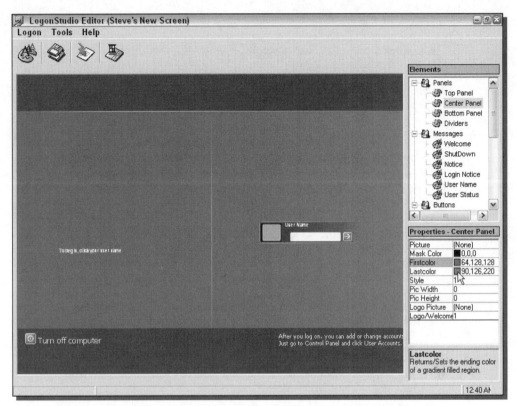

FIGURE 1-15: LogonStudio Editor showing how to change the color.

appear in the Properties browser. Just click the three dotted icon in the Properties browser. A new dialog box will pop up, giving you the option to edit or browse. If you click Edit, the image will open up in MS Paint for you to edit it. If you already have a new image that you want to use, then just click Browse and select the replacement.

Tip   When you are creating graphics for your Welcome screen and want parts of the image to be transparent, such as the background around a button you made, just paint the background with the light pink color (Red: 255, Green: 0, Blue: 255). This is the default color for transparency in Windows.

6. You will not always want some elements in the Welcome screen. For example, you probably won't want the dividers that appear in the center of the screen and the dividers at the top and bottom sections. These dividers are just images. One easy way to get rid of them is to click the center divider line to bring up the Dividers property browser, then just click the three dotted icons and uncheck the Use Picture box when the dialog box pops up.

7. Editing the text of the Welcome screen is just like editing the text in any word processing program. Just click the text, and you will see all of the properties in the Property browser for the font, size, and color. You can even change what the text says by modifying the Caption property.

8. The area that displays the users account, known as the User Account element, may take the most time to get it looking the way you want. Dozens of different properties are in this area, one of which specifies the location of the user's accounts on the Welcome screen. This property is called the Account property. It shows a number that signifies a region on the screen. Click the button to the right of the number and you will get a visual map of the different locations. Select a location by clicking it. Another type of property in this section is the Alpha properties, which has three subproperties. These have to do with how visible the accounts are at different stages. 0 is not visible at all and 255 is completely visible. The Alpha Mouse subproperty is used to adjust the Alpha levels when the mouse is hovering over the name block. Alpha Selected is when the user has clicked the name and Alpha Normal is when the name has not been selected and the mouse is not hovering over it. BackColor is the name of another property in the section as well, which sets the background color for the account. When using this part of the editor, I discovered a small bug in the preview window. For some reason, the preview does not show the back color of the user's account. Instead, it just displays the blue gradation bitmap from the default Welcome screen. Don't worry too much about this bug, because it is only in the preview screen and will not affect your Welcome screen when it is in use. Once you change the color, the color change is saved, just not displayed.

9. You now know about all of the different parts of the editor and the basics of how to make a good-looking Welcome screen. Once you are finished, click the Save button (the two disks) and you are finished. If you want to save and view the Welcome screen at the same time, click the Logon menu bar item and select Save and Apply.

You now know the ins and outs of creating your own Welcome screen using LogonStudio. I personally use the method to create and manage my Welcome screens. It is just easier than using the resource hacker and I can live without the added flexibility that the resource hacker provides.

LogonStudio also has a feature that allows you to import hacked system file Welcome screens that you used in the first section on changing the Welcome screen. Although this feature makes it a little easier to convert the Welcome screen to the new format by extracting the images, usually the layout and all of the strings are messed up and require adjustment. If you have a lot of free time, try experimenting with this feature. I have not yet been able to get it to work 100 percent of the time.

Working with the classic logon screen

The classic logon screen, also known as the Windows 2000 style screen, has many benefits over the new Welcome screen for some users. Users that are concerned about the security of their system often do not want a list of all of the user's accounts to be displayed when they turn on the computer.

In corporate environments, the classic logon screen provides the capability to log into domains (Windows network security servers), although the Welcome screen does not have this capability. Additionally, some people just do not like change that much and they do not like the new Welcome screen. Also, if you are a minimalist and like to keep things simple and uncluttered, you may like the classic logon screen better because it is very simple and only takes up a small amount of your screen.

This next section is dedicated to showing you how to turn on the classic logon screen as well as customize it a bit.

Switching to classic logon

The classic logon can always be reached on the Welcome screen by pressing Ctrl+Alt+Delete two times. If you want to completely get rid of the Welcome screen, doing so is very simple. Before you disable the Welcome screen, you should also be aware that doing so will disable Fast User Switching. Fast User Switching gives you the ability to switch between accounts on your computer without having to log out of one account to log on to another. Most users never use this feature, so having it disabled will not change anything. Follow these steps to kill the new Welcome screen:

1. Click the Start menu and select Run. Then type **nusrmgr.cpl** in the box and click OK. This will start up the User Accounts control panel applet.

2. Once you see the User Accounts app, click Change The Way Users Log On Or Off. Then, uncheck the box next to Use The Welcome Screen, as shown in Figure 1-16, and click Apply Options.

3. Now, you will no longer see the Welcome screen.

If you ever want to use the Welcome screen again, just go back into the User Accounts control panel applet and check the box for the Use The Welcome Screen.

Now that you have the classic logon screen activated, there are a few things that you can do to make it look a little better and unique.

Changing the logon screen background color as well as the visual style and color scheme of the logon screen are all examples of ways you can hack the classic logon screen to make it unique.

Changing the Logon Background

Ever want to change the background color of the classic logon screen from light blue to some new color? Windows makes this difficult, because there are no options anywhere in graphical user interfaces of Windows to change it. However, with the help of the Registry Editor, you can easily change the color of the logon screen. To get started, follow these steps:

1. First, you will want to start up the Registry Editor by clicking the Start menu and selecting Run. Then type **regedit** in the box and click OK.

2. Once the Registry Editor starts up, you will want to expand HKEY_USERS, .DEFAULT, Control Panel, and then Colors.

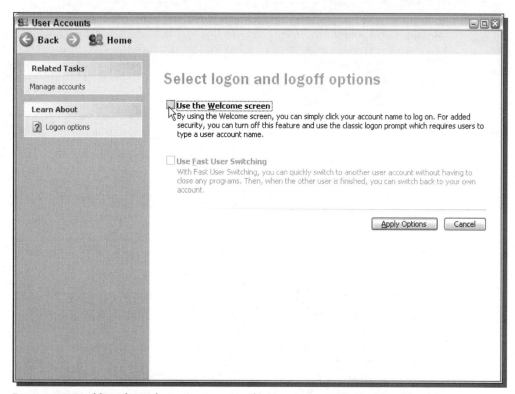

FIGURE **1-16: Disabling the Welcome screen using the User Accounts Control Panel applet.**

3. Once you have expanded the Colors key, you will see all of the different default user settings. These are all of the settings that are used on the logon screen. The entry that you will be interested in is called Background. You will notice that the background entry has a value that contains three different numbers. Each of these numbers represents a different color makeup in the RGB color format. The first number is red, the second is green, and the third is blue. The numbers can range from 0 to 255. A RGB Value of "255 255 255" is white; "0 0 0" is black. Changing the color is not as simple as replacing the numbers with the word red; first you have to convert the color that you want to use to the correct RGB numbers.

Tip

An easy way to convert a color to a RGB number value is to use Microsoft Paint, which can be found in the Start menu under Accessories. Once you have Paint up and running, double-click one of the colors in the color palette; this will bring up the Edit Colors window. Next, click the Define Custom Colors button. This will expand the window and will show you the Red, Green, and Blue values for any color you select. Click the boxes in the Basic Colors section to see their RGB values or if you do not see a color you like, use your mouse to click around on the color image to the right to get a custom color. Once you have found a color you like, just write down the number of Red, Green, and Blue. These values can be found in the lower-right corner of the screen.

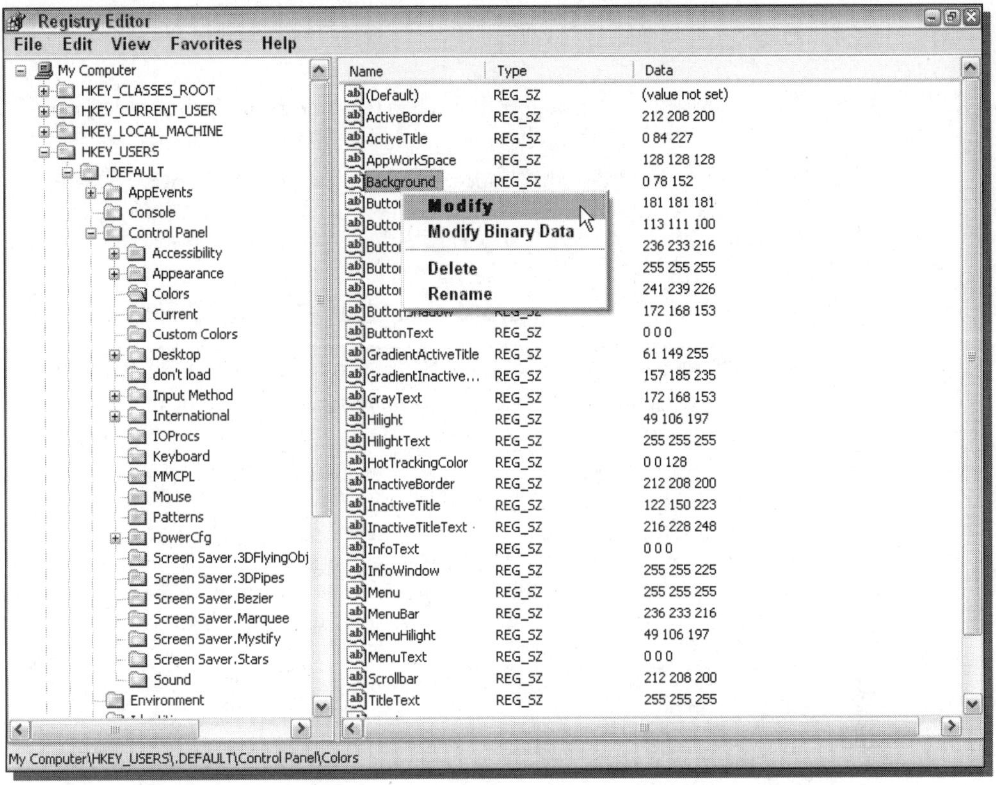

FIGURE 1-17: Changing the background color of the logon screen with the system Registry Editor.

4. When you have found the color that you want to use as the background and have also converted it to the Red, Green, and Blue format, you are ready to edit the entry. Right-click the entry, as shown in Figure 1-17, and select Modify.

5. In the Edit String box, replace the numbers so that the first number is the number of red, followed by a space. Then, repeat that format for the other two colors so that your entry looks something like this entry for orange, "255 128 0". Click OK when you are finished to save the change.

Once you change the color, the next time you reboot and the classic logon screen is displayed, you will see your new background color.

If you ever want to revert your computer back to the default blue color, repeat the steps above to change the color and set the value of the background entry to "0 78 152".

Setting a background image for the logon screen

If you do not want to change the color of the screen, perhaps you have an image that you would like to set as the background to appear behind the logon window. Once again, the only way to set this is to use the Registry Editor to hack the default user settings which are displayed on the logon screen. To get started, follow these steps:

1. Click the Start menu and select Run. Then type **regedit** in the box and click OK. This will start up the Registry Editor.

2. Once the Registry Editor has loaded, you will want to expand HKEY_USERS, .DEFAULT, Control Panel, and the Desktop key. Next, you should see all of the different entries for desktop properties. The entries that you will be interested in are Wallpaper and WallpaperStyle.

3. Right-click the Wallpaper entry and select Modify. Then type in the full path to the image that you want to use on your computer. Let's assume that you want to set the nice grassy hills photo as your background. This file is located at `C:\WINDOWS\Web\Wallpaper`. The name of the file is `bliss.bmp`. Therefore, the full path of the image file is `C:\WINDOWS\Web\Wallpaper\bliss.bmp`.

4. Once you have the path to the file set, you can click the OK button to save the change. Now you can change the WallpaperStyle entry if you want to change how the wallpaper will be displayed. You have three different options: 0 = centered, 1 = tiled, 2 = stretched to full screen. If you want to change the way it is displayed, just right-click the WallpaperStyle entry and select Modify, then enter the corresponding number value for the style you want to use. Click OK to save, and you are finished!

Now you have worked with customizing the look of the background, let's move on to changing the way the sign-in box looks.

Changing the visual style and color scheme

Changing the visual style and color scheme can greatly increase the visual appeal of the classic logon screen. Instead of using the default blue Windows XP style on the screen, you can specify any style that is installed on your computer as well as the different color schemes that some styles have. This hack works great in combination with setting a background image. You can create a nice clean look that still looks good without using the Welcome screen.

To get started, you will be using the Registry Editor again. Also, before you can change the visual style, you should be aware that you will need to apply a patch to your system so that you can run Visual styles that other people have made for Windows XP. More on this in Chapter 4, where you will find out where to get Visual styles from and how to install them. Just be aware that you will not be able to change the visual style of the classic logon window until you have read Chapter 4. If you attempt to change it now, on an unpatched system, you will run into problems. However, if you just want to change the color scheme of the default Windows XP style, then you will have no problems right now at all. Now that I have warned you about the possible problems you may encounter, let's get started:

1. Click the Start menu and select Run. Then type **regedit** in the box and click OK.

2. Once the Registry Editor is open, navigate through HKEY_USERS, .DEFAULT, Software, Microsoft, Windows, CurrentVersion, and ThemeManager. You will now see all of the theme properties for the logon screen. The two entries that you will be working

with are ColorName and DllName. ColorName specifies the color scheme of the current visual style that is specified in the DllName property.

3. First, let's change the color scheme of the default Windows XP style. You have three different choices for the ColorName value: NormalColor (default blue look), Metallic (silver), Homestead (olive green look). To change this property, just right-click it and select Modify. Then change the value to the corresponding value for the color scheme you want to use, such as Homestead, as shown in Figure 1-18. For example, if you want to use the olive green look on the classic logon screen, you will want to set the ColorName value to Homestead.

4. If you want to change the visual style of the classic logon screen, and have already read Chapter 4 and have patched your computer, then you will want to edit the DllName property. Right-click it and select Modify. Then, type in the path to the visual style you want to use. The path for the default Windows XP style is `%SystemRoot%\Resources\themes\Luna\Luna.msstyles`. The `%SystemRoot%` in the path is just an environment variable that the system interprets as `C:\Windows` or whatever folder where you

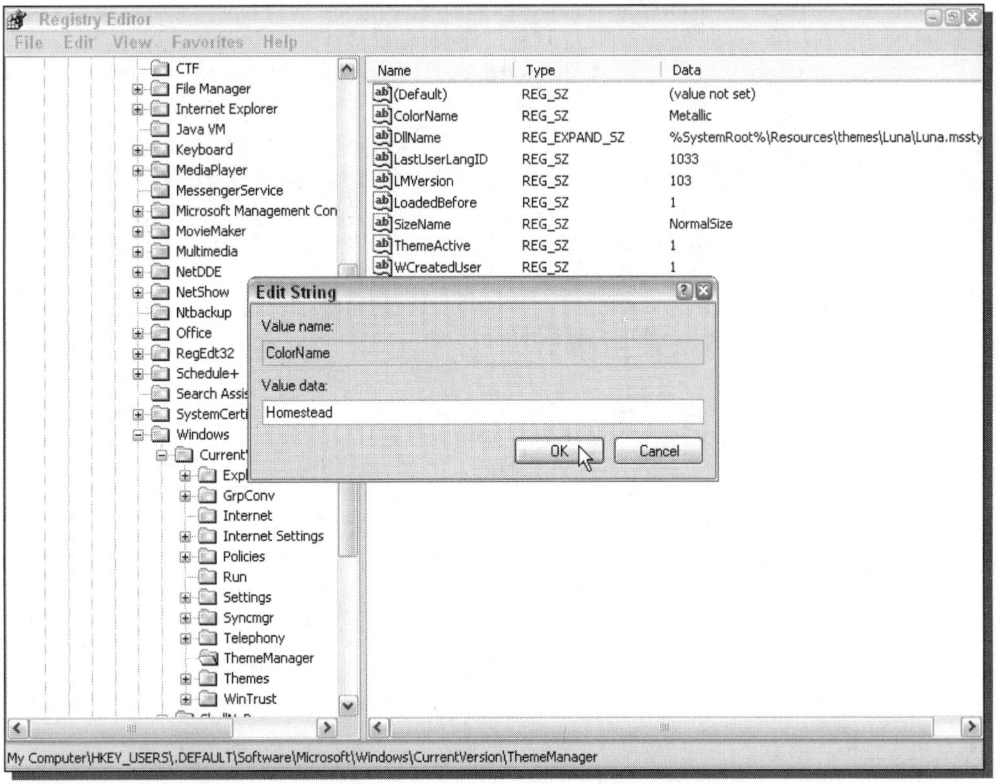

FIGURE 1-18: Modifying the color scheme of the default Windows XP visual style with the Registry Editor.

installed XP. Once you have the new path entered that points to the visual style that you downloaded or made, click OK to save your changes.

5. When you have changed the visual style, you will also have to update the `ColorName` property to reflect the names of the different color schemes within the visual style. By default, you should set this property to `NormalColor` for most Visual styles. Once you have completed this, you are finished!

Once you reboot or log out, you will see the changes that you made. If you are having display problems after you install a new visual style, make sure that you have properly patched your computer. Remember, you have to patch your computer, not just install a program like Style XP. Refer to Chapter 4 for much more information on Visual styles.

Clearing the last user logged on

Every time a user logs into your computer, their username is stored, and that name is displayed the next time the classic logon screen is displayed. This can be a nice feature, but it also can be a feature that causes a security problem. Knowing a user's username is half the battle of breaking into a computer. If you have sensitive information on your computer, I suggest that you follow these instructions to hide the last user logged on:

1. Start up the Registry Editor again by clicking the Start menu and selecting Run. Then type **regedit** in the box and click OK.

2. Navigate through HKEY_LOCAL_MACHINE, SOFTWARE, Microsoft, Windows, CurrentVersion, policies, and system. Locate the DontDisplayLastUserName entry.

3. Right-click the entry and select Modify. Then type in a 1 to activate the feature, as shown in Figure 1-19. Click OK, and you are finished.

If you ever want to reverse this hack, just repeat the instructions above and replace the **1** with a **0** for the value of DontDisplayLastUserName.

Global logon/Welcome settings

A few hacks can modify the system logon for users of both the Welcome screen and the classic logon interface. These features can improve the quality of the screens, turn on different key-locks, and fine-tune other settings such as the screensaver.

Turn on clear type

Users of flat-panel LCD monitors as well as users of laptops can take advantage of a cool new feature in Windows XP called ClearType. This new technology is an advanced version of the font-smoothing technologies that existed in previous Windows versions. When this new font-smoothing technology is turned on, the entire screen will look significantly better.

Normally, this feature is only available after a user logs into the computer, but with the help of a cool registry hack, you can enable this feature to start up before a user logs in. Follow these steps to get started:

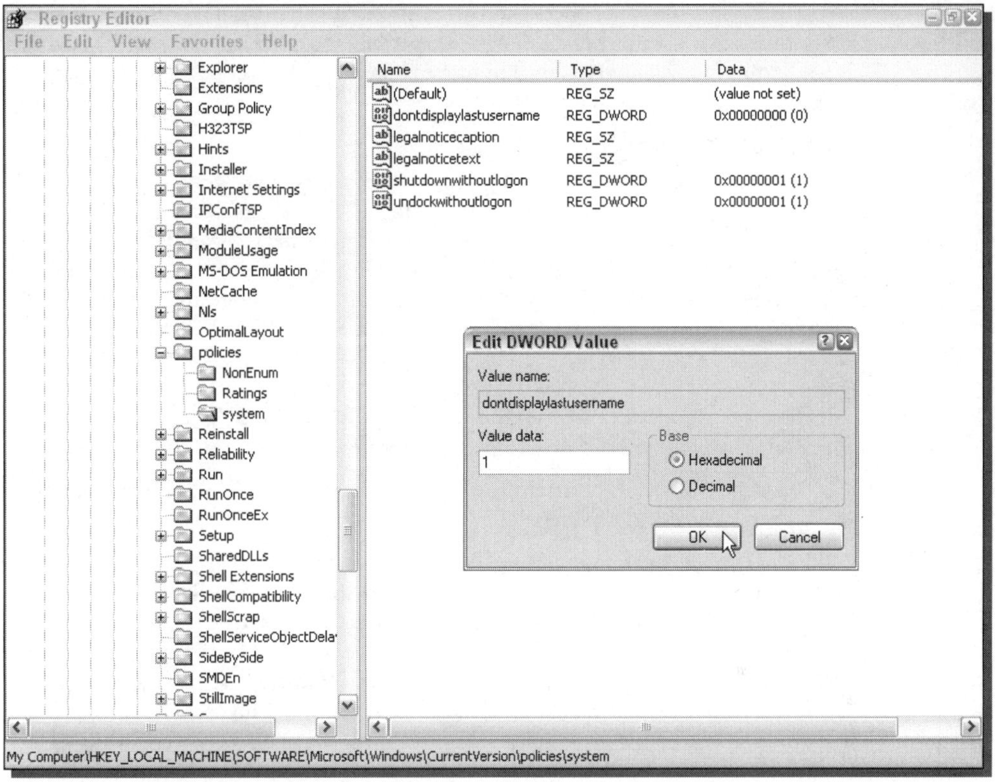

FIGURE 1-19: Making the computer clear the last user that logged on using the Registry Editor editing the DontDisplayLastUserName entry.

1. Start up the Registry Editor by clicking the Start menu and selecting Run. Then type **regedit** in the box and click OK.

2. Once Registry Editor starts up, navigate through HKEY_USERS, .DEFAULT, Control Panel, and Desktop.

3. Locate the ForegroundFlashCount entry and right-click it and select Modify. There are three different options for the value of this property. 0 indicates that font smoothing will be disabled, 1 indicates to use standard font smoothing, and 2 indicates to use ClearType font smoothing.

4. Replace the value of the property with 2 to enable ClearType and then click OK to save the change.

That's it—you are finished. You will notice that your logon screen is now much smoother than before. Some users do not like this new smooth look, so if you are one of those that miss the extra-crispy look, repeat the preceding instructions but replace the 2 with a 1 to set it back to the default settings.

Users of CRT monitors (the once-standard cathode ray tube-based monitors) can attempt to use this tweak, but ClearType was designed especially for LCD monitors, so if you are using a CRT monitor, you will not see much improvement, if any. But it doesn't hurt to try!

Working with the screensaver

If you do not sign on to your computer after a specific amount of time, it will turn on the screensaver. Changing the screensaver and modifying its settings is not as easy as changing the screensaver that is displayed when you are already logged on. You can not change the screensaver of the Logon/Welcome screen from within Display properties as you would normally change a screensaver. The only way to edit these settings is through registry hacks. Follow these steps to change the screensaver as well as the inactivity time before the screensaver is activated:

1. First, you will need to start up the Registry Editor. Click the Start button and select Run. Then type **regedit** in the box and click OK.

2. Once the Registry Editor starts up, navigate through HKEY_USERS, .DEFAULT, Control Panel, and Desktop.

3. First, change the amount of time the system waits after the last activity detected before starting the screensaver. To do this, right-click the ScreenSaveTimeOut entry and select Modify. The amount of time to wait is stored in seconds. By default, the system will wait 600 seconds (10 minutes) before starting up the screensaver. If you want to change this value to something shorter, such as 1 minute, then just enter in a new value, which for one minute would be 60. Next, click OK to save your changes.

4. Next, change the screensaver that is displayed. By default, the boring flat Windows XP logo screensaver is displayed. Try something a little more exciting, such as the 3D flying Windows logo. To change the screensaver that is displayed, you will want to modify the SCRNSAVE.EXE entry. Right-click this entry and select Modify. You will want to change the value of logon.scr to reflect the name of the file for the screensaver that you want to use that is located in the C:\Windows\System32 directory. Because I did not know the name of the file for the 3D Windows XP screensaver, I had to do a search for all of the files on my computer that had a .scr extension by using the search feature in the Start menu and searching for *.scr, as shown in Figure 1-20. The name of the .scr files are usually very descriptive, so you will have no problem finding the right file. If for some reason you do, just double-click each file to launch a preview of the screensaver. After the search, I identified that the file for the 3D Windows screensaver was named 3D Windows XP.scr. One you have the name of the screensaver that you want to use, just replace logon.scr from the value window with the name of the file you want to use, such as 3D Windows XP.scr.

5. Click OK to save your changes, and the next time that your computer boots up, your new screensaver will be shown.

You can also use other screensavers that you have downloaded from the Internet. If the .scr file for the screensaver is not located in the Windows or Windows\System32 directory, you will have to enter in the whole path to the screensaver file instead of just the name.

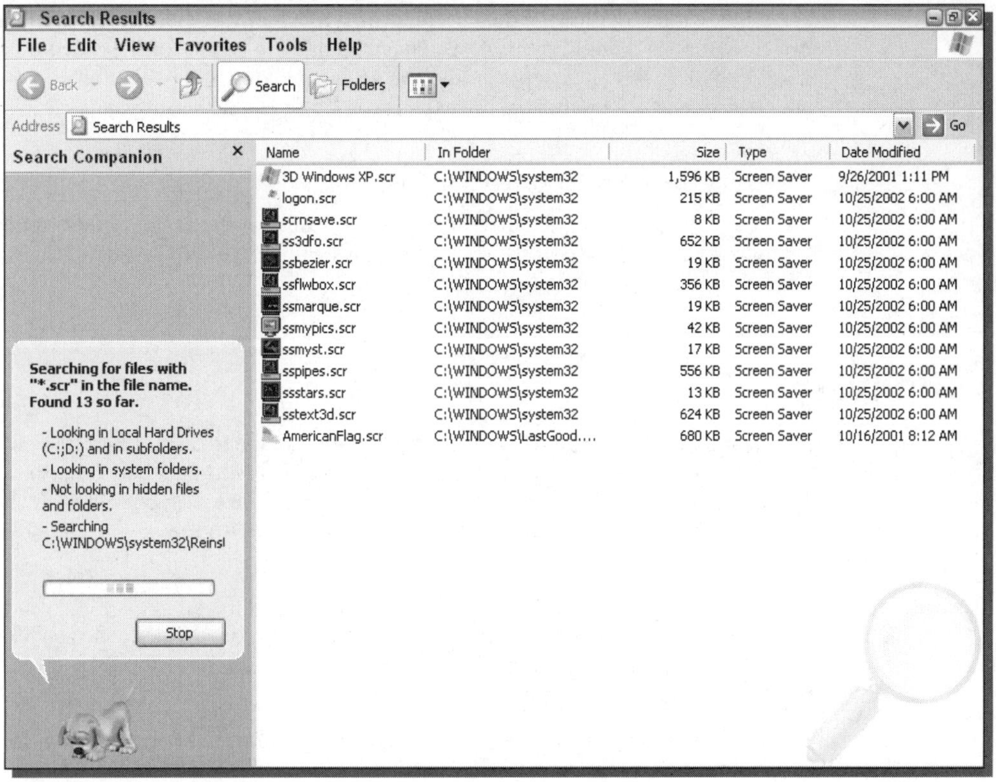

FIGURE 1-20: Using the search feature of Windows XP to find the filenames of the installed screensavers.

Enable Num Lock to be turned on by default

If you have a password that has both numbers and letters and you frequently use the number pad to enter in part of your password, this hack is for you. I cannot count the number of times that I started to type in my password and then was faced with a logon error screen telling me that my password was not correct. I would sit there staring at the screen for a second before I realized that my Num Lock on my keyboard was not on.

This is a great hack for every desktop computer with a full-size keyboard with a separate number pad. Turning on the Num Lock by default on a laptop may not be a very good idea, because usually most laptops do not have a separate number pad. Enabling this feature on a laptop will result in almost half of your keyboard to function as the number pad and you would just be much better off using the numbers above the letters.

1. Start up Registry Editor by clicking the Start menu and selecting Run. Then type **regedit** in the text box and click OK.

2. Once Registry Editor loads, navigate through HKEY_USERS, .DEFAULT, Control Panel, and Keyboard.

3. Next, locate the InitialKeyboardIndicators entry, right-click it, and select Modify. You can enter various codes into this property, but all of them except for the code for Num Lock are pointless. For example, would you want your computer to start up caps-lock, which is code 1? Of course not. To enable Num Lock, you will want to enter **2** into the box.

4. Then click OK to save the changes, and that's it!

If you are on a laptop and you attempted to enable Num Lock even though I told you not to and need to fix your system, repeat the above directions but replace the value of InitialKeyboardIndicators to **0** to disable the feature.

Summary

This first chapter can be thought of as the first step in the complete customization of every aspect of your Windows XP. It started from the very beginning with the boot screen and worked through the different logon methods and how to customize each one. Then, it showed you how to make your computer even better by using a few nifty features to make it look and act great.

The next chapter will pick up on the next part of customizing your computer. First, you will learn all about customizing the new Windows XP Start panel. This chapter will show you how to get the most out of this new feature. Then, it will show you how you can revert to the old Start menu style and customize that as well.

After you have customized the heck out of your Start menu, you will be shown many cool ways to customize and improve the taskbar. Changing the makeup of the taskbar and the text of the Start button are a few sample topics from this section.

Customizing User Navigation

Customizing user navigation is the next stop on the Windows XP customizing road trip. In the last chapter, with the help of some cool hacks, you were able to change and improve the boot and logon screens. This chapter will pick up where Chapter 1 left off and will show you how to customize and improve the visual navigation elements of Windows XP.

This chapter starts off with customizing the look and contents of the cool new Start panel. This new screen can show a lot more than just your recently run programs. If you do not like the new Start panel, you can find out how to get the old classic Start Menu back. Then, you will learn some cool hacks to improve and customize the classic Start Menu. You cannot customize the Start panel and then leave out customizing the program listings. I will show you some cool hacks that will customize this as well.

To finish this chapter up, you'll learn how to customize the taskbar on the bottom of your screen. The taskbar is a very essential part of navigating your computer. I will show you how to customize and improve its features and will give you some new ideas on how you can use it that may dramatically improve your experiences with Windows XP.

Customizing the Start Panel

The Start panel is what I call the new replacement for the traditional Start Menu that we are all familiar with from using previous versions of Windows. I call this the Start *panel* because it is not just a *menu* anymore. It is now a collection of various links and features all thrown onto one panel that pops up. It offers many new features, such as a dynamic list that places your most frequently run programs on the panel so that you can easily access them without having to navigate throughout the entire program listings. Additionally, the Start panel has replaced all of the icons on the desktop except for the Recycle Bin so that your desktop will look much cleaner and uncluttered.

Different tools and hacks are available that will allow you to customize the Start panel. Almost everything on it is customizable. You can add and remove items that are displayed, and you can even change the way it looks. With the many different options available, you can customize the way that different parts of the panel works. For example, you can change the number of frequently run programs that are displayed.

When you have finished reading these next few sections, you will have transformed your Start panel into something that is even more useful for your everyday tasks.

Using Group Policy Editor to customize the Start panel

The Group Policy Editor is a great tool that makes customizing the Start panel a snap. It is a very powerful tool that was not originally designed to be a tool that can customize but a tool for workplace management. Group policies were originally designed so that administrators can limit what a user can do on their computer. Let's say you are responsible for hundreds of Windows machines at work. Most likely, you will want to limit what users can do on their computers so that they don't accidentally install a harmful program or change a system setting that renders their computer useless. Group policies make it possible to limit a user's access to critical areas of the operating system.

The most common use of the Group Policy Editor is to edit policy information on a domain controller. The domain controller can be thought of as a computer on a corporate network that is in charge of security. It is like a database of usernames, passwords, and configuration information. The Group Policy Editor is used by administrators to modify the user configuration data. The next time a user logs onto their computer, new policy information is downloaded and applied. Now the user is limited in what they can do on their computer.

Although the Group Policy Editor is primarily used for computer management in a business, it can also be used to customize an individual computer running Windows XP Professional. Because Microsoft wanted to support both small and large businesses, they have included a copy of the Group Policy Editor with every copy of Windows XP Professional. With that inclusion, even if a company was not large enough to have a domain controller, they could still limit and fine-tune a user's experience. Unfortunately, Windows XP Home does not come with a copy of the Group Policy Editor. This exclusion was not by accident. Microsoft chose not to include a copy of this utility with XP Home because the Group Policy Editor was designed to be a business utility. And, well, XP Home is meant for use in the *home*.

Think you can get the Group Policy Editor to work by copying over the program file to a computer running Windows XP Home? Sorry, but I tried doing so, and the program would not start. So, the discussion in this section will only apply to those working with Windows XP Professional. If you are running XP Home, you will not be missing out on too much; the next section about adding and removing the different navigation icons will be compatible with your version.

Now that you know all about the Group Policy Editor, it is time to learn how you can use it to customize the Start panel. The Editor will enable you to enable and disable various different features. First, you're going to find out how to get the Editor up and running. Then, you can check out a list of all of the relevant features you can use to customize the Start panel.

To begin customizing, follow these steps:

1. Click the Start Menu and select Run. Then type **gpedit.msc** into the box and click OK. This will start up the Group Policy Editor. If you get an error, make sure that you have typed the name of the file correctly and that you are running Windows XP Pro.

2. Now that you have the Group Policy Editor up and running, you will want to navigate to the Start Menu and Taskbar settings. This can be done by expanding the User Configuration, Administrative Templates, and the Start Menu and Taskbar folder.

3. Once you have navigated through the Editor, you will see a list of all of the different features of the Policy Editor, as shown in Figure 2-1. A number of features listed will only apply to the taskbar. Table 2-1 lists all of the relevant features and provides a description of what they will do. For the sake of demonstrating how to use the Editor, let's assume that you want to remove the username from appearing on the top of the Start panel. Use your mouse to locate Remove User Name from the Start Menu list. Right-click it and select Properties.

4. The Remove User Name from the Start Menu Properties window will load. Then, to turn the feature on, just click the circle (known as a radio button) next to Enabled, as shown in Figure 2-2.

5. Then, just click OK and you are finished.

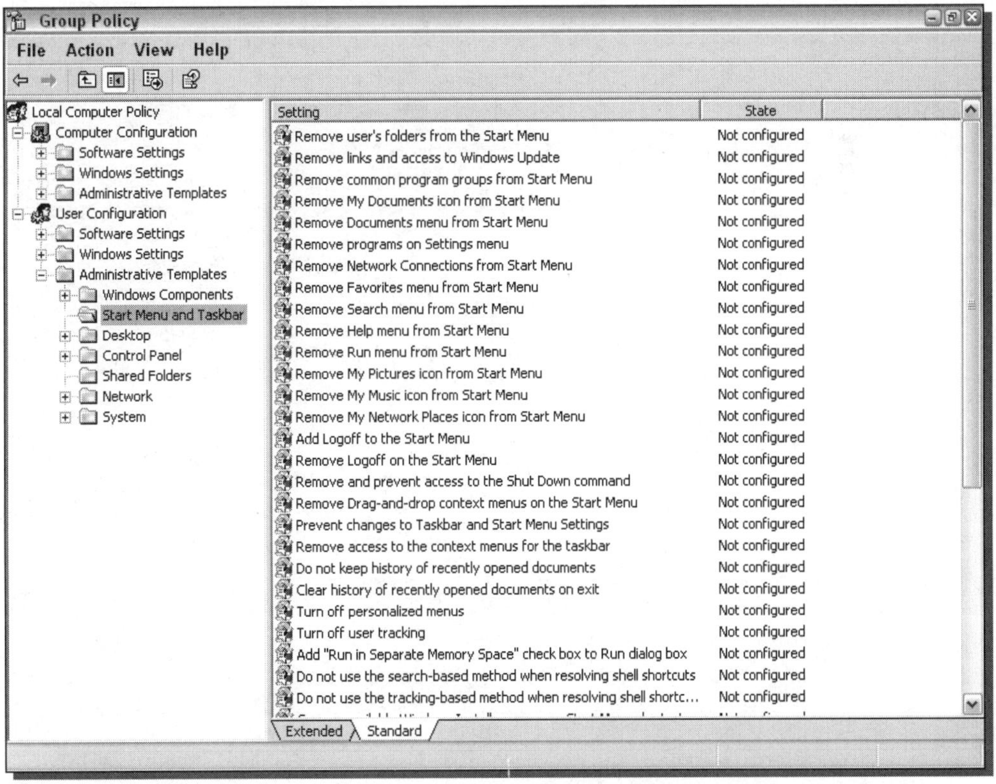

FIGURE 2-1: The Group Policy Editor displaying a list of all of the different features it provides for customizing the Start panel.

Table 2-1 Group Policy Features to Customize the Start Panel

Feature Name	Description
Add Log Off to Start Menu	If you do not have the Log Off button on your Start panel, this feature will display it when you set it to Enable. Some installations of Windows XP do not have this feature enabled by default. With these, the only way to log off your computer when the button is not displayed is to first click the Shutdown button and then click the Log Off button from the Shutdown menu that pops up. It is much easier and faster to just click the Log Off button in the first place
Remove All Programs list from the Start Menu	This feature will take out the All Programs link that displays the list of all of the applications installed on your computer. This feature is useful if you want to limit the programs someone has access to on your computer, or if you just want to do away with the old menu altogether. Set this feature to Enable and say goodbye to your program list
Remove Logoff on the Start Menu	This feature will remove the Logoff button from the Start panel. If you are one of the lucky users and your installation of Windows XP includes the button to log off, you can enable this feature to get rid of the button, if you have no use for it
Remove pinned programs from the Start Menu	Pinned programs are the list of programs that appear in the top left corner of the Start panel. By default, programs such as Internet Explorer and either Outlook Express or Microsoft Outlook are displayed in this area, which shows the list of frequently run programs. If you would like to remove these links to programs so that you will have more room to display frequently run programs, as shown in Figure 2-3, set this feature to Enable and you are set
Remove user name from Start Menu	You already have experience with this setting from the procedure I walked you through. If you do not want your username to be shown on the top of the Start panel, then enable this feature. This may seem like a useless hack at first, but it may be useful in a variety of cases (such as if you are concerned about the security of your computer). Anyone that clicks your Start button will be shown your username. If you operate an Internet café or manage public computers, you are strongly advised to enable this feature
Prevent changes to Taskbar and Start Menu Settings	Once you get your Start panel and taskbar (see *Customizing the Taskbar*) looking the way you want, a good way to lock in your changes is to enable this feature

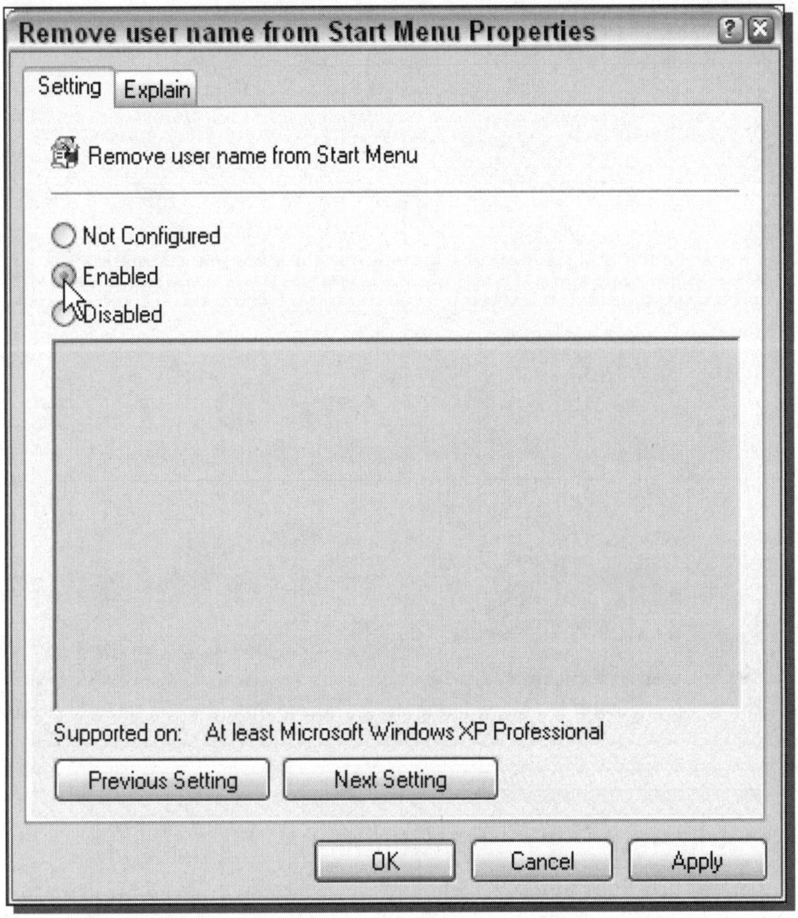

Remove user name from Start Menu Properties   [?] [X]

Setting | Explain

Remove user name from Start Menu

○ Not Configured
○ Enabled
○ Disabled

Supported on: At least Microsoft Windows XP Professional

| Previous Setting | Next Setting |

| OK | Cancel | Apply |

FIGURE 2-2: Enabling Remove User Name from the Start Menu Properties feature.

If you want to get your username back, just repeat the above directions but select the Disable Radio Button instead and then click OK.

Table 2-1 shows a list of all of the great features that will help you customize your copy of Windows XP Pro.

 Caution

Wait to enable the feature that allows you to prevent changes to the taskbar and Start Menu until you have finished reading Part 1 of this book. Otherwise, you may run into unexpected programs as you are customizing various parts of your computer.

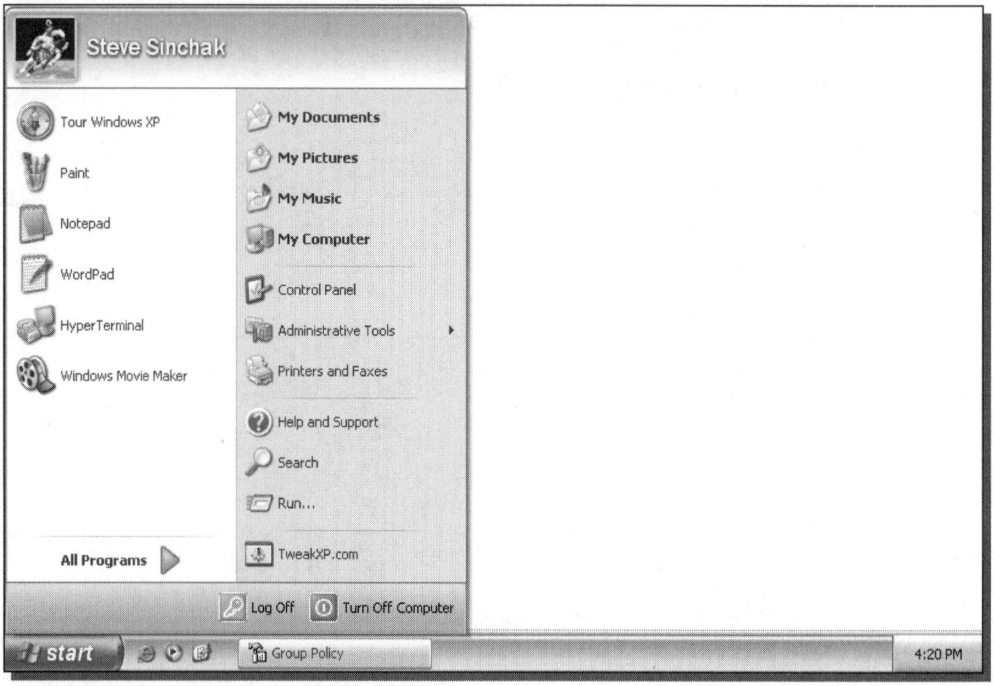

FIGURE 2-3: The Start panel with the pinned programs removed from the left side of the panel.

Adding and removing navigation icons

Many icons on the new Start panel will help you navigate through Windows in a way you have never done before. All of the icons that are displayed can be customized to fit your needs so that you can have one-click access to several different parts of your computer. Icons such as My Computer, My Music, Network Connections, and many more are now placed right on the Start panel. Windows XP gives you the capability to add even more. Additionally, these icons can be transformed into pop-up menus that expand and show the details. For example, instead of just displaying the My Computer icon, when you move your mouse over the icon, it can pop up a menu that will display shortcuts to each of the separate drives on your computer.

These new features allow you to be much more efficient when working with your computer. You can save yourself a lot of time by enabling the auto-expanding pop-up menu feature on many of the utility icons such as Control Panel. This way, you can have access to all of your Control Panel applets with just one click on the Start Menu.

Windows XP makes it possible to edit most of the navigation icons right from within the user interface so you don't have to worry about hacking the registry in this section. To get started, follow these steps:

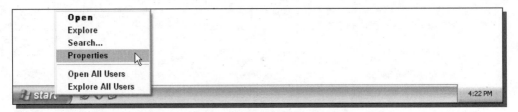

FIGURE 2-4: How to view Start Menu properties by right-clicking the Start button.

1. Right-click the Start button and select Properties, as shown in Figure 2-4.

2. You should now see the Taskbar and Start Menu Properties window. Next, click the top Customize button, and the Start Menu settings will load.

3. The Customize Start Menu is where you can change many aspects of the Start panel; for now, click the Advanced tab. You will learn about some of the items on the General tab in the next few sections.

4. Once you have the Advanced tab displayed, you will see the Start Menu items scroll box. In this box you will see a list of all of the different features for the icons that can be displayed on the Start panel. Table 2-2 lists in detail all of the different features and their separate options. For demonstration purposes, let's make the My Computer icon expand automatically to show all of the drives. Scroll down in the box until you see the My Computer title.

5. Then select the Display as a Menu option, as shown in Figure 2-5, to enable the Auto Expand feature.

6. Click OK twice, and your change is now complete.

As you can see, making changes to the items on the Start panel is quite simple. Take a look at Table 2-2 for more information on all of the navigation icons that you can customize with the method just described.

Switching to small icons for frequently run apps

The new Start panel includes a neat little feature that will keep track of all of the programs that you run and will place the most frequently run programs directly on the Start panel. I use this list of programs on the Start panel even more often than I use the All Programs pop-up menu because it is just much faster. One way that I like to customize my Start panel is to decrease the size of the icons on the left so that you can fit more icons on the screen. This way, more frequently run programs can be displayed. Figure 2-6 shows the difference between a Start panel that has been switched to use small icons compared to the normal Start panel.

Table 2-2   Start Panel Features

Feature	Description
Control Panel	By default, the Control Panel shortcut is shown and is selected to Display As A Link. I like selecting the Display As A Menu option, because it turns on the auto-expanding menu feature that displays all of the Control Panel applets without even having to open up the Control Panel. Doing so saves me a lot of time and is well worth it. If you do not want the Control Panel to be displayed, just click the Don't Display This Item option
Help and Support	There's not a lot that you can do with this one. If you use Help and Support frequently, let this one be; otherwise, uncheck it to free up some space on your Start panel
My Computer	The My Computer icon is one of the best candidates to enable the Display as a Menu feature so that it automatically expands to show you all of your drives. If you do not have any drives on your computer, feel free to disable the My Computer icon by selecting Don't Display This Item
My Documents	By default, the My Documents shortcut is displayed just as a link. I suggest that you leave this feature set this way if you have a lot of documents in your My Documents folder. Enabling the Display As A Menu option when you have a lot of documents is just not worth it, because it gets so hard to find what you want. If you do not like the My Documents menu on the Start panel, just click the Don't Display This Item option
My Music	The My Music folder is great, but most of us that have music on our computers have a lot more than just a few songs. I recommend that you leave this one alone as well, because enabling the Display As A Menu feature is counterproductive when you have more than a few songs. If you are like me and do not use the My Music folder, then click the Don't Display This Item option and you will have made some more room on your Start panel
My Network Places	This is the icon that you can use to browse your local area network if your computer is on any type of local area network (LAN). If you want to connect to a remote computer to view their shared files, you will want to have this option selected. If you do not have a network card, and just use a modem, then I suggest that you uncheck this item because you will never use it
My Pictures	My Pictures is a nice link if you use the My Pictures folder to store your photos. But forget about enabling Display As A Menu on this one. Doing so will just give you a list of file names. With today's digital cameras' number schemes, you will never find the

Feature	Description
	photo you want unless you can see a thumbnail. If you don't use the My Pictures folder, click Don't Display This Item and the shortcut will be removed
Network Connections	The Network Connections item can be very useful. If you have a dialup connection or even if you have a network adapter and are on a LAN, the network connection shortcut, when set to Display As A Menu, will allow you to easily access all of your connections to view and set properties as well as connect right from the Start panel
Printers and Faxes	No Printer? Uncheck this box
Run Command	I recommend that you leave this box checked, as you will be using this button in various directions throughout this book
Search	Search for files a lot? If not, get rid of this shortcut to save yourself some room
Set Program Access and Defaults	You all probably know about Microsoft's antitrust problems with the government. Part of their settlement required Microsoft to provide users an easy way to switch between default applications on their computers such as the default Web browser and Mail Client. This shortcut is useful, but it does not deserve to be on your Start panel. Uncheck this box to free up some room. You can access this feature later from within the Add and Remove Programs Control Panel applet
System Administrative Tools	The System Admin tools are the most useful tools besides the Control Panel. I highly recommend that you include this item on your Start panel in both the All Programs menu and the Start Menu by selecting the middle, all-inclusive option

Changing the icons is very easy. You just need to change one setting within the Start Menu properties. To do so, follow these steps:

1. Move your mouse over the Start button and right-click it with your mouse and then click Properties.

2. This will bring up the Start Menu Properties menu that you used in the last section. Here, you will want to click the Customize button.

3. On the General tab, you will see two options under Select An Icon Size For Programs. This is where you can change the icon size. Select Small Icons and then click OK.

4. Click OK once more and you are finished.

Now you will have made some more room so that you can display more frequently run programs on the Start panel. When you click the Start Menu, you may notice that there aren't any

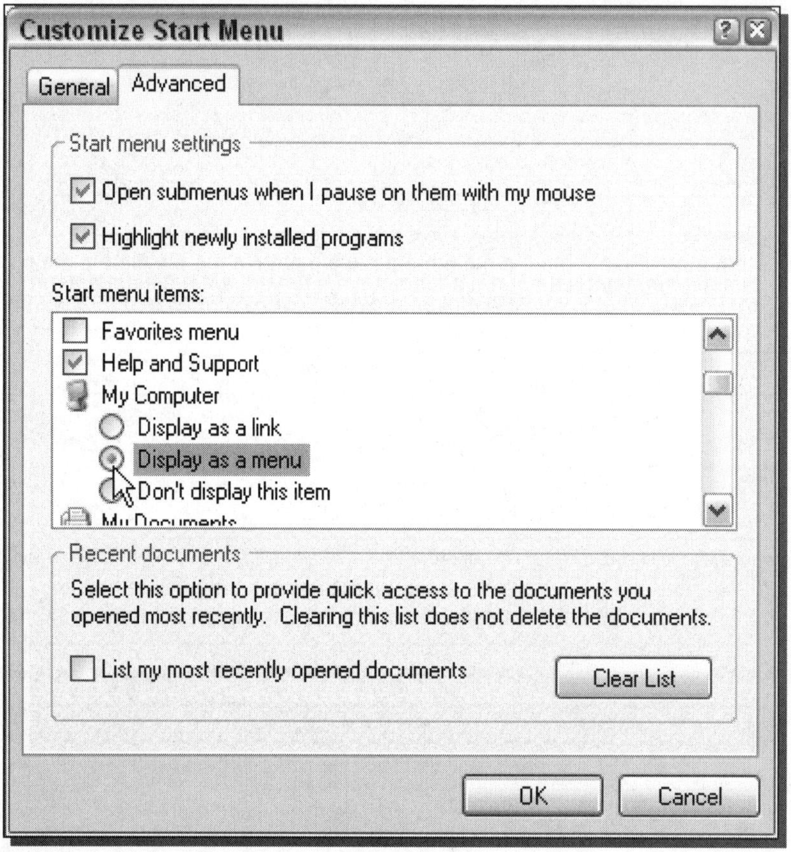

FIGURE **2-5:** Customizing the Start panel by enabling the Display as a Menu feature for the My Computer icon.

more programs showing up. That is because you also have to adjust the number of programs that will appear. The next section will show you how to adjust how many program shortcuts are displayed.

Increasing number of recently run programs displayed on the Start panel

By now, you have changed the icon size of the frequently run programs list so that you can fit more icons on the screen. Now, you can increase the number of programs that will be displayed so that your list of programs will become even more useful. If you decided that you did not want to change the size of the icons, don't worry—you can still change the number of programs that are displayed. You just won't be able to display as much.

FIGURE 2-6: The difference between the two Start panel icon sizes.

Changing the number of programs depends completely on personal preference. Do you like having a huge Start panel that stretches from the taskbar to the top of the screen? Do you like a Start panel with a small footprint? By design, the Start panel cannot contain more than 30 programs on the list. Very few users can display 30 items at once, because they must have their screen resolution set at a minimum 1280 × 1024, assuming that they are using the small icons. That high resolution is usually only used by owners of screens larger than 17 inches. The most common computer screen resolution is 1024 × 768. At that resolution, 22 programs can fit on the Start panel when the small icons are used. If you have an older computer or just a small display and your screen resolution is set for 800 × 600, then you will only be able to display 15 programs on your Frequently Run Programs list.

The resolution settings of your screen will determine the maximum number of programs that can be displayed. If you accidentally choose too many programs, Windows will let you know by giving you a friendly error message once you try to click your Start Menu after the change.

Now that you have an idea of the number of programs that your computer can display, you are ready to get started. To increase the number of programs, do the following:

1. Right-click the Start button and select Properties to bring up the Taskbar and Start Menu Properties settings.

2. Next, click the Customize button to show the Customize Start Menu options.

3. On this screen, locate Number of Programs on Start Menu on the text box. You can adjust this value by clicking the up and down buttons or just by selecting all of the text and entering in a new number.

Tip If you ever want to clean your list of frequently run programs, just click the Clear List button on the Customize Start Menu screen. This will reset all of your program run counts so that your list will be rebuilt over time just as it was the first time you used your computer.

4. Once you have entered the number of programs you want displayed, click the OK button to save your changes.

5. Then click the OK button once more and you are finished.

The best way to set the number of programs is to experiment with several different values until you get your Start panel looking the way you want. After you find the value that is just right, you will have a much-improved Start panel.

Hiding programs from appearing in the Start panel

So you have a top-secret program that you do not want anyone else to know you have. Every time you run a program on your computer, Windows XP keeps track of it and will place it on your frequently run programs list as a convenience to you. Sometimes, this feature is not always a convenience and is, instead, like a chronic medical problem that will not go away.

For example, let's use the situation of a guy named Larry. Larry plays Solitaire all the time on his computer when he is at work. It is not the best game, but it will help him pass time and it's a great alternative to actually doing work. Every time Larry plays Solitaire, Windows XP automatically puts the game into the frequently run programs list. This tracking is a problem for Larry because he is concerned that one of his fellow employees might see the program on the list and report him. What should he do? First, Larry should buy a copy of *Hacking Windows XP* and then he should follow these steps:

1. Click the Start Menu and select Run. Type in **regedit** and click OK to start up the Registry Editor.

2. Next, expand the HKEY_CLASSES_ROOT folder.

3. Search through the list of folders until he finds the folder called Applications and expand that as well.

4. Now he will see a list of every executable file for the programs installed on his computer. To hide a program from the frequently run programs list, he will want to expand the folder that is the executable for the program. To hide Solitaire, he will want to expand the sol.exe folder.

Tip If you do not know the name of the executable file that a program shortcut points to, you can easily look this up by right-clicking the shortcut and selecting Properties. In the Properties box, you will see a full path to where the file is located as well as the name of the file. When you right-click the shortcut in the Start Menu for Solitaire, you will discover that the name of the executable for the game is sol.exe.

5. Can't find a folder called `sol.exe`? That's because some Windows applications are not listed. If his application was listed, he needs to skip this step. Otherwise, he will need to create a folder. To do so, he selects the Applications folder with the mouse. Then he right-clicks and selects New and then Select Key. Then he types in the name of the executable for the name of the key. For Solitaire, he will want to name the key **sol.exe.**

6. Now that he has found the folder for the application or has created one, he expands it so that he can see all of its values. Then, he right-clicks the executable's folder that he just created or found in the registry. Select New and then select String. Next, he types in **NoStartPage** as the name of the string variable.

7. He closes the Registry Editor and logs off and then back in. He will never see Solitaire in his frequently run programs list again.

Now Larry can play as much Solitaire at work as he wants without having to worry about it showing up in his frequently run programs list. Don't get too confident after completing this hack. Remember, people can still look over your shoulder and see your computer screen. To solve that problem, I recommend using a cardboard box to build a shelter over your cubicle to block spying eyes. This will also limit the number of people that can ask you questions, which will allow you to better concentrate on your game of Solitaire.

Pinning your programs

I use the Calculator application all the time when I am using my computer. My desk calculator is always lost somewhere in my drawers and I don't even want to waste my time looking for it when I just want to do a quick calculation. Every time I want to use the Calculator application, I have to click the Start Menu, then select All Programs, and then navigate up through the Accessories menu until I finally can click the Calculator app. There is a much better way that I can access this program.

Instead of navigating through the programs listings, I can just pin the program to the Start panel. Pinning a program is a very simple task that allows the program that you pin to appear on the Start panel just above the frequently run programs. If you pin a program shortcut, it will appear just below the Internet Explorer and e-mail icons in the Start panel.

Navigating through the entire Start Menu to launch a program you use all the time is a waste of time. Pin your most commonly used programs today!

Are you excited yet? No? Okay, well let's get started:

1. Start your pinning adventure by navigating through the Start Menu as you normally do to launch a program. Navigate to a program that you use all the time, such as the Calculator application in the Accessories menu.

2. Once you have the item highlighted with the mouse, right-click the item and select Pin to Start Menu. That's it, your program will now appear directly on the Start panel.

Now let's say that you got a little too excited and pinned too many applications and want to remove some. What should you do? Just click the Start button once more to bring up the Start

Menu and highlight the program you want to un-pin from the Start panel. Next, just right-click the item and select Unpin from Start Menu.

Pinning your favorite programs is a simple solution to speeding up your access to your programs.

Adding Web site links to your Start panel

Do you have a Web site that you visit frequently? How would you like to place a link to that Web site directly on your Start panel? With the help of a registry hack, it is possible to place a shortcut on the bottom-right side of your Start panel, as shown in Figure 2-7.

Adding a link to a Web site is a great way to get to your favorite Web site fast. Also, if you run your own Web site, you can make your own registry file that you can distribute to your visitors so they can add your site to their Start Menu. I will show you how to make a quick script from your registry once you have made the changes on your computer.

Now that I have told you the basics of this hack, let's get started:

1. Click the Start Menu and select Run. Then type **regedit** to launch the Registry Editor.

2. When the Registry Editor has launched, you will want to expand the HKEY_CLASSES _ROOT folder and then the CLSID folder.

3. Next, you will want to scroll through the list of Class IDs until you find {2559a1f6-21d7-11d4-bdaf-00c04f60b9f0} and expand it as well.

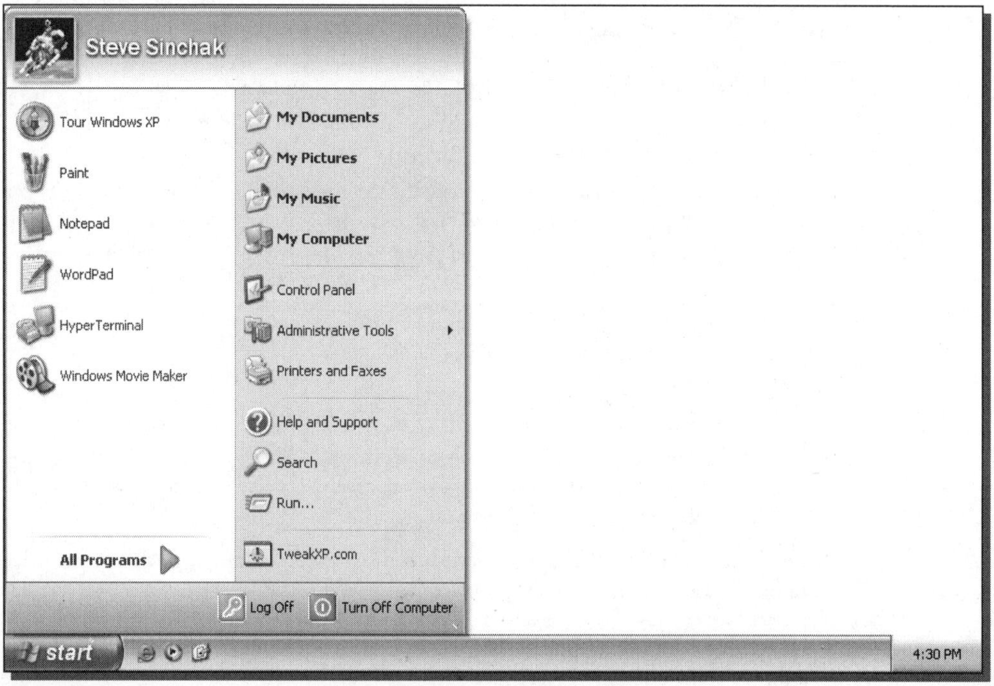

FIGURE 2-7: A hacked Start panel showing a new link to TweakXP.com.

4. Start your modifications by naming this class. Right-click the (default) entry within the {2559a1f6-21d7-11d4-bdaf-00c04f60b9f0} folder and select modify.

5. Then type **TweakXP.com** in the value data box and click OK to save your changes.

6. Now you are going to set up the icon that will be displayed on the Start panel next to the name. To do this, you will need to create a new folder. Select the {2559a1f6-21d7-11d4-bdaf-00c04f60b9f0} folder again and right-click it. Then select New and then Key. This will create a new subfolder that you should call DefaultIcon.

7. Right-click the DefaultIcon folder that you just created and create a new string value by expanding new and selecting string value. Name this new value (Default). The value of this string will be the location of the icon that you want to use.

8. I like using the system icons which are stored in the shell32.dll. To use these icons, right-click the new (Default) string value that you created and select modify. Then type **%SystemRoot%\\system32\\shell32.dll,-47** in the value box and click OK to save. The 47 in that line is the index of the icon that I wanted to use for my link to TweakXP.com. If you want to use a different icon, replace the 47 with the icon index number you want. You are free to use any icon that you want, including icons that are not in the shell32.dll file. If you want to use an icon that you downloaded or made, just enter the full path to that icon in place of the line mentioned above.

Caution

If you do not know what icons are in the shell32.dll file, take a look at a program called IconXpert created by Xpert-Design to browse through the system icons located inside the file. This free application can be downloaded from their Web site, located at www.XpertDesign .de/English/. Once you have IconXpert installed and running, browse over to the Windows and then the System32 folders to find shell32.dll. Once you select Shell32.dll, you will be shown all of the icons stored within the file. If you want to use a specific icon, just note its index number and use that in place of the 47 in the (Default) entry that you created above.

9. Now that the shortcut is set up, specify what it is supposed to do. To do this, expand the Instance folder that is inside the {2559a1f6-21d7-11d4-bdaf-00c04f60b9f0} folder and then expand the InitPropertyBag folder.

10. Inside the InitPropertyBag folder, you will be making the last changes for this hack. To start off, you will want to create a new string value and call it Command. You can create this by right-clicking the InitPropertyBag folder and selecting New, and then String Value.

11. Right-click the new string value that you created and select modify. Key in **TweakXP.com** in the value data box and click OK. This value will be the text that is displayed on the Start Panel.

12. Now you are almost finished. Create one more string value in the InitPropertyBag folder and name it Param1. Then right-click the string value, select Modify, type **www.TweakXP.com,** and click OK to save.

You are now finished! Once you log off and log back on, the changes will be activated. If you wish to make a shortcut that points to a different Web site, just replace all of the TweakXP.com's to the name of the site that you want it to point to. Also you will have to modify the value of the Param1 string value to hold the address of the new Web site. Be sure to always include http:// in front of your URLs so that the shortcut works properly.

On the CD A registry import file can be found to automate the preceding process in the Chapter 2 folder of the companion CD-ROM, called `website_link.reg`. Just right-click the registry file and select import to automatically merge the file with your registry. If you do not like the effect, I have created an easy undo file that will remove the link in your Start panel, called `remove_website_link.reg`.

Also, as I mentioned before, if you own a Web site, creating a Start panel button would be a cool feature to give your visitors. You can create a registry file of your registry that you can distribute to other users. Then, all they have to do is double-click the file and click Yes on the import screen. To make a registry file, just select the {2559a1f6-21d7-11d4-bdaf-00c04f60b9f0} folder and right-click it. Then select Export from the menu and save the file. The file should only be a few bytes, so it will be easy to distribute the file on the Web. Keep in mind that this registry file will only work on Windows XP machines, so be sure to relay that information to visitors of your Web site if you choose to offer your registry file up for download.

Customizing the Classic Start Menu

The classic Start Menu, also known as the Windows 2000/98 style, has its advantages and also its share of downfalls. It provides a clean and small interface to your programs but does not offer nearly as much access to your computer as the new Start panel does. Some users like the old Start Menu and dislike the big bulky Start panel. If you are one of those users, these next few sections are for you.

Turning the classic Start Menu back on

Don't like the new Start Menu? The new Start panel can be overwhelming for some users and is just not as clean looking as the old Start Menu. Getting the old Start Menu back is actually very simple. There must have been mixed emotions within the Windows XP team about the new Start Menu because they still included the classic Start Menu and made it so easy to change. To get started, just follow these steps:

1. Right-click the Start button and select Properties.
2. Then select Classic Start Menu as shown in Figure 2-8 and click OK.

Now that you have the classic Start Menu back, you can begin customizing the way it looks and what it includes.

Customizing the classic Start Menu

Just as it is possible to customize the new Start panel, it is possible to make changes to the classic Start Menu to make it look the way you want. Not as many things can be done to customize the classic Start Menu as can be done to customize the Start panel, but still a handful of features can be customized.

To get started, assume that you want to display your expanding Internet Explorer Favorites menu directly on your Start Menu. I will walk you through how to turn this feature on or off and will then provide you with more information on all of the different features that are available on the same screen. Follow these steps to start customizing:

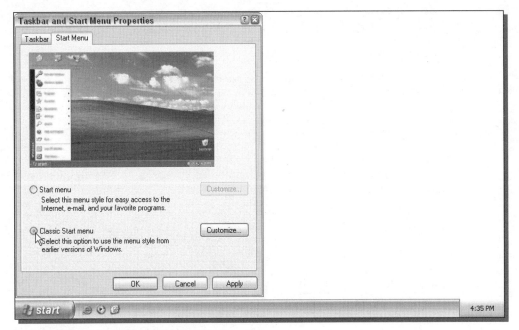

FIGURE 2-8: Turning on the classic Start Menu.

1. Use your mouse to right-click the Start Menu and select Properties. This will bring up the Taskbar and Start Menu Properties screen.

2. Click the lower Customize button to bring up the Customize Classic Start Menu properties.

3. Now you will see a list of all of the different features available in the Advanced Start Menu options box. You can scroll through this box to view all of the different features. Locate the Display Favorites option and check it to enable it.

4. Click the OK button to save your changes.

5. Click the OK button once more to exit the Properties window.

That's it. As you can see, customizing the Start Menu is very easy. If you want to disable a feature, just uncheck it.

Table 2-3 gives a list of all of the different features and a description of what they can do.

Customizing the Start Menu/Panel Program Listings

Now that you have selected what you want your Start Menu to display as well as customized it to suit your needs, you are ready to move on to customizing the way the programs are listed. There are a variety of features that will impact the way the programs are listed on the screen.

Table 2-3   Customizable Features of the Start Menu

Feature Name	Description
Display Administrative Tools	The administrative tools provide users with even more control over their system. I suggest that you enable this feature by checking the box so that you will be able to take advantage of the easy access to your system controls
Display Favorites	The favorites can be useful depending on how often you use them in Internet Explorer. If you are like me, and do not use your favorites very often, then consider leaving this one off. If you would like to add your favorites to your Start Menu, then this will place an expanding menu that will display all of your links
Display Run	This feature will display the Run command on the Start Menu. I do not recommend that you remove this from the Start Menu because it is used throughout this book in almost every chapter to start up hidden programs
Expand Control Panel	I like this feature the most out of all of the features that you can customize. Enabling this feature will make the Control Panel automatically expand and show you each of the Control Panel applets. This way, you can get almost anywhere in your computer controls easily without even having to load the Control Panel first. You can jump directly to where you want to go instead
Expand My Documents	I personally do not use this feature because I have way too many documents in the My Documents folder. Trying to find the correct document is a waste of time when you have to scroll through the list. It is must faster to leave this one alone and then just browse through the icons when you open up your documents
Expand My Pictures	As I mentioned before when I covered this option as a feature on the Start panel, this feature is pretty much useless when you have more than a few photos. Because most pictures that you take are saved in a numbered fashion, it is very hard to find a particular photo. Instead, don't enable this one so that it remains just a link. That way, you will be able to take advantage of the new filmstrip view when browsing your photos
Expand Network Connections	I recommend that you enable this feature because it will allow you to easily access and connect to your various communications devices. If you use a dialup connection, your dialup connection will be displayed and you can connect by right-clicking the name and selecting Connect. If you have a network adapter, you can access your network properties and status easily from this menu as well

Feature Name	Description
Expand Printers	Have a lot of printers installed on your computer? Or, do you use a lot of network printers? This is an easy way to access all of the different printers that you use. You can view the print queue as well as delete jobs for a specific printer
Show Small Icons in Start Menu	This is my favorite feature on the list. This basically shrinks your whole Start Menu by removing the Windows XP banner from the left and replacing the large icons with small icons. This allows the Start Menu to take up far less space than before. Take a look at Figure 2-9 for a comparison between when this feature is on and off

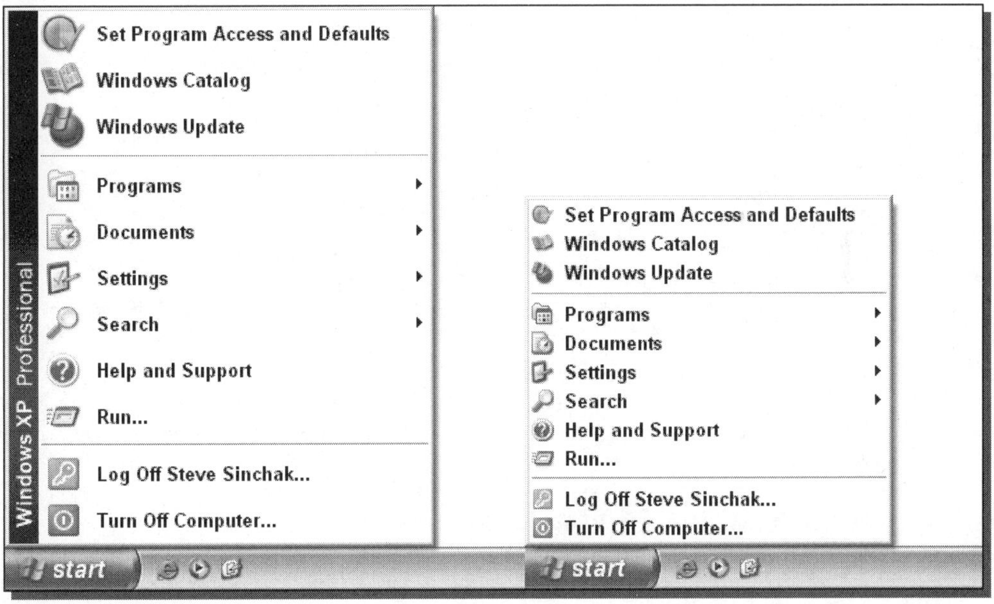

FIGURE 2-9: Comparison between the normal and small Start Menu, with the Show Small Icons setting enabled.

These next few sections will help you get rid of some of the new annoying features, such as the personalized menus and the scrolling program listings.

There are basically two slightly different program listing methods. When you are using the new Start panel, the programs listing is slightly different in the way it looks and acts when compared to the classic Start Menu listing. Follow the corresponding sections below for the menu option that you are running.

Changing program listing display options for users of the Start panel

As I mentioned earlier, the Start panel All Programs listing works a little differently than its classic counterpart. The new program listing has some features that the classic version does not and that is why it is necessary to have two different sections. In the following sections, you will find two very common topics that users are interested in changing.

Disabling new program highlights

One of the features I thought was a great idea when I first started to use Windows XP was the program highlight feature. This feature will automatically highlight any new programs that you install so that you can easily find them on the Start Menu the first few times that you want to run the application. After I started to use XP for a few months, I noticed that this feature did not always work correctly. Some programs that I install never get highlighted, although others seem to be highlighted for weeks after I have installed them.

After a while, I decided that I had enough of this highlighting, so I decided to turn the feature off. Thankfully, Microsoft has made turning off this feature fairly simple. Just follow these steps to get rid of those annoying highlights:

1. Right-click the Start button and select Properties.
2. Click the top Customize button for the Start panel.
3. Click the Advanced tab.
4. Uncheck Highlight Newly Installed Programs, as shown in Figure 2-10.
5. Click OK to save your changes.
6. Click OK once more to close the Properties window.

Now you will not have to worry about the programs that sometimes seem to be highlighted randomly.

Fun with the Scroll Programs feature

Some people love the program scroll feature, and others hate it. Personally, I don't like this feature that much. I like to see all of my programs installed on my screen at once instead of having to move the mouse to the bottom of the list and clicking the down arrow or waiting for the list to move up automatically when the feature is enabled.

If you do not like having your menus take up a lot of space on your screen, enabling the scroll programs feature will cut your programs list down in size dramatically if you have a lot of programs installed.

Some computer manufacturers ship their machines with this feature automatically enabled; other don't have it enabled. So if this feature sounds interesting to you, feel free to try it out by following these steps. If you hate this feature, then follow these steps to remove it:

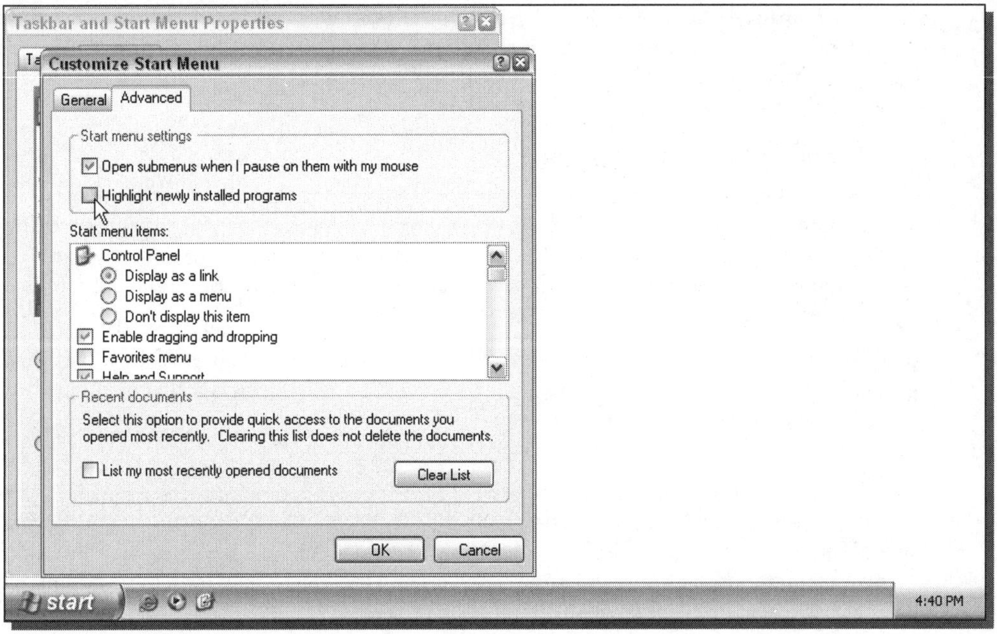

FIGURE 2-10: Customize Start Menu window showing how to turn off program highlights.

1. Right-click the Start button and select Properties.

2. Click the top Customize button for the Start panel settings.

3. Next, click the Advanced tab.

4. Locate the Start Menu items scroll box in the middle of the window and scroll down all the way to the bottom until you locate the Scroll Programs entry.

5. Check the box to enable; uncheck to disable.

6. Click OK to save your changes.

7. Click OK once more to exit the Start Menu settings.

Now you will have full control over your scrolling program list.

Changing program listing display options for users of the classic Start Menu

The classic Start Menu has some of the features that were in older versions of the Windows operating system, such as the personalized menus feature. This feature can be more of an annoyance than a convenience, so I have dedicated a whole section to it. Also, you will learn how to manage the scroll programs feature for the classic menu users because it is slightly different than for users of the Start panel. Before you get started, make sure that you have the classic Start Menu enabled in order to use the following hacks.

Disabling personalized menus

Personalized menus is a feature in Windows that has been around for a little while. It uses your program run history to hide all of the other programs in your Start Menu program listing that you don't use or don't use often. After a user has used his computer for a short while, Windows will hide all of the programs that the user does not run so that he can find his most frequently run programs more easily.

Personalized menus sound like a great feature, but really think about it. Why would you have programs in your Start Menu that you don't use? If there is a program that is installed and never used on my computer, I uninstall it. You don't need to be wasting your storage space with useless programs.

Additionally, I have had experience with some beginning computer users complaining that Windows deleted all of their programs because they are no longer showing up in the Start Menu programs listing. Well as you probably know, they are still listed; the user just didn't realize that if they click the down arrow, it will expand the Start Menu back to its original size so they can view all the programs.

When considering all of these issues with personalized menus, I can't see why you would want to have this feature enabled. Follow these steps to take back your computer:

1. Right-click the Start Menu and select Properties.

2. Click the bottom Customize button to bring up the Customize Classic Start Menu window.

3. Locate the Advanced Start Menu options box, and scroll down all the way to the bottom.

4. You should now be able to see the Use Personalized Menus setting. Just uncheck the box to disable the feature.

5. Click OK to save your changes.

6. Click OK once more to close the Taskbar and Start Menu Properties window.

Now you will no longer have to deal with your programs disappearing. I highly recommend that you disable this feature on any beginner computer user's computer as well, to save yourself a headache explaining to them that Windows didn't really delete everything.

Working with the scroll programs feature

The scroll feature works the exact same as when it is enabled for users of the new Start panel. Instead of showing all the programs on your list on-screen at once, it will show only one column of programs that you will be able to scroll through.

Some computer manufacturers ship their systems with this feature enabled, although some have it disabled. Follow these steps to modify this feature for your computer:

1. Right-click the Start button and select Properties.

2. Click the Customize button at the bottom.

3. Then locate the Advanced Start Menu Options box and scroll all the way to the bottom again.

4. Locate the Scroll Programs feature and check it to enable; uncheck it to disable.

5. Click OK to save your changes.

6. And click OK once more to close the Properties window.

Now your program scrolling is under your control.

Removing pop-up Help for users of both the Start panel and Menu

Ever notice that when you hover your mouse over a program listing in the Start Menu, a little yellow Help box will pop up? This Help feature is called balloon help. If a user does not know what a program does, she can hold the mouse over the program for a second or so and a little message will fade in telling her what it is, if the programmer has set up this feature of the user's program. For other programs that do not have this feature set up in their shortcut, it will just tell the user where the program is located on her computer.

This feature can be very useful for a beginning computer user. Sometimes the pop-up Help can become an annoyance and just blocks your screen. If you do not need this feature, why not disable it? Follow these steps to get rid of this feature:

1. Click the Start Menu and select Run and then type **regedit** in the box and click OK.

2. Once the Registry Editor is loaded, navigate though HKEY_CURRENT_USER, Software, Microsoft, Windows, CurrentVersion, Explorer, and Advanced.

3. Right-click the entry called ShowInfoTip and select Modify.

4. Set the value equal to 0 to disable this feature, and click OK.

5. Close the Registry Editor and log off and back so the feature can be removed.

You are now finished with the last section on customizing the Start Menu and program listing. Now on to customizing the taskbar.

A registry file can be found in the Chapter 2 folder on the companion CD-ROM that will allow you to easily undo the pop-up Help hack. It is called `restore_popup_help.reg`.

Customizing the Taskbar

The Windows XP taskbar has many new features, such as the ability to group programs and the new system tray that automatically hides icons that are not active. On top of these new features, there were enhancements such as new animations and graphical refinements that make the taskbar look so much better.

The taskbar normally is used to switch between active programs and provides some system information, such as the current time and other system events in the system try. Now it can be used for so much more, as you will see in the next few sections.

Using and adjusting program grouping

The program grouping feature can be very useful, or it can be an annoyance. When you have more than just a few programs open, the taskbar can become cluttered. To fight this, as the taskbar fills up, programs that have more than one window open are grouped together. If you have a bunch of Internet Explorer windows open, they will all be grouped together into one entry on the taskbar. Then, if you want to switch between them or close one, you have to select the entry on the taskbar and a new menu will pop up showing you all of the different windows open for the specific application.

One great feature of grouping is it gives you the ability to close several windows at once. When all of the Internet Explorer windows are grouped together, you can just right-click the entry on the taskbar and select Close Group. Doing so will automatically close all of the browser windows at once.

The downside to this is it takes an extra step to navigate through the grouped program items. Some people do not like this option very much and would rather have a taskbar that is more cluttered, because they will be able to switch between programs faster.

You can do a number of different things to customize this feature. Using a program called Tweak UI, which is a PowerToy released by Microsoft for Windows XP, you can easily change the behavior of how programs are grouped. But first, I am going to show you how to enable program grouping, if it is not set up on your computer. You'll also find out how to disable it, if you do not like it. Follow these steps to enable/disable program grouping:

1. Right-click a blank part of the taskbar and select Properties.

2. This will bring up the Taskbar and Start Menu Properties window that you used previously. This time, you are going to be concerned with what is on the Taskbar tab. Locate the Group Similar Taskbar Buttons item in the taskbar appearance section.

3. Check the box to enable this feature and uncheck to disable.

4. Click OK to save your changes.

Now that you have the feature turned on, you are ready to use Tweak UI to customize the way it behaves. First, download a copy of Tweak UI from Microsoft's PowerToys Web site, located at www.microsoft.com/windowsxp/pro/downloads/powertoys.asp. Make sure that you download the normal version of Tweak UI and not the version for Itanium-based systems unless you have a 64-bit system. When you have Tweak UI installed, follow these steps:

1. Launch Tweak UI by clicking the Start button, selecting All Programs, and then PowerToys for Windows XP.

2. When Tweak UI is started, expand Taskbar and Start Menu and select Grouping.

3. You will be shown three different options that determine the behavior of the grouping feature. Group Least Used Applications First will group the applications that are the oldest on the taskbar and have more than one window open. Group Applications With The Most Windows First will just group programs that have the most windows open when the taskbar starts to become cluttered. Group Any Application With At Least X Windows is the setting that gives you the most control over grouping. Select this behavior and then enter the number of windows an application must have open before they are grouped. I personally prefer this feature and set it to a value of 4 so that when I have a lot of Internet Explorer windows open, I can still switch between them quickly when I have a few open, but it groups them when I have a lot open so my taskbar is not all cluttered.

4. Once you have selected the behavior you prefer, click the OK button on the bottom of the window to save your changes.

Once you log off and back on or reboot, your changes will be active.

Quick Launching your programs

The Quick Launch bar is a great way to start up your programs. You can completely bypass the Start Menu and launch your programs with just one click. By default, the Quick Launch bar is not enabled. This section will show you how you can enable the Quick Launch bar and how you can make it very useful. First, enable the Quick Launch bar and then customize it by doing the following:

1. Right-click an open space on your taskbar and expand Toolbars and then select Quick Launch. This will make the Quick Launch bar appear.

2. By default, there are three icons on it: Internet Explorer, Show Desktop, and Windows Media Player. You can easily add more icons to the Quick Launch bar by just dragging them onto the toolbar. You can even specify where you want the icon to be placed by dragging the icon between two icons. The best way to add programs to your Quick Launch bar is to browse through your Start Menu and drag icons to the bar while holding down the Alt key. Holding down the Alt key will ensure that you create a copy of the shortcut in the Start Menu to be placed on the Quick Launch bar. Otherwise, when you drag a shortcut from the Start Menu, it will be removed from the Start Menu and placed only on the Quick Launch toolbar. I like to add my drives from My Computer to my Quick Launch bar as well for easy access. Just open up My Computer and drag them on down to the toolbar.

3. Once you have all of the icons set up on your Quick Launch bar, have some fun changing the position of the bar. To do this, you will have to unlock your taskbar. Right-click an

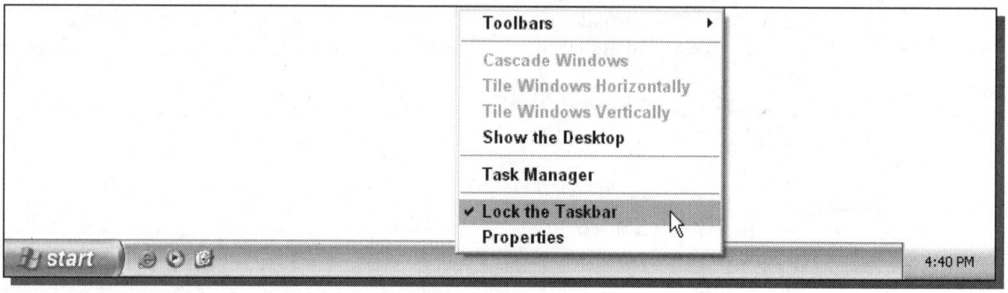

	Toolbars ▶
	Cascade Windows
	Tile Windows Horizontally
	Tile Windows Vertically
	Show the Desktop
	Task Manager
	✓ **Lock the Taskbar**
	Properties

start ... 4:40 PM

FIGURE 2-11: Taskbar properties, showing the taskbar locked.

open part of the taskbar and select Lock the Taskbar only if there is already a check next to it, as shown in Figure 2-11. If there is not a check, then your taskbar is not locked and you are ready to proceed.

Now that you made sure that the taskbar is not locked, you are ready to move the bar around. Let's expand the taskbar up so that you can have one row of Quick Launch icons and then your open programs will be listed below. You can do this by placing and holding down the left mouse button on top of the taskbar, as shown in Figure 2-12, and moving the mouse up, while still holding the button down on the mouse, until the taskbar expands upward.

Once the taskbar moves up one notch, you can move the Quick Launch bar up. You can do this by grabbing the left side of the menu on the dotted vertical line with the mouse and moving the mouse up while holding down the left mouse button. When you are finished, your taskbar should look like what's shown in Figure 2-13. Notice that when you have expanded your taskbar up one notch, the system clock expands to show the date as well as the day.

4. When you have the taskbar unlocked, you can easily change the size of the icons that are placed on the Quick Launch bar. This can be done by right-clicking somewhere on the bar that is taken up by an icon, and selecting View. You will then see two choices: large and small icons. By default, the Small Icons are shown. The Large Icons look pretty cool because they make your taskbar look very different. I suggest you play around with this feature and get your icons looking the way you like them best.

5. Once you are finished making all of your changes to the taskbar, I suggest that you lock it again so that you won't accidentally move things around the taskbar.

Now you have customized your Quick Launch bar and have greatly improved your navigation by creating your own list of programs. This will speed up the amount of time it takes to start up any program.

Hacking the Start button to replace the Start text

One of my favorite hacks for Windows XP is the Start button hack. It is possible to use resource editing tools such as Resource Hacker as well as a bunch of other adjustments to

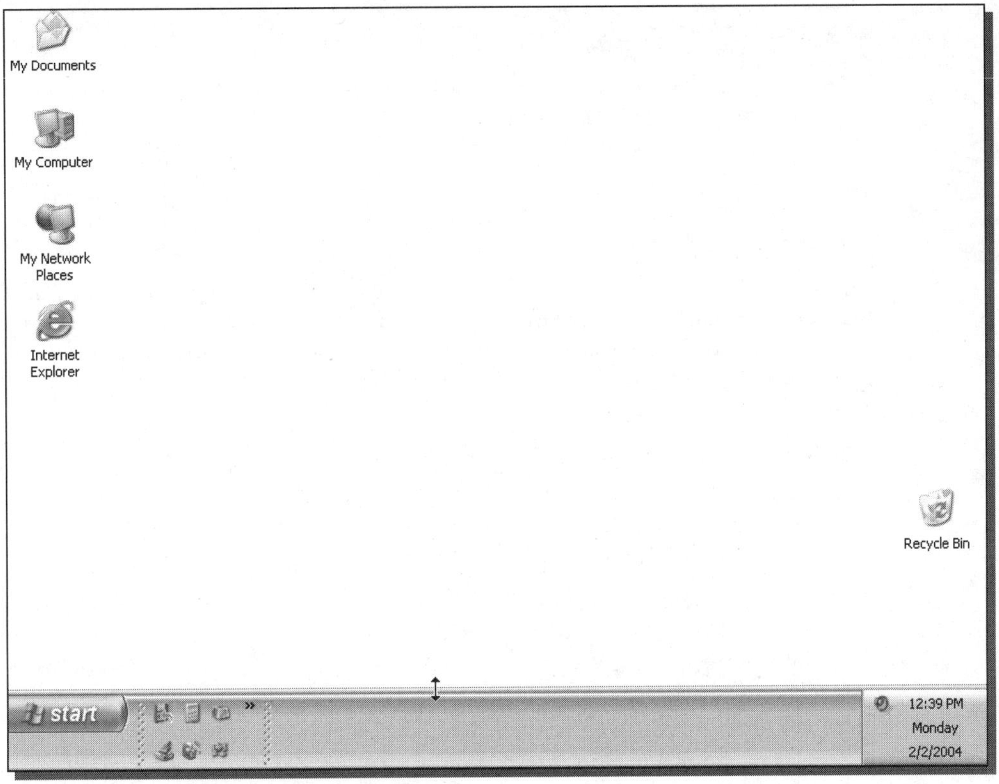

FIGURE 2-12: Expanding the taskbar by placing the mouse on top of the taskbar and moving the mouse up when the left button is held down.

replace the Start text to anything that you want. I changed my Start Menu button on Hacking Windows XP, as shown in Figure 2-14.

You can edit the text on the Start button in a number of different ways. The most popular method is to use a hex editor. First, open up the Windows Explorer file and edit the string (a string is computer lingo for text), if you can find it in the file. Then, you will have to make some changes to the system file protection to allow you to run a hacked version of Explorer. After you have made those changes, you have to boot into Safe mode and swap the Explorer

FIGURE 2-13: What the taskbar can look like when you have finished moving it to the Quick Launch bar, adjusted the taskbar size, and added more programs to your Quick Launch bar.

FIGURE **2-14: The Start button text changed.**

file with the version that you hacked. Additionally, with that method, you are limited to only five characters on the Start Menu button.

That method is just too complicated and has a lot of unnecessary steps. After experimenting with several different ideas that I came up with, I discovered an even better way to change the Start button text. Using my method, you will not have to mess with the system file protection at all, boot into Safe mode, or even be limited to five characters on the Start button. Sound good? Okay, let's get started:

1. First, you will need to start up the Resource Hacker that you used in Chapter 1. If you no longer have a copy of Resource Hacker, you can download another copy from www.users.on.net/johnson/resourcehacker. Once you have Resource Hacker started up, go to the next step.

2. You are going to want to open up the Windows Explorer main file, called explorer.exe. This file is stored in the C:\Windows directory. To open the file up, click the file menu bar item and select Open, then just navigate over to the Windows directory and select explorer.exe.

3. When explorer.exe is loaded, you should see a bunch of folders on the left side of the screen. Expand the String Table folder and then expand the 37 folder and select 1033.

4. You will not see a bunch of text on the right side of the screen. Locate where it says Start, and replace it with the text that you want to use. I am going to replace it with "Hacking Windows XP." Make sure that you only enter your text between the quotes; see Figure 2-14 for more clarification.

5. Next, you will have to click the Compile Script button, as shown in Figure 2-15.

6. Now, you have to save the file that you just edited and recompiled. Click the File menu bar item again and this time select Save As. Then save the file with a name other than explorer.exe. I suggest you call it "ExplorerHacked.exe." Make sure that you add the .exe to the end of the file name or else it will not work.

7. You are now finished hacking the Explorer file. You can close the Resource Hacker. Now you just have to tell Windows to use your new Explorer file the next time you log in. To do this, click the Start button and select Run.

8. Type **regedit** in the box and click OK.

9. Next, when the Registry Editor is loaded, expand HKEY_LOCAL_MACHINE, SOFTWARE, Microsoft, Windows NT, CurrentVersion, and Winlogon.

10. Inside the WinLogon folder, you will want to look for the Shell entry. Right-click it and select Modify, as shown in Figure 2-16.

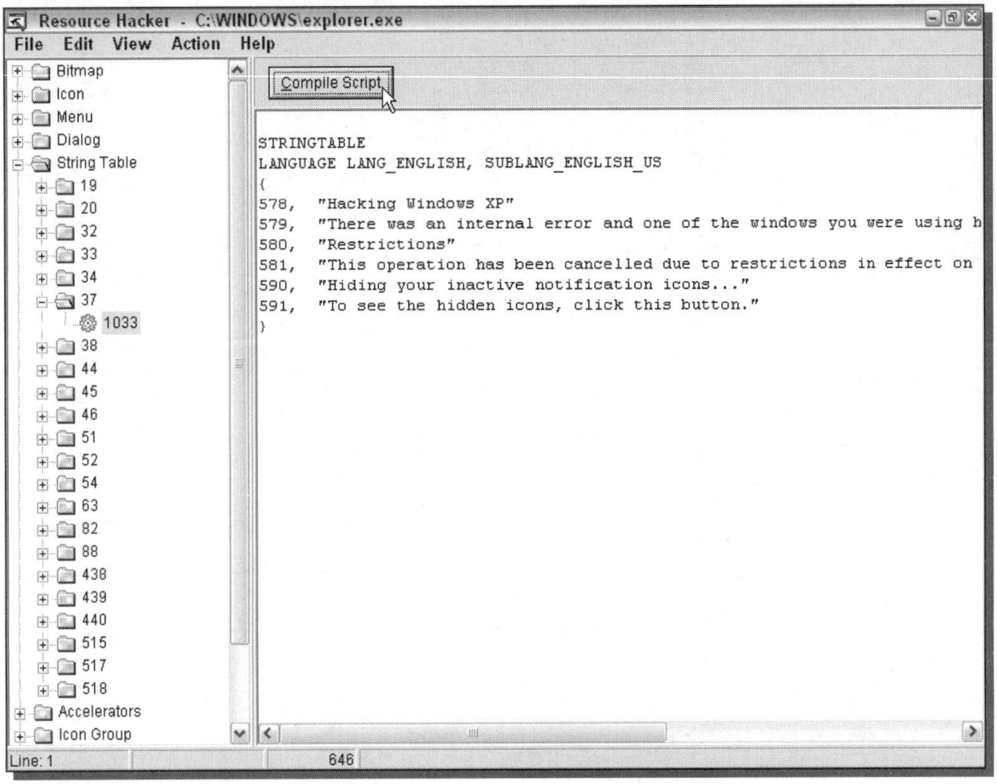

Resource Hacker - C:\WINDOWS\explorer.exe

File   Edit   View   Action   Help

- Bitmap
- Icon
- Menu
- Dialog
- String Table
  - 19
  - 20
  - 32
  - 33
  - 34
  - 37
    - 1033
  - 38
  - 44
  - 45
  - 46
  - 51
  - 52
  - 54
  - 63
  - 82
  - 88
  - 438
  - 439
  - 440
  - 515
  - 517
  - 518
- Accelerators
- Icon Group

Compile Script

```
STRINGTABLE
LANGUAGE LANG_ENGLISH, SUBLANG_ENGLISH_US
{
578,   "Hacking Windows XP"
579,   "There was an internal error and one of the windows you were using h
580,   "Restrictions"
581,   "This operation has been cancelled due to restrictions in effect on
590,   "Hiding your inactive notification icons..."
591,   "To see the hidden icons, click this button."
}
```

Line: 1   646

FIGURE 2-15: Using Resource Hacker to recompile explorer.exe to rename the Start Menu button.

12. Type in the name of the file that you saved in Step 6. I used "ExplorerHacked.exe," so that is what I will replace all of the text with.

13. When you are finished, click OK to save your changes. You may now close the Registry Editor because you are finished with the hack.

Just log off and log back on or restart to see the new changes in effect. If you did not edit the registry correctly, such as specifying the exact correct file as the value for shell, you will not be able to use your computer properly because Explorer will not load. If that is the case, after you log on, eventually you will be shown just your background image. You will need to start up Explorer manually by pressing Ctrl+Alt+Delete to bring up the Task Manager. Once the Task Manager is displayed, click the New Task button on the Applications tab and type in **regedit**. This will launch the Registry Editor again so that you can edit the shell entry again. Go back through Step 9 to get back to the shell entry. Make sure that you type in the full correct file name with the extension as the value. If you want to revert to the original Windows Explorer with Start as the text on the Start button, just change this value back to **explorer.exe**. Then just log off your computer by using the shutdown menu bar item in the Task Manager and you will be back to normal when you log back on.

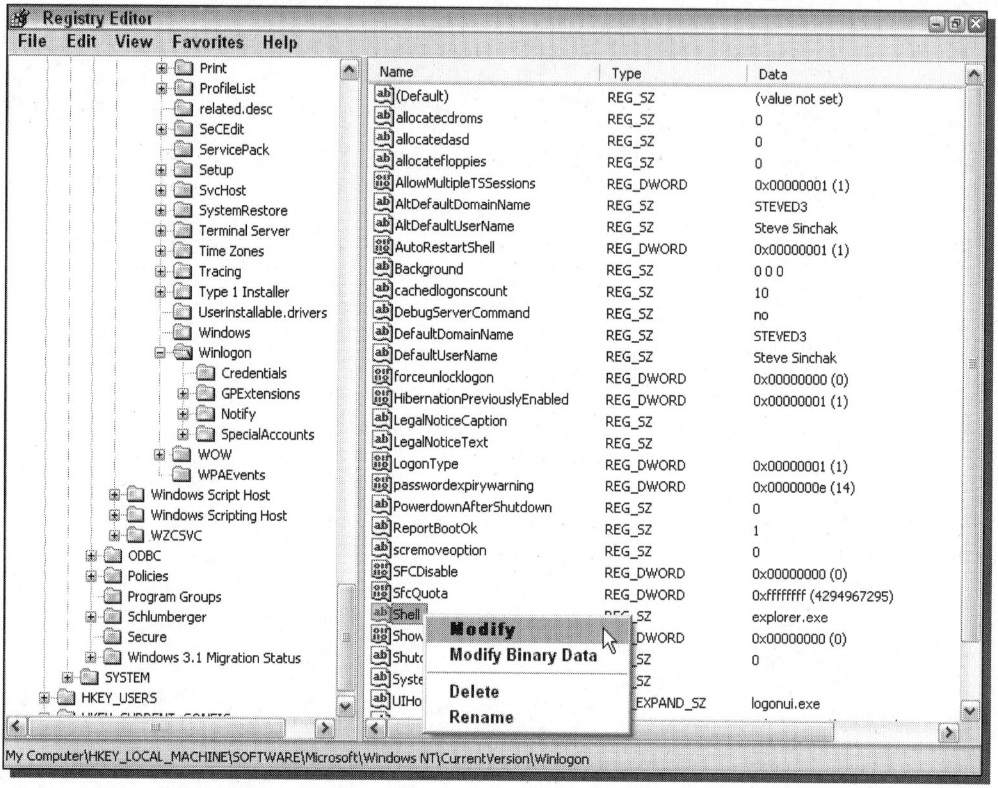

FIGURE 2-16: Using the Registry Editor to replace the original Explorer shell.

Modifying the taskbar location

You always see the taskbar appear on the bottom of your screen. That does not always have to be the case. It is possible to move the taskbar to every side of the screen. This allows you to really change the look of Windows XP. Figure 2-17 shows what your screen could look like if you moved your taskbar to the left side of the screen.

Moving the taskbar is very simple. There are just three basic steps:

1. You will want to unlock the taskbar if it is already locked. Right-click an open part of the taskbar and select Lock the Taskbar, if there is a check next to the entry.

2. Click and hold your mouse on any part of the taskbar where there are no icons, such as the system clock, and drag the taskbar to different sides by moving your mouse in the general direction.

3. When you have the taskbar where you want it, you may want to readjust your toolbars inside the taskbar, such as the Quick Launch bar. Then lock it back up again by right-clicking it and selecting Lock the Taskbar.

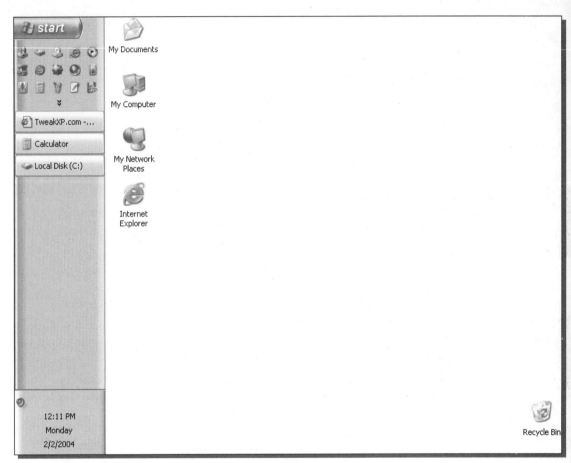

FIGURE 2-17: Windows XP with the taskbar on the left side of the screen.

Using the Taskbar Magnifier PowerToy

Microsoft has released many different PowerToys, some of which we have already used (Tweak UI). Another PowerToy that is pretty cool is the Taskbar Magnifier. The Taskbar Magnifier turns the mouse into a magnifying glass. When you activate the Taskbar Magnifier, a new bar will be displayed in your taskbar that is like a little TV screen, as shown in Figure 2-18. It will display a magnified image of what the mouse is currently over. If you know someone whose eyes are not as good as they used to be, the Taskbar Magnifier is a good aid for them. Also, if you do a lot of graphic work and care about the details of your work, instead of having to zoom in all the time, you can use the Taskbar Magnifier to see a zoomed-in view that will reveal details.

Getting the Taskbar Magnifier PowerToy setup is easy; just download it from Microsoft's PowerToys Web site, located at www.microsoft.com/windowsxp/pro/downloads/

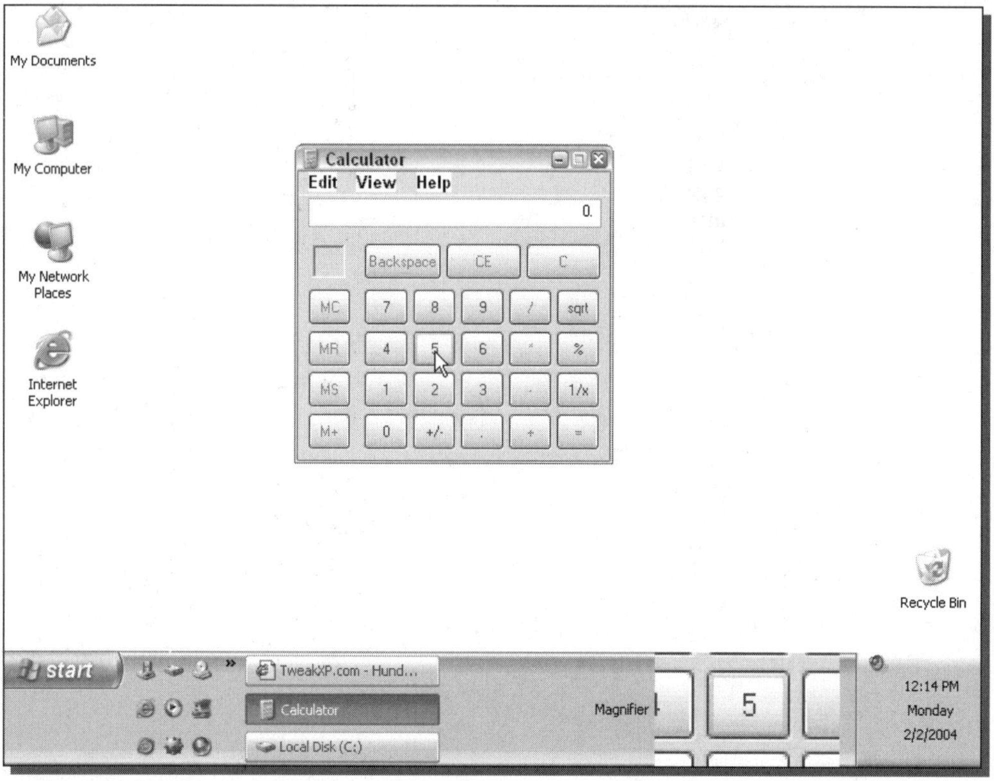

FIGURE 2-18: The Taskbar Magnifier PowerToy.

powertoys.asp and follow these steps:

1. Once you have the PowerToy installed, you just have to enable the toolbar on the taskbar. First, you will have to unlock your taskbar.

2. Next, right-click an open part of the taskbar and expand Toolbars and then select Taskbar Magnifier. This will cause the Taskbar Magnifier to show up on the taskbar.

3. You may want to resize the taskbar a little, such as dragging the t of the bar up to make it a little larger so your magnifier screen is bigger.

4. Also, you can remove the text next to the magnifier by right-clicking the magnifier object on the taskbar when the taskbar is unlocked and selecting Show Title to unselect it.

If you ever want to remove the Taskbar Magnifier, just right-click an open part of the taskbar and expand the toolbars menu again and select Taskbar Magnifier to uncheck the item.

Removing the notification area

The notification area is the right side of the taskbar, where all of the little system tray icons are located. This item is not critical to the operation of the system and can be removed if you want more room for your open programs and other toolbars. However, any program such as an instant messenger program, that might minimize itself to the notification area will be a little more difficult to get to. The only way to remove the notification area is to use the Group Policy Editor. Unfortunately, this will only work if you are using Windows XP Pro. If you are running Windows XP Pro, then follow these steps to remove the notification area:

1. Launch the Group Policy Editor by clicking the Start button and then selecting Run. Type **gpedit.msc** in the box and click OK.

2. Once the policy editor has loaded, expand Administrative Templates, and then select Start Menu and Taskbar.

3. Locate and select Hide the Notification Area. Right-click it and select Properties.

4. Then, just click Enable and click the OK button to save your changes.

The next time you log on, your notification area will be gone. If you want to free up even more room, consider removing the clock by reading the next section.

Removing the clock from the taskbar

The clock can be very useful if you don't have any other clocks in the same room as your computer. Otherwise, it is just taking up space. After all, how many clocks do you really need? If you want the maximum amount of space for your toolbars and open programs on the taskbar, I suggest that you also remove the clock.

Removing the clock is extremely simple. Follow these quick instructions:

1. Right-click the system clock and select Properties.

2. Then, under the Notification Area on the Taskbar and Start Menu Properties window, uncheck Show the Clock.

3. Click OK to save your changes and the clock will be gone.

Summary

This chapter has taken you through the steps of customizing the Start Menu and then onto the task bar. You made your Start panel work the way you want it to and made it even more convenient. If you liked the classic Start Menu, you were shown how to change the settings so that you could use it. Then you were shown how to customize and improve the way the taskbar works.

The next chapter will concentrate on customizing the desktop. You'll find out how you can use great tools, such as the multiple desktop PowerToy, to create several different desktops for one user. Then, you will learn how to change other desktop settings to customize your desktop.

Hacking the Desktop

chapter

3

S tudies have shown that customizing your desktop will result in a 64 percent increase in productivity as well as a 248 percent increase in happiness levels of computer users. I was unable to contact the institute where these numbers purportedly came from to confirm this information, but even if these numbers are slightly off (or completely made up), customizing the desktop is still very beneficial.

This chapter will show you some cool tricks and tools to make your desktop look and work much better so that you can also benefit from a customized desktop. Starting with the icons, it will show you how to remove, enlarge, replace, and adjust the special effects, such as the drop shadows. Then, it will move on to customizing the way your desktop behaves and operates by using Active Desktop and a cool desktop PowerToy.

The desktop seems like a pretty simple part of the operating system, but there is a lot you can do to it to make using your computer more efficient as well as fun.

Customizing Desktop Icons

The first time I started up Windows XP, I was shocked to find only the Recycle Bin icon on the desktop. Where were the rest of the icons? Did the install screw up? Microsoft is starting to transition away from the desktop that we are all used to with previous versions of Windows. With the introduction of the Start panel, the same icons on the desktop are just not needed. Now, the desktop looks much cleaner and more visually appealing because there are not 50 icons on the screen blocking your view of the wallpaper.

I have to admit, I like the clean interface, but I miss some of the icons that used to be on the desktop. Thankfully, you can do a number of different things to customize the desktop to bring back some of the old icons and also customize them so that you can preserve the clean look while restoring functionality. The next several sections will show you how you can get your desktop looking the way you want it to by taking advantage of hidden features and tricks.

Removing all icons from the desktop

No matter how hard I try, I always end up with a lot of junk on my desktop. From programs that I download and documents that I was too lazy to save elsewhere as well as new program links that seem to pop up from nowhere, there is never an end to the war that I fight with my desktop to keep it clutter-free. I like to be able to see my desktop wallpaper and not have my view of the wallpaper blocked by useless icons. One great way to win the never-ending desktop war is to just disable the desktop's ability to show the icons and instead place the most common desktop icons, such as My Computer and the Recycle Bin, on the Quick Launch bar.

Disabling the icons on the desktop is actually a very simple task. Most people never know about this feature, because it is placed where you would really never expect it. To get started, just right-click Desktop. Then expand Arrange Icons By and select Show Desktop Icons to unselect it. After a few seconds, the icons will disappear.

Don't worry, the icons and folder on your desktop were not deleted. If you ever want to turn the icons back on, just repeat the preceding steps once more.

This is a very simple way to quickly clean up the desktop. It's sort of like sweeping the dirt under a rug. The desktop clutter is still there, but you just can't see it.

Customizing the icon drop shadow effect

One cool new feature of Windows XP is the Use Drop Shadows for Icon Labels on the Desktop. This new effect really makes the icons stand out from your wallpaper and makes them much easier to read when you are using a background, such as a photo, that has both light and dark spots. Unfortunately, depending on your computer's hardware configuration, you may or may not be able to experience this cool new effect. If you have a newer computer that has an average graphics card, you will have no problem using this feature. But if you have an older graphics card, then you may be out of luck.

The Use Drop Shadows for Icon Labels on the Desktop can be turned on or off. Depending on the wallpaper that you are using, you may like or dislike the feature. I really like the new effect, but if you like having a clean and crisp interface, I recommend disabling the effect. Follow these steps to turn the feature on or off:

1. Click the Start button, and select Run.

2. Key in **sysdm.cpl** and click OK to launch system properties.

3. Click the Advanced tab, and then click the Settings button under the Performance section.

4. While on the Visual Effects tab, scroll down to the bottom of the box.

5. Locate Use Drop Shadows for Icon Labels on the Desktop, as shown in Figure 3-1, and check or uncheck the value, depending on what you would like to do.

6. Click OK to save your changes.

7. Click OK once more to close the System Properties window.

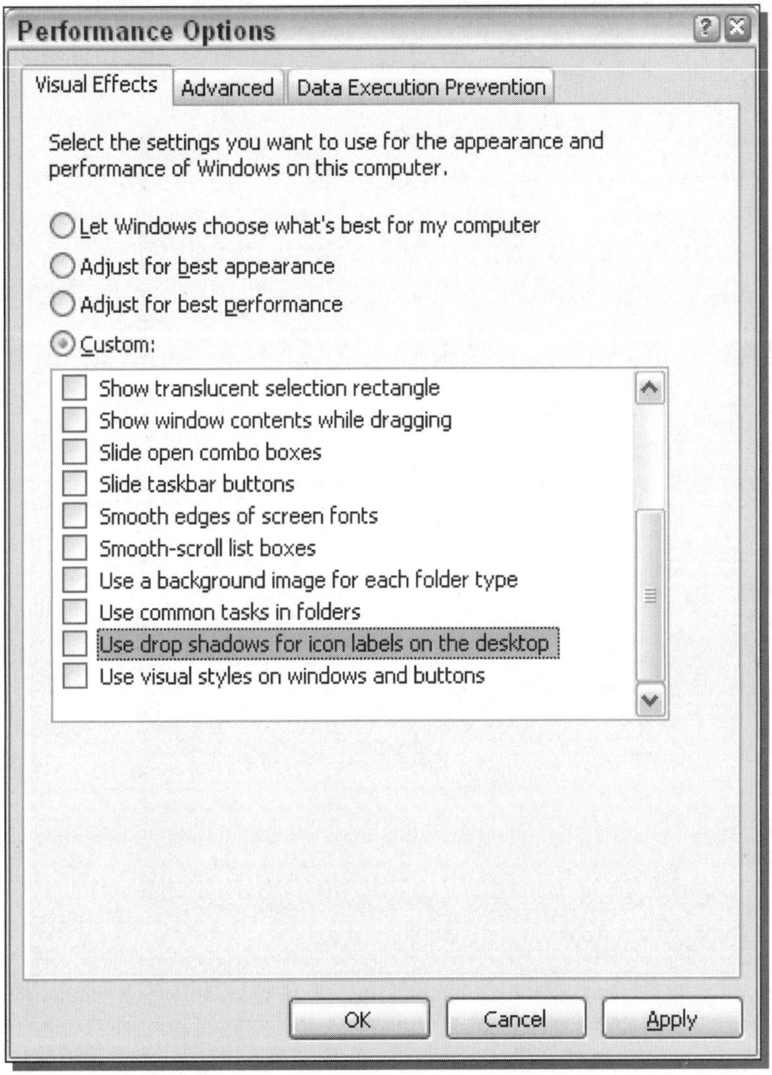

Performance Options

Visual Effects | Advanced | Data Execution Prevention

Select the settings you want to use for the appearance and performance of Windows on this computer.

○ Let Windows choose what's best for my computer

○ Adjust for best appearance

○ Adjust for best performance

◉ Custom:

☐ Show translucent selection rectangle
☐ Show window contents while dragging
☐ Slide open combo boxes
☐ Slide taskbar buttons
☐ Smooth edges of screen fonts
☐ Smooth-scroll list boxes
☐ Use a background image for each folder type
☐ Use common tasks in folders
☐ Use drop shadows for icon labels on the desktop
☐ Use visual styles on windows and buttons

OK | Cancel | Apply

FIGURE 3-1: Turning the drop shadow effect on and off for icons on the desktop.

If you enable the effect by checking the box and the effect still does not show up after you reboot your computer, this is a sign that your computer does not support the feature.

Displaying the traditional Windows icons

Now that Windows XP includes the new Start panel with shortcuts to My Computer, My Documents, My Network Places, and Internet Explorer, the shortcuts on the desktop are less important and Microsoft decided to remove them. If you are a user that doesn't like clutter on

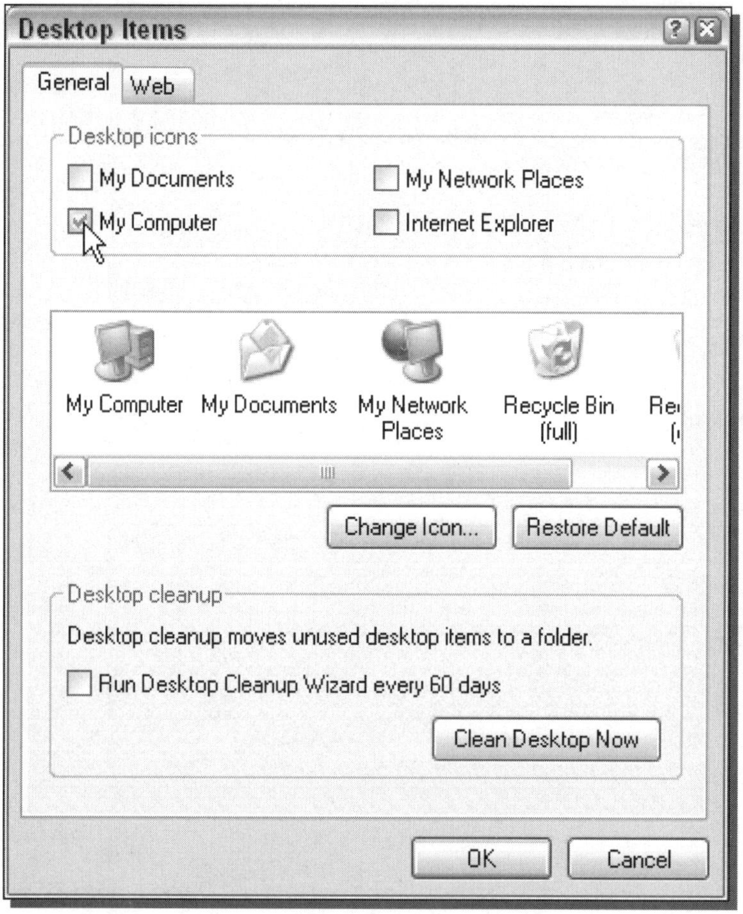

FIGURE **3-2: Selecting which icons to display on the desktop.**

your desktop, then this feature is great for you. But if you like the old way of using Windows, and like the desktop to be the center of your navigation instead of the Start panel, then you are out of luck.

However, just as with other new features in Windows XP, with the desktop you can revert to the old way of doing things. Turning the desktop icons back on involves a little more effort than just switching back to the classic Start Menu, but doing so still is not very difficult. Follow these steps and you will be able to select which icons you want back:

1. Right-click the desktop and select Properties.

2. Click the Desktop tab and then click the Customize Desktop button at the bottom of the window.

3. Then, on the General tab, just select the check box next to the icons you want to display, as shown in Figure 3-2.

4. Click OK to save your changes.

5. Click OK once more to close display properties.

You will see the icons on your desktop immediately after you complete the steps.

Enabling large icons on the desktop

Windows XP has support for larger and more colorful icons than any other previous Windows version. The support for high-quality graphics is one of the reasons why Windows XP looks so much better than previous versions of Windows. This section will show you how to take advantage of the new graphical enhancements to make your desktop look cool.

Two different sizes of icons are used on the Windows XP desktop. The normal size for icons in Windows XP is 32 × 32 pixels. Windows XP also has support for larger icons, which are 48 × 48 pixels. Figure 3-3 shows the difference in size between the two icons. Use of the larger icons will not only help your vision but will also make your desktop look more visually pleasing, because the larger icons are more detailed.

I recommend that you turn the large icons on, to see how you like it. If you have a large monitor, chances are that you will love the large icons. Some of you, however, may not like them because they take up more space than the smaller icons and decrease the amount of icons that can fit on your desktop. Although this is a tradeoff, I feel the high-resolution icons are worth it. To get started, follow these steps:

1. Right-click the desktop and select Properties.

2. Click the Appearance tab and then click the Effects button.

3. Check the Use Large Icons box, as shown in Figure 3-4.

4. Click OK to save your changes.

5. Click the OK button again to close display properties.

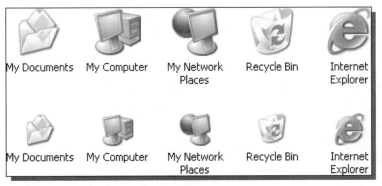

FIGURE 3-3: Large and normal size icons.

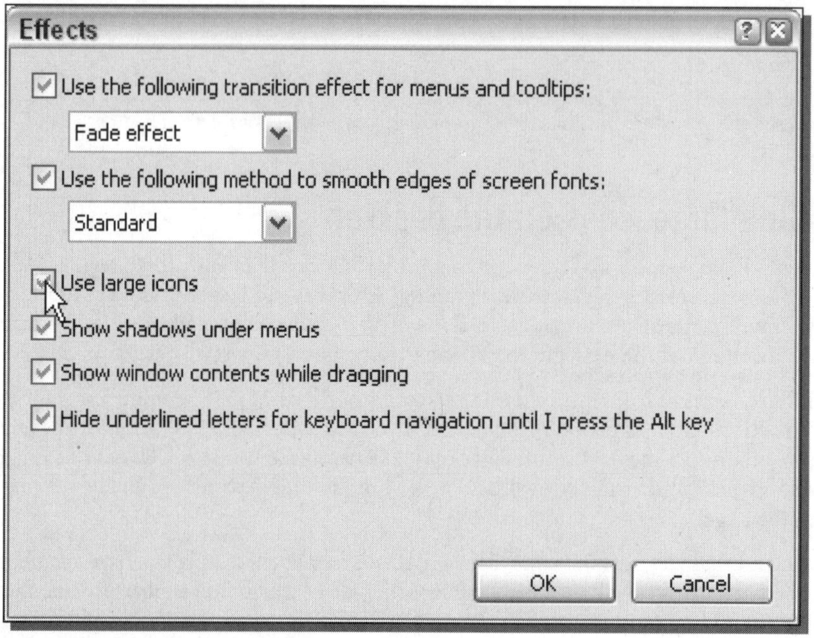

Figure 3-4: Enabling large icons.

The large icons should be displayed immediately after the change. You will notice that some other icons will also enlarge. This is a side effect of using this tip, because it is impossible to adjust just the size of the icons on the desktop. However, only the icons that you see when you browse your computer and use the Control Panel are slightly larger. None of the other icons are changed.

To revert to the normal-sized icons, just repeat the preceding step and uncheck Use Large Icons.

Removing the text below the icons

Icons and text always go together. Every single icon on your desktop has to have a label below it. If you have a lot of icons on your desktop, the text under the icon is very valuable. However, if you have few icons on your desktop, you can get away with just using the icons alone. Doing so will result in a much cleaner interface. Amazingly, your desktop will look much simpler and cleaner without the labels below the icons.

How is it possible not to display the text? Well, it is actually just a trick. You are not really removing the text under the icons. Instead, you are replacing the name of the icon with some characters that the computer will not display. Renaming the icons would be very easy if all that was involved was clicking the name and pressing the spacebar a few times. Unfortunately, that is not the case, because Windows does not allow you to enter in a space with the spacebar. Instead, you can use the ASCII code for a space. Every character that is used in the computer is stored in the PC as a code for a character. For example, the ASCII code for an *s* is 0115, the ASCII code for a copyright sign is 0169, and so on. You will be interested in the ASCII code for a character that shows up as a blank space, which is 0160. Now that you know the basics of ASCII, let's rename some files.

1. Start with the first icon that you want to rename: right-click it and select Rename.

2. Select all of the text, and erase it with the Backspace key.

3. Now, enter in the ASCII code for the space, so make sure your Numlock is on, and just press and hold the Alt key while typing in **0 1 6 0** on the numpad on the right of the keyboard.

4. When you have finished typing in **0 1 6 0**, let go of the Alt key and the blank space will be inserted.

5. Then, just press Enter to save the new name.

If you want to remove the text of multiple icons, then you will have a problem with the instructions because each shortcut or item must still have a unique name. One easy workaround is to enter in the ASCII code as the previous directions indicate, and then add a space using the spacebar after it. The first icons will have the ASCII space code + one space, the second icon will have the ASCII space code + two spaces, and so on.

Removing the text below the icons also allows you to do some fun things with the placement of your icons. Try removing the name of several icons. Then, turn on large icons, if you have not already done so, and line them up just above the taskbar, as shown in Figure 3-5. This will give you a setup that is similar to the bar on Apple's OS X. Although your icons won't be animated and bounce around, you will be able to set up your interface so that it looks like the OS X setup.

Renaming the Recycle Bin

The Recycle Bin is a great feature of Windows, but it is very difficult to customize the name. Unlike other system icons on the desktop, you cannot just right-click it and select Rename. The only way to rename the Recycle Bin is to hack the Registry. This is not as simple as the method for the other icons, but you can easily get through it. To get started, let's assume that you want to rename the Recycle Bin as Trash Compactor:

1. Click the Start button and select Run.

2. Then type **regedit** in the box and click OK.

3. When the Registry Editor is started, you will want to expand the HKEY_CURRENT _USER, Software, Microsoft, Windows, CurrentVersion, Explorer, CLSID, and {645FF040-5081-101B-9F08-00AA002F954E} folders.

FIGURE 3-5: Icons placed to look like the OS X bar.

4. When you have expanded the last folder, you should see an entry called (Default) that has no value. Right-click that entry and select Modify.

5. Next, just type **Trash Compactor**, or any other name, in the box and click OK. If you want to hide the text under the Recycle Bin icon, you will still have to specify a name. Instead of typing in a word, just click the spacebar once and then click OK. You do not have to worry about entering in the ASCII code for a space when editing the registry.

6. Close the Registry Editor and press F5 when viewing your desktop to see your changes. If that does not work for your computer, then you will have to log out and log in to activate the changes.

Now your Recycle Bin is no more. Hello Trash Compactor!

 If you want to undo this hack, just import the registry file on the companion CD-ROM located in the Chapter 3 folder called `undo_recycle_rename.reg`.

Removing the shortcut arrow from icons on the desktop

One thing that I always hate about Windows is the shortcut arrow. Sure, it is good to be able to tell if a shortcut is actually a shortcut, but I think I know that the applications that I put on my desktop are already shortcuts. This feature can be annoying as well as problematic. One example of this is when you use the large icons. Any icon that is a shortcut has a stretched version of the arrow in the lower-left corner of the icon, making the icon look pixelated.

A number of different solutions to the shortcut arrow problem are available. You can replace the big white square with a smaller semi-transparent arrow, use your own icon file, or you can disable it completely. The best way to change the shortcut arrow setting is to use the most popular Microsoft PowerToy, Tweak UI. You should already have a copy of Tweak UI installed on your computer, if you followed my suggestions and instructions from Chapter 2. But just in case you don't, you can get a copy of it from the PowerToys Web page, located at `www.microsoft.com/windowsxp/pro/downloads/powertoys.asp`. Follow these steps to change the shortcut arrow settings:

1. Click the Start Menu and expand All Programs, PowerToys for Windows XP, and then select Tweak UI to start it up.

2. Once Tweak UI is started, expand the Explorer entry and select Shortcut.

3. You will now see four different icon Shortcut Overlay options. I recommend you try using the light arrow options first. Then if you still don't like it, click None, as shown in Figure 3-6, to remove the shortcut arrows.

4. Once you have made up your mind and selected the Overlay option, click OK to save your changes.

You may now close Tweak UI. Your changes will show up after you reboot.

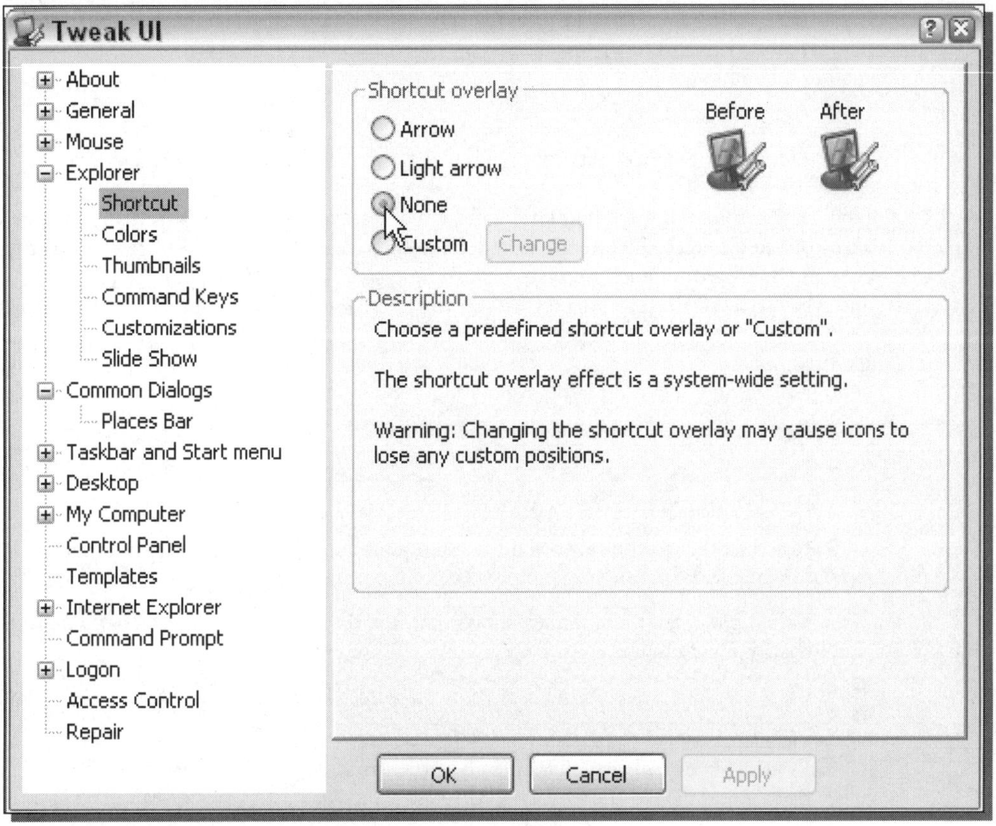

FIGURE 3-6: Using Tweak UI to customize the shortcut overlay.

Changing the icons on the desktop

The new icons that come with Windows XP provide a much-needed change from the boring low-resolution icons of previous Windows versions. The new icons have started a whole breed of icons, known as the XP-style icons. There are now hundreds of Web sites started by artists where you can download their personal XP-style icon creations. My favorite site is www.foood .net, which offers hundreds of very well-designed XP icons for free. Now that there are so many cool XP icons floating around on the Web, why not replace your desktop icons for a fresh new look?

Changing the desktop icons is very simple in Windows XP. The most difficult part of the process is finding good XP icons. To help you out on your hunt for cool XP icons, I have created the following list of some of my favorite icon Web sites:

- *Iconica*: www.marvilla.us

- *I heart NY*: www.iheartny.com/xicons

- *WBC Icons*: www.wbchug.com

- *Foood's Icons*: www.foood.net

- *I-cons*: http://i-cons.tk/

- *xIcons*: http://xp.xicons.com

Now that you have a few good sites to start your search, it is time to actually change the icons on the desktop. As already noted, changing the icons is easy. But if you want to change the icon of one of the system shortcuts, such as the My Computer, My Documents, and My Network Places icons, as well as the Internet Explorer and Recycle Bin icons, then you have to follow a special procedure. Follow these steps to change any of the system icons:

1. Right-click the Desktop and select Properties.

2. When Display Properties loads, click the Desktop tab and click the Customize Desktop button at the bottom of the window.

3. Just click the icon that you want to change, as shown in Figure 3-7, and then click the Change Icon button.

4. When the change icon screen shows up, click the Browse button and navigate to the icon that you want to use.

5. Once you have selected the icon that you want to use, just click OK and your icon should change in the preview box.

6. When you are finished changing all of the icons, click OK to save your icon modifications and return to the Display Properties window.

7. Now, just click OK once more to save your changes.

Changing the system icons is pretty simple, but changing other icons on your desktop, such as program shortcuts and folders, is even easier. Just follow these steps:

1. Right-click the item for which you want to change the icon and select Properties.

2. If you right-clicked an application shortcut, then you will see the Change Icon button at the bottom of the window. If you are trying to change the icon of a folder on your desktop, you will have to click the Customize tab first and then you will see the Change Icon button at the bottom of the window as well.

3. Once you are finished changing the icon, click OK to save your changes.

Tip If you want to change other system icons, such as the Internet Explorer icon, Drive icons, or the Folder icons, you will have to use a special utility. Many programs on the Web will allow you to do so, but the two that I like to use are called Microangelo (www.microangelo.us) and Icon Packager (www.stardock.com/products/iconpackager/).

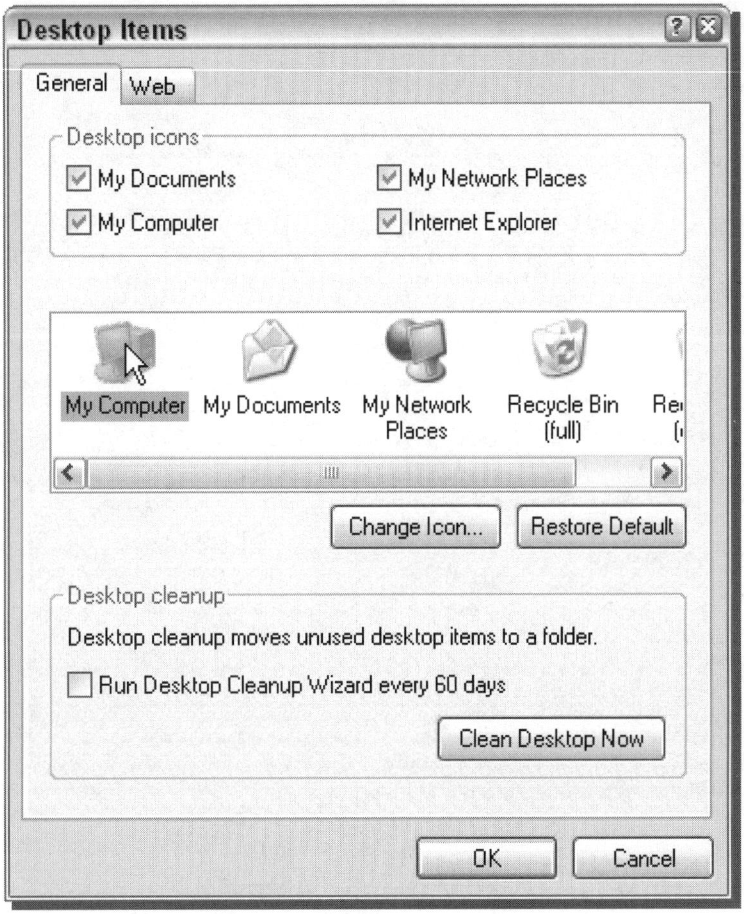

FIGURE **3-7: Changing the My Computer icon.**

Now you will be able to benefit from all of the cool icons that are available for free on the Web. Because you have now finished customizing the look of your desktop icons, let's move on to customizing the desktop.

Customizing the Behavior of the Desktop

The desktop is a pretty simple part of Windows XP. You really can't do much to customize its looks besides changing the wallpaper. However, several different tools are available that you can use to add features to the desktop and to take advantage of some of its lesser known features. These next few sections will show you how you can use these tools to do cool things such as use multiple desktops or create a special Web page that will display live data, such as a weather report, from the Internet on your desktop.

FIGURE 3-8: The Windows XP Virtual Desktop Manager PowerToy.

Using the Virtual Desktop Manager PowerToy

Throughout my computing career, I have used several different computing platforms that run all sorts of different window environments. Of all of them, KDE, which is a window environment for Unix and Linux, has become my favorite because of its implementation of the virtual desktop feature. If you are like me and do several different things at once on your computer, you can use virtual desktops to switch between groups of open programs rather than relying on the taskbar.

A couple of months after Windows XP was released, Microsoft released a Virtual Desktop Manager PowerToy. I was extremely happy to be able to get this feature on Windows XP. Although it is not exactly the same as the KDE version because it does not show a preview of what is going on in the window, it allows you to switch between desktops. The Windows XP Virtual Desktop PowerToy works by adding a new toolbar to the taskbar, as shown in Figure 3-8.

You can easily switch between your desktops by clicking the numbered buttons. Also, you can click the Preview button to see a four way split-screen of all of your desktops so that you can view what is open on all of them at once, as shown in Figure 3-9.

FIGURE 3-9: The Virtual Desktop Manager PowerToy split-screen preview.

Let's get started with setting up the Microsoft Virtual Desktop Manager (MSVDM) on your computer. First, download a copy of the Virtual Desktop Manager from the Windows XP PowerToys Web site, located at www.microsoft.com/windowsxp/pro/downloads/powertoys.asp. Once you have a copy of the PowerToys installed, follow these steps to get it up and running:

1. Once you have installed the PowerToy, you will want to unlock your taskbar so that you can place the Virtual Desktop Manager on it. Right-click your taskbar and select Lock the Taskbar Item only if there is a check next to the text. Otherwise, your taskbar is already unlocked.

2. When you have your taskbar unlocked, right-click the taskbar again, in the general location that you want the Virtual Desktop Manager to appear, and select Toolbars and then Desktop Manager.

3. This will make the Virtual Desktop buttons appear on your taskbar. I always like to get rid of the label to the left of the buttons. To do this, right-click the Virtual Desktop Manager and select Show Title to disable the label. This will only work when the taskbar is unlocked.

4. Now that you have the Virtual Desktop Manager set up on the taskbar, customize the way it works. Set up the background for your different virtual desktops so that you can easily determine which one you are on. To do this, right-click the Virtual Desktop toolbar and select Configure Desktop Images. Then, on the MSVDM Settings window, just select the desktop number with your mouse and then select the background image you want to use. Click OK when you are finished to save your changes.

5. The next feature of the Virtual Desktop Manager that I always like to customize is the shared desktop feature. This allows you to access the same taskbar on every desktop. There are times when it is nice to have this feature disabled so that your taskbar on the different desktop is nice and tidy, but that makes moving windows that you already have open on one desktop to another impossible because there is no way to right-click a window and send it to a specific desktop like with other Virtual Desktop Managers in different window environments. You can easily enable or disable the shared desktop feature by right-clicking the Virtual Desktop Manager and selecting Shared Desktops. I suggest you experiment with this feature to find the best setting for your personal taste.

6. The last feature that I like to modify is the animation feature of the preview screen. Every time you click the preview screen, your screen will slowly shrink up into the four-way split-screen preview. Then, when you select a desktop, it will slowly expand to full screen. This is a nice feature, but unfortunately the quality of the animation is not very high. On computers that have larger monitors, the animation looks pretty bad and just becomes a delay that you have to wait for every time you want to use the preview screen. One easy way around this is to simply disable animations by right-clicking the Virtual Desktop Manager and selecting Use Animations.

The virtual desktop feature is now set up on your computer. Have fun playing around with the feature. Once you get used to it, you will find that it can help you when you are doing several things on your computer at once.

Fun with Active Desktop

Active Desktop has been a feature of Windows ever since Windows 98. Over time, it has changed a lot and has become a very powerful feature when it is used to its full potential. I use the ability to display a Web page file as my background feature of Active Desktop to customize the way that I use my computer. Because you are able to display a Web page, the kind of information that you can display on your desktop is only limited to your knowledge of HTML (HyperText Markup Language), which is the language used to create Web pages. If you are new to HTML, then I suggest you get a book on it, such as *Creating Web Pages For Dummies*, or at least read a lot about HTML on the Web. For the purpose of this section, I am going to assume that you know a little HTML, or at least know how to use an HTML editor such as Microsoft FrontPage.

To give you an idea of what you can do with Active Desktop, I have written a short little Web page in HTML that I could use to help me get to work the best possible way. Currently, I live in the suburbs of Chicago and commute to work every day. During the summer, I like to take the train instead of driving to avoid wasting my time in traffic. However, because I have a long walk to get to work once I get off the train, I have to listen to the weather report to see if I should drive because I don't want to be soaked when I get to work if it rains. To speed up my routine in the morning, I could use Active Desktop to display the Web page that I created, which displays a live Chicago weather radar image on the desktop, as shown in Figure 3-10. This way, I don't even have to waste time going to any Web site; I just have to look at my desktop on my computer and I can instantly judge for myself if it looks like it is going to be raining in the near future.

There are actually even cooler things that you can do with your Web page if you know HTML well enough. You can add links to your Web page that you can access on your desktop to launch programs or visit Web sites. Additionally, if you are very talented in HTML and other Web technologies such as ASP, you could write a Web page that is one big frame that points to an Active Server Page on an external Web server. Then you can program that external page to do almost anything you can think of, such as gathering news headlines or other data.

Okay, now that you know what you can do with this cool feature, I am going to show you how you can take advantage of it as well. The first part of using this feature is coming up with a Web page to set as your background. The following is the source code for my Web page that I am using to display my weather radar:

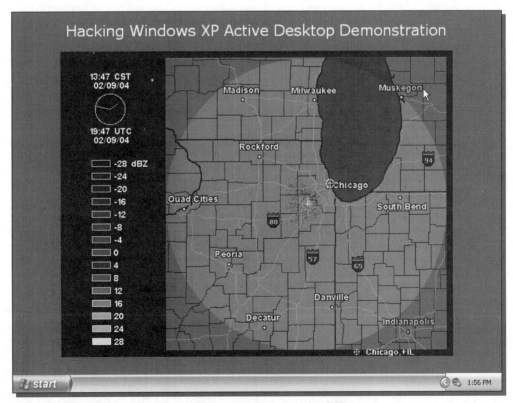

FIGURE 3-10: Using Active Desktop to display a Web page as the desktop.

```
<html>

<head>

<META HTTP-EQUIV="Refresh" CONTENT="10">

</head>

<body bgcolor="#0066CC">

<p align="center">

<font color="#FFFFFF" size="5" face="Verdana">

Hacking Windows XP Active Desktop Demonstration

</font>

<br>

<img src="http://radblast.wunderground.com/cgi-bin/radar/
WUNIDS?station=LOT&brand=wui&num=1&delay=15&type=N0R&frame=
0&scale=&noclutter=0&t=1076307247&lat=41.88650131&lon=
-87.62449646&label=Chicago,%2BIL">

</p>

</body>

</html>
```

This is the content of my Web page file that is saved as `radarpage.htm`. Basically, the most important line in the code above is the META Refresh line. This is the line that automatically tells my browser, or Active Desktop, to refresh the page every 10 seconds. That way, I will always have an up-to-date radar image displayed on my desktop. All of the other lines are just standard HTML tags.

If you want to create a file like this, just open up Notepad and type in your HTML code and then save the file with an `.htm` extension.

Now, once you have your Web page made in either Notepad or a nice HTML editor, you are ready to set it up to be used as your desktop. To do this, follow these steps:

1. Right-click your Desktop and select Properties.

2. Next, click the Desktop tab and then click the Browse button that is located on the middle-right side of the window.

3. Navigate through your computer and select the Web page that you created to use as your background and then click OK to select it.

4. Click OK once more to save your changes and you are finished.

You will have to wait a few seconds as Active Desktop loads your desktop for the first time. After that, the display properties window will go away and you should see your new desktop.

Have fun with this feature. If you learn HTML well enough, you can even start to include images that you make yourself to really give your computer a customized look and feel.

Using the wallpaper PowerToy

We all like changing our wallpaper every once in a while. We get tired of staring at the same old photo or pattern and like to select a new image that we downloaded on the Web or made

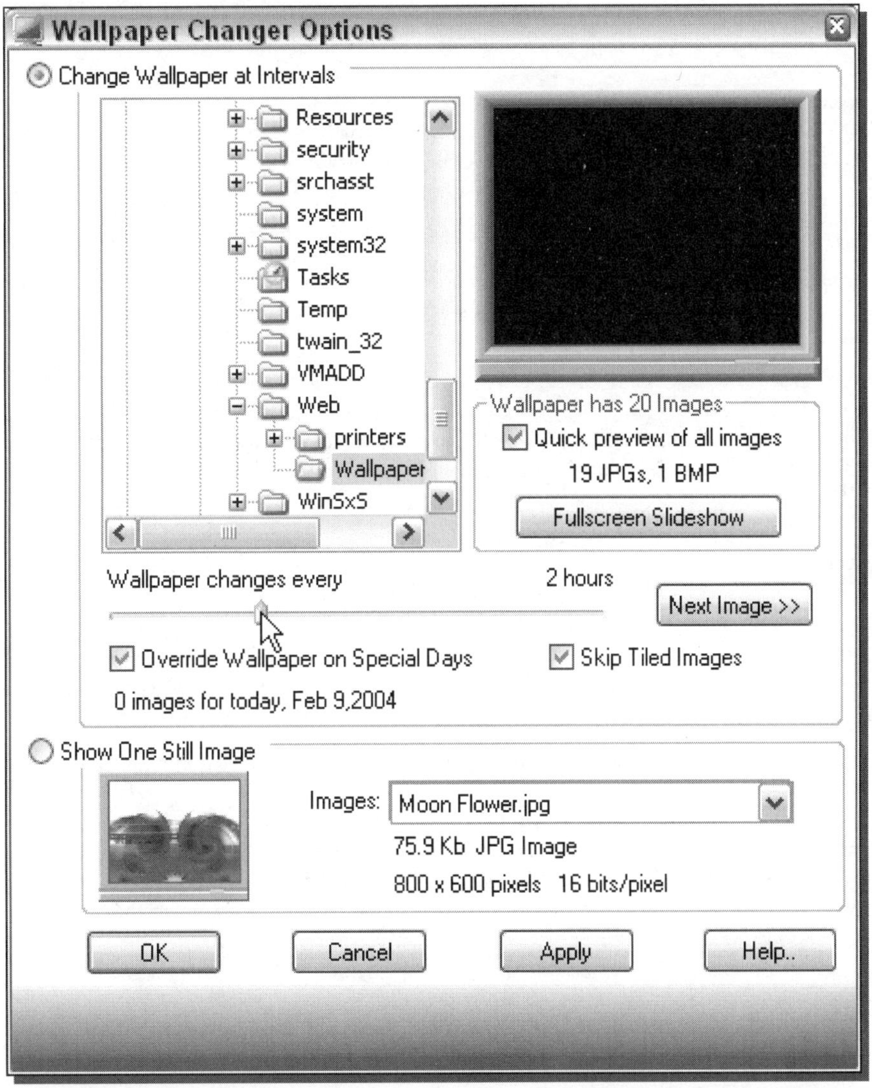

FIGURE 3-11: Using the Wallpaper Changer PowerToy to customize the desktop by adding rotating wallpapers.

ourselves. Back in April of 2003, Microsoft released a series of creativity fun packs that included all sorts of neat things, such as different types of themed templates as well as a few new PowerToys. One of those PowerToys was called the Wallpaper Changer. This PowerToy is an application that will automatically rotate your wallpaper over a given period of time that you set. Additionally, you can specify a folder of images to use so that you can control which images are rotated.

I like to use the Wallpaper Changer to change my wallpaper weekly, although it is possible to set it up to change your wallpaper every 15 minutes. If the Wallpaper Changer is something that interests you, visit `www.microsoft.com/windowsxp/experiences/downloads/create_powertoy.asp` to download a copy yourself. Then, follow these steps to configure it.

1. Once you have installed the Wallpaper Changer PowerToy, you can start it up by clicking the Start Menu, navigating to All Programs, expanding PowerToys for Windows XP, and then selecting Wallpaper Changer.

2. When the Wallpaper Changer has loaded, select the folder that you want to use as your source of the images using the browsing box.

3. Then, just set the interval between wallpaper changes by sliding the marker across the line, as shown in Figure 3-11.

4. Once you have the interval set, just click OK and your settings will be saved.

The Wallpaper Changer will allow you to customize your desktop like never before. Now you will always have a nice-looking desktop that is always new.

Summary

Through this chapter, you have learned how to customize the icons on your desktop in many different ways as well as make the desktop a little better. The icons on your desktop are by far the most important part, but the desktop itself can be customized. I have shown you three different ways to customize your desktop and make it function even better.

The next chapter will be one of the most important chapters on customizing. I will be showing you how to change the visual style of Windows XP to make it look completely different. There are many high-quality visual styles to be found on the Web, produced by many talented artists. I am going to show you how to take advantage of those visual styles and put them to use on your computer. But that's not all. I'm also going to show you how to make your very own visual styles. The next chapter will be a must for anyone that wants to customize the most visible part of Windows XP.

Customizing the Appearance of the Windows Interface

In the last few chapters, you customized little parts of the operating system starting with the boot screen. Then you moved onto customizing the logon screen, which led to customizing the Start panel/menu. After the Start panel/menu was customized, you found out how to customize the taskbar and the desktop. This next chapter will show you how to customize the entire user interface by changing the theme or visual style.

The material in the paragraphs that follow show you how to make major alterations in the way your computer looks—more so than all of the material that has been presented thus far. First to be examined is the difference between a theme and a visual style, to clear up any possible confusion that you might have. Next comes a discussion of the use of themes and how you can make your own. Then, you will learn how to use visual styles, as well as how to make your own. You will find out about some alternatives to using themes and visual styles so that you know about all of your customizing options.

Working with Themes

Themes have been a part of Windows for a very long time. Ever since Windows 95 was released, themes made it possible to save the configuration of the fonts, colors, visual style, wallpaper, mouse cursors, and even the sounds that are used. Throughout the years, not a lot has changed in the theme world. Originally, you had to have Microsoft Plus to use themes, but now, the ability to use themes is included in all of the latest Microsoft operating systems. Additionally, when themes were first developed, they did not keep track of visual styles, just because they didn't exist. Now, the theme format has expanded to allow for the new Windows feature.

Why are themes still important to talk about even though they have been around so long? Because they provide a unique way to save all of your computer's visual settings as well as audio settings so that you can easily change all of them at once. You don't have to customize each of the different elements of the windows such as the font and colors every time you use them. Themes make your life easier. These next few sections are going to show you how you can use themes and make your own so that you too can benefit from the convenience they offer.

Changing the current theme

When you install Windows XP, Microsoft includes two themes: Windows XP and the Windows Classic theme. By changing the themes, you can turn on and off the new Windows XP look. Also, remember that you can make your own themes, which I will get to in the next section, so that you can easily switch between your own theme sets. When you do so, after you spend time customizing the look of XP, making changes to window metrics, sounds, visual style, cursors, wallpaper and so on, they can be saved to a theme file so that you will never lose your changes.

Changing the themes is actually pretty simple. It is all done through the Display Properties Control Panel applet. To change themes, follow these steps:

1. Right-click the desktop and select Properties.

2. Display Properties will then load and will be displaying the Themes tab.

3. Next, just expand the drop-down box under Theme, as shown in Figure 4-1, and select the theme that you want to use.

4. When you have selected the theme, click OK to save your changes.

Once you have hit the OK button, the new theme will be applied. This process may take a few seconds while the changes are being made.

Now that you know how to change a theme, it is time to make your own.

Making your own themes

Making your own theme will allow you to easily back up your visual changes to XP so that you can distribute your settings to other computers or on the Internet. Making your own theme is actually just like changing the theme. The most difficult part of the process is customizing all of the little aspects of the visual elements that make up the user interface. The next few sections will walk you through the process of fine-tuning the user interface and will then show you how to save your changes and make your own theme file.

Modifying the window metrics and fonts

What the heck are window metrics? Well, it is the fancy way of talking about how big everything is. There is actually a whole lot that you can adjust that will affect the size of user interface elements such as the title bar of a window and other window elements such as buttons. Almost everything on a window has a size that can be adjusted. This section will show you how to alter your visual style or classic Windows interface look by fine-tuning the different components of the window.

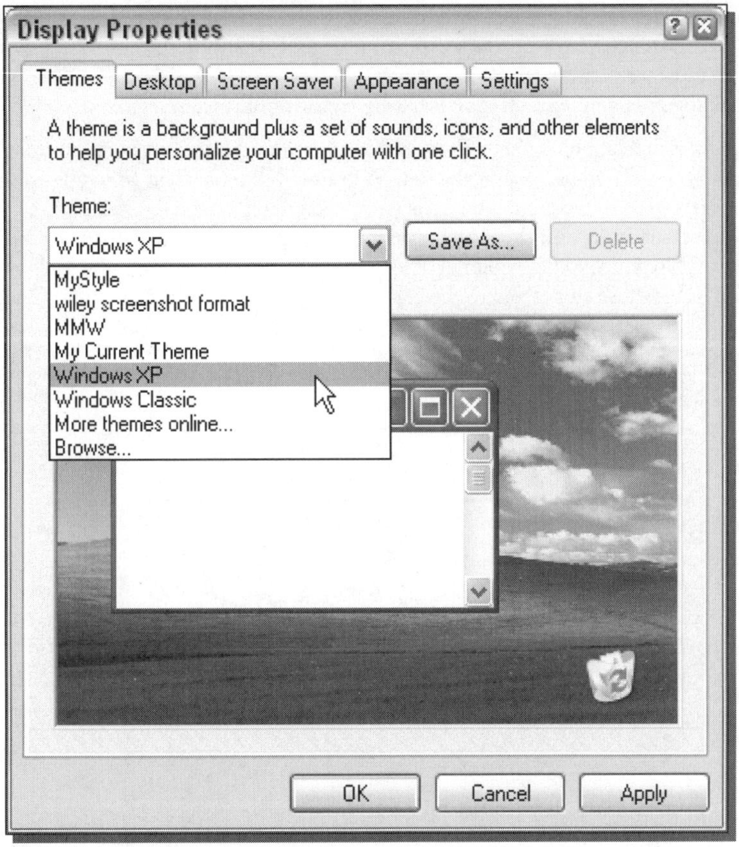

FIGURE 4-1: Changing the active theme.

Another possibility is to fine-tune the fonts that are used. You can change the size of the font displayed, the style, and even the actual font that is used.

To get started, you will be using Display Properties again to make the changes:

1. Right-click the desktop and select Properties.

2. Click the Appearance tab and hit the Advanced button located on the bottom-right of the window.

3. The Advanced Appearance window will show up. This location is where you can change the size as well as the font for all of the different aspects of a window. You can make changes in two different ways. The first way is to use the Item drop-down box. Just expand it and select the item that you want to modify. The other way is to click the object that you want to customize on the Preview picture. This will automatically select the item from the Item drop-down box for you. Either way, select an item that you want to change. For purposes of demonstration, I suggest that you click or select Active Title Bar.

4. Once you have selected an object that you want to change, use the Size, Font, and Color settings to customize your window, as shown in Figure 4-2. The Active Title Bar is a good item to experiment with the size. Try playing around with this one and see how you can change the way a visual style looks by adjusting this value.

5. When you are finished changing the sizes of the window items, try changing the fonts and colors as well. If you are using the new Windows XP look, then adjusting the colors on this screen will not matter, because visual styles ignore these color settings and use their own that are built into the visual style file. However, if you are using the classic Windows XP look, then these color settings are critical to customizing the look of Windows XP because this is where the classic look gets its color information. Once you are done, click OK to save your changes.

6. You will have to click OK once more to activate your changes and close the Display Properties window.

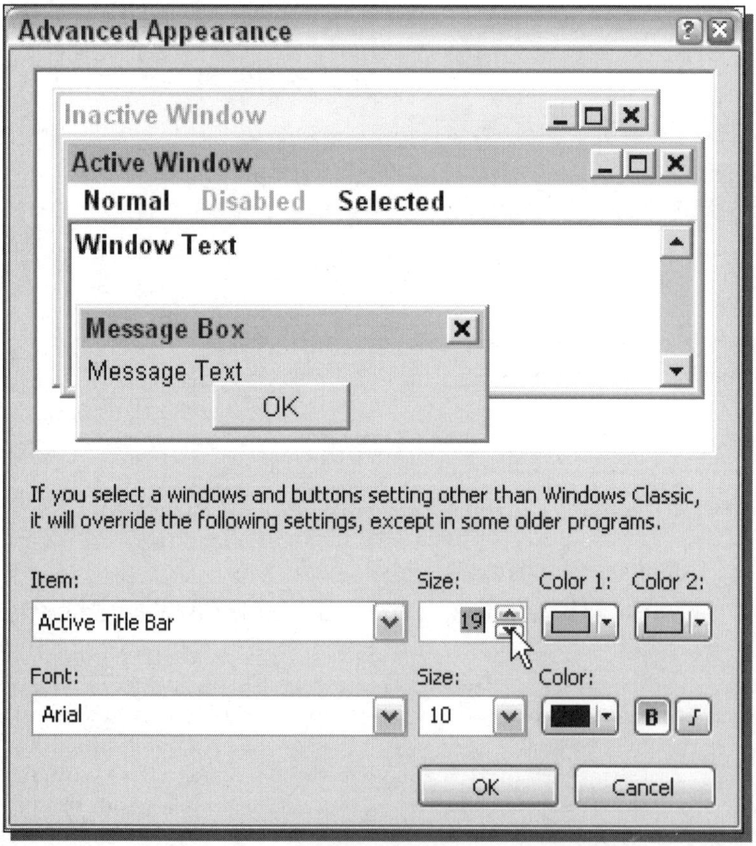

FIGURE 4-2: Customizing the sizes and fonts of the user interface.

You can do a lot of interesting things to make your computer look unique. One thing I always like to do is decrease the size of the Active Title Bar so that it is as small as it will allow me to make it. Doing so makes the Maximize, Minimize, and Close buttons smaller too. It is a nice look that makes your windows look like they have lost some weight. Of course, you could increase the size as well and make the buttons so big you could operate your computer 10 feet away from your monitor.

Modifying the system sounds

The sound file Windows plays when you log in, log out, minimize and maximize a window are saved inside a theme file. Because I am taking you through all of the different things that a theme file will save the settings for, I will go over how to change the settings for the sounds that Windows XP uses so that you can customize this aspect of your computer as well.

Changing the event sounds is very simple. Just follow these steps to launch and configure the Sound Properties:

1. Click the Start Menu and select Run.

2. Type **mmsys.cpl** in the box and click OK to launch the system Sounds and Audio Devices Properties.

3. Once the Sounds and Audio Devices Properties loads, click the Sounds tab.

4. Next, to adjust the sound clip for a specific event, click the event that you want to mod-ify, as shown in Figure 4-3, by navigating though the Program Events box.

5. Once you have an event selected, the Sounds drop-down list will become enabled and you will be able to select the sound clip that you want to use. You can select (None) from the top of the list if you do not want to use a sound for a specific program event. If you cannot find a sound that you like on the list, you can use the Browse button to pick a specific sound file on your computer to use.

6. When you are finished with your changes, just click OK to save your work.

You are now finished with customizing the sound events on your computer. The next step is to customize the cursors of the mouse so that they too will be included in your theme file.

Customizing the mouse cursors

The mouse cursors are yet another item that is saved in the Theme file. Many different pointer schemes are included with Windows XP. Although not all of them may be the nicest-looking cursors, they can really help out in some situations. Additionally, Windows XP includes special large mouse cursors so that the cursors will be easier on the eyes of some people.

To get your cursors set perfectly for your Theme file, do the following:

1. Click the Start button and select Run.

2. Type **main.cpl** and click OK to open up Mouse Properties.

Sounds and Audio Devices Properties [?] [X]

| Volume | Sounds | Audio | Voice | Hardware |

A sound scheme is a set of sounds applied to events in Windows and programs. You can select an existing scheme or save one you have modified.

Sound scheme:

[   ] [v]

[Save As...] [Delete]

To change sounds, click a program event in the following list and then select a sound to apply. You can save the changes as a new sound scheme.

Program events:

| Select |
| Show Toolbar Band |
| Start Windows |
| System Notification |
| Windows Logoff |
| Windows Logon |

Sounds:

[Windows XP Start] [v] [▶] [Browse...]

[OK] [Cancel] [Apply]

FIGURE 4-3: Modifying the sound for the Start Windows event.

3. Next, click the Pointers tab.

4. Once you are there, you have two options to customize the cursors: You can use the drop-down Scheme box to change all of the pointers at once to different styles, by selecting a different cursor scheme from the list shown in Figure 4-4. When you select the different schemes, all of the cursors will change automatically. Alternatively, if you do not like the cursor schemes, you can individually select a cursor from the customize box list by scrolling through the list and selecting the cursor you want to change. Then, hit the Browse button to change it.

5. When you are finished customizing your cursors, just hit the OK button and you are finished.

Now you are ready to move on to customizing the visual style that the theme will be using.

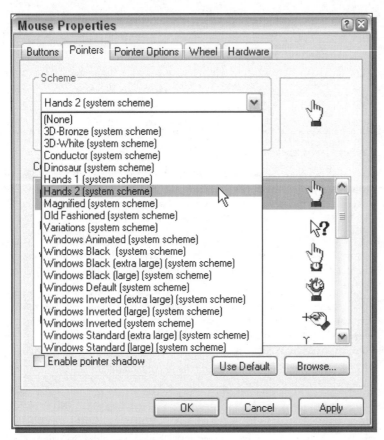

FIGURE 4-4: Changing the pointer scheme.

Choosing the visual style the theme will use

Windows XP introduces the new way of skinning the Windows interface (applying a new skin/look to the interface) with files called visual styles. The visual style files are like one file with all of the different images in it that make up the way the interface looks. Windows XP only includes one visual style, which is called the Windows XP style. The second half of this chapter, which is all about visual styles, will show you how you can get more visual styles.

Each visual style usually contains different color schemes. The Windows XP style that comes with Windows XP has three: Blue, Olive Green, and Silver. The color schemes of the Windows XP style do not change the shape of the windows, just the color, since this is what a color scheme is designed to do. Unlike the classic windows interface, changing the colors of the window elements is not as simple as selecting a new color. Instead, a visual style has to have a whole new set of graphics created and then imported into the file. Because of that, each of the different color scheme options of a visual style are actually completely separate visual styles. Because each of the color scheme options of a visual style require a whole new set of graphics, authors of visual styles on the Web often use the color scheme settings to store slightly different versions of their visual style. Not only do the different versions often have new colors, but they also have minor physical tweaks and differences.

Now that you know the basics of the visual style, it's time to tweak the visual style settings so that when you make your Theme file in the next sections, it will be included with your sound and mouse settings:

1. Right-click the desktop and select Properties to bring up the Display Properties window.

2. When this is displayed, click the Appearance tab.

3. In the bottom half of the window, you should see the Windows and Buttons drop-down list. This will include all of the visual styles properly installed on your computer. By default, with a new Windows XP install, you will have two choices: Windows XP Style and Windows Classic Style, as shown in Figure 4-5.

4. Once you have your visual style picked out, play around with the color schemes and see which one you like best. Remember, if you have already installed some visual styles that you downloaded from the Web, changing the color scheme may reveal different variations of a visual style that can look completely different from one another.

5. The font size settings are also fun to play with, but most users have little use for them because the author of a visual style usually picked what looks best with the style of the skin. However, if you do not like the author's choices, this is where you can customize the look to suit your taste. When you are finished customizing your visual style settings, click OK to save your changes.

Changing the wallpaper

You all know how to change wallpaper on your desktop, but I am going to show you a great little trick that you can do to change your wallpaper even faster and also one that will allow you to easily change it on multiple computers without having to go to Display Properties all the time.

The trick? Just create a registry file that you can import into the registry that will overwrite your current wallpaper information. Doing so is actually very easy; just follow these steps to create your very own file:

1. Open up Notepad (located in Start Menu in the Accessories folder).

2. Type in the following code:

```
Windows Registry Editor Version 5.00

[HKEY_CURRENT_USER\Control Panel\Desktop]
"Wallpaper"="C:\\windows\\MyWallpaper.bmp"
"WallpaperStyle"="1"
```

3. You will want to replace the `C:\\windows\\`... with the path and filename to the bitmap that you want to use. Note that in the path, wherever there is a \, you have to put two of them in the registry file you are creating because the registry editor requires all paths to be in that format. You can change the `wallpaperstyle` property that will allow

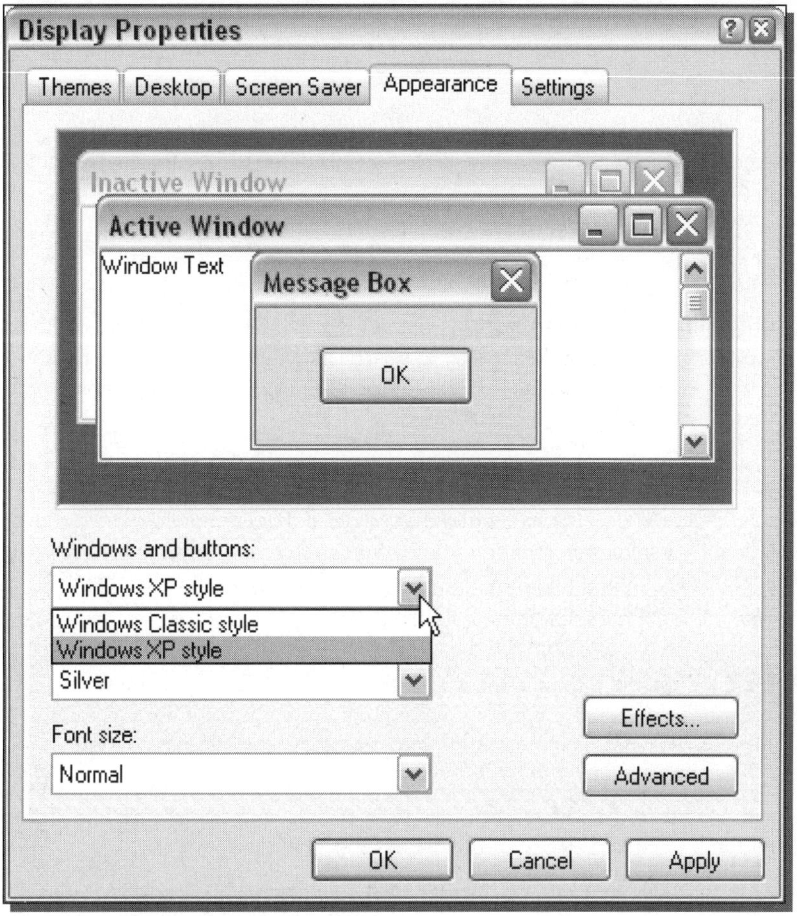

FIGURE 4-5: Adjusting the window style.

you to control how the bitmap image is displayed on your computer. Setting the value equal to 0 will center the image on the screen. Setting the value to 1 will display the image as if it was tiled or repeated across the entire screen. Setting the wallpaperstyle value to 2 will stretch the image to fit the entire screen.

4. When you have the text in Notepad looking like the code in Step 2 but with your changes included, you are ready to save the file. Go to the File menu bar item and select Save As, then select Save As Type. In the File Name box, type **wallpaper.reg**. Keep in mind: You need to have the .reg at the end of the filename so your computer knows to import the file into your registry using the Registry Editor.

5. Once you save the file, just go to the location where you saved it, and double-click the file. A screen will come up asking you if you want to import the file into the registry;

click Yes. Then, you will be presented with a confirmation screen informing you if the update was successful.

You will have to log out and log back in if you want to see your changes take effect.

 On the attached companion CD-ROM, you will find a copy of the registry to change the desktop wallpaper in the Chapter 4 folder.

Saving your changes to a theme file

You have now customized all of the aspects for which the Theme file will keep track. Now you will be able to make your own theme file, one that you can use as a backup or give to other people so that they can replicate your changes.

Before I go any further, I want to make it clear what exactly the theme file saves. The theme file will save the configuration of all of the different parts of Windows XP that you just modified; however, it will not save the actual files that you used. For example, if you decide to change the sounds of a program event on your computer, then you will also have to include that sound clip to anyone or any computer to which you want to apply the theme file that you made. A theme file just saves the settings, nothing else.

Now that you understand what the theme file format is, you are ready to get started. Making your own theme file is just as easy as changing one. To do so, follow these steps:

1. Right-click the desktop and select Properties to get to the Display Properties.

2. On the Themes tab, you will see that it now says the name of the original theme that you started along with "(modified)" attached to it. To save your new theme, just hit the Save As button located to the right of the theme drop-down box.

3. Enter in the name that you want to save the theme file as and the destination. By default, you will be pointed to your My Documents folder. That location is a good place to store your theme files so that you can easily access them later to delete or distribute them to other users.

You have now created a backup of your theme so that you can easily change back to it when you customize the user interface. Now it's time for you to explore the world of visual styles. Learn all you can about how you can make Windows XP look its best.

Modifying the Visual Styles

Windows XP includes a new skinning engine built into the operating system, which it uses to display its own skin format, known as visual styles. Visual styles are responsible for transforming the boring old Windows classic look into the colorful and visually pleasing Windows XP look. Unfortunately, Microsoft has decided to keep the format of visual styles secret and built the skinning engine to only accept Visual styles that are digitally signed by Microsoft. This decision puts a big roadblock in the path of creating your own visual styles. On top of that, Microsoft decided that they were not going to release any more visual styles, so we are all stuck with the default Windows XP look.

This presented a problem to the Windows XP tweaking community. Everyone wanted to take advantage of the new visual styles engine that was built into Windows XP and create his or her own visual styles. When I first started to use Windows XP, I spent a lot of time trying to figure out how to create my own visual styles. I tried using Resource Hacker on the visual style file that came with Windows XP to replace the bitmaps inside the file. I was sure that this attempt would work, but when I tried to view the visual style in Display Properties, the rendering was very strange in the Preview window, and when I tried to apply it, the computer would revert to the classic Windows interface. After spending some time browsing the Web and reading forums, I found out that the reason why my new visual style was not working was because the file was not digitally signed by Microsoft. Apparently, even if you modify a file that was signed by Microsoft, the signature is broken because the checksum of the file changed when you replaced the bitmaps.

What would be the next step? Well there were two options: either try to fake a digital signature on the theme file or just remove the digital signature requirement from the visual style engine. Faking a digital signature is very difficult, if not impossible, so removing the digital signature requirement was the only plausible choice. This was the limit of my skills. I had no clue how to remove the requirement other than opening the file up in the hex editor and starting to delete random bytes.

Thankfully, someone else figured it out. A company called TGT Soft (www.tgtsoft.com) released a program called Style XP, as well as a free patch that you could use. All you would have to do is run the patcher on your computer and let it go loose on your uxtheme.dll file, which is the heart of the visual style engine, and it would remove the digital signature requirement. You'll soon learn how to use the Style XP shareware for making lots of interesting changes, in the section entitled *Installing New Visual Styles*.

The development of Style XP and its runaround of the Windows XP signatures created shockwaves in the skinning community. It would now be possible to use different visual styles to take advantage of the new skinning engine. Sites such as ThemeXP.org sprung up, offering hundreds of visual styles that XP users all over the world made. Everyone was happy, except for Microsoft.

Eventually, TGT Soft found itself in a little trouble when Microsoft found out that they released a program that bypassed the requirement. Microsoft could have blown this company out of the water, but they were very generous and allowed TGT Soft to continue to develop its product and helped them write a service that ran in the background so that they would no longer have to hack the system file.

Nowadays things have changed a little bit. TGT Soft still offers its Style XP application that can be used to unsign visual styles, but it is still shareware. Thankfully, there is an application called the UXTheme Multi-Patcher, which will patch the skinning engine just like the old TGT Soft patch. More will be discussed about the patchers shortly, in the section entitled *Using UXTheme Multi-Patcher to enable use of non-Microsoft Visual styles*.

Note It is a little unclear what Microsoft thinks about users of Windows XP bypassing its digital signature requirement for the visual style engine, using applications such as UXTheme Multi-Patcher. Taking a look at the whole situation, they really do not have a reason to be upset because it is not like the Multi-Patcher is contributing to software piracy. Additionally, the ability to use thousands of visual styles available on the Web with the fast native visual style engine is a great reason to upgrade to Windows XP. From a marketing standpoint, Microsoft should just forget about the stupid protection. It would make users of Windows XP happier because they would be able to customize their computers easier.

So, you've now learned a brief history of how one of the best new features of Windows XP became unlocked. These next few sections will show you how to install and use new visual styles on your computer to completely transform the way the user interface looks.

Installing new visual styles

Currently, you can use new visual styles on XP in two different ways. Both options work around the requirement that visual style files must be signed. First, I am going to explain how to use, as well as the benefits of using, TGT Soft's Style XP to use new visual styles. Then, I am going to show you how to use patcher XP as well as the benefits of using it. But first, I am going to show you where to download visual styles that can be used on your computer.

Downloading visual styles

Many cool sites on the Web offer thousands of visual styles to download. Unlike boot and logon screens, you do not need to worry about the version of a visual style because they are not system-critical files and their format does not change when service packs are released. This capability makes downloading them even easier, because you don't have to worry about screwing up your computer.

Check out the following list of my favorite sites from which to download visual styles. I think you will find them very helpful.

- ThemeXP.org (www.themexp.org) offers well over 1,100 visual styles for Windows XP. It is, by far, the leader in the XP visual style world.

- XPTheme (www.xptheme.info) offers over 300 visual styles.

- NeoWin (www.neowin.net/forum/index.php?showforum=36) offers a great theme forum that has a lot of quality visual styles.

- deviantART (browse.deviantart.com/skins/windows/visualstyle/) is another good site for visual styles that has an easy to use navigation system that shows 24 thumbnails of visual styles at once.

- TSS2000 (www.tss2000.nl) is a great site from which to get quality visual styles. Although they require you to register on their site to download a visual style, this requirement is worth it. They also have a large collection of Apple OS X-looking visual styles.

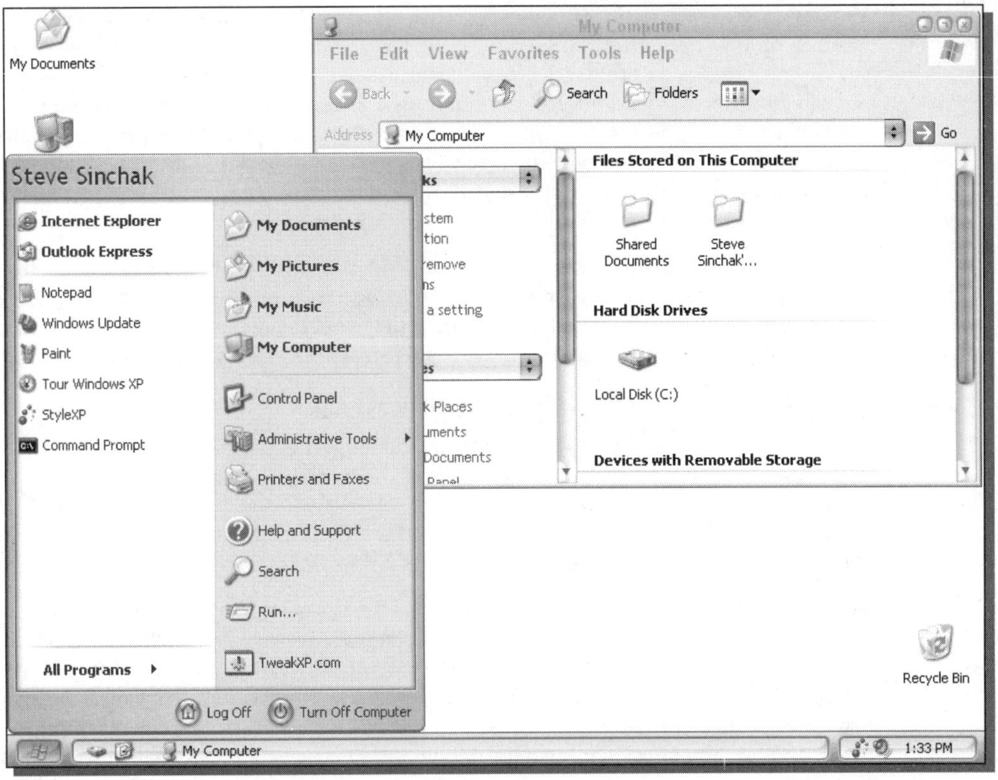

FIGURE 4-6: Changing the look of Windows XP by using the iBar 4 visual style created by Dartbra, which gives the desktop a nice gray metal look with light blue accents.

I personally like the look of the Apple OS X visual styles but do not like trying to make my PC look like a Mac. My favorite visual style is called iBar 4 set on the WinFlag color scheme, which is shown in Figure 4-6. It is a nice blend between the OS X look and a Windows visual style. The iBar 4 visual style can be downloaded from www.deviantart.com/deviation/ 4650418/.

On the CD In the Chapter 4 folder, you can view a full color screenshot of the iBar 4 visual style created by Dartbra.

Many more sites are available from which you can download visual styles, but the sites mentioned previously will give you plenty of styles, more than you are likely to ever go through or use. Once you have downloaded a few visual styles that you would like to use from the Web, you are ready to extract them and place them in the appropriate place on your hard drive.

Windows stores the default Windows XP-style visual style at `C:\Windows\Resources\Themes` on your hard drive. This is also where you should extract all of your visual styles that you downloaded inside a folder that has the same name as the `.msstyles` file. If the folder is not named correctly, Windows XP may not recognize the visual style. Also, you will find that when you extract some ZIP files where there was a visual style, there may be a folder called shell. This folder contains other visual style data and should be put in the same folder as the visual style file. If you also have a `.theme` file included with the visual style download, you should place that in the themes folder instead of inside the visual style folder.

When you have finished installing all the visual styles that you have downloaded to the themes folder, you are ready to set up your computer so that you can use the visual styles. The next two sections will show you how to install them using the two different approaches already mentioned: using the shareware Style XP and using freeware patches such as UXTheme Multi-Patcher.

Using Style XP to use non-Microsoft visual styles

Style XP, which is made by TGT Soft, was the first program that allowed Windows XP users to use non-Microsoft visual styles. Style XP and the free patch that TGT Soft also released are responsible for creating the visual style world on the Web. In this section, I am going to show you how to use this interesting app to install and use all of the thousands of visual styles available on the Web to transform the way Windows XP works.

Style XP 2.0 offers a lot of new features, such as icon packages, as well as logon and boot screen management. However, we are just going to focus on the visual style feature because that is what made this program famous. To get started, you will need to get a copy of Style XP 2.0 from TGT Soft. Visit `www.tgtsoft.com/download.php` to get a copy of Style XP. Once you are on their site, you will notice that they offer a couple of different download packages. Make sure that you download Style XP 2.0 full install. They offer two different versions of this install, one for men and one for women. The two versions are the exact same version of Style XP except they have different visual styles included as a convenience if you have not already downloaded other visual styles. But because you have already downloaded some visual styles, you don't really have to worry about that.

Once you have Style XP 2.0 downloaded and installed, you are ready to get started using it. Follow these steps to get Style XP up and running:

1. Click the Start button and navigate to All Programs, then look at the top of your Start Menu when all programs are expanded by Windows Update. Expand TGT Soft to run Style XP.

2. When Style XP loads, click the Visual Styles button and Style XP will search your Theme folder for new visual styles.

3. You will see a list of all of the different visual styles on your computer in the middle of the window. A preview will be shown when you click the different visual style names.

4. Once you find the visual style that you want to use for the whole user interface, click the Apply Style to Current Theme button, as shown in Figure 4-7.

5. Your new visual style will now be applied. If you are satisfied with the new look, close Style XP and you are finished. If you're not satisfied, go back to Step 3 and start over.

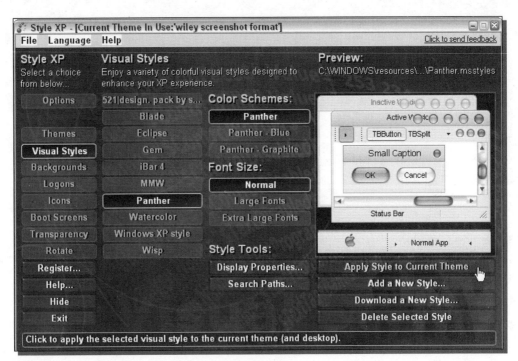

FIGURE 4-7: Using Style XP 2.0 to change the visual style.

As you can see, Style XP provides a very easy mechanism to change the current visual style that the Windows XP skinning engine is using. If you decide to download more visual styles, just install them and restart Style XP so that it can detect the new visual style. Then you will be able to change the visual style just as you have done previously.

Using UXTheme Multi-Patcher to enable use of non-Microsoft visual styles

Style XP 2.0 is not a free program. It provides an easy way to change the visual style, as well as a bunch of other features such as the ability to use visual styles without having to modify any skinning engine to accept non-Microsoft signed visual style files. With this convenience comes a price that you have to pay, if you want to use the program for more than 30 days.

If you would like a free solution to using non-Microsoft signed visual styles, then the best option is a program called the UXTheme Multi-Patcher, which will allow you to patch the visual style engine. This patch will remove the code in the engine that checks for a Microsoft signed file, which will then allow you to use any visual style that you want.

Another program that will also patch the visual style engine is known as Patch XP. However, there are various versions of XP, such as Original, Service Pack 1, and Service Pack 2. Each of these versions has a slightly different visual style engine, and that requires a program to be written for each specific version. I like to use the Multi-Patcher because it can patch different versions of Windows XP, unlike Patch XP, which requires a specific version for each Windows XP version.

UXTheme Multi-Patcher is developed by an XP user known as Windows X and can be downloaded at their Web site located, at www.windowsx.org/enhance/myvs/uxtheme.html. Download a copy now and perform the following steps to patch and change the visual styles on your computer without having to use Style XP:

1. Once you have downloaded the latest copy of the Multi-Patcher, double-click the Exe to start up the program.

2. When the Patcher loads, you will see the main program screen. Hit the Patch button, as shown in Figure 4-8.

3. The OS Detection screen will pop up, asking you to confirm the Windows XP version that you are running. If the information is correct, click OK to continue.

4. When the patch is complete, you will be prompted with a screen asking you if you want to restart. Click Restart, if you want to restart now, or you can always restart at a later time. However, the visual style engine needs to be reloaded in order to accept non-Microsoft visual styles.

5. Shortly after the restart screen is shown, a Windows File Protection window may show up. Windows XP has detected the change in the system file and wants to replace the system file with an unpatched version. Click the Cancel button so that Windows XP does not replace the patched file with the original file. Windows will make you confirm your

UXTheme Multi-Patcher v1.5

UXTheme Multi-Patcher (Windows XP/SP1/SP2 Beta, 2003) By Windows X, original sources Vorte[x]

This program will patch your uxtheme.dll file so you can use any 3rd party visual style on Windows XP, Windows XP SP1, Windows XP SP2 and Windows Server 2003. File protection dialogs should be cancelled and a reboot is required after using this patch.

Patched Windows XP or Windows Server 2003 systems can be unpatched by running this program again.

By Windows X
Website: http://www.windowsx.org
E-Mail: deadknightz@hotmail.com

[Patch]   [Cancel]

FIGURE 4-8: Using UXTheme Multi-Patcher to patch the visual style engine.

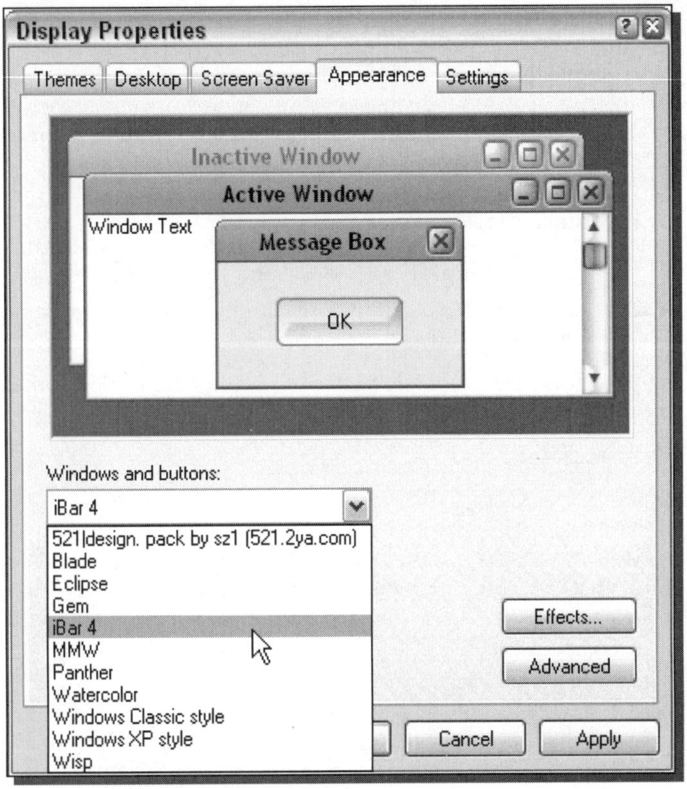

FIGURE 4-9: **Changing the visual style.**

decision by popping up another window; click Yes so that you keep the patched version of the file.

6. Once you reboot, you will be running the patched version of the visual style engine. To change the active visual style, right-click the desktop and select Properties.

7. Then, click the Appearance tab and adjust the visual style by changing the Windows and Buttons drop-down box, as shown in Figure 4-9.

8. After you change the visual style, also consider adjusting the color scheme. Many of the visual styles that you download have different versions stored as different color schemes.

9. Once you are finished changing the visual style, just hit the OK button to save your changes and view the new visual style.

If you have problems with the UXTheme Multi-Patcher after running the patch, you can always revert to your original system file by running the Multi-Patcher again. Doing so will display an option that allows you to revert to the original visual style engine file.

Tweaking the visual styles

Now that you have finished changing the visual styles using one of the two methods that I described, you can customize the look of your computer a little more by tweaking the visual style. One thing that I always like to customize after I change the visual style is the title bar height. You can easily do so by changing the window metrics:

1. Right-click the desktop and select Properties.

2. Then, click the Advanced button on the Appearance tab.

3. Click either the active or inactive title bar of the preview image and then adjust the Size setting next to the Item drop-down box.

4. While you are changing the size, you might want to also customize the fonts. You can do so by clicking the text for which you want to change the font, and then selecting the font.

5. Click OK to save your changes.

6. Click OK once more to close Display Properties and activate the new changes.

Customizing the way a visual style looks is always refreshing. Usually when you install any system, you find a few things that you wish were just a little different. Now you know how to refine your desktop to look its best.

Making your own visual styles

You now know how to install and use custom-made visual styles, but did you ever wonder how other people make visual styles? This next section will take you through the process of creating your own visual style as well as the history of how people started making them.

It all began before people could actually use the visual styles. Curious users snooping around their Windows XP files discovered that Windows XP had a skinning engine just like many other applications that had the whole look of the operating stores in a file on the hard drive in the themes folder called luna.msstyles. This file contains all of the data for the new Windows XP look.

Then, just as with the boot and logon screens, people started to use resource hacking tools such as Resource Hacker to open up luna.msstyles and replace the bitmaps stored within the file with image files they made. Additionally, you could use programs like Resource Hacker to edit the settings files stored within the visual style as well to edit all of the sizes of the different Windows components.

The possibilities that applications such as Resource Hacker gave users were unlimited, except for the fact that there still was no way to test and use the new user-made visual styles because they were not digitally signed by Microsoft. Eventually, that all changed, as you know from the last few sections, and users were able to use their own visual styles.

Now there are several different ways that you can make your own visual style. You can use the Resource Hacker approach and manually open up your luna.msstyles file and replace bitmaps in the file with ones you made yourself. This process can be a very long and difficult one when you are trying to design a completely different visual style. This method would really only make sense to use if you just wanted to replace one part of a visual style, such as the green Start button.

If for some reason you just don't like the green Start button, then you can open up the file in Resource Hacker and look for the bitmap on which to work. First, you will probably want to extract the bitmap from the file so that you can work on it in your favorite image editing program. Then, once you are finished, just replace the bitmap in the file with your modified version. Hit Save As, give the file a new name, and you are finished once you create a new folder for the name of the visual style.

If you want to make a completely new visual style with a new look or modify an existing one beyond changing one little component, then using a commercial editor is a must. TGT Soft, the company that brought you Style XP and the first patch for the visual style engine, has come out with an editor known as StyleBuilder.

StyleBuilder is an amazing program that TGT Soft created after they found out how the visual style file was compiled. It provides the user with an easy-to-use visual front for editing the visual style files. Instead of using a resource hacker and searching for a specific bitmap to replace, you can just navigate through the menus and click the object that you want to replace within the editor. This saves a lot of time and makes it feasible to create a whole visual style from scratch.

To get started, download a copy of StyleBuilder from TGT Soft's Web site, located at www.tgtsoft.com/download.php. Sometimes, the best way to learn something is to start by modifying a visual style. Once you download and install a copy of StyleBuilder, perform the following steps to learn how to import an existing visual style, make changes to it, and then save it for use on your computer and distribution on the Internet:

1. Start up StyleBuilder by navigating though the TGT Soft folder in the Start Menu and selecting StyleBuilder.

2. Say that you'd like to import the iBar 4 visual style that you use on your computer and want to make some changes to it. When StyleBuilder is starting up, click the File Menubar item and select the Import .msstyle file.

3. Next, you will have to fill in the two boxes on the import window. Specify the .msstyles file of the visual style that you want to import to modify. Then specify the folder that you want all of the settings and images to be extracted to so that StyleBuilder can edit the files.

4. When you are finished filling in the two boxes, hit the OK button to start the import process.

5. After a few seconds, the import should be done and you will be notified if the import has been successful or not. If it has, you will have the option to open up the newly created StyleBuilder files to edit the visual style. Click the Yes button so that you can edit the files.

6. StyleBuilder will now open up the imported visual style for editing. First, get familiar with the interface. Figure 4-10 is what the StyleBuilder interface looks like when you

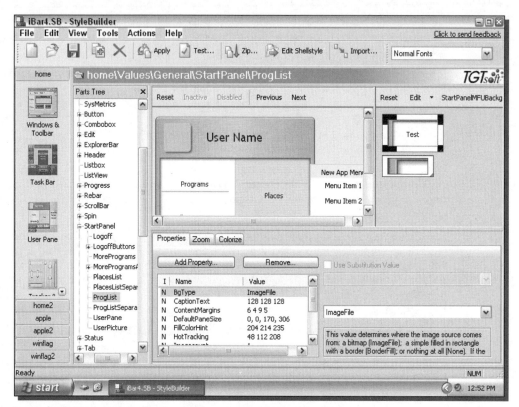

FIGURE 4-10: Using StyleBuilder to modify a visual style from the Web.

have a visual style open for editing. On the left-hand side of the screen are the buttons that you use for navigating between different parts of the visual style to edit, such as the Task Bar, User Pane, and Tracker & Progress. Also, you will see different section header buttons that indicate the current color scheme of the visual style that you are editing. In Figure 4-10, those buttons are labeled Home, Home2, Apple, Apple2, and so on.

7. Editing the different settings and images is easy with StyleBuilder. Just click the object that you want to edit with your mouse in the preview window. Alternatively, you can navigate through the setting tree to easily get to a specific items settings.

8. To edit an image, just right-click it and select Edit. If you want to use a specific program, you will have to set up your graphic editors in StyleBuilder by right-clicking an image and selecting Edit With from the menu. Additionally, you can specify a different image file by clicking the ImageFile entry on the list and then hitting the Choose button, as shown in Figure 4-11.

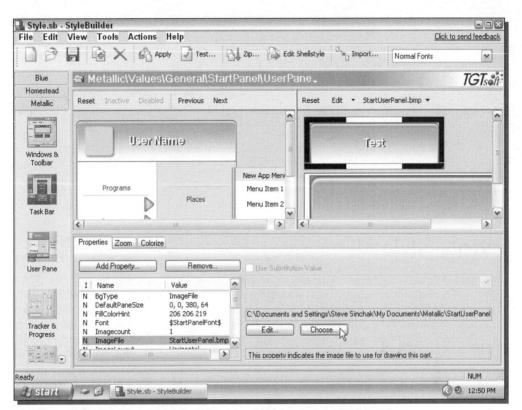

FIGURE 4-11: Changing the image of an object in a visual style using StyleBuilder.

9. Once you have your images replaced, you can play around with the settings for the visual style, such as the object sizes, borders, and fonts. All of these settings can be adjusted by selecting an object from the list on the Properties tab and editing the values on the right in the textboxes.

10. As you are working on your visual style, you may want to test it to see how it looks, as the Preview window doesn't always give you an accurate depiction of how it will look on your computer. You can do so by clicking the Apply button on the toolbar. Included is also a cool test feature that will allow you to view the current visual style applied on a window that has every possible window object that you can think of so that you can see how your visual style will look in all varieties of applications.

11. When you have finished modifying a visual style, and have created your own custom style, you are ready to compile it and, if you want, export it for distribution on the Web. Click the Actions menu bar item and select Compile. You will be asked to name your visual style; once you name it, it will be compiled and placed in your documents folder. If you would like to distribute your visual style on the Web to share with your friends or

the rest of the world, click the ZIP file from the toolbar on the top and specify what you want to include and click OK. Then, you can e-mail your friends this ZIP file, which, by default, is saved in your documents folder, or you can submit it to Web sites such as themexp.org.

Making your own visual style from scratch requires a lot of graphical and artistic skills. But if you just want to tweak your favorite visual style, then you will have no problem doing so with the help of StyleBuilder.

You have now mastered the world of visual styles. You have discovered how you can make your system accept non-Microsoft visual styles so that you can take advantage of the new skinning engine built into Windows XP. And now you also know how to modify and make your own visual styles.

Visual Style Alternatives

Before visual styles were a part of Windows, only one way existed to change the way Windows looked. That was accomplished by using a program called WindowBlinds, which is made by Stardock (www.windowblinds.net). WindowsBlinds is a classic Windows program. Back when it first came out, it transformed the boring gray interface of Windows into an attractive and colorful experience. Now that Windows XP includes its own skinning engine, products like WindowBlinds, which have their own skinning engine, become less necessary. So why am I even mentioning this application? Because there are some things that it brings to the table that visual styles do not.

Because WindowBlinds is a completely independent skinning engine from the Microsoft visual style engine, it has some features that the native engine does not have. One of these features is the ability to skin parts of the operating system that the native skinning engine cannot. The most talked about application that has this problem is the Command prompt in Windows. For some reason, Microsoft's engine just does not apply visual styles to this window. Instead, it is displayed using the classic Windows interface. WindowBlinds will allow you to skin this app as well.

WindowBlinds has a very strong skin base. A lot of very talented people have created XP skins for WindowBlinds that just look great. One benefit of using WindowBlinds to change the way your computer looks is the set of additional features that it provides, one of which is the ability to "roll up" a window so that just its title bar is shown. This is a great feature that can be activated by just double-clicking the title bar on skins that support the feature.

Another benefit of using WindowBlinds is its ability to skin applications that were not made to be skinned. This is a nice feature, but can also result in some applications looking a little strange because their buttons and other visual elements are replaced, which often throws off the spacing and placement of controls.

The one controversial topic about WindowBlinds is its effect on system performance. Because it runs on top of your computer's visual system and uses special system calls to change the way the computer looks, it takes up more system resources compared to the native visual style engine. Some users have a fast experience with WindowBlinds, although others do not. It really depends on your computer's hardware.

My personal experience with WindowBlinds has not indicated that they have set any record-setting speeds. I have run WindowBlinds on my computer a lot and have only noticed a decrease of performance in certain situations when I have used it with slower hardware. But my experience does not mean that you too will notice a slowdown. The speed of its operation seems to depend a lot on the specific hardware configuration of your computer, such as your video card and CPU. Also, even if you do notice a slowdown, it might be worth it if you find a really cool skin for WindowBlinds. Either way, I suggest that you give WindowBlinds a shot.

Using WindowBlinds to change the way Windows XP looks

WindowBlinds 4.2 is the latest version of this skinning app that will help you change the way Windows XP looks. Follow these steps to get that version of WindowBlinds set up on your computer so that you can start experimenting with it:

1. Visit www.WindowBlinds.net or http://download.com.com/3001-2326-10251037.html for a direct link to download a copy of WindowBlinds. Proceed to step 2, when you have finished installing it.

2. The best way to get to WindowBlinds is by right-clicking the desktop and clicking the Appearance tab when Display Properties loads. Then, click the WindowBlinds button.

3. The WindowBlinds Advanced Configuration will load, as shown in Figure 4-12. In this window, you can change the active skin. Browse through the skins that came with WindowBlinds when you installed it by scrolling the horizontal scrollbar. Click a skin to see it in the Preview box.

4. Just like visual styles for the native skinning engine, WindowBlinds skins include slight variations of a specific skin in one file. This can be thought of as the different color schemes that you worked with earlier. Not all WindowsBlinds skins have different versions included, but those that do can be changed by selecting the version from the drop-down box, as shown in Figure 4-13.

5. Once you are satisfied with a particular skin, click the Apply This Skin Now button.

6. WindowBlinds will then load the skin and apply it to the whole user interface. If you are happy with the way it looks, close the configuration editor and you are finished. Otherwise, select a different skin and try it again.

WindowBlinds may be a good alternative to the built-in visual style engine if you like the skins better and the extra features that it adds. Stardock has a more advanced version of WindowBlinds, called WindowBlinds Enhanced, which offers even more features and control over the themes. However, that version is not freeware, so the decision as to whether or not to use it is up to you. The question really boils down to whether or not you would use the extra features that WindowBlinds Enhanced provides.

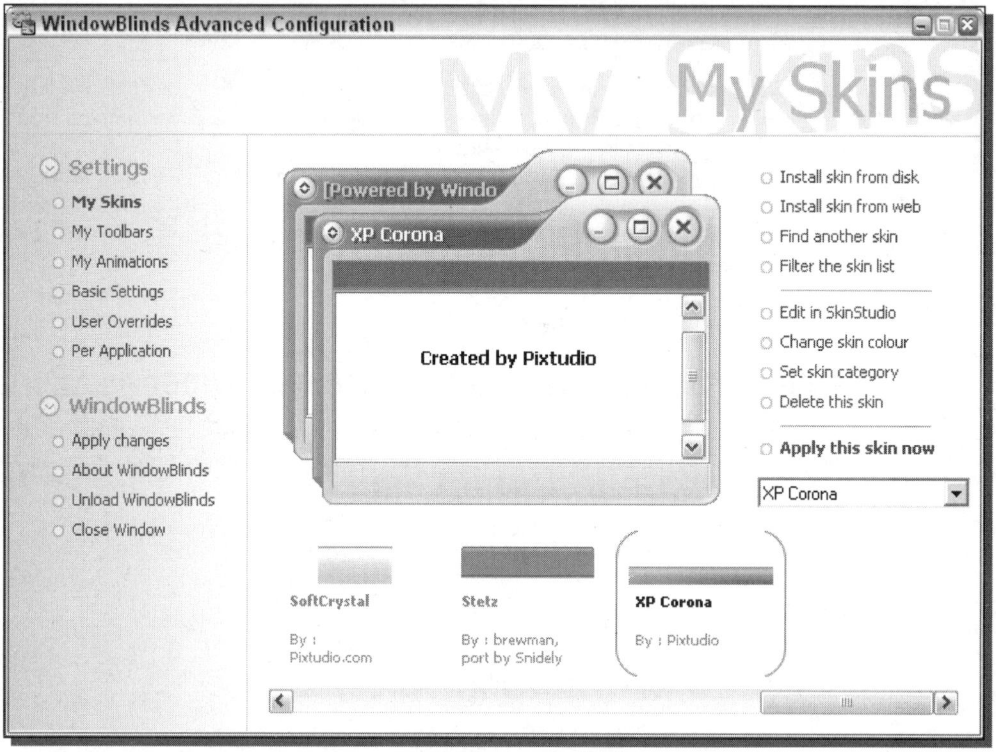

FIGURE **4-12**: Using the WindowBlinds Advanced Configuration editor.

If you ever decide that WindowBlinds is not for you, just go to the Control Panel and select Add Or Remove Programs. Then uninstall WindowBlinds by selecting it from the drop-down list that appears. This method provides an easy way to completely remove WindowBlinds from your computer if you decide that it is just not working out for you.

Installing additional Windows XP skins for WindowBlinds

One of the benefits of using WindowBlinds is how easy it is to add and use additional skins. Stardock operates an excellent Web site for thousands of WindowBlinds skins called WinCustomize, located at www.wincustomize.com.. To get started, open up your Web browser and visit www.wincustomize.com/skins.asp?library=1 for a list of all of the skins available.

Once you see the list of skins, to install one just hit the Download link and it should automatically start to download. When it is finished, WindowBlinds will automatically load it and will prompt you by asking if you would like to apply it. Once the skin is installed, you will be able to go back into the Advanced Configuration Editor to browse through the

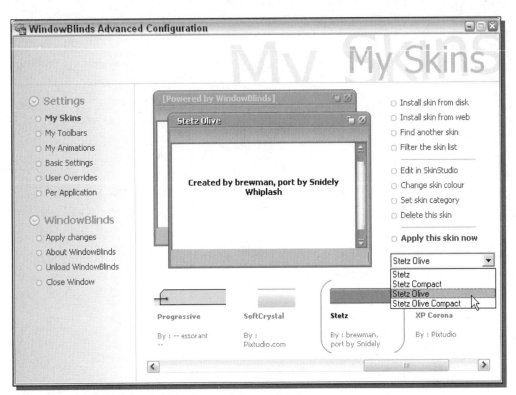

FIGURE 4-13: Selecting different subversions of a particular skin.

different versions and colors of the skin (assuming, of course, that the skin *has* multiple versions).

Summary

This chapter has focused on the most important part of customizing your computer. The visual interface is by far the part of the operating system that has the most impact when it is customized. Using the tools and techniques presented in this chapter, you can completely change the way Windows XP looks. You are no longer limited to using the default Windows XP style and can now use the thousands of visual styles and skins available on the Web.

The next chapter will be all about customizing the Windows Explorer, which is the program that you use to browse through all of the files on your computer. I will show you how you can customize the way it looks and works so that you can maximize the functionality to meet your needs.

Hacking Windows Explorer

The Windows Explorer is one of the most used parts of Windows XP. Every time you go to My Computer and browse through files on your computer, you are using Explorer. Using the icons on the desktop, right-clicking Files and Folders, copying and pasting files are all examples of using the features that the Explorer provides.

Many of the features that Windows Explorer provides can be easily customized to make Windows XP even better. This chapter will show you how you can change many of the features and how to take advantage of some of the new, lesser known features. It will start off with showing you how to customize the way you interact with files and then how you view your files. By the end of this chapter, you will have completely customized all of ways that you use Explorer to browse through and create files on your computer.

Hacking File Associations

Every time you click a file, Windows looks up what the default program to open for the file is from the registry. Then, Windows loads that application and tells the app what file to open up. This is something that we encounter almost all the time when we are using our computer. Often, when you install many programs on your computer, programs start to compete over which is going to be the default program to open up a file.

This commonly occurs when you install various music applications on your computer. I used Winamp to place CDs and MP3s on My Computer almost all the time. But when Apple released iTunes for Windows, I switched to that right away because of the cool library. Once I installed iTunes on My Computer, it took over all of my music files. Whenever I would insert a CD into my drive, iTunes would automatically load and start playing it. When I would click a MP3 file on my hard drive, the same would occur.

What happened to My Computer when I installed iTunes is not always a bad thing. However, there are situations when I wanted to use Winamp to play my MP3 files. One big reason for this is that when I click an MP3 file and it plays in iTunes, it is automatically added to my library. When I am sorting through my collection of songs that I ripped from my old CDs, I don't always want to add all of the songs to my library in iTunes because there are usually just two or three clicks on a 14-track CD. One easy solution to this problem is to change the file association back to Winamp so that when I click a file, it will be played in Winamp. Then if I like it, I can always add it to my library later within iTunes.

These next two sections will show you how to customize the default launch application for all of the different file types on your computer, as well as how your file types look.

Changing the default launch app

The information that Explorer looks up to find which program should be used to launch specific file types is stored in the System Registry under the HKEY_CLASSES_ROOT section. Using the Registry Editor, it is possible to browse to that key and then find the file type that you want to change and edit some keys, but there is a much easier way in Windows XP to accomplish the same task.

Hidden away in Folder Options within any Explorer window resides a useful utility to change the default application easily without having to worry about application IDs and file association structure. Just follow these steps to change any File Types default launch app:

1. Open up My Computer by clicking the desktop icon or on the icon in the Start panel.

2. When you have My Computer displayed on your screen, click the Tools menu bar item and select Folder Options.

3. Once the Folder Options window appears, click the File Types tab.

4. Navigate through the list of file extensions until you find the extension of the file for which you want to change the default app. Because I want to change my MP3 player default launch app, I am going to select the MP3 file extension. When you find the file extension that you want to change, select it by clicking it.

5. Click the Change button once you have your extension selected, as shown in Figure 5-1. The Open With properties window will load, asking you what program to load it with. It will show a list of common programs that you can choose from, but you are not limited to just those programs. Click the Browse button to navigate to any executable file on your computer to specify exactly what program you want to use if it is not on the list.

6. Once you have the application selected that you want to use, just click the OK button to save your changes. You are now finished with changing the launch app.

Your changes to file launch apps are activated immediately after you click OK to save your changes. Now you will no longer have to worry about applications taking control of your files.

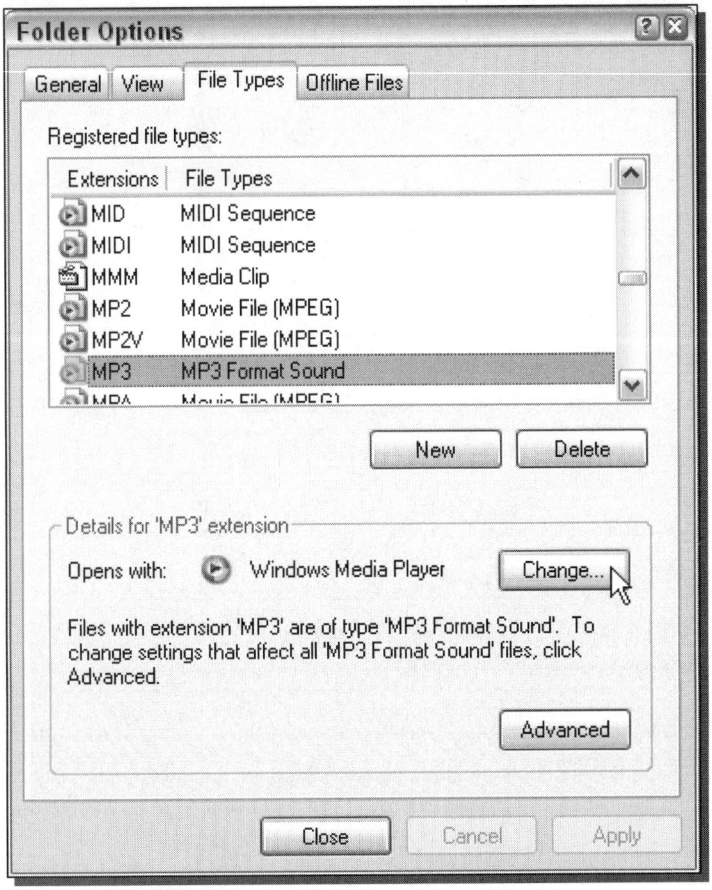

FIGURE 5-1: Changing the default launch app for MP3 files.

Changing the icon of any file type

So far, you have learned how to change the icons of the desktop icons. This next section will show you how you can change the default icon that is displayed for any file type on your computer. Changing the icons is actually very easy; the most difficult part of the process is trying to figure out what icon to use. Additionally, keep in mind that you can use any of the new high resolution icons that you can download from the sites mentioned in the *Changing the Desktop Icons* section in Chapter 3.

To get started changing your icons, you are going to want to use the Folder Options feature you used in the last section. Follow these steps to begin:

1. Open up Folder Options again by clicking My Computer. Then when it launches, click the Tools menu bar entry and select Folder Options.

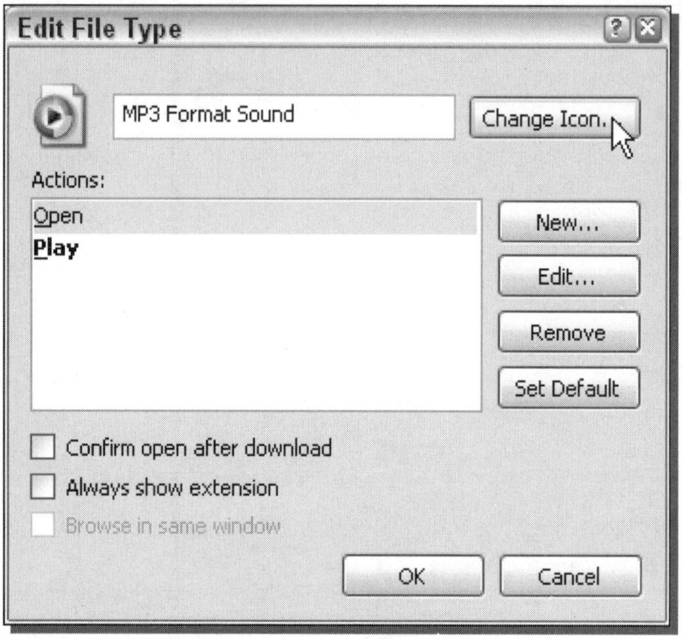

FIGURE 5-2: Changing the icon of a specific file type.

2. Inside Folder Options, click the File Types tab to reveal the list of all of the different file extensions on your computer.

3. Browse through the list and select the extension for which you want to change the icon.

4. Once you have the entry selected, click the Advanced button.

5. On the Edit File Type screen, click the Change Icon button, as shown in Figure 5-2.

6. The Change Icon screen will be displayed. Here, you will be shown various system icons from which you can choose. If you do not find any that you like, just click the Browse button and select an icon that you downloaded on your computer.

7. Once you find the perfect icon, click OK to select the new icon.

8. Then click OK once more to save your changes.

You don't have to reboot after you make your changes, because you will see your changes immediately after you click OK to save them.

Hacking the Context Menu

What is the context menu? This is the menu that pops up when you right-click a file on your computer. Over the years, these menus have become more and more useful. However, with the extra entries in the context menu, they often become cluttered with options and features that you just don't need. These next few sections will show you how to get your menus back under control as well as how to take advantage of the new features to make your own context menu entries.

We will start off by removing items from the context menus and will then move on to adding and customizing the components of the menus.

Removing items from the context menu

Over time, your context menus can become cluttered with program entries from old programs that you may not use any more. Sometimes, you may experience programs that take over all of your context menus. Compression apps such as Winzip or Picozip always end up adding program entries to all of the context menus. I have Picozip installed on My Computer and every time I right-click any file or folder, I see five entries from Picozip giving me different compression options. This can be a convenient feature, but if you don't compress and extract ZIP files very often, then you might not need the added convenience. Instead you could remove these entries from your context menu, which will give your system a cleaner interface as well as a small performance boost if you have a lot of extra entries in your context menu.

Before editing your registry, you would be wise to create a system restore point by using system restore. Doing so will provide an easy method to revert to your original configuration before you made any changes just in case you accidentally delete or modify something that hurts your computer.

Actually removing these programs from your context menus can be a little tricky, because they are spread in different places in the registry. Also, the easy-to-use context menu editor that you used in the last section to change the icon and default launch app for certain file types is not robust enough to allow you to remove entries from programs that take over all context menus such as Picozip. The only way to remove these types of entries is to edit the registry directly. If you want to remove an entry on a context menu that does not appear on every context menu and just appears on one or a few other file types, then you can still use the easy-to-use editor. Because of that, I have provided you two different sets of steps depending on what you want to do. When you are ready, follow these steps for the corresponding type of entry to remove it for good.

Removing entries that appear in all context menus

This set of steps will show you how to remove entries in the context menu that appear in all menus for all file types that were put there by programs such as Picozip.

1. Start up the Registry Editor by clicking the Start button and selecting Run. Then type **regedit** in the box and click OK.

2. When the Registry Editor appears, expand the HKEY_CLASSES_ROOT folder. You will now see a list of every file type that is set up on your computer.

3. If the entry that you want to remove from the context menu appears in all context menus, such as the preceding Picozip example, you will have to expand the * folder.

4. Now that you have the correct folder expanded, expand the Shellex and ContextMenu Handlers folders. Your registry path should look like HKEY_CLASSES_ROOT*\ shellex\ContextMenuHandlers.

5. Look through the list until you find the entry that you want to remove. Right-click the folder of the entry and select Delete. You will find that identifying some of the programs is easy. For example, Picozip is labeled Picozip. However, you may run into some items that are listed using their application ID number or a vague name. If that is the case, copy (Ctrl+C) the application ID, which is formatted like this—{XXXXXXXX-XXXX-XXXX-XXXX-XXXXXXXXXXXX}—to the clipboard. You may have to expand the folder to see the ID. Then, once you have the ID copied to the clipboard, press Ctrl+F to bring up the Search box in regedit and paste the ID in the box. Next, just click Find and you should be able to find some other references to that same ID in your registry that also might give you some clues to what it is. If that does not work, try doing a search on Google to see if that turns up anything.

6. Once you are finished removing all of the entries from your context menus, just close Registry Editor and you are finished. Your changes will be in effect immediately.

Removing entries that appear only under certain file types

If you want to remove an entry on a context menu that appears on just one file type or a few different file types, this section will show you how to easily remove it by using the context editor in Folder Options.

1. Open up My Computer by clicking the icon on the desktop or by clicking the Start Menu.

2. Once My Computer appears on the screen, click the Tools menu and select Folder Options and click the File Types tab.

3. Scroll through the list of file types and select the extension that you would like to modify.

4. Click the Advanced button to bring up the Edit File Type window, where you will see a list of all of the different entries that will show up in the context menu, as shown in Figure 5-3.

5. Select the item that you want to remove and click Remove.

6. Click OK and you are finished.

If you ever want to revert to your original context menus, you can just restore your computer to an earlier checkpoint. Or, if you didn't create a system restore checkpoint, you can just reinstall the app and that should take care of it.

Adding your own items to the context menu

Now that you have removed all of the extra clutter from your context menus, why not add some useful entries to your menus? You can add a lot of interesting things to your context menus that can enhance your experience with your computer. My favorite item to add to the context menus is a "Send Attached to Message" entry. This entry in my context menu grew out of a need to find a better way to e-mail files. I send a lot of messages every day, often just

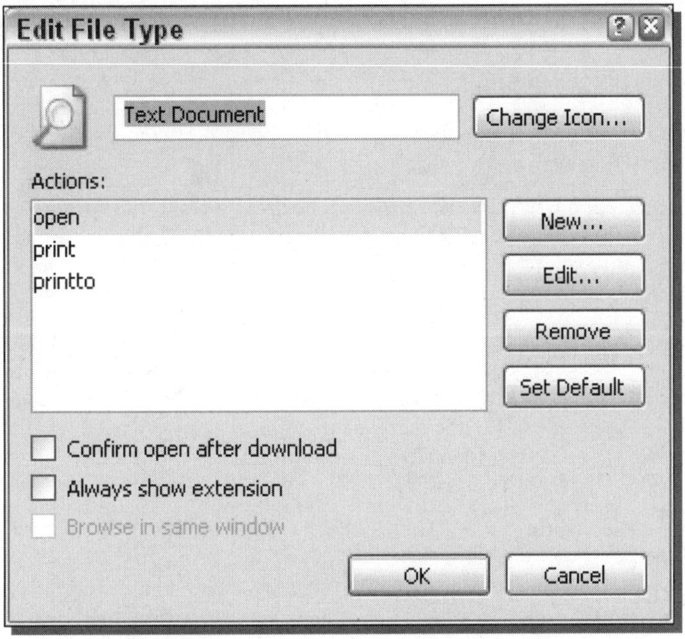

Edit File Type

Text Document   Change Icon...

Actions:

open
print
printto

New...
Edit...
Remove
Set Default

☐ Confirm open after download
☐ Always show extension
☐ Browse in same window

OK   Cancel

FIGURE 5-3: Edit File Type window displaying a list of all of the entries in a text document's context menu.

for the purpose of sending a file. I thought to myself, wouldn't it be simple if I could just right-click a file and select some option that would automatically open up Microsoft Outlook, create a new message, and attach the file? That would streamline the whole process by knocking out a few steps.

Adding an entry to a context menu is very simple. The most difficult part of solving my little puzzle was figuring out how to launch Outlook so it would automatically create a message and attach the desired file to it. After a few minutes on Google researching, I came across Outlook-Tips.net, which is a great resource for just the information that I was looking for. According to `www.outlook-tips.net/howto/commandlines.htm`, I just had to launch Outlook with the /a switch and the name of the file. Once I had this information, I had all of the pieces of the puzzle and was ready to start putting it together. Perform the following steps to learn how to add your own item to any File Types context menu:

1. First, open up a copy of My Computer by clicking the icon on the desktop or Start panel.

2. Click the Tools menu bar item and select Folder Options.

3. Then, click the File Types tab to expose all of the different file types on your computer.

4. Because I usually send Word documents, I scrolled down the list of file types and selected the .doc file extension. Pick any other file extension for which you would like to add an entry.

5. Then, once you have the entry selected, click the Advanced button to bring up the Edit File type window.

6. Click the New button to add an entry.

7. In the Action box, type in the name that you want to appear on the menu. I typed in **Send Attached to Message.**

8. Then, in the Application Used to Perform Action box, you will want to specify the application and any switches that you want to use for this new entry. Click the Browse button to easily browse to an executable. I navigated until I found OUTLOOK.EXE inside the OFFICE11 folder.

9. When you click OK, the path to the executable will fill the box. Now you will want to add any application flags at the end of the line. To tell Outlook to create a new message and attach a file to it, I had to add **/a-** after the path, followed by **%L.** The %L is a system variable that holds the name of the file that you are right-clicking. When I was finished, my box looked like the following (including the quotes): "C:\Program Files\Microsoft Office\OFFICE11\OUTLOOK.EXE" /a "%L".

10. When you are finished editing your new entry, click OK to save it.

You are now finished adding an entry to a specific File Types context menu. If you followed all of the previous steps to add the Send Attached to Message entry, every time you right-click a Word document, you will now see the new entry, as shown in Figure 5-4. If you want to add

FIGURE 5-4: What the context menu will look like after the Send Attached to Message is attached.

the same entry on other file types, just repeat the previous directions by selecting a different file type in step 4.

You can do even more things with the context menus. If I wanted to, I could use the different switches that I found on the Outlook Tips Web site (www.outlook-tips.net) to make my entry send the file to a specific person instead of leaving the To field blank in Outlook. Once you know the %L variable, you can send the name of the file to any program, given that you know the correct switches with which to launch the program.

 I have included a registry file that you can import to easily set up your context menu with the Outlook Send To hack that will display the shortcut on all context menus for Microsoft Word documents. Outlook_sendto.reg is located in the Chapter 5 folder of the companion CD-ROM.

Modifying the Send To menu

The Send To menu is one of the features of my context menus that I use the most. The ability to right-click any file and have a shortcut of it sent to the desktop is invaluable. All of the other features are very useful as well. How would you like to make it even more useful? It is very easy to add your own items to the Send To menu, such as folders that you can send files to. Do you have a folder that you store all of your music in? How about a folder that you store all of your digital photos in? Just follow these quick steps to add anything that you want to your Send To context menu entry.

1. Open up My Computer and browse to the C drive, or whatever drive you have Windows installed to.

2. Then browse through Documents and Settings, your user name, and the Send To folders.

 If you do not see any of the folders that are required in this section, you may have hidden files turned on. Because these folders are hidden by default, you will have to tell Windows to show all files. To do this, refer to the section on working with hidden files towards the end of this chapter.

3. When you are looking at C:\Documents and Settings\Username\SendTo, you will see all of the files that appear in the Send To menu. If you want to add an entry to the menu, just copy a shortcut to this folder.

4. Let's say that you want to add your Digital Photos folder to your Send To menu. Just navigate to your Digital Photos folder and right-click it and select Send To desktop. Then just cut and paste the shortcut that was created from your desktop into the Send To folder.

5. If you ever want to remove some items from the Send To menu, just delete them from the Send To folder.

It is that simple. You are now finished with customizing your Send To menu. Now you will be able to fine-tune all of the different features of your context menus so that you can get the most out of your Windows XP experience.

Customizing Your Folders

The folders of Windows XP can be customized in ways that were never before possible. You can easily change the icon of the folder as well as the way the folder behaves once you open it up. These next few sections will show you how to take advantage of the great new folder features of XP.

Changing a folder icon and picture

Changing the icon that is displayed for a folder is one of the easiest ways to customize how it looks and make it stand out from the rest of your folders. Windows XP also includes a new way to apply pictures to the front of your folders when you are using thumbnail view. This next section will show you how to change the way your files and folders look as you browse through them by taking advantage of the new high-resolution icons.

Changing the folder icon and the folder picture are done within a folder properties menu. For the sake of demonstrating what you can do with these new features, create a new folder on one of your hard drives and call it Downloads. This can be a folder to which you can save all of your downloads so that they do not clutter up your desktop. Follow these steps to change the way this folder looks:

1. Right-click the new folder that you just created, or on any folder that you want to customize, and select Properties.

2. Next, click the Customize tab to reveal all of your customizing options.

3. The particular view you are currently using, whether it be the Icons, Tiles or Thumbnails view, will determine what you can customize. First, customize the icon, because that is the most popular way to customize the look of the folder. To do that, click the Change Icon button on the bottom of the window.

4. Now you will be able to browse through the list of available system icons or you will be able to specify your own by clicking the Browse button. Personally, the system icons are good enough for this folder, so I would select one of the globe icons for the Downloads folder.

5. Once you have selected the icon that you want to use, just click the OK button to return to the Customize screen. Then click Apply to see your changes.

6. If you are using Thumbnail view to view your icons, you can customize the folder by making an image appear on the front of the folder so that it can be used as a reminder of what is in the folder. To do that, just click the Choose Picture button on the Customize screen and specify a bitmap to be displayed on the file.

7. Once you are finished selecting the image, click OK to save your change. Then click Apply on the Customize screen to see your changes. Remember that you will only see your change if you are using the Thumbnails view. The view can be changed to Thumbnails view by clicking the View menu bar item.

When you are finished changing the way your folder looks, just click the OK button to save your changes and exit the folder properties window.

Changing the template of a folder

Windows XP has several different ways to display the contents of a folder. Specifically, XP has many new ways that different types of data inside a folder can be viewed. For example, if you have a folder filled with MP3 files, Windows can display new information, such as the title of the song, artist, year, track #, bitrate, duration, and other data from the ID3 tags (special data that keeps track of the title of the songs, artist, album, etc.) that are stored within a MP3 file when displaying the file in Details view with the music template selected. Another example is the new Filmstrip and Thumbnails view that can be selected to easily browse through your photos on your computer.

To get started customizing the folders on your computer so that they can take advantage of the new features, you have to set the template of the folder so that Windows Explorer knows how

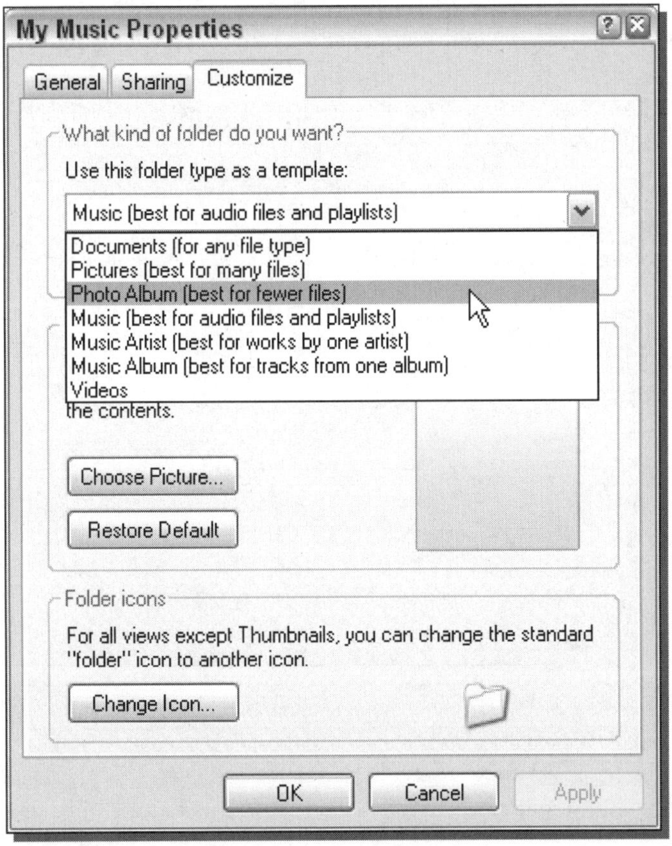

FIGURE 5-5: Changing the template of a folder.

to display its contents. This can be done by using the Customize tab in Folder Properties. Follow these steps to specify the template that should be used for a specific folder:

1. Navigate to the folder that you want to modify and right-click it and select Properties.

2. Then click the Customize tab.

3. Next, select the template that you want to use by expanding the drop-down box, as shown in Figure 5-5. The default template that is used is the Documents template. Other template options include Pictures, Photo Album, Music, and Videos. There are actually a few different subsets of music as well, but it really does not matter which one you select because most likely you will be customizing the look further in the next section. The main purpose of changing the template is so that you will have a different set of features with which you can work and customize.

4. Also, if you have a lot of folders within this folder with the same type of content, click the Also Apply This to All Subfolders check box so that your changes will be propagated to all subfolders.

You have now customized the template of the folder and are ready to customize the view.

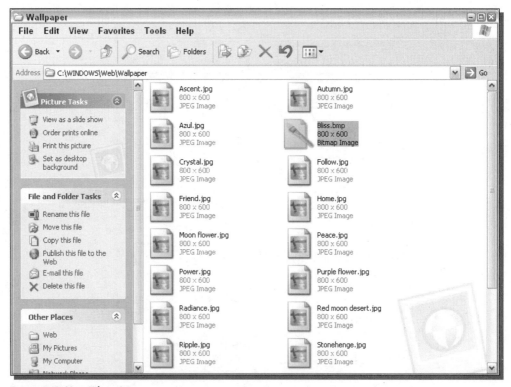

FIGURE 5-6: New Tiles view.

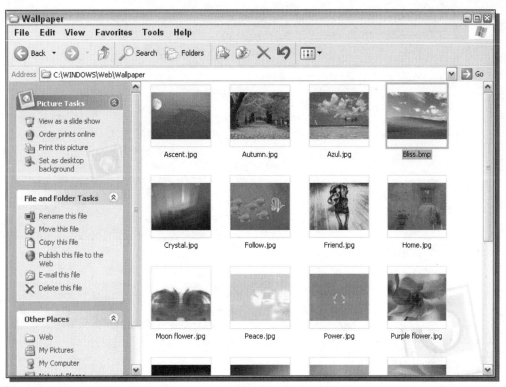

FIGURE 5-7: New Thumbnail view.

Customizing the view folder

Now that you have a specific template selected for your folder, you will have a more advanced feature list to work with so that you can display a lot of useful information about the file in your folder. First, you need to be aware of the new views that you can use in Windows XP:

- The default view of Windows XP is the Tiles view, as shown in Figure 5-6. This view is basically the same as the Icons view, but the icons that are displayed are just a little bigger.

- The Thumbnails view is one of the most useful new views of Windows XP, as shown in Figure 5-7.

- The Filmstrip view is another very useful view that makes it easy to browse through photos on your computer. It gives you the ability to see a large sample of the image, as shown in Figure 5-8, so that you can see a more detailed preview without having to open up the file.

FIGURE 5-8: New Filmstrip view.

- The Details view is not exactly a new view, but it has been expanded to include many new fields that display useful file information, such as ID3 tags and image data like dimensions and camera info.

The Details view can be customized like no other view can. All of the columns that are displayed can be resized, removed, rearranged, and more can be added. This can all be accomplished by using some of the lesser-known tricks of the interface. To start off, customize a folder that contains a bunch of MP3 files. By now, you should have already changed the template for this folder to one of the music templates so that you can use the advanced music specific features. If you have not already done that, go back to the last section to find out how. When you are ready, follow these steps to customize all of the different parts of the Detail view:

1. Start off by resizing the columns. To do so, just place the mouse on the vertical line that is displayed between the columns and click and hold the left mouse button while you drag the mouse back and forth.

2. Now, add some of the new columns that display information from the ID3 tags from the MP3 files. Just right-click the column heading and select one of the many new options, such as bit rate. You can even select more items to add from the bottom of the pop-up

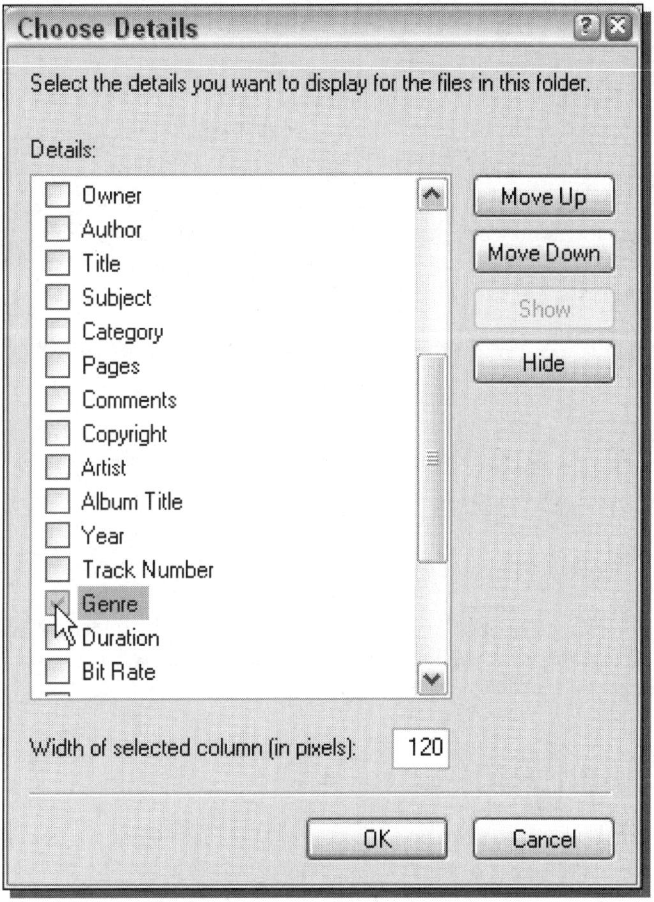

FIGURE 5-9: Adding new columns to the detailed view.

menu, as shown in Figure 5-9. Repeat this step until you have added all of the new columns that you want.

3. Most likely, there will be some columns that you just don't need. To remove these columns from the Details view, just right-click the column heading and select the item once again to uncheck it. This will instantly remove the column from view.

4. The last part of customizing the view is to set the order of the columns in a way that you like the best. To change the order of a column, just grab the column header and drag it around by holding down the left mouse button and moving the mouse.

If you want to customize the detailed view of a folder that contains other multimedia files such as videos or photos, just repeat the previous steps and you will see additional column features with which you will be able to customize your detailed view.

Applying your folder settings to all folders

When you first use Windows XP, all of the folders are configured to use the Tiles view. Personally, I don't always like to use the Tiles view for my folders. It takes up so much screen space and I usually end up scrolling through the long lists while trying to find the file that I want. Instead, I like to use the Detail view on all of the windows by default.

To do this, you could change the settings of every folder, but there is a much easier way. Instead, just customize one folder on your computer using the preceding sections so that you can get it looking great, then follow these steps to apply the same configuration to all of the other folders on your computer.

1. While the folder that you customize is still open, click the Tools menu bar item and select Folder Options.

2. Next, click the View tab.

3. Click the Apply to All Folders button and click Yes on the confirmation screen. Also, keep in mind that when you do that, you will overwrite your configuration on all of the other folders on your computer.

4. Click OK to close the Folder Options window and you are finished.

If for some reason you don't like what you did and want to restore all of the folders on your computer to the original look, just click the Reset All Folders button that was next to the Apply to All Folders button on the View tab in Folder Options.

Working with Hidden Files

Just like every other Windows version, Windows XP likes to hide files. When you are interested in tweaking and customizing your computer, this hiding of files can become problematic, as many of the system files with which you want to work are often hidden. These next two sections will show you how to make Windows XP display all hidden and system files as well as the super hidden files.

Unhiding hidden files

When you are tweaking your computer, you often need to edit different configuration files for different applications. This can cause a problem because those configuration files are often hidden. The only way to edit them would be if you knew the exact file name and typed it in the Browse box manually. Otherwise, you would be out of luck.

Telling Explorer to show hidden files and folders is the only solution to this problem. Making Explorer show hidden files is just a matter of getting to the right place. Follow these steps to show all hidden files:

1. Open up a copy of Explorer My Computer by clicking the icon on the Desktop or Start panel.

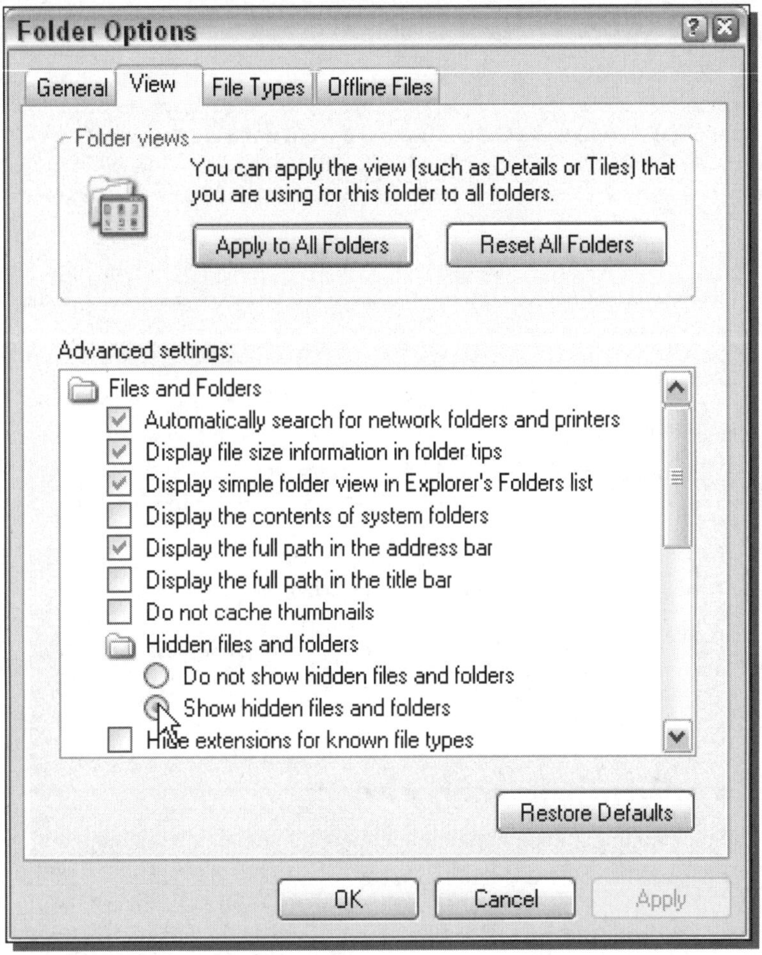

FIGURE 5-10: Revealing hidden files.

2. Then go to the Tools menu bar item and select Folder Options.

3. When the window appears, click the View tab to see all of the different file display options.

4. Scroll down the list until you see the entries for Hidden Files and Folders. Select Show Hidden Files and Folders, as shown in Figure 5-10.

5. When you are finished, just click OK to save your changes and exit the configuration window.

You should now see all of the hidden files on your computer that are hidden using the +h file attribute. However, you may notice that there still are some files that are not showing up. These are the system files. To show these files, continue on to the next section.

Revealing the super hidden files

Microsoft has added many features to Windows XP to protect the critical files of the operating system. The system file checker, for example, continually monitors the system files versions to ensure that no application will replace your system files with a version that Windows XP was not designed to work with. The new super hidden files feature allows Windows to protect itself even further by hiding some of its most critical files from the user. If they can't get to it, they can't hurt it, right?

Revealing the super hidden system files is not very difficult at all. You can uncheck the box on the list on the View tab of Folder Options, but where is the fun in that? Use the Registry Editor to turn this feature off:

1. Click the Start button and select Run.

2. Type **regedit** in the box and click OK to start up the Editor.

3. Once regedit appears, navigate through `HKEY_CURRENT_USER\Software\Microsoft\Windows\CurrentVersion\Explorer\Advanced`.

4. Right-click ShowSuperHidden and select Modify.

5. Change the value to **1** and click OK to save your changes.

Now you will be able to see all of the files on your computer, including the super hidden system files.

Disabling the Common Tasks Pane

Every time you use Explorer, you are forced to view the new Common Tasks pane. The Common Tasks pane is the new panel that is displayed on the left side of the screen that provides you with links to various parts of the operating system as well as useful utilities. This new feature looks visually pleasing and seems to be a very nice and useful feature. However, that is not always the case. I do not think that I have ever used any link on my tasks pane or any of the other information that is shown on it. If you are like me and do not use your Common Tasks pane, why not remove it to recover some space that could be used to display more icons on your screen?

Removing the Common Tasks pane is very easy using the Folder Options that can be accessed in any Explorer window. Follow these steps to remove the Common Tasks pane from your windows:

1. Click the Tools menu bar item from any open Explorer window and select Folder Options. If you do not have an open Explorer window, just open My Computer.

2. On the General tab, just select Use Classic Folders under the Tasks settings on the top.

3. Click OK to save your changes.

You have now removed the Common Tasks pane from all of your Explorer windows.

Summary

This chapter has shown you many different ways to customize how Explorer looks and works. You discovered how to change file associations as well as how certain file types look when viewed in Explorer. Then, you found out how to customize the context menu as well as how to clean it up. The last part of this chapter showed you how to customize the different views of Windows XP so that you can take advantage of the cool new features and increase your productivity as well.

The next chapter will be the last chapter in Part I of this book. In it, you will discover many more ways to customize the interface of Windows XP, including many interesting utilities, such as the graphical task switcher and effects apps, that will make your computer look great. Additionally, it will show you how you can customize Internet Explorer and refine other elements of Windows to complete this customizing journey.

Exploring Other Windows Enhancements

Welcome to the last chapter of Part I of this book, which deals with customization. So far, you have found out how to customize the way your computer looks from the moment you hit the power switch to the moment you start running your favorite applications. This chapter will show you even more ways to customize your computer by customizing Internet Explorer and several other little tweaks that will fine-tune your PC.

Customizing your computer is a great way to be more productive—and simply makes your computer look great. The next few sections will show you how you can customize the toolbars of Internet Explorer, as well as some cool address bar tricks that you can use to change the way you browse the Web. Then, you will discover some different ways that you can expand functionality, as well as add some fascinating special effects, to the windows. The chapter will finish up by going over customizing the last bits and pieces of the user interface, such as branding your computer and adjusting the clear type effect. When you are finished with this chapter, you will have completed one of the most thorough customizations of Windows XP possible.

Modding Internet Explorer

Most of us spend a lot of time with Internet Explorer (IE) as an Internet browser. IE can be customized a few ways. The most popular tweak to Internet Explorer is to change the Windows logo animation. It's time to get started with customizing Internet Explorer by changing the animated logo.

Changing the logo animation

Every time you submit data on a Web page or visit a new page, your browser will start the animation of the Windows flag (also known as a throbber) in the upper-right corner of your screen. The Windows flag is a nice animation, but why not replace that animation with one you made yourself? Many very cool animated GIFs are available on the Web that you can download for free. This section will show you how to use those animated GIF image files that you can download as a replacement for the Windows flag.

To do this, you will need to have two applications downloaded and installed. The first application is Microsoft's Tweak UI PowerToy. This can be downloaded at the PowerToy's Web site, located at www.microsoft.com/windowsxp/pro/downloads/powertoys.asp. The other application that you will use is a free app called BitStrip, which is developed by Darrell L. A copy of this free application can be downloaded from his site at www.virtualplastic.net/redllar/bitstrip.html. Once you have installed Tweak UI and extracted BitStrip, you are ready to get started.

To change the throbber, perform the following steps:

1. First, find the image that you want to use as your new animation. Many animation sites can be found on the Internet. My favorite site is called the Animation Factory. Located at www.AnimationFactory.com, you will find thousands of high-quality animated graphics. The default size of the small animation is 26 × 26 pixels (this is the default animation that is shown on most computers). The large animation is 38 × 38. You will want to find an image that is smaller than or the same size as those dimensions. If you can only find a large image, try resizing the image with an animated GIF editor. If you cannot properly resize the image, you will not have any problems other than it just might look a little strange. Once you have found an image that you want to use, you are ready to prep the image file.

2. Internet Explorer only accepts replacement animations in a specific format. All replacement animations must be saved as a bitmap. However, bitmaps cannot be used to store animations like GIFs can. To solve that problem, Internet Explorer reads the bitmap like it is a film projector. Therefore, we need to convert the animated GIF file into one tall bitmap image that has all of the frames arranged vertically. To do this, use the BitStrip program. Start up BitStrip and open up your source animated GIF that you want to convert by clicking the Browse to GIF File button.

3. Once you have the image file selected, click the Vertical button and you should see a preview similar to Figure 6-1 on your screen.

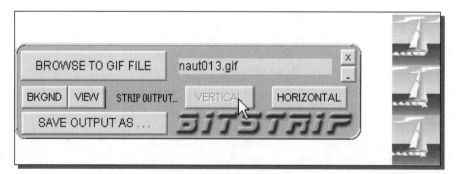

FIGURE 6-1: A compatible bitmap file.

4. If it looks good, then save the file as a bitmap by clicking the Save Output As button.

5. You now have converted your animated GIF into a format that the browser can read. The next step is to tell the browser to use the new file. To do this, you will want to start up Tweak UI, which is listed in the Start Menu under Windows XP PowerToys.

6. When Tweak UI has started up, expand Internet Explorer and select either small or large animation depending on which one your computer is currently displaying. By default, Windows XP shows the small animation unless you have changed it.

7. You will now see all of the throbber settings for Internet Explorer. Click the Custom radio button, as shown in Figure 6-2, so that you can specify your own file to use for the animation.

8. Next, click the Change Busy Image button and select the bitmap file that you just converted in step 4.

9. After you have selected your image, it should show up in the Preview box. If the image looks good, click the OK button to save your changes.

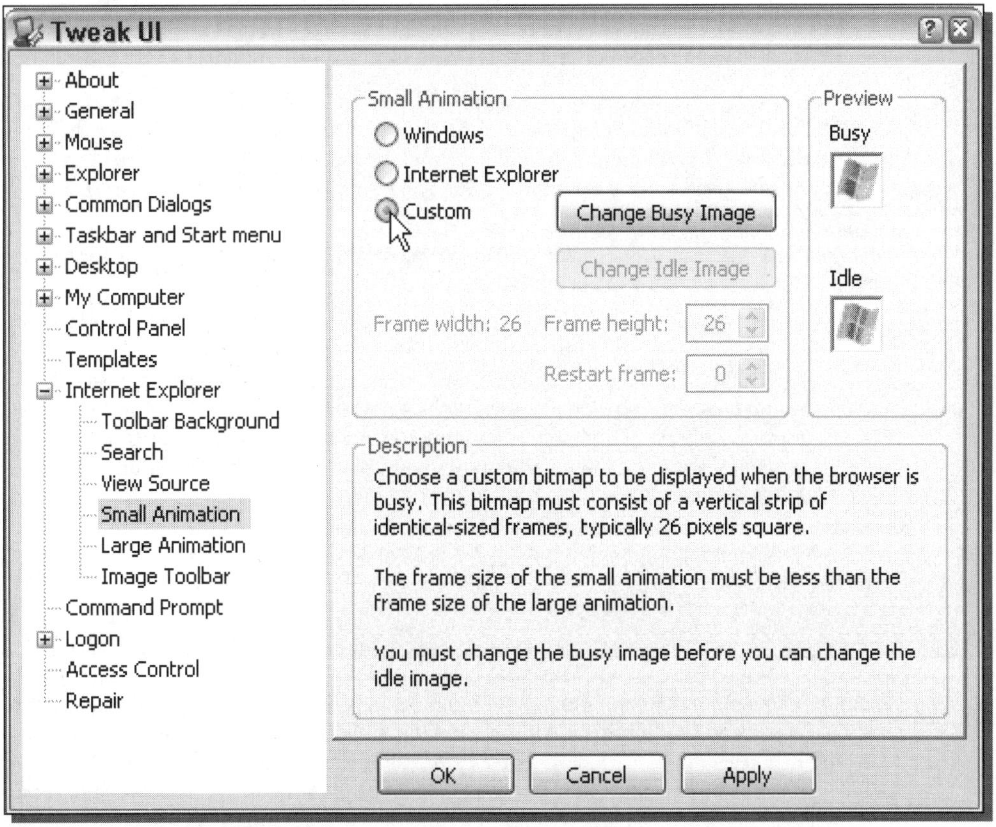

FIGURE 6-2: Using Tweak UI to change Internet Explorer's animation/throbber.

You are not done with changing the browser animated logo. To see the new animation in action, you will have to restart all instances of Internet Explorer that were open while you were changing the animation. The next time you start up IE, the new animation should be displayed. If that is not the case, then try using BitStrip again on the source animated graphic file to create a new bitmap and then repeat step 8.

Changing the toolbar background

Changing the background of the toolbar is one of the oldest tweaks for Windows. It has been around ever since Windows 95 and still works on the latest version of Windows. Because I am writing a book on customizing Windows XP, I just had to include this classic.

Back in Windows 95, the only way to display an image as the background for the menu bar and toolbar of Internet Explorer was to hack the registry. Now, using Tweak UI, changing the toolbar background is very easy. If you do not already have Tweak UI, download a copy now. If you already have it or have just finished installing it, you are ready to get started:

1. Start up Tweak UI from the PowerToys for Windows XP entry in the All Programs menu of the Start Menu.

2. Next, expand the Internet Explorer item from the list and select Toolbar Background.

3. You will be shown two different options. You can specify a bitmap to be shown just on the Internet Explorer toolbar or you can specify a bitmap to be shown on the Explorer windows (My Computer, My Documents, and so on.). For the purpose of this section, you will just be using the first option. The next step is to check the Use Custom Background for Internet Explorer Toolbar.

4. Once you have put a check in the box, the Change button will become active. Click the button and select the image bitmap that you want to use. You can use any bitmap image on your computer. However, certain files, such as photos, don't always look the best. I like to create my own bitmap using Adobe Photoshop and making a simple image that is just a gradation. This gives a nice appearance as the back of the toolbar, as shown in Figure 6-3. You don't have to use Adobe Photoshop to create an image that is a simple gradation of two shades of a color; you can use any image editing program that has the gradient feature. Just about all popular Paint programs have that feature.

Once you have picked out or created your image file and have selected it with the Change button, you are finished and will be able to see your new toolbar background by opening up a new instance of Internet Explorer.

Making your own quick search address command

You can do a lot of interesting tricks with the Address bar. One of my favorite hacks is to add a special command to the address bar interpreter that will allow you to visit a Web site just by typing in a keyword. This alone is a nice feature, but to make it even better, you can set it up so that you can even pass other words to that Web page. For example, it is possible to set up your browser so that when you type **Google TweakXP**, it will automatically go to google.com and do a search for TweakXP. This can be a very convenient feature if you do a lot of searches on the Web. It basically eliminates the first step of going to the Web site.

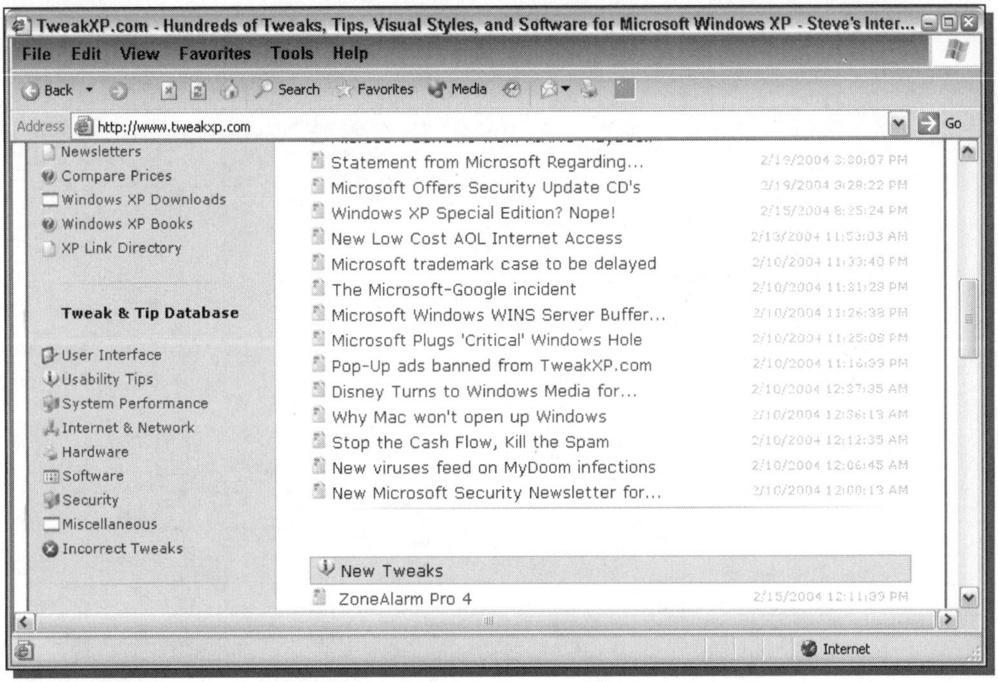

FIGURE 6-3: Internet Explorer with an image used at the background of the toolbar

To add this cool feature to the address bar, you will need to use our favorite utility, Tweak UI. By now, you should have Tweak UI installed, but if you don't, go to www.microsoft.com/ windowsxp/pro/downloads/powertoys.asp and download a copy. Once you have Tweak UI installed, follow these steps:

1. Start up Tweak UI by expanding the PowerToys for Windows XP entry in the All Programs menu and selecting Tweak UI.

2. Expand the Internet Explorer entry and select Search.

3. Click the Create button on the bottom right of the Search Prefixes box.

4. Now you will want to enter the name of the command that you want to type in the pre-fix box. This is where you should type in Google, Search, or whatever you want your command to be called.

5. Next, in the URL box, you will want to add **www.google.com/search?q=%s** so that your command points to Google's site, as shown in Figure 6-4. Notice the %s in the URL? That is a system variable that catches all of the text to the right of your command (where the search words are).

6. When you are finished filling in both boxes, click OK and your new command will be created.

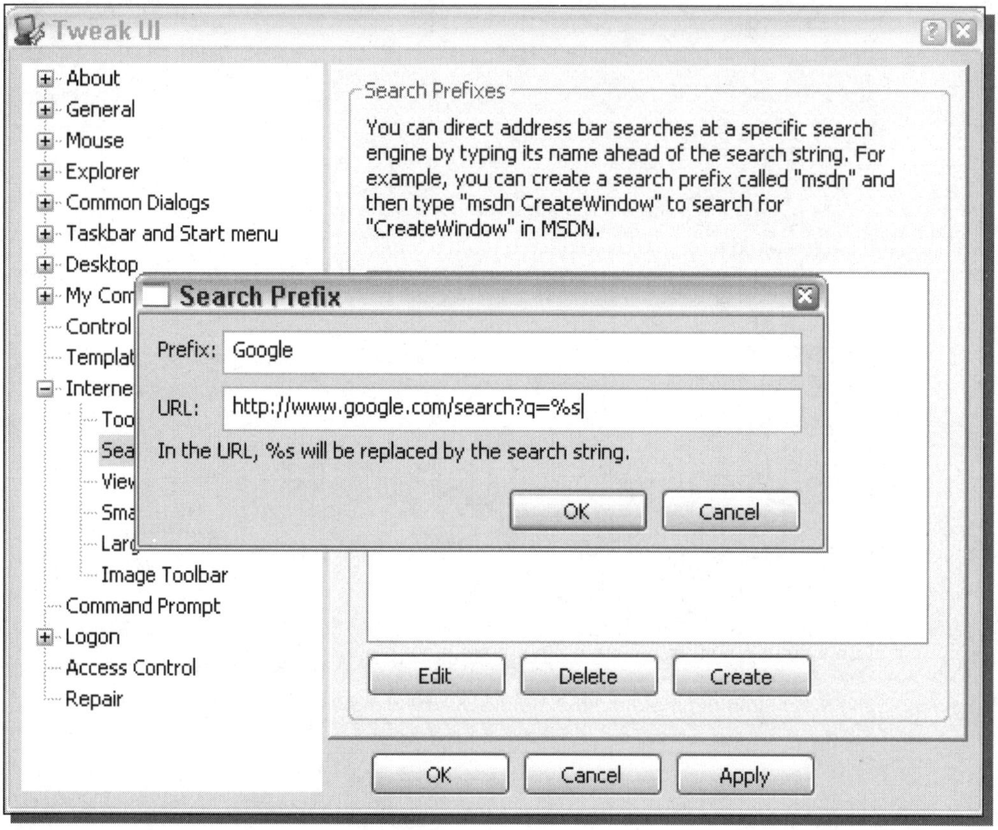

FIGURE 6-4: Creating an address bar command.

You are now finished and can close Tweak UI. To test your new command, just open up a new instance of IE and type in Google search terms. You should be taken to Google with your search terms displayed as the results.

If you like the new command, you can always make more for other search engines or for quick links to Web sites. I also like to create a command called weather. I just type in **weather** followed by a ZIP code and then am taken to the weather channel's site. To make this work, I have my URL set to http://www.weather.com/weather/local/%s.

Other Visual Enhancements

A few more hacks and utilities can enhance and customize the different visual elements even further. These next few sections will show you some great apps that will add interesting special effects to your user interface as well as a few hacks that will help you fine-tune other elements of your computer.

Replacing the task switcher

The task switcher is the little application that pops up when you press Alt and Tab to switch between active applications. To use it, just hold down the Alt key and press Tab. Then keep the Alt key held down and tap the Tab key to select a different app to switch to. The task switcher is a no-thrills app that just shows you the icon and the name of the application when it is displayed. Most people rarely use the task switcher to switch between programs because the taskbar is usually much easier. However, Microsoft has released a new PowerToy that is a replacement for the task switcher that might make you think twice about using the taskbar to switch between apps because of its cool new appearance and features.

The new replacement task switcher, shown in Figure 6-5, is updated to reflect the new XP look and includes a new image preview of the application that you can switch to. Operating the replacement task switcher is exactly the same, just use Alt and Tab.

Now that you know a little about the new task switcher, it's time to get it installed on your computer. Installing it on your computer is very easy. Just download a copy of the app from the PowerToys Web site, located at `http://www.microsoft.com/windowsxp/pro/down`

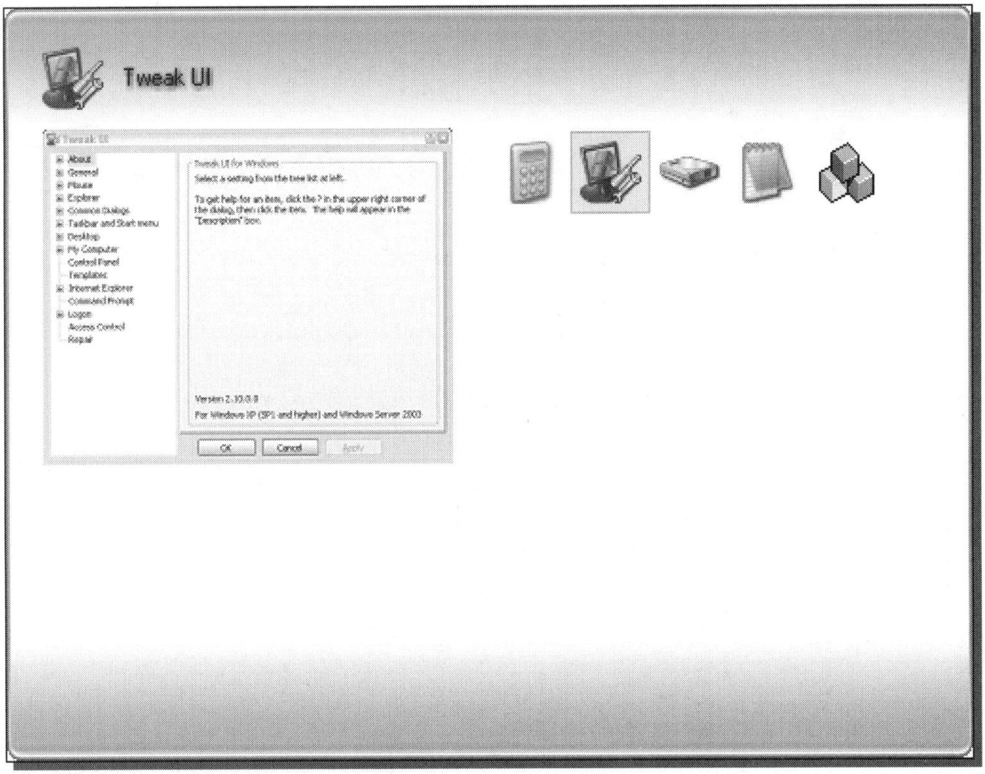

FIGURE 6-5: Microsoft's new Alt+Tab replacement.

`loads/powertoys.asp`. It is located on the top of the list on the right side of the page. When you have finished downloading it, open up the file and keep clicking Next to install it. When the installation exits, the new task switcher is ready to be used without a system reboot. Just click the Alt and Tab keys to see the new task switcher on your computer. Remember, the task switcher will not function if you have just one app open. It requires a minimum of two applications to be open in order for it to work. After all, why would you need to switch between apps if you have only one app open?

Adding Special Effects to your Windows

Thousands of tiny apps are available on the Web that will add both visual effects and features to your windows. Three nifty apps are a must for any user who is interested in customizing her or his computer and making it unique. I have selected a few of my favorite apps that represent several different special effects, such as animation, fades, shadows, and more.

Using WindowsFX

WindowsFX is a program developed by Stardock that offers a suite of special effects that will help make your computer look great. It gives users the ability to add drop shadows on all active windows, window transitions, and transparency. But the most impressive feature, and the reason why I am including this app, are the animations that appear when you drag a window around on the screen. As shown in Figure 6-6, when you drag a window across the screen, the window has an effect as if it is some sort of gelatin.

This is an effect that you will really have to experience first hand to understand. Therefore, follow these steps to get WindowsFX installed on your computer and the dragging effect up and running:

1. Visit Stardock's Web site at `www.stardock.com/products/windowfx/` and download a copy of WindowsFX.

2. Once you have WindowsFX installed, start it up by expanding the Object Desktop entry in the All Programs menu and select WindowsFX.

3. Under the side menu for 2000 / XP Only, select Window Dragging to bring up the settings.

4. On the Window Dragging screen, select Basic Swaying Windows, as shown in Figure 6-7.

5. Once you have selected Basic Swaying Windows, click Apply Changes, located in the lower-left portion of the window just under WindowFX.

Once you have applied your changes, you will notice the new effect when you drag windows around on the screen. A lot of different dragging effects are available that you can use, but unless you purchase the full version of the app, those will not be available to you.

Adding shadows to your windows

Drop shadows are a cool feature to add to your windows. They make your applications stand out a lot more when you have a lot of windows open and make Windows XP look like OSX or

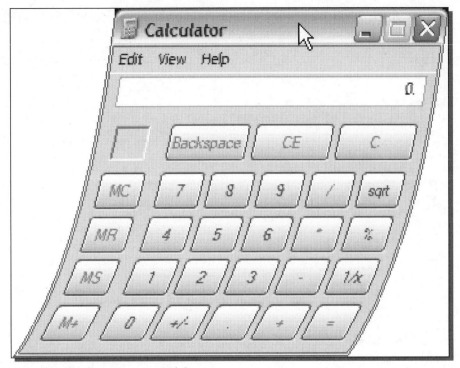

FIGURE 6-6: WindowsFX's animated drag.

as they are expected to look in Longhorn, the next Windows operating system due out within a few years. Drop shadows are possible through a variety of applications on the Web. My favorite application to use for this is called Lokai Shadows XP. This free application, written by Brandon Sneed, can be downloaded from his Web site at http://redf.net/download.php?view.2. One of the reasons why I like this application so much is because it works (a lot of them I could not get to work) and because it also can run as a service in the background. The quality of the drop shadows on the windows is also of high quality, as shown in Figure 6-8.

Visit the author's Web site and download a copy of Lokai Shadows XP and follow these steps to install the app and get it up and running:

1. Once you have downloaded Lokai Shadows XP, extract the ZIP file to a permanent home on your hard drive. Make sure that you do not put it in a directory that has a space in the name or else you will have a problem with step 2.

2. Now that you have extracted the files for the app, you have to register it on your computer as a service. Let's assume that you extracted the shadow app to c:\ShadowXP. Click the Start button and select Run. Then type **c:\ShadowXP\ lokaishadow_svc.exe /install** in the box and click OK. If everything went OK, then you should get a pop-up confirmation box telling you it was installed successfully.

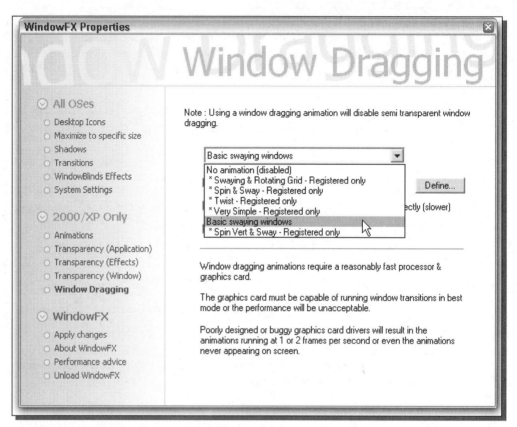

FIGURE 6-7: Selecting Basic Swaying Windows to enable the dragging animation.

3. Now that you have registered the service, turn it on. Click the Start Menu again and select Run. Type **services.msc** in the box and click OK.

4. The Services dialog box should load. Look through the list of services and right-click Lokai Shadows XP and select Start.

5. Close the Services dialog box and you are finished.

After the service is started, any new windows that you open up will automatically have drop shadows displayed. Also, do not worry about having to manually start the service each time you turn on your computer. By default, the service is set to Automatic. That tells the computer to start it up every time the computer boots.

Using Glass2k to make your windows transparent

Would you like to see through your windows? Do you often have to rearrange windows on the screen to get to information that is hidden below another window? I always run into that

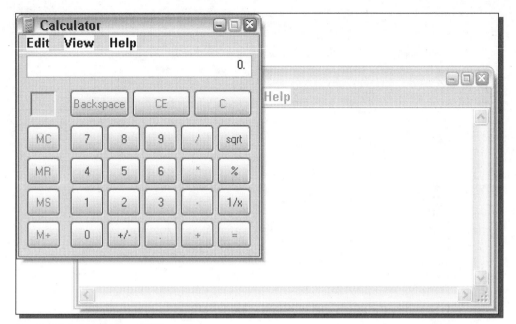

FIGURE 6-8: Lokai Shadows XP in action.

problem when I am doing a lot of tasks on my computer at once. Being able to make a window or application transparent, as shown in Figure 6-9, by just clicking a few hotkeys on your keyboard is an easy and cool-looking solution to that problem.

Windows XP has transparency, also known as alpha settings, built into the operating system but it does not use any of these features on windows or the taskbar. Programs that add the transparency capability are just turning this feature on for use on other parts of the user interface, such as the windows and the taskbar. My favorite app for making windows transparent is called Glass2k, developed by Chimes Software. This is a great little app that is free and is also very simple to use and install. The whole program consists of just one file that you don't even have to worry about extracting from a ZIP file. Follow these steps to get Glass2k installed and running on your computer:

1. Visit the Glass2k Web site at www.chime.tv/products/glass2k.shtml and download a copy.

2. Once you have a copy on your computer, just double-click the app to start it up.

3. You will see the Glass2k setting screen, as shown in Figure 6-10, when it has started up. Here you will see several options. If you want the app to start up every time the computer starts up, check the Auto-Load box.

4. One of the most valuable features of the Glass2k is the ability to remember the application's transparency settings. Check this feature box to make sure that this feature is turned on for you.

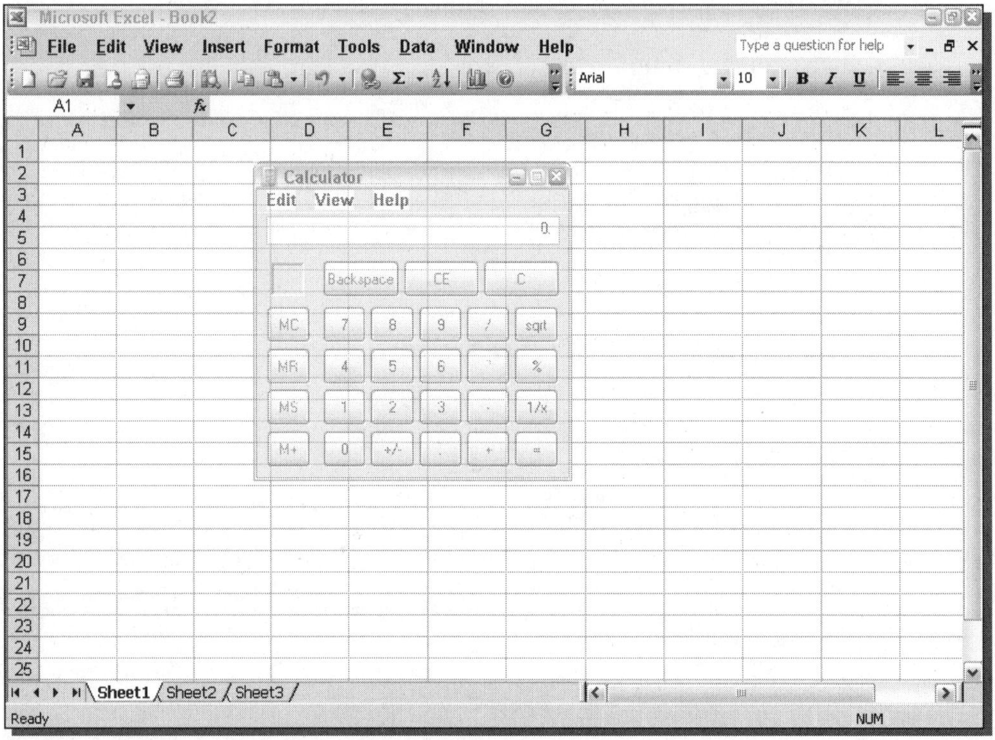

FIGURE 6-9: Using Glass2k to make windows transparent.

FIGURE 6-10: Glass2k settings screen.

5. The transparency pop-up menu allows you to right-click any open application or window and a menu for Glass2k will be shown, along with any normal right-click menu. I recommend that you disable that option because I find it to be more of an inconvenience than a convenience. To disable it, just select Disabled from the top of the drop-down list.

6. Taskbar transparency is another feature of Glass2k that looks great but has little purpose. To enable this feature, just click along the horizontal bar to the right of the taskbar transparency label. The further you click to the right of the bar, the less transparent it is.

7. Once you have your settings all figured out and set up the way you want, you are ready to start using the app to make windows and apps transparent. Before you can do that, you should click the Save button to save all of your changes.

8. Making an app or window transparent is very easy. When Glass2k is running, just hold down the Ctrl and Shift buttons and press a number (0—9: 0 = solid, 1 = lightest, 9 = darkest) when any window or app is displayed.

Now that you know how to change the transparency of a window, have fun changing all of your applications. If you ever want to make adjustments to the settings of Glass2k, just right-click its icon (the three stacked cubes) in the system tray and select Settings.

Glass2k is a great app that will change the way you use your computer. It may take a little time to get used to the new Ctrl and Shift shortcuts, but once you get that down, you will be flying through your windows.

Making your windows roll up

How would you like to make your windows roll up as if they were shades? If you own an Apple computer, you will know that this is one feature that Apple has had for a long time. Unfortunately, for legal or other reasons, Microsoft has decided not to implement a rollup feature in Windows XP. However, with the help of an interesting utility called FreeShade, developed by hmmnsoft, it is now possible to make your windows roll up into the top bar of the window. This is a great feature because it allows you to easily hide apps temporarily so that you can see what is behind them or organize them on the screen.

FreeShade by hmmnsoft works just like other rollup apps on different operating systems. Just double-click a window and it will roll up into the title bar, as shown in Figure 6-11. Then to pull the shade back down, just double-click the title bar again and the window will be restored. When you are ready, follow these steps to get FreeShade up and running on your computer:

1. Visit FreeShade's Web site at www.hmmn.org/FreeShade/ and download a copy of the latest version. Once you have downloaded the file, double-click it and follow the onscreen directions to install it.

FIGURE 6-11: A window that has been rolled up.

Table 6-1   FreeShade Keyboard Shortcuts

Keys	Result
ALT + 5 on num pad	Rollsup/unrolls window
ALT + "+" on num pad	Displays FreeShade properties
CTRL + ALT + "-" on num pad	Closes FreeShade
ALT + 1 on num pad	Moves window to lower-left of screen
ALT + 2 on num pad	Moves window to bottom of screen
ALT + 3 on num pad	Moves window to lower-right of screen
ALT + 4 on num pad	Moves window to left of screen
ALT + 6 on num pad	Moves window to right of screen
ALT + 7 on num pad	Moves window to top-left of screen
ALT + 8 on num pad	Moves window to top of screen
ALT + 9 on num pad	Moves window to top-right of screen

2. After you have installed FreeShade, you will have two icons on your desktop, one that will start the app, and one that will stop it. Click the FreeShade icon to start up FreeShade. Nothing visually will happen, but when you double-click a window you will notice that it now rolls up.

3. If you ever want to close FreeShade, just click the Stop icon that is located on your desktop or in the Start Menu.

FreeShade also offers a few other enhancements that affect how the window is sized. In order to use the other enhancements, you will have to use special keyboard shortcuts. Refer to Table 6-1 for a list of the keyboard shortcuts and what they will do.

Fine-Tuning ClearType

One of the best features of Windows XP is the new ClearType font smoothing engine. This new font smoothing feature uses a graphic technique known as anti-aliasing, which smoothes all of the rough edges of the fonts on the screen and greatly improves the look of Windows XP for users of LCD flat panel monitors. If you are an owner of a LCD monitor, you should definitely turn on this feature, as it will make your screen look amazing. Figure 6-12 shows a comparison between when the feature is turned on and when it is turned off. The image on the bottom, which has ClearType enabled, may look a little blurry on the page, but on a LCD the image looks very sharp.

If you do not have ClearType enabled, follow these steps to get it turned on:

1. Right-click the desktop and select Properties.

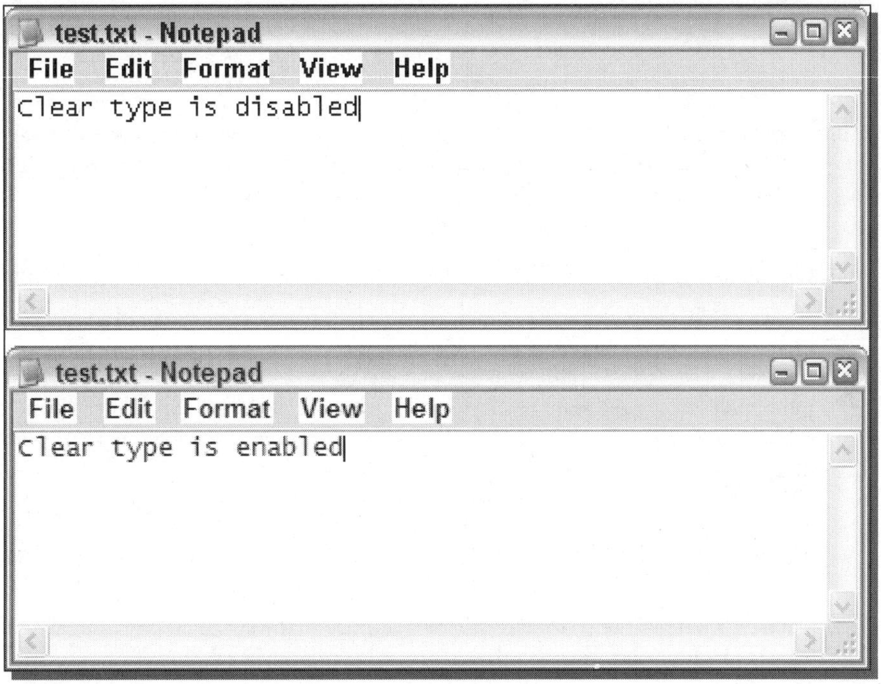

FIGURE 6-12: Normal font smoothing versus ClearType.

2. Click the Effects button on the Appearance tab.

3. In the second drop-down box, select ClearType under Use The Following Method To Smooth The Edges Of The Screen Fonts.

4. Click OK to save your changes.

5. Select OK once more to close Display Properties and to apply the new settings.

Now that you have ClearType turned on, it's time to fine-tune its settings. Some users complain that the new ClearType feature causes the text on their screen to look a little blurry compared to standard font smoothing. ClearType was designed to smooth the fonts on the screen replacing jagged edges. If you are one of the users that do not like how ClearType looks, with the help of a very cool online tool, you can customize how ClearType looks. Using the online tool that is developed by Microsoft, it is possible to change the darkness and thickness of the text. This will allow you to make the text that appears on your monitor look crisper. Follow these steps to fine-tune your ClearType settings:

1. Open up Internet Explorer and browse to www.microsoft.com/typography/cleartype/.

2. Navigate to the ClearType Web interface to fine-tune the settings located on the right side of the Web page.

3. As the ClearType Web interface is loading, you will be prompted to install the ClearType Tuning Control. Click Yes on your screen so that this component will be installed.

With the release of Windows XP Service Pack 2, Internet Explorer was locked down to provide better security. If the ClearType Tuning Control does not automatically download and install, then you may need to adjust your ActiveX security settings in Internet Options.

4. On the step 1 screen, click Next to move to the next step, because you already have ClearType started.

5. On step 2 of the ClearType Tuning Control, you have to select if your monitor uses a red-green-blue (RGB) color scheme or a blue-green-red (BGR) scheme. All LCD computer monitors are made up of very tiny vertical lines of alternating colors. There are two different ways that monitors lay out the lines on the screen. Some monitors alternate red, green, and blue lines (RGB) on the screen, whereas other monitors alternate blue, green, and red lines (BGR). ClearType has recently been updated to also support the BGR format, and now users that have BGR monitors can select this feature. Don't know which one to select? It's easy; just select the option that looks sharper on your screen and then click Next.

6. On step 3, you will be shown six different settings that you can choose to fine-tune ClearType. Just select the item that looks best to you and click Finish.

Your new settings will instantly go into effect. If you do not like the changes, just follow the preceding instructions and start over. If you notice that the coloration of some of the characters on your screen is a little strange, specifically the I's, then you might have the wrong screen mode selected. Follow the preceding instructions again and select the other color scheme.

If you don't own a LCD monitor, you can still try to use ClearType. It will not create any problems but also might not help out all that much either. I recommend that you still experiment with it. You might be surprised.

Branding Windows XP

Did you ever notice how when you buy a computer from one of the big computer manufacturers your computer has their name and logo in many different parts of the computer? How would you like to replace their branding information with your own? Or if you built your own computer, why not brand it? These next two sections will show you how you can brand the system information screen and Internet Explorer.

Branding system properties

Every time you right-click My Computer and select Properties or click the System applet item in the Control Panel, you will be shown branding information on the general information screen of System Properties. This screen is usually customized by computer manufacturers to display their logo, as well as general information such as the model number and support notes. If you would like to change this information or brand a PC that you made yourself, this section will show you how to accomplish this in just a few easy steps. To get started, assume that your computer is not branded and that you are going to be doing this for the first time. If your computer was already branded, then instead of creating the files that I will mention, just replace them with your versions. Follow these steps to do branding of your own:

1. There are two parts to branding your computer. The first part is creating an image to be displayed on the System Properties General tab. The image must be a bitmap and be no larger than 180 × 115 pixels. Once you have created your file, name it **oemlogo.bmp** and save it in C:\Windows\System32 folder.

2. Now that you have to get the logo out of the way, you will need to create a file with all of the text that you want to appear on the screen next to it. To do this, open up Notepad and key in the following code. Feel free to replace the text to the right of the = with anything you want.

```
[General]
Manufacturer=StevePC
Model=HighwaySpecial 18G
[Support Information]
Line1=No support is provided in English
Line2=Guaranteed to work for at least 5 days
Line3=87% restocking fee for all returns
Line4=Returns only accepted at Kuznetsk warehouse in Russia
```

3. Once you have your text in the right format, click the File menu bar item and select Save As.

4. Save the file as **oeminfo.ini** in your C:\Windows\System32 folder. Make sure to change the Save As file type to All Files instead of .txt so that the file is saved with the correct file extension.

On the CD

A copy of the oeminfo.ini file can be found in the Chapter 6 folder on the book's companion CD-ROM.

If everything went well, the next time you look at the System Properties screen, you should see your new branding information. Figure 6-13 is an example of what my branded screen looks like.

Branding IE

Internet Explorer is another part of the operating system that is often branded by computer manufacturers and Internet Service Providers. Not a lot can be done to brand Internet Explorer other than to add some text to the title bar of the browser. Back when dialup Internet was the only means of accessing the Net, I remember trying to figure out how to remove text that the dialup software distributed from providers such as CompuServe and Prodigy. Every time I would open up Internet Explorer, it would say Prodigy Online along with Microsoft Internet Explorer as the title of the window. Back then, the only solution for getting rid of the excess type was to manually hack the registry and fix the entry responsible for storing the name of the

FIGURE 6-13: Creating your own branded system screen.

window. Now a really great utility is available, called Rebrand, by Advent Code, that greatly simplifies the editing of the Internet Explorer window title. Follow these steps to edit your title bars:

1. Visit Advent Code's Web site at www.adventcode.net/rebrand.html and download a copy of Rebrand. Then, run the file and extract the files to your computer.

2. Start up Rebrand by browsing to the directory from which you extracted it and clicking on rebrand.exe.

3. To change the title of Internet Explorer, just type new text in the top box, as shown in Figure 6-14, and then click the Apply button to save your changes.

Once you are finished editing the title and have clicked the Apply button, you can close Rebrand. Your changes should take effect immediately.

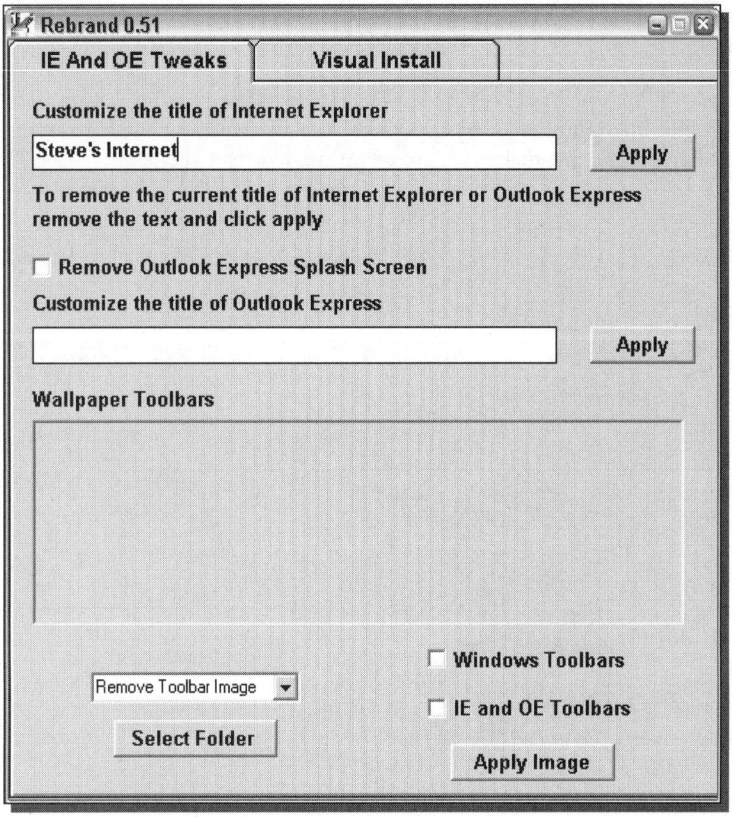

FIGURE 6-14: Using Rebrand to change the title of the Internet Explorer window.

Rebrand also offers a few other features, such as the ability to change the title of Outlook Express and the ability to change toolbar backgrounds. The Outlook Express feature is cool, but I like using Tweak UI to change the backgrounds of toolbars.

Summary

So ends the customizing portion of *Hacking Windows XP*! You have seen many ways that you can completely change the way Windows XP looks from the moment you turn on your PC. This chapter has focused on adding cool effects and features that will make Windows XP look high-tech, state-of-the-art, and visually attractive—a winning combination.

Part II of *Hacking Windows XP* is all about making your computer perform better than ever before. When I first started working with computers several years ago, I was always working with the slowest and oldest hardware possible. I spent countless hours trying to figure out ways to make Windows run just a little bit faster on my POS machine. Even if I could just shave a few microseconds off of something, it would all add up in the end. Now that I can afford better hardware, speed is still something that I am very concerned about. Making Windows XP run as fast as possible is something that I have spent a great deal of time researching and testing. This next part will help you, too, make your computer run like never before.

Increasing Your System's Performance

part

Analyzing Your System

D id you ever wonder how fast your computer actually is? Sure, it says that it is a Pentium 2.8 Ghz on the box the system came in but the speed of the CPU is not the only factor in determining how fast your system actually is. The true speed of your computer is determined by the speed of all of your hardware, such as the speed of data written and read from the hard drive, the speed of the RAM, and the speed of the front side bus of the motherboard. This chapter will help you analyze your system to determine exactly how fast it is and how you can make it faster.

Before you start to make your computer run faster, you need to understand the limitations of your hardware and also to be able to identify possible bottlenecks in your system. The situation is just like what would happen before you go to the hospital to have an operation. It is usually better to have some tests completed first so that the doctors know exactly what to do. Using the tools discussed in this chapter, you will be able to run different tests that will help you in the upcoming chapters decide which hacks will work best for your computer.

Monitoring Your System Hardware

Monitoring the status of the system using various tools will help you understand what is going on behind the scenes, much like monitoring the instrument panel on your car will help you understand what is happening to the vehicle at all times. For example, regular monitoring will reveal if you are running low on memory, if your CPU is overloaded, or if your system has too many programs running at the same time. These are all useful and important things to know, and having that information available will enable you to check your system's operation and change settings to get optimal performance. There is a variety of performance monitoring software available on the market. However, Windows has many great monitoring applications built in that provide adequate reporting to analyze your system.

Using performance

Built into Windows is a great little tool called the *Performance system monitor*. The system monitor is a sleek tool that will allow you to easily monitor hundreds of different statistics about all areas of the operating system. Similar to other system monitor tools, its purpose is to help you detect problems and improve your system performance. The easiest way to start the performance application is by the command line or by using the Run command in the Start Menu. To start the performance application:

1. Click the Start Menu and select Run.

2. Then type **perfmon.msc** in the text box and click the OK button.

An icon for the application can be found in the Administrative Tools folder located in Control Panel. But for most users, running the preceding command will be the easiest method of starting the program.

Tip   The Performance application gets the data for its performance counters from the System Registry. If you would like to change the source of the data so that it will get the data directly from the Windows Management Interface instead, simply start the performance counter with the "/sysmon_wmi" flag. Then type **perfmon.msc /sysmon_wmi** in the text box on the Run dialog box.

Once the program is started, you will be greeted with a graph of data as well as a list of active counters. You will see a graph of the % Processor Time as well as memory Pages/sec and the avg. Disk Queue Length. These are all great stats, but the Performance application has quite a few more from which to choose. In order to add more performance counters, simply click the icon with the + symbol on it or press Ctrl+I and the Add Counters window will appear, as shown in Figure 7-1.

Once the Add Counters window is shown, you will notice where it states "Performance Object." In the drop-down menu list box below this is a list of all of the possible items that you are able to monitor. Depending on the services that your computer has installed, such as the Web server IIS, you will have more or less items available. Take a few minutes to browse through the list. You will notice that when you select a different item subject, you will be shown a new list of detailed counters in the box below. You have the option to add all counters or you can select only specific counters from the box by pressing the Ctrl key to select multiple items. Additionally, to the right of the listing box is another box which lists the instance of the object you are going to monitor. This gives you the ability to define the scope of the counter so that you can monitor only one specific device instead of monitoring all devices. For example, it is possible to monitor the queue length of just one hard drive instead of the total file access queue length.

Once you are finished selecting all of your counters for a specific object, click the Add button. Once you are finished adding counters for all of the objects you are interested in, click the Close button.

Viewing the data

The performance counter allows you to view the data in many different ways. The default screen is the line graph, as shown in Figure 7-2. This display method is adequate for a few performance counters, but when you have more than three or four, figuring out what line is for what counter starts to become a little confusing. Fortunately, the employees at Microsoft

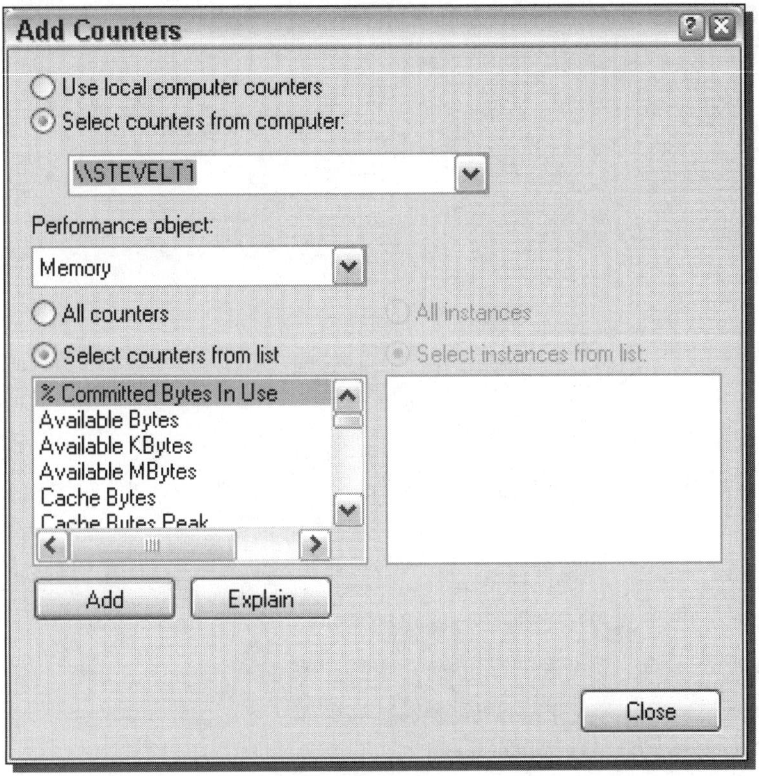

FIGURE 7-1: Add Counters window listing all available items to monitor.

that made the performance counter application provided us with two other methods of viewing the data.

Another method of viewing the data is by using the histogram display, as shown in Figure 7-3. To change to this display method, simply press the Histogram icon on the menu or, on the keyboard, press Ctrl+B. This method of displaying the data is not much better than the default. But because it relies on one scale, counters that report small numbers will be dwarfed by the counters that report large numbers. This limitation makes it almost impossible to read some of the counters.

To make everyone happy, there is also a Report viewing method which simply lists the counter numbers in text, as shown in Figure 7-4. Activate this viewing method by clicking the icon which looks like a notebook or pressing Ctrl+R.

Setting update interval

Now that you have all of your counters set up and displaying data, you need to select the interval time of how often the data will be updated. How often you want the counters to be updated depends on your reason for monitoring your hardware. For example, if you are trying to

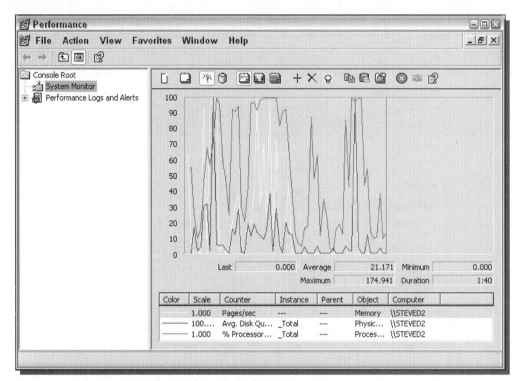

FIGURE 7-2: Default screen of the Windows XP Performance counter.

track how much data your computer is sending through your network adapter every day or hour, it is not necessary to have that counter update every second. You will just be wasting CPU cycles because you are making the computer constantly update that counter. However, if you are interested in current memory or CPU utilization, you will want a much faster update time.

To change the update interval, click the Properties button, which looks like a hand pointing to a notebook. Alternatively, you can press Ctrl+Q. Once the System Monitor Properties window loads, locate where it states, "Sample automatically every" and update the value in the text box, as shown in Figure 7-5.

Configuring alerts

If the hundreds of performance counters are not enough for you, Microsoft has also included the ability to set alerts that are fully customizable and can be set for any performance counter. In order to set up an alert for a specific performance counter:

1. Start the Performance application if it is not already started, then once it is started, expand the Performance Logs and Alerts item.

2. Next, click the Alerts item and you will see a list of active alerts set up on your system in the window on the right.

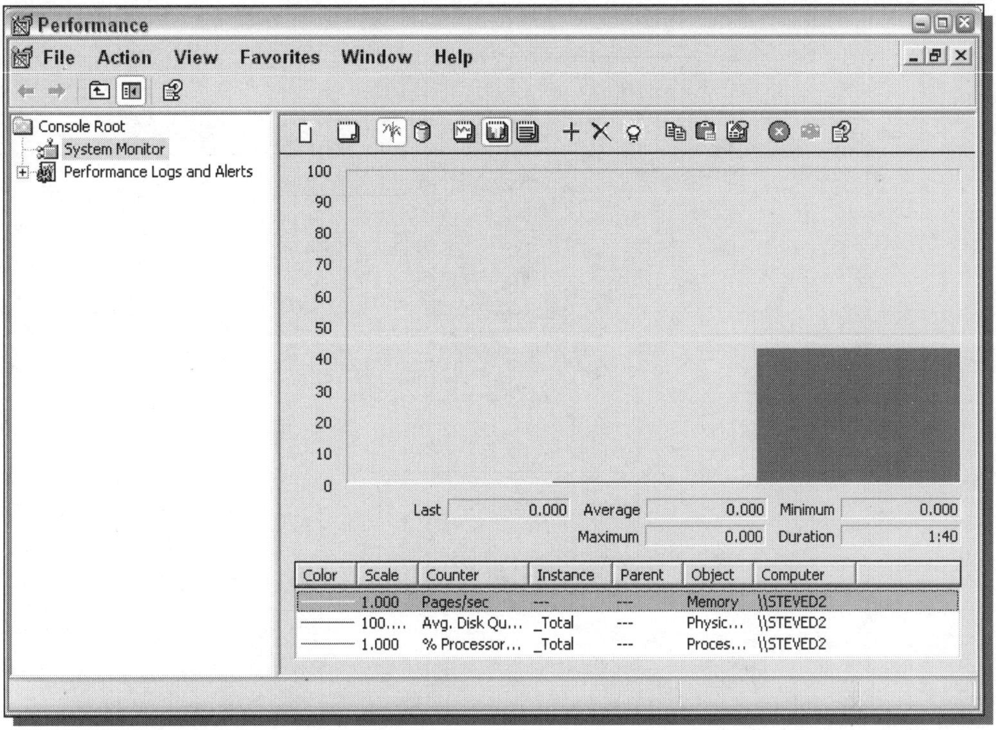

FIGURE 7-3: Performance's Histogram view.

3. Right-click in the open window on the right-hand side of the screen and select New Alert Settings.

4. Type a name for your new alert in the dialog box and click OK.

5. Next, on the alert settings page, click the Add button to add a performance counter to be monitored.

6. Once you have finished adding a performance counter, close the Add Counters window. Then, fill in the settings for the alert event trigger such, as the limit that will trigger the alert.

7. Also, take a look at the Sample Data Every section to set this area appropriately.

8. Click the Action tab to specify what you would like to be done when and if the alert is triggered.

9. Also, take a look at the Schedule tab to specify when the alert should be started and the duration of the alert.

10. Once you are satisfied with all of the settings, click the OK button and you are finished setting up an alert.

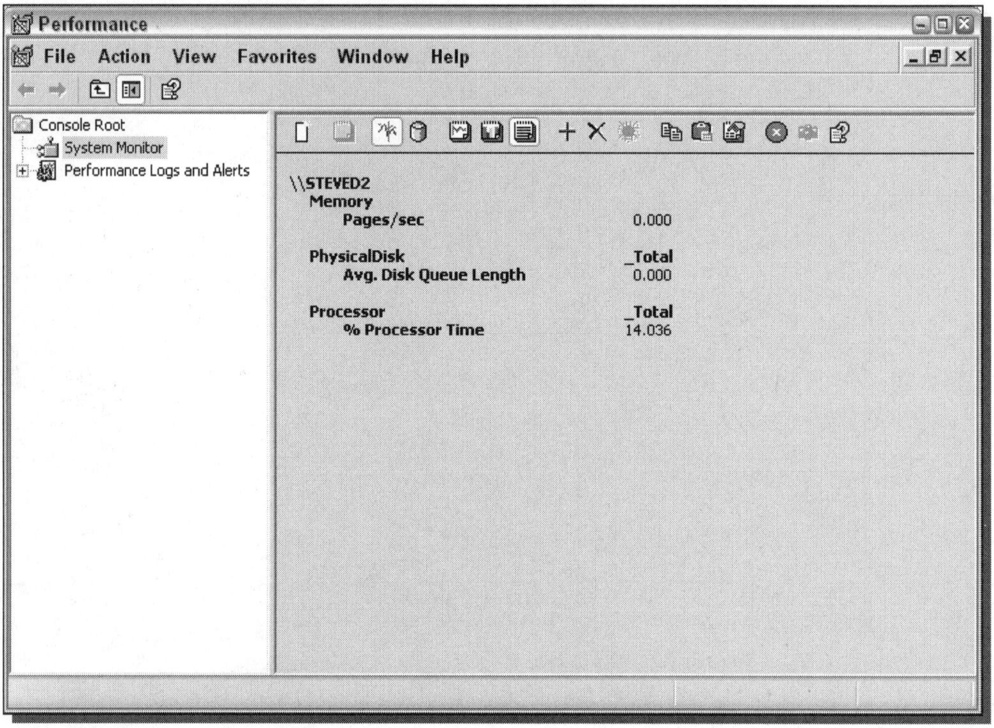

FIGURE 7-4: Performance's Report view.

At any time, it is possible to make changes to the alerts by right-clicking them and selecting Properties.

Analyzing and detecting problems

Use of the performance application and the various performance counters makes it possible to detect many problems and shed light on how to make your system run faster. You should familiarize yourself with a handful of tips that deal with specific performance counters; these will prove to be invaluable in your analysis and decision making. The following are some of the things to look out for when monitoring your system:

- *Physical Disk: Disk Read Bytes/sec & Disk Write Bytes/sec.* These two performance counters can tell you if your physical disk is set up and functioning correctly. In order to determine this, consult the Web site or the manual of the manufacturer of your hard disk. Look up what the range of read/write speeds are. If the readings that you are getting are far below what you should be getting, then your hard disk could be damaged or set up incorrectly. Run diagnostic software on the disk and make sure that it is set up properly in device manager with the correct transfer mode. Remember that most hard drives read at different speeds when they are reading from different parts of the disk. This is why there may be some discrepancies between your readings.

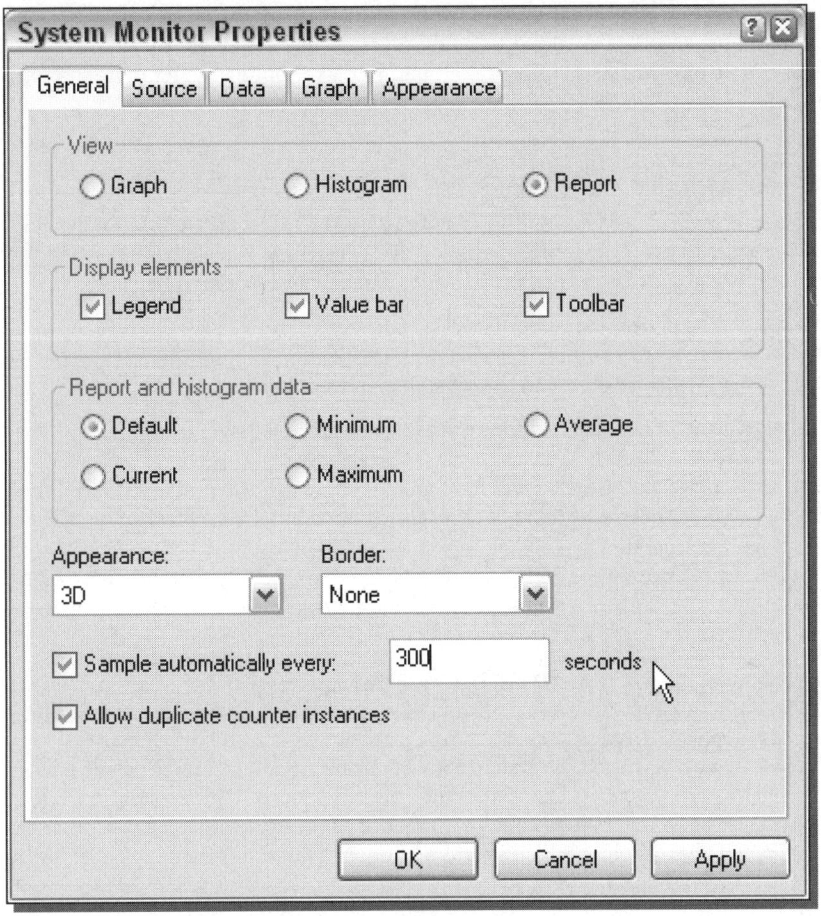

FIGURE 7-5: Updating the update interval value.

- *Paging File: % Usage & % Usage Peak.* These two performance counters can tell you how well your system is using the page file. If you set the size of the page file manually, then these counters are very critical to deciding what size the page file should be. As a rule, if the page file % Usage is above 95 percent or if the Usage Peak is near 100 percent, consider increasing the size of the page file if you have set the size manually.

- *Memory: Available MBytes & Paging File: % Usage.* These two performance counters will help you decide if you should put more RAM in your computer. If your available megabytes are under 5 and your paging file usage percentage is very high, then you should consider purchasing more RAM for your computer.

- *Processor: % Processor Time.* This performance counter monitors the activity and work your processor is doing. If your CPU is consistently working at or above 85 percent, and you are not running any computation-intensive applications in the background, this would indicate that you should consider upgrading your CPU. The CPU is having a hard time keeping up with all of your programs. You could also try closing open applications that are running in the background to make your computer more responsive and faster.

Saving your performance counter setup

Once you have spent some time adding all of the performance counters that you would like to use, it is possible to save this configuration so that every time you start the performance application, your performance counters will automatically be loaded.

In order to save the performance counters selected:

1. Click the File menu object on the menu bar and select Save As.

2. Then type in a file name and specify a location and click Save.

This will save a new `.MSC` file that will have all of your performance counters saved in the file. The next time you want to load all of your performance counters, simply open up the new file that you saved by either double-clicking it or making a shortcut to it and placing it in your Start Menu. If you open up the performance application in the way that was shown earlier, you will not have your performance counters loaded automatically.

Using Bootvis to analyze your system start

Bootvis is an application released by Microsoft that allows users and developers to debug and detect issues that occur during the system start up. Contrary to what most people believe, Bootvis is not a performance enhancement tool, but a diagnostic and reporting tool. Running Bootvis will not speed up or change the performance of your system in any way other than what the system does automatically. Therefore, running Bootvis for the purpose of having it automatically speed up your system is pointless. However, the information that the Bootvis reports can be invaluable to improving the performance of your system.

What exactly is Bootvis? Bootvis is a tool that will trace all of the different stages of the system start such as the system kernel, then the device drivers, and then the start up of processes. If you are wondering why your computer is taking so long to start up, then Bootvis will provide you with many answers.

Installing Bootvis

Bootvis is not included with Windows and must be downloaded from the Web. Currently, Microsoft has removed the link to download the program from their Web site. According to the Web page at Microsoft at which the tool originally could have been downloaded (`/www.microsoft.com/whdc/hwdev/platform/performance/fastboot/bootvis.mspx`), "The `Bootvis.exe` tool is no longer available from this site." Microsoft has never made a public statement explaining exactly why the utility was removed. Nevertheless, based on messages that I have read in Microsoft's Windows XP newsgroups and other sites, this is what most users close to the issue believe:

Microsoft has removed this tool from their site because users have been using it for the wrong purpose. Ever since the tool was first discovered on Microsoft's Web site, users would use Bootvis because they thought that it would speed up their computer's boot time. That misconception arose because Bootvis is capable of starting some of Windows XP's boot optimization features that are normally run by the operating system after it has fully analyzed the boot. However, Bootvis was designed to be a performance analysis and diagnostic utility, not a speed boosting app. Because users were using Bootvis for the wrong reason, and because use of its advanced boot optimization features could possibly do more harm than good, Microsoft decided to remove the tool from their site.

Microsoft's removal of the tool from their Web site is unfortunate, because it really can give you a lot of useful information about your boot. Fortunately, several Web sites exist from which users of Windows XP still download Bootvis, namely:

- *SoftPedia*: `www.softpedia.com/public/cat/12/2/12-2-1.shtml`.

- *Major Geeks*: `www.majorgeeks.com/download.php?det=664`

- *Old Microsoft Download Link* (Still works but not listed on any page):
  `http://download.microsoft.com:80/download/whistler/BTV/1.0/`
  `WXP/EN-US/BootVis-Tool.exe`

If the above links no longer work. Check out `TweakXP.com` and you will find more links from which you can download Bootvis.

The latest version of Bootvis that Microsoft released is version 1.3.37.0. This version is compatible with Windows XP Service Pack 1, but it is not known yet if it will work for Service Pack 2.

Once you have downloaded a copy of Bootvis, install it by double-clicking the file. A new entry will be made in the Start Menu under All Programs, labeled Microsoft Bootvis.

Tracing your system start

Now that you have Bootvis installed, you are ready to start analyzing your system. Start the application from the shortcut located in the Start Menu. Once the application has started, you will see an empty Bootvis interface. To initiate a new trace, click the Trace item on the menu bar and select Next Boot + Driver Delays, as shown in Figure 7-6. This will pop up a new window, asking you how many times you would like the trace to be run. It is often a good idea to run the trace more than once to see if the items that are slow in your startup are consistently slow. Select the number of repetitions by using the arrow buttons. Once you click OK, your computer will automatically start the process of tracing and will reboot your computer.

Make sure that you do not have any unsaved work on your system, as you could lose anything that you have been working on if you do not save your work before the system restarts.

When you are ready, click the OK button and you will see a countdown window counting down from 10 seconds until the system will reboot. If you choose, you can click the Reboot Now button if you do not want to wait for your system to reboot automatically.

Once your system starts to reboot, it will start the tracing process. Do not press any buttons on your computer during the tracing process other than to log onto your computer, if your

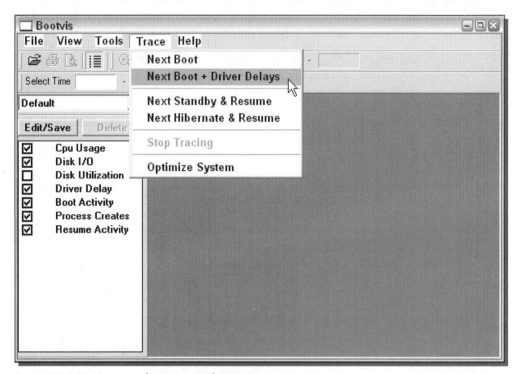

FIGURE 7-6: Initiating a new boot trace with Bootvis.

computer is set up that way. After the log on screen, Bootvis will display a message on the screen telling you not to do anything on your computer.

Once the trace is complete, the computer will automatically reboot and will repeat this process the number of times you selected to repeat earlier. When the process is all finished, your computer will automatically load the trace file. If you performed more than one trace, you will have to manually load one of the trace files.

Analyzing the Bootvis trace file

To view a report, you will have to launch Bootvis again if you performed more than one trace. If you decided to just do one trace, skip this paragraph. When Bootvis finishes loading, click the File menu object and select Open. Navigate to C:\ Documents and Settings and then expand the folder named after your username. There you will find all of the trace files with a .BIN extension. Select the file that you would like to analyze and select Open. Bootvis will load the trace file and display the results of the trace, as shown in Figure 7-7.

Now that you have all of the data, it is time to analyze it. The most important information that the Bootvis application provides is *Driver Delay information*. The drivers are the most time-consuming portion of the system boot. Identifying slow device drivers can help you speed up your system. Scroll down so that the Driver Delay window is displayed. Each device driver that is loaded during setup is sorted into different categories and is represented by a

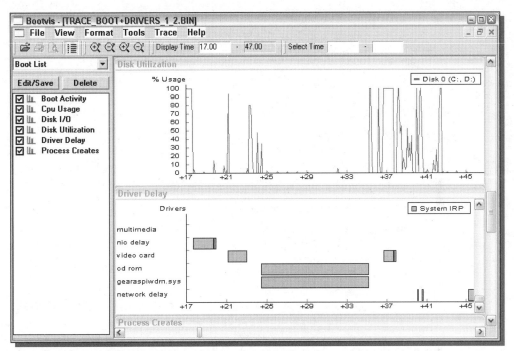

FIGURE 7-7: Bootvis displaying trace results after boot analysis.

green rectangle. Move your mouse over a rectangle and the name of the driver, as well as the estimated time it took to load, will be displayed. Scroll horizontally to see the different drivers that are loaded over time.

If you find a driver that is taking a long time to load and initialize, it could be configured incorrectly or the driver itself could be poorly written and may have problems. Make sure that you have the latest device drivers from your equipment manufacturer to ensure that you have the best version of the driver code.

Tip You can make sure that you have the latest drivers installed on your computer by visiting your hardware manufacturer's Web site and downloading the latest drivers. This will ensure that you have the best performing drivers and trouble-free operation.

Bootvis displays many other graphs besides the driver information. The other graphs are less useful when viewed separately, but can be valuable when viewed in conjunction with other graphs. Looking at the CPU utilization and disk utilization at the same time one of the drivers is initializing can give you valuable information, such as why the device driver could be taking so long to initialize. For example, if the CPU is maxed out and the disk utilization is very high, it might not be the driver's fault for taking so long to initialize. Instead, it is all of the other background processes running at the same time that is slowing everything down.

Bootvis also offers a feature that allows you to trace what is going on when your system is resuming from standby or starting up from hibernation. To run these types of traces, simply click the Trace menu bar item again and select either Next Standby and Resume or Next Hibernate and Resume. Then, after the traces are complete, just open up the trace files as you did previously for a normal boot trace.

Using Task Manager

The Windows Task Manager is a critical part of Windows that makes it possible for users to have full control over what their system is doing. Providing the ability to monitor individual programs and control any program or process, the Task Manager is very useful. In order to use Task Manager, no special software must be installed. Just push Ctrl+Alt+Delete keys on your computer and the Windows Task Manager will be loaded. On some computers, you may have to click the Task Manager button in the window that pops up in order to start it.

Once Windows Task Manager has started, you will notice a list of active applications running on your computer. Additionally, you will see five tabs that will list processes, CPU performance data, networking performance data, and active user data.

Monitoring processes

All the applications on the computer that are running, those that are hidden and those that are not, can be found on the list under the Processes tab. On this list, you will be able to see how much memory each process is using, as well as how much of the CPU each process is using. By clicking the column headings, you can sort the rows in numeric or alphabetical order, as shown in Figure 7-8.

There are many useful columns on the Processes tab, such as the Image Name column, which gives you the name of the process. The User Name column shows who started the process. The CPU column shows what percentage of the CPU the process is using and the Mem Usage column shows how much memory a process is using.

If you find a process that is taking up a lot of your memory or eating up a big portion of your CPU, then you may want to consider ending the process if it is not a critical one. Ending a process is very easy; just select the row of the service you want to end, and click the End Process button.

Viewing performance data

When you visit the Performance tab, as shown in Figure 7-9, you will notice that it shows a lot of the same information that the Performance application shows. This tab is another place that you can view memory and CPU information but in a far less detailed manner.

The Networking tab is a great way to monitor the current network activity. Each networking device on your computer has its own graph, showing the percent that it utilized. Although it does not keep track of bandwidth sent and received, it does show the speed at which the hardware is working and if it is connected.

Configuring Task Manager to display CPU monitor

When the Windows Task Manager is started, a small histogram is displayed in the system tray that shows the CPU utilization. This little feature can be very useful if you would always like to

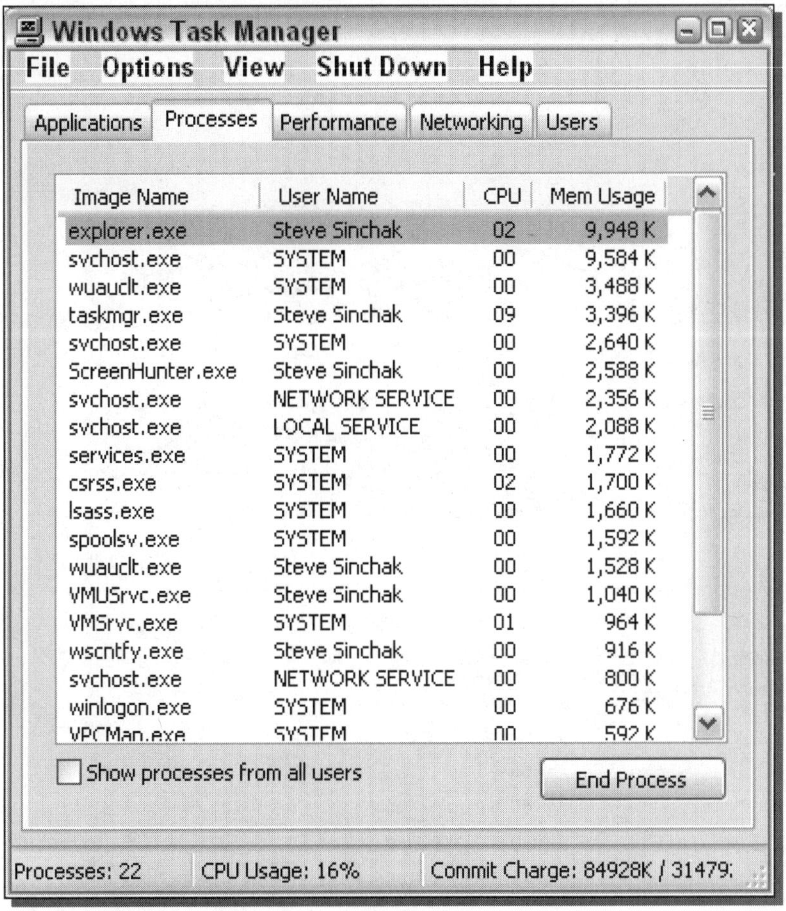

Windows Task Manager

File Options View Shut Down Help

Applications | Processes | Performance | Networking | Users

Image Name	User Name	CPU	Mem Usage
explorer.exe	Steve Sinchak	02	9,948 K
svchost.exe	SYSTEM	00	9,584 K
wuauclt.exe	SYSTEM	00	3,488 K
taskmgr.exe	Steve Sinchak	09	3,396 K
svchost.exe	SYSTEM	00	2,640 K
ScreenHunter.exe	Steve Sinchak	00	2,588 K
svchost.exe	NETWORK SERVICE	00	2,356 K
svchost.exe	LOCAL SERVICE	00	2,088 K
services.exe	SYSTEM	00	1,772 K
csrss.exe	SYSTEM	02	1,700 K
lsass.exe	SYSTEM	00	1,660 K
spoolsv.exe	SYSTEM	00	1,592 K
wuauclt.exe	Steve Sinchak	00	1,528 K
VMUSrvc.exe	Steve Sinchak	00	1,040 K
VMSrvc.exe	SYSTEM	01	964 K
wscntfy.exe	Steve Sinchak	00	916 K
svchost.exe	NETWORK SERVICE	00	800 K
winlogon.exe	SYSTEM	00	676 K
VPCMan.exe	SYSTEM	00	592 K

☐ Show processes from all users   [End Process]

Processes: 22   CPU Usage: 16%   Commit Charge: 84928K / 31479:

FIGURE 7-8: Sorting processes by memory usage.

keep an eye on your CPU utilization but do not want Task Manager always on top of all of your windows. With a little bit of work, it is possible to start up the Windows Task Manager automatically and run it minimized and hidden from the taskbar except for the system tray.

1. Click the Start Menu and navigate to All Programs and locate the Startup listing.

2. Right-click where it says Startup and select Open. A new window will open up with the contents of your personal startup folder. Any shortcuts that you place in this folder will be automatically loaded with Windows when it starts up.

3. Once the Startup folder is opened, right-click in the open white space and select New and then navigate to Shortcut.

4. When the new shortcut wizard loads, type **taskmgr.exe** in the text box asking for the location of the file. After typing in the file name, click the Next button.

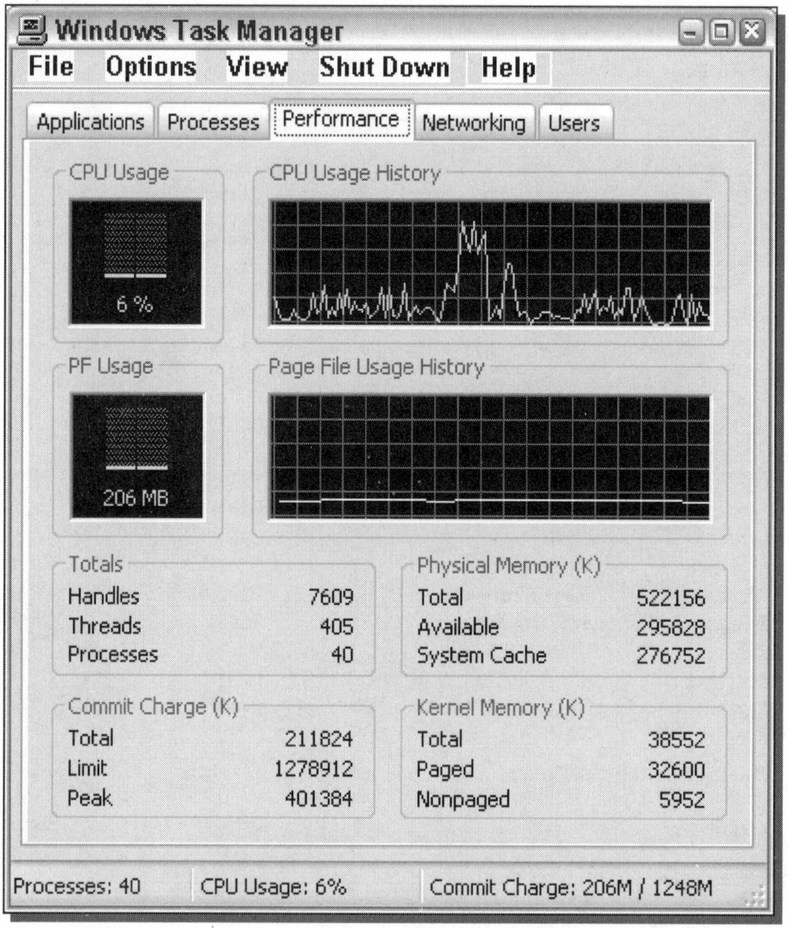

FIGURE 7-9: Windows Task Manager Performance information.

5. Type in a name for the shortcut and click the Finish button.

6. Now you will be shown the startup folder again and a new icon for the Task Manager. In order to make Task Manager start minimized, right-click the new icon and select Properties.

7. Change the Run type where it says Normal Window to Minimized and click OK.

8. Now the shortcut is all set up. However, there is one last change to make and you will need to open up Task Manager to do this. Once you have opened up Windows Task Manager, click the Options menu bar item and select Hide When Minimized so that when the program starts, the CPU histogram will only be shown and the program will not appear on the taskbar.

Your system is not configured to start up the CPU meter on every boot in the system tray. Should you change your mind at a later time and no longer want the Task Manager CPU meter to show up, simply delete the shortcut from the Startup folder.

Other performance monitoring utilities

On top of all of the Microsoft applications, there are various third-party applications that provide system information. One of my favorite monitoring utilities is an open source program called CoolMon. CoolMon is a highly customizable program that allows you to display a wide range of information about your computer, such as:

- System Temperature (Requires additional Mother Board Monitor application)
- Fan Speeds (Requires additional Mother Board Monitor application)
- Network Information
- Memory Information
- System Uptime
- CPU Information
- Physical Disk Information
- Power and Battery Information

CoolMon can be downloaded from `http://coolmon.arsware.org`.

Once you have installed CoolMon, you are ready to start configuring it. Everything about the appearance can be changed by navigating through the Layout menu that can be accessed by right-clicking the CoolMon icon in the system tray.

If you would like to change the information that is displayed, simply right-click the CoolMon icon in the system tray and select Display Items. You will then see a new window called Options that looks like a text editor. The CoolMon program uses its own markup language to establish how the information will be laid out. Browse through the drop-down box located in the middle of the window to select different items that can be displayed. Once you have selected the item that you want to add, click the Add Tag button and the text above will be updated. When you are finished with the layout, click the OK button to see the new information.

Benchmarking Your System

Benchmarking means testing your computer and assigning some sort of score to your computer's configuration. The score could be an amount of time, such as the amount of time it takes your computer to solve a complex math problem. The score could also be a calculated point value that is determined by running a variety of tests, such as hard drive transfer speeds. The test could read and write files to your hard drive and then calculate a weighted score depending on how each test went. The amount of time or calculated point value have very little value on their own; it is when they are compared to other results of the same test that they become valuable.

It is important to get an initial benchmark score for your computer so that you can compare your computer's initial performance to benchmark scores from tests that you may run at a later time. It would be nice to know how much of a difference some of the hacks in this book actually helped your system. Or, if you upgraded the amount of RAM your computer has, it would be helpful to see how it impacted your system performance. By running an initial benchmark, you will have a score that you can compare all of your benchmark scores to after you make changes to your computer.

How to benchmark your system

In order to benchmark your system, you will need the help of a benchmarking application. There is a wide variety of different software programs that can benchmark just about every part of your system. If you are interested in benchmarking the abilities of your 3D video card, there is software for that. If you are interested in benchmarking your hard disk speeds, then there is special software for that task as well. On top of the individual tests, there are a lot of benchmarking suites on the market. One is known as Sandra Standard and is published by SiSoftware. The next section will show you how to use Sandra Standard to benchmark your computer.

 You will find several links to different benchmarking applications that you can use to benchmark specific hardware components of your computer in the Chapter 7 folder of the companion CD-ROM.

Using Sandra Standard to benchmark

Sandra Standard is a great program to use to benchmark your computer because it has a wide variety of individual tests, and it's free. To get started, you will need to download a copy of Sandra Standard from the Web site located at www.sisoftware.co.uk. Once you have Sandra Standard installed, you will be able to begin testing and benchmarking your system. To start Sandra Standard, click the Start Menu and expand All Programs and SiSoftware Utilities (Win32 x86), then click SiSoftware Sandra Standard (Win32 x86 Unicode) to launch Sandra. Once Sandra is started, and you have closed the Tip of the Day, you will see a list of different information and testing modules, as shown in Figure 7-10.

In order to run a benchmark, just double-click the icon of the benchmark you would like to run. For an example, let's run the CPU Arithmetic Benchmark. Scroll down on the list and list of icons until you find the CPU Arithmetic Benchmark icon and then double-click it. Once it loads, click the blue Refresh arrow button or press F5 on your keyboard to start the benchmark. Once the benchmark starts, the Analyzing window will be shown that indicates the progress of the test. Do not touch your keyboard or mouse while the test is running. On some benchmarks, the status bar does not update very frequently, so don't get worried if the benchmark seems to be frozen; most likely it is not. The vast majority of the benchmarks take only a few minutes to run, although a few may take up to 10 minutes. When the test is over, the results will be displayed in comparison to other hardware configurations.

CPU Arithmetic Benchmark

The CPU Arithmetic Benchmark will run a series of standard CPU benchmarks, such as the Dhrystone (integer arithmetic such as whole number addition) and Whetstore (floating point

FIGURE 7-10: Sandra Standard benchmark modules.

arithmetic such as decimal addition) benchmark tests. This test takes about 30 seconds to run but is repeated several times to get an accurate test result. All together, this test takes between two to five minutes to run. This test is not very useful for measuring how much faster you have made your computer but it is useful to compare how fast your CPU is compared to other systems. Within the module, the results of the test will be compared against other similar systems and you can select any processor to compare it against.

CPU Multimedia Benchmark

The CPU in your computer is a lot more advanced than CPUs from 20 years ago, which just did basic computer functions. With the growing need for high-performance multimedia applications such as 3D games and DVD players, CPU manufacturers started to include advanced instructions in the design of the chip that would allow for special multimedia performance increases. The CPU multimedia benchmark is designed to test the most popular multimedia extensions that your computer is equipped with, such as MMX, 3DNow, SSE2, and SSE3. The test will take about 20 seconds but it will repeat a few times to get reliable results. During the test, a fractal is generated and other objects using the multimedia extensions. The results are then calculated and repeated for both integer (whole numbers) and floating point (decimal) calculations and displayed in comparison to other systems.

Removable Storage/Flash Benchmark

The Storage/Flash Benchmark will measure the speed of the flash-based storage devices, such as USB pen drives and compact flash-based cards, used in many digital cameras. The benchmark module tests the read performance, write performance, as well as the delete performance. Then, based on the performance in each area, the drive is given a drive index score. After the test, the actual data speeds are available and the device can also be compared to similar devices. This test can take up to 10 minutes to complete and cannot be canceled while it's performing.

File System Benchmark

The File System Benchmark is similar to the flash storage benchmark but is designed for different hardware, such as hard drives. The File System Benchmark tests the drive by doing a series of read tests that test reading data from random locations, reading data from a series of adjacent locations, and reading data from the disk buffer. Additionally, the file system benchmark tests the writing speed by writing data to random locations, writing data to a series of adjacent locations, and writing directly to the disk buffer. To finish the benchmark, the application completes a seek test and then calculates a drive index score based on the results of the three types of tests. The data is then displayed in comparison with similar types of drives.

CD-ROM/DVD Benchmark

The CD-ROM/DVD Benchmark test is similar to the file system benchmark but is designed for the optical drives. In order to run the test on a data CD drive, you must place a CD that has at least 600MB of data on it and contains large files that are greater than 64MB each. For a video CD or DVD, any VCD movie or DVD movie will do for the test. After the test is completed, which usually takes about 10 minutes, the results will be displayed in comparison with other drives.

Memory Bandwidth Benchmark

The Memory Bandwidth Benchmark tests the system memory using the popular STREAM memory benchmark. This benchmark tests the storing and retrieving of data of both integer and floating point operations. Once the test is completed, usually after two minutes, the results will be displayed. The "ALU" results are from the integer arithmetic tests and the "FPU" results are from the floating point tests. If you would like to learn more about the STREAM memory benchmark, visit www.streambench.org to find out how it works.

Cache & Memory Benchmark

The Cache & Memory Benchmark tests the CPU cache and memory using floating point operations. The test is designed to make it possible to compare different CPU configurations. After the test is run, which usually takes about 10 minutes, the results will be given in a graph that shows how effective the cache is at different text block sizes, as shown in Figure 7-11. This test is great for determining exactly how CPUs of the same speed but different cache sizes are different.

Network/LAN Bandwidth Benchmark

The Network/LAN Bandwidth Benchmark will measure how fast your local area network is. The test will ping and transfer data from another machine on your network to test for response time and for maximum speed. Although this test is limited to the maximum speed of the

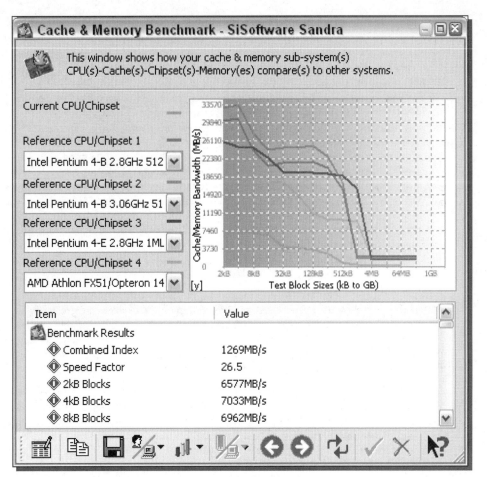

FIGURE 7-11: Results of the Cache & Memory Benchmark test.

hardware that the test is testing across the network, the benchmark is still effective when used to detect how fast your network can really go. The test may take a while to load, as it needs to search your local area network to find another machine that it can connect to so that it can run the network benchmark. Once the module loads, and the test is run, the results will be displayed within 5 minutes.

Internet Connection Benchmark

The Internet Connection Benchmark attempts to measure the speed of your Internet connection link. The test will detect the first gateway of your ISP and measure the speed of the data transferred to and from. Then the test measures the latency of your connection by pinging the gateway. The tests are run a number of times and the mean of the results is what is reported. This benchmark is useful for comparing your results against other types of connections on which the test was run. However, the numbers generated by the benchmark are not the true

Internet connection speed. In order to test your Internet connection for its maximum speed, run a search on Google looking for "Speed tests" and you will find numerous sites that will help you test the maximum speed.

Internet Peerage Benchmark

The Internet Peerage Benchmark basically measures the quality of your Internet Service Provider. Peering is what a connection between other networks is called. When one ISP connects its network to another ISP, the connection is known as *peering*. The Internet is made up of the peering of different networks. The overall speed of your Internet connection can depend on the quality of peers your ISP has linked up with as well as the number of peers. When you browse the Web, a request is sent to the Web server of the Web site. The Web servers are located all over the world in different places. Therefore, the speed of connecting to one Web site could be different than the speed of connecting to another Web site. The speed of the peers determines the speed of your Internet connection. The peerage benchmark attempts to measure the speed of a variety of popular Web sites and then calculate an average speed. The test only takes a few minutes. Once the test is completed, the results will be displayed in comparison to other ISPs and connection types.

Using Bootvis to benchmark

Bootvis is a great diagnostic tool that is good for zeroing in on problematic drivers and services that are resident in the system startup. Finding a new device driver or a different application version is one solution when you have a driver that is taking a long time to start up. Before you update the device driver or application service, you really should set a benchmark to see if the new driver or application has made a difference or if the new driver or application has decreased performance further.

New problems often arise in new drivers and versions of applications. Upgrading the latest version of the drivers and applications will help in the majority of cases. However, sometimes they may not, and may even prove to be detrimental. In those cases, you should be able to see what the net effect of the change is. One easy solution to finding the net effect on the change would be to benchmark the driver loading time.

This can be done manually by running a trace on the boot, as was discussed earlier in this chapter, and then running some simple calculations to get an accurate benchmark number. Follow these simple steps:

1. Start up Bootvis and set up a Next Boot + Driver Delay trace. You really should set the boot trace to repeat at least three times to get an accurate benchmark.

2. Once the system has restarted and traced the boot the number of times you have specified, open up each file and determine how long a specific driver took to initialize by looking at the Driver Delay window and moving the mouse cursor over the green rectangles, as shown in Figure 7-12.

3. Keep track of all of the different delay times for each of the boot trace files. Then once you have a minimum of five different times, throw out the extremes and calculate the mean of the remaining values. Save the value that you calculate so that you will have something to compare it to later.

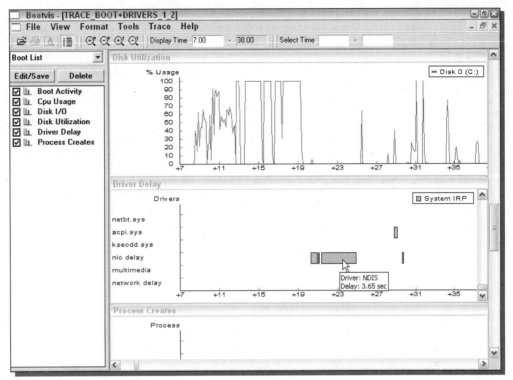

FIGURE 7-12: Determining how long a driver took to initialize by positioning the mouse over the driver rectangle.

4. Once you have updated the device driver, repeat the previous process to calculate a new benchmark value that you can compare to the original value that was calculated.

Benchmarking with PCMark04

PCMark 2004 edition, from Futuremark Corporation, is one of the most popular benchmarking programs for power users available. PCMark 2004 has a cool online component that allows you to view your benchmark data on their Web site and compare it to other users' computers. The PCMark04 application is a great way to provide your computer with an overall score. This score can be used to compare your system to other systems. The comprehensive score that is assigned to your system is the result of numerous test results testing various parts of your computer.

A copy of PCMark04 can be downloaded from www.futuremark.com/download/.

On the CD A link to the Futuremark Web site, where you can download PCMark04, is found on the CD-ROM at the back of the book.

The user interface of PCMark04 is very simple and easy to use. Simply click the Run PCmar button to start the tests. Included with the free version are only the basic system tests that are run to simulate normal computer usage. The basic system tests include the following:

- File compression and decompression benchmark tests, which test the CPU's ability to do integer calculations by compressing and then extracting a text file similar to using applications such as WinZip to put your files in a compressed ZIP file.

- File encrypting and decrypting benchmark tests, which encrypt and decrypt both an image and audio file. This test uses the popular blowfish encryption algorithm to encrypt the files and measure how long it takes your computer to encrypt and decrypt the files.

- Virus Scanning benchmark tests, which test the computer's ability to scan files. This test simulates an anti-virus program to see how fast your hard drive is as well as the CPU's performance as it scans document, executable, and image files.

- Grammar Check benchmark tests, which test the speed of the CPU by simulating the common task of using a word processor. For example, it took your computer 24 seconds to check a document's grammar.

- Audio Conversion benchmark tests, which are used to test the CPU floating point performance by converting a wav audio file into an ogg vorbis (a new audio compression format similar to a MP3) file.

- Image processing benchmark tests, which test the CPU performance by reading and decoding JPEG image files to get an elapsed time reading.

- Web Page rendering benchmark tests, which test the CPU and system memory by loading several Web pages to calculate how many sample Web pages can be rendered per one second.

- WMV Video Rendering benchmark tests, which are used to test how fast the computer can encode a video clip at 320 x 240 resolution at 1000 kbps rate in Windows Media 9 format.

- Divix Video Rendering benchmark tests, which check how fast the computer can encode a video clip at 720 x 480 resolution in the popular Divix codec.

- Physics & 3D benchmark tests, which test the gaming abilities of your PC by running a 3D test that measures frames per second while calculating many physical objects.

- Graphics Memory benchmark tests, which check the memory on the video card as well as the AGP bus speed by running read/write tests directly in the memory over the AGP bus.

Once you click the Run PCmark button, the system tests will begin, as shown in Figure 7-13.

Once the benchmark tests are completed, you will be shown your system's overall score. To view the detailed scores of the different tests, you will have to register on Futermark's Web site via the link on your results window. This is a slight letdown, but registering on the site allows you to compare your system against other systems. You can find out what hardware really performs and what hardware you should avoid. Overall, the PCMark04 Web site adds a great amount of value to the application.

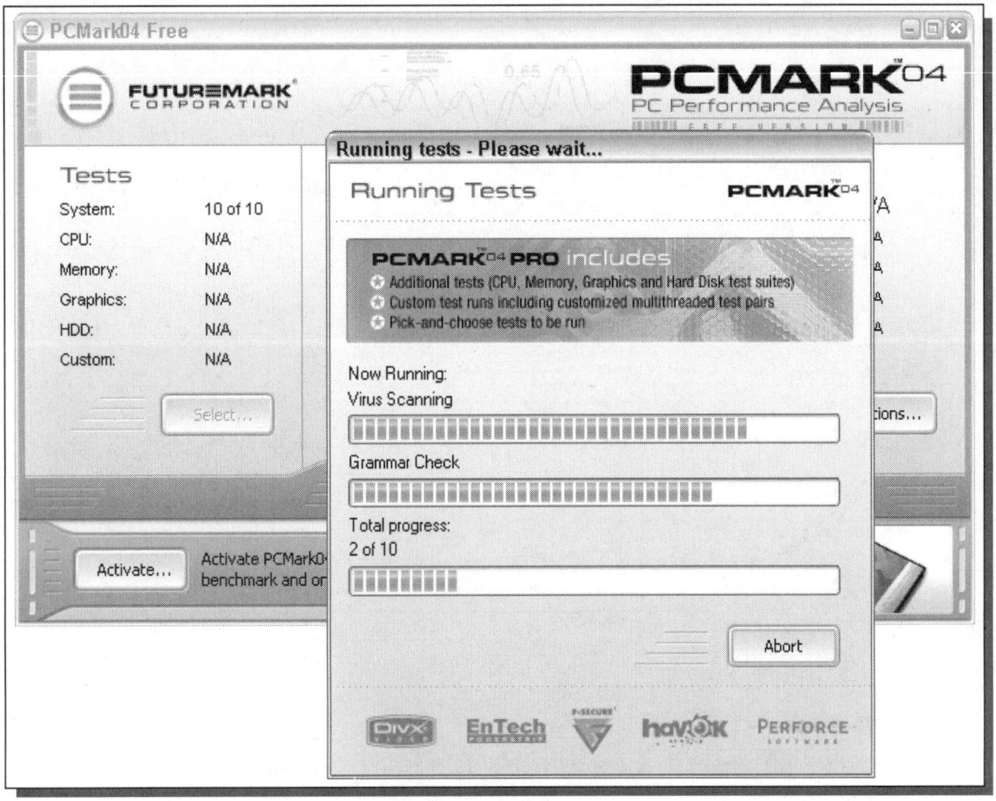

FIGURE 7-13: PCMark04 running the system benchmark test.

Summary

This chapter was meant to be an introduction to the world of benchmarking. Before you can make your computer faster, it is very helpful to know what your computer doesn't perform well with. This chapter showed you how to discover bottlenecks using applications such as Performance, Bootvis, Sandra Standard, and PCMark04. Use the information that you gained from this chapter to get the most out of the upcoming chapters. For example, if your computer's video card does not perform all that well compared to other computers, then you should definitely try decreasing some of the graphical visual effects of Windows XP, as will be shown in the upcoming chapters. The next chapter will start to optimize the speed of your computer from the very beginning, the system boot.

Speeding Up the System Boot

N o doubt you are surprised at how fast Windows XP boots up compared with other Microsoft operating systems. I certainly am, every time I start up the PC. This bootup time is something that everyone is becoming more concerned about as the need for PC speed becomes increasingly more important. Despite the relatively fast speed of Windows XP bootup time, this chapter will guide you through the steps of making the system boot up even faster. The changes discussed here should help you realize your bootup speed dreams. Your friends will then no doubt be impressed by your PC's superfast operation.

Windows XP has a lot of great features and visual enhancements that make it the most attractive OS from Microsoft to date. However, with all of the new features and attractive effects, the operating system has a higher system overhead, which means your hardware has to work even harder. If you are like me, and do not always have the fastest hardware, this chapter will help you get the most out of your current hardware by reducing the heavy workload put on it during the bootup process.

Working with BIOS

Every personal computer has a system basic input/output system, or BIOS, which is what takes control of your computer the moment you turn it on. The screen that you first see when you turn on your computer is called the *power on self-test screen*, better known as the *POST screen*. If you purchased your computer from one of the major computer manufacturers, this screen is often hidden by the manufacturer's logo. To get rid of this logo from the screen, just press the ESC button on your keyboard; you'll then see what is going on in the background. At this stage in the system boot, the BIOS is probing the hardware to test the system memory and other device connections. Once the POST is completed, the BIOS proceeds to look for a device to boot from. Once it finds your hard drive, it will begin to load Windows.

The BIOS also acts as a main system component control panel, where low-level settings for all of your hardware devices are made. The device boot order, port addresses, and feature settings such as plug and play are all found in the BIOS setup screens. For example, if you want to change the order of the drives that your computer checks to boot from, then you will want to modify the device boot order. I have to modify this setting almost every time I install Windows because I want my computer to boot off of the CD-ROM to launch the Windows XP setup application instead of booting off of the operating system on my hard drive.

BIOSs on each and every PC may be made by different companies or accessed in different ways. Nevertheless, the most common way to access the setup screen is to press F2 or the Delete key when the POST screen is displayed. Some computers even tell you which key to push to enter setup, as my Notebook does. If your PC doesn't allow you to access the setup screen in this way, consult your computer documentation or contact your computer manufacturer for instructions.

While you are making changes in the BIOS, make sure you do not accidentally change any other settings. If you accidentally change a value of a setting and do not know what to change it back to, simply exit the BIOS setup screen as the on-screen directions indicate and select Do NOT Save Changes. Then just reboot and re-enter the setup screen and continue hacking away at your system.

Changing the boot order of your drives

Most computers are set up so that when you first turn on your computer, it will check to see if you want to boot from other drives besides your hard drive. It will automatically check to see if you have a bootable CD in your CD drive. If your computer has a floppy drive, it will check to see if you have a boot disk in the floppy drive. Then, once it has checked all possible locations for a boot disk, the system will default to your hard drive and start booting Windows.

What are the benefits of changing the boot order of your system devices? If you modify the order of the boot devices so that the hard disk is placed at the top of the list, the system does not have to waste time checking other devices for boot records. Just by changing the order of the devices, you can shave anywhere from one to several seconds off of your boot time, depending on the speed of your hardware.

To change the boot order (or sequence, as some call it), you will have to enter the BIOS setup screen that was mentioned earlier.

1. Press F2, Delete, or the Correct key for your specific system on the POST screen (or the screen that displays the computer manufacturer's logo) to enter the BIOS setup screen.

Working in the BIOS setup screens will allow you to change many critical values that could affect the performance and the stability of your computer. Be careful which settings you decide to change because they may cause device resource conflicts as well as render your hardware unusable. However, there are very few settings in the BIOS that, if set incorrectly, will lead to physical hardware damage. The only feature that my BIOS has that can do that is the CPU overclocking functions. If I set those values too high, my CPU could burn up. Changing basic feature settings such as the boot order will only result in a minor inconvenience if it was set incorrectly. To fix a problem, you will just have to go back into the BIOS and set the right value and everything will be back to normal.

2. Look for where it says Boot and enter the sub menu.

3. Select Boot Sequence, and press Enter. Figure 8-1 shows an example of the boot sequence screen.

4. If your screen looks similar to that shown in Figure 8-1, then you are in the right place. Next, navigate to where it states "first device" and cycle through the list to where it states "Hard Disk Drive" or "IDE0" (assuming that your hard drive is connected to IDE0). If your setup screen does not specifically state "first device" but rather just lists all of the devices, then all you have to do is select the hard disk and move it to the top of the list. That can be done by using the change values keys, which for my BIOS (made by Phoenix) is the spacebar to move an item up and the minus symbol key to move an item down. The specific keys are different on almost every system but the basic concepts are the same. You want to get your hard disk to the top of the list or listed as the first device from which to try to boot.

5. Once you have made the changes, exit the BIOS by pressing the Esc key and making sure that you select to save your changes upon exit. Once you reboot, the new settings will be in effect.

What are the consequences of changing the boot order? Changing the boot order will not hurt your system in any way if you do it correctly. If, by accident, you remove your hard drive from the list and save the BIOS settings, you will get a pleasant surprise when your computer

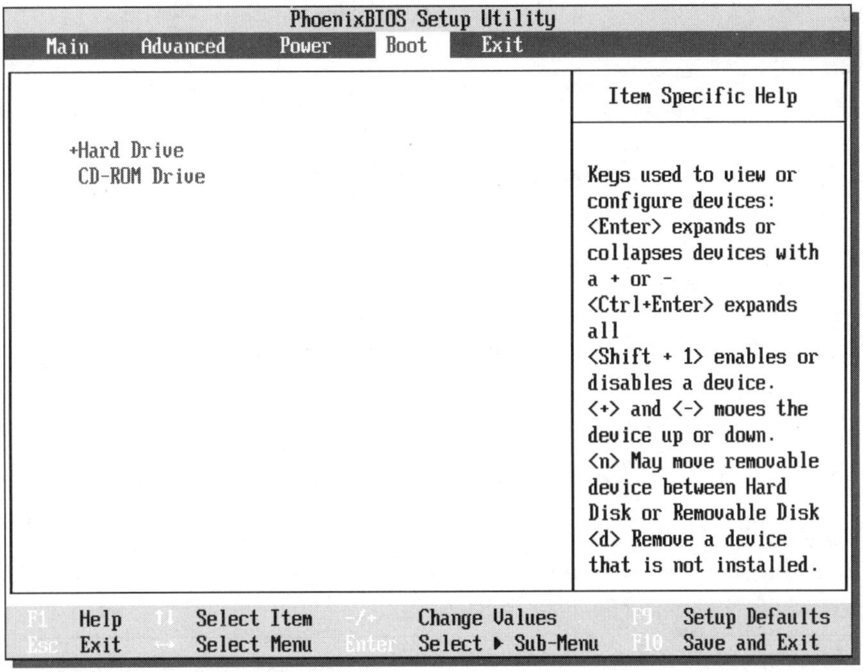

```
                    PhoenixBIOS Setup Utility
   Main      Advanced      Power      Boot      Exit
 ┌──────────────────────────────────────┬──────────────────────┐
 │                                       │  Item Specific Help  │
 │                                       │                      │
 │     +Hard Drive                       │  Keys used to view or│
 │      CD-ROM Drive                     │  configure devices:  │
 │                                       │  <Enter> expands or  │
 │                                       │  collapses devices wi│th
 │                                       │  a + or -            │
 │                                       │  <Ctrl+Enter> expands│
 │                                       │  all                 │
 │                                       │  <Shift + 1> enables or
 │                                       │  disables a device.  │
 │                                       │  <+> and <-> moves the
 │                                       │  device up or down.  │
 │                                       │  <n> May move removable
 │                                       │  device between Hard │
 │                                       │  Disk or Removable Disk
 │                                       │  <d> Remove a device │
 │                                       │  that is not installed.
 ├──────────────────────────────────────┴──────────────────────┤
 │  F1  Help    ↑↓  Select Item   -/+   Change Values   F9  Setup Defaults
 │  Esc Exit    ←→  Select Menu  Enter  Select ▶ Sub-Menu F10 Save and Exit
 └──────────────────────────────────────────────────────────────┘
```

FIGURE 8-1: The boot sequence setup screen.

reboots—a statement that the computer cannot find any operating system. If you happen to get that message, then just reboot by pressing Ctrl+Alt+Delete and go back into the BIOS settings and make sure that you select your hard drive as a boot device. Once you have done that, your system will be back to normal.

Another possible issue that you may encounter is simply a matter of inconvenience. Once you change the boot order of the system devices so that the hard drive is listed first, you will no longer be able to use system restore CDs or floppy boot disks. If something has happened to your computer and you need to boot off of those drives to restore your system or run diagnostics, just go back to the BIOS and lower or remove the hard disk from the first boot device.

Using the quick boot feature of the BIOS

All systems initialize in more or less the same way. During the power on self-test mentioned earlier, the BIOS checks the hardware devices and counts the system memory. Out of all of the different types of system memory, the random access memory, better known as RAM, takes the longest to be counted. Counting the RAM takes time, and on a machine that has large amounts of RAM, this calculation can take several seconds. For example, a machine that has 512MB of RAM may take up to 3 seconds just to count the memory. On top of the RAM counting, a few other tests need to be done because your computer wants to make sure that all of the hardware in your computer is working properly.

All of these system tests are not needed every time you boot, and can be turned off to save time. Most BIOS's offer a feature called quick boot. This feature will allow the user to turn off these tests. Other BIOSs only allow you to turn off the memory check, which will still cut down on a lot of time.

To turn on the quick boot feature or turn off the memory check, just do the following:

1. Enter the BIOS again by pressing F2 or the correct system setup Enter key upon the POST screen.

2. Once you are in the BIOS setup, locate where it states Quick Boot or Memory Check, as shown in Figure 8-2. Navigate with the arrow keys until the option is highlighted.

3. Use the Change Value keys to cycle through the options and select enable for the quick boot feature or disable if your BIOS has the memory check feature.

4. Once you have made the changes to the setting, exit the BIOS by pressing the Esc key and make sure to save the changes upon exit.

Use of the quick boot feature or the disabling of the memory check will not harm your system. In fact, there are even some computer manufacturers that ship their computers with these settings alread1y optimized for performance. The only downside to disabling the tests is the rare situation in which your RAM self-destructs; the BIOS will not catch it and you may receive errors from the operating system or your system could become unstable. If you notice that your system becomes unstable and crashes frequently or will not even boot, try going back into the BIOS and re-enable the tests to find out if your system's memory is causing the problems.

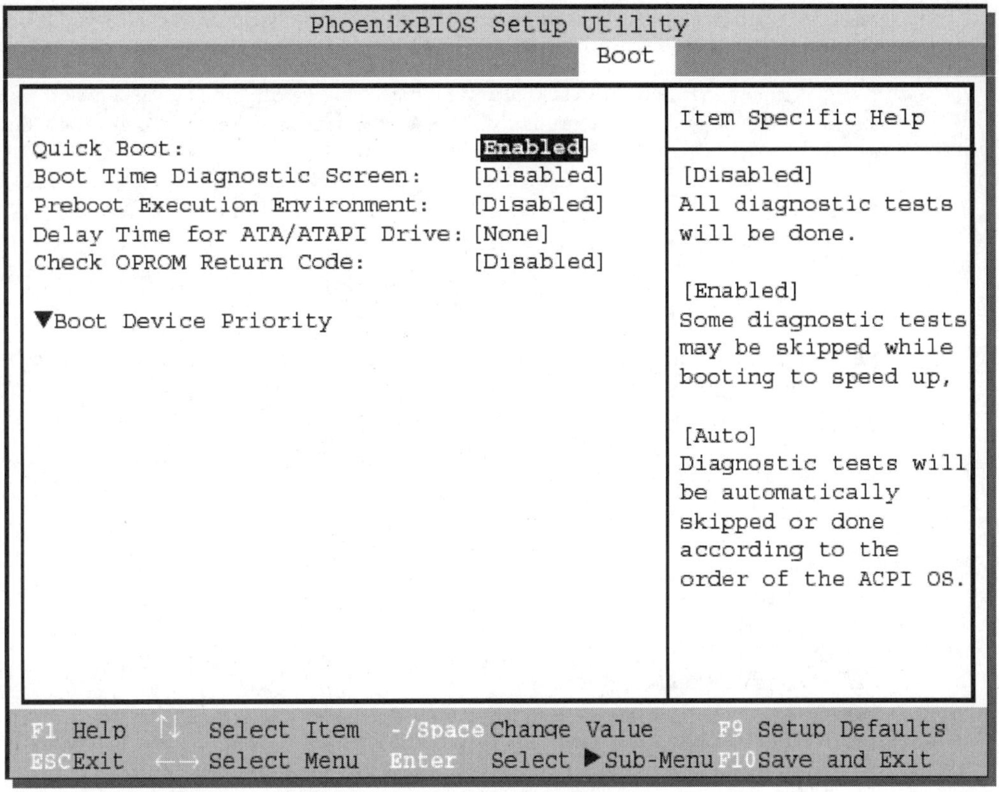

```
                     PhoenixBIOS Setup Utility
                                    Boot

                                                    Item Specific Help
      Quick Boot:                    [Enabled]
      Boot Time Diagnostic Screen:   [Disabled]     [Disabled]
      Preboot Execution Environment: [Disabled]     All diagnostic tests
      Delay Time for ATA/ATAPI Drive: [None]        will be done.
      Check OPROM Return Code:       [Disabled]
                                                    [Enabled]
      ▼Boot Device Priority                         Some diagnostic tests
                                                    may be skipped while
                                                    booting to speed up,

                                                    [Auto]
                                                    Diagnostic tests will
                                                    be automatically
                                                    skipped or done
                                                    according to the
                                                    order of the ACPI OS.




      F1 Help   ↑↓  Select Item   -/Space Change Value    F9 Setup Defaults
      ESC Exit  ←→  Select Menu   Enter   Select ▶ Sub-Menu F10 Save and Exit
```

FIGURE 8-2: BIOS setup screen displaying the quick boot feature.

Modifying the Operating System Boot

Other hacking methods are still available that will shave a few more seconds off the boot time. For example, you can cut timeout values and slim down the system to get rid of all of the extra features and services that you do not use or need. Check out the following ways to do so.

Lowering OS timeout values

If you have more than one operating system installed on your computer, you'll have to deal with the OS Selector that the Microsoft installer configures during installation of another operating system. By default, the OS Selector gives you 30 seconds to select an operating system before it reverts to the default operating system. The only way not to wait 30 seconds is to select the operating system you want to use right away. If you use one operating system most of the time, you would definitely save time if you set that operating system as the default and lowered the timeout value to 1 or 2 seconds. That way, you would not have to select an operating system every time you turned on your system or wait 30 seconds before doing so.

With Windows XP, both Professional and Home, changing the timeout value is simple if the operating system that you use primarily is already the default. If it is, just follow these directions:

1. From the Start Menu, select Run and type **MSCONFIG** and press OK. This will load the System Configuration utility.

2. Once the System Configuration utility has loaded, click the tab labeled BOOT.INI, as Figure 8-3 shows.

3. Locate the Timeout text box and replace 30 seconds with 1 or 2 seconds—or any number that gives you enough time to select the other operating systems on your system. The amount of time that you select to be your timeout value is not the amount of time you have to select the operating system. Rather, it is the amount of time you have to click any key and then select the operating system. So don't be afraid of setting this timeout value too low.

4. Once you have made the change, click the OK button, and you are finished.

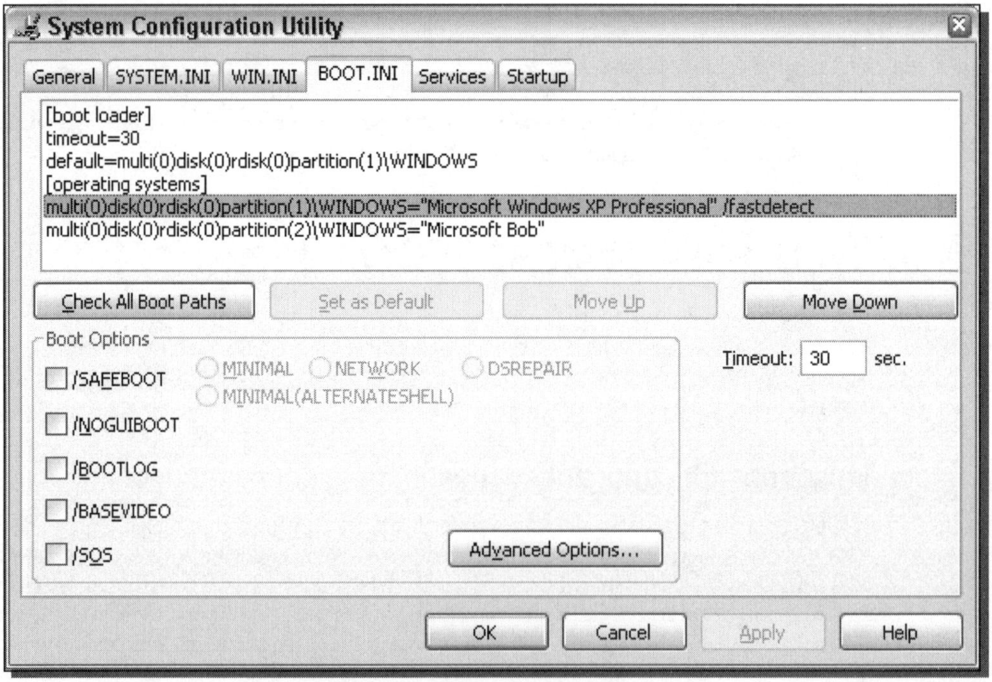

FIGURE 8-3: Microsoft System Configuration Utility boot settings.

If, after testing out your change, you feel that you gave yourself too much or too little time to select the other operating system, repeat the directions above to fine-tune your timeout time.

If you don't have your primary operating system as your default timeout operating system and you want to do so, load Notepad from the Accessories menu in the All Programs section of the Start Menu. Once Notepad is loaded, do the following to set the default:

1. Select File from the menu bar and select Open, and navigate to your root system drive. Type **Boot.ini** in the File Name text box and click the Open button.

2. Under the [operating systems] heading, you will see your operating systems listed. You will notice some disk and partition information that has an equal sign after it that then has the title of the operating system in quotes. Copy all of the disk and partition information to the left of the equal sign (such as "multi(0)disk(0)rdisk(0)partition(1)\WINDOWS") to the clipboard by highlighting the text with the mouse and then pressing Ctrl+C.

3. Then locate where it states default in the boot configuration file. Paste the new disk and partition information over the old information to the right of the equal sign by highlighting the old information and then pressing Ctrl+V.

4. Save the file and close Notepad. That's it!

You can also change the default timeout value editing the boot.ini file in Notepad. But using the System Configuration Tool is much easier for doing so. The System Configuration Tool has a lot of other useful features. I'll go into more detail about them in Chapter 9.

Disabling the system boot screen

So, are you enjoying the fun blue bars moving across your screen when your system starts up? Not? Are you finding that you can live without the daily reminder that you are running Windows XP? If so, then you might want to consider removing the boot screen. One added advantage to doing so: You will be getting a boost of performance in return.

Disabling the boot screen might only save you a fraction of a second off your boot time. But keep in mind, every fraction of a second counts. And when you apply all of the performance hacks listed in this part of the book, you will see a definite performance increase.

This performance improvement works on a very simple principle. It takes time for the computer to do anything. Taking away some work that it has to do, such as loading the boot screen, will free time that it can spend loading your system files instead.

The process for disabling the system boot screen is similar to the process for modifying the default operating system in the boot file. If you do not have any other operating systems installed on your system, then you will have to create your own boot.ini file to place in your drive root (that is, the c:\ drive). I am going to show how to create a file first, and will then show how to modify the boot.ini file if you already have one in your drive root or have multiple operating systems installed.

Creating the boot.ini file

This section will show you how to create a boot.ini file for your computer if you have just one operating system installed and you do not already have a boot.ini file in your drive root. To get started, let's go over what the boot.ini file looks like.

The boot.ini file that disables the boot screen looks like the following:

```
[boot loader]
timeout=0
default=multi(0)disk(0)rdisk(0)partition(1)\WINDOWS
[operating systems]multi(0)disk(0)rdisk(0)partition(1)\WINDOWS=
"Microsoft Windows XP Professional" /fastdetect /noguiboot
```

The above boot.ini file is pretty standard except for the addition of the /noguiboot to the last line of the file. That is the parameter that tells Windows to start up without using the graphical user interface boot screen. To get started, open up a copy of Notepad, found in the Accessories menu of the All Programs entry, in the Start Menu and follow these steps:

1. On the first line of the file, type in **[boot loader]**.

2. On line 2 of the file, key in **timeout=0** so Windows does not show the boot selection screen at all. You don't want this anyways because you only have one operating system installed on your computer.

3. On line 3 of the file, type in **default=multi(0)disk(0)rdisk(0)partition(1)\WINDOWS** so that Windows knows where to look on your hard drive to start the operating system.

4. On line 4, type in **[operating systems]**.

5. On line 5, type in **multi(0)disk(0)rdisk(0)partition(1)\WINDOWS="Microsoft Windows XP Professional" /fastdetect /noguiboot** to start up Windows with the /noguiboot parameter to disable the boot screen.

Tip If you upgraded your computer from Windows 2000 or any other NT-based product and your root Windows directory is not Windows, then you will have to make one change to the boot.ini file to correct where the path of the Windows files are located. On Lines 3 and 5, replace all references to \WINDOWS to \WINNT or the name of the directory to which you installed Windows. This will set your system to boot from the right folder.

6. Click the File menu bar item and select Save As.

7. Type **Boot.ini** in the File name box and change the Save as type to All Files.

8. Then, change the Save in directory to your drive root, which is usually Local Disk (C:).

9. Click the Save button and you are now finished.

You can now close Notepad. The next time you reboot your computer, you will not see the boot screen.

A sample `BOOT.INI` file can be found on the companion CD-ROM in the back of the book in the Chapter 8 folder.

Modifying an existing boot.ini file

If you have a multi-boot system or already have a `boot.ini` file, then all you have to do is open up your `boot.ini` file in Notepad and follow these steps:

You should make a backup copy of your existing `boot.ini` file just in case you make a mistake editing the file. To make a backup, just open up My Computer to your root drive where the `boot.ini` file is located, then right-click it and select Copy. Next, right-click the white background of the folder and select Paste. This is an easy way to make a backup copy of the file that will be automatically named copy of `boot.ini`.

1. Locate the Windows XP line in your `boot.ini` file that will look similar to "multi(0)disk(0)rdisk(0)partition(1)\WINDOWS="Microsoft Windows XP Professional" /fastdetect".

2. Type **/noguiboot** at the end of the line one space after `/fastdetect`.

3. Click File and select Save.

These instructions will remove your boot screen. But should you change your mind after you made the change, it is very easy to get the boot screen back. Simply remove the `/noguiboot` from the `boot.ini` file. If you are working from the file that you created yourself or copied from the CD-ROM, just delete it.

Disabling unneeded hardware devices

Every time you turn on your computer, it has to load and initialize all of your computer hardware. Keep in mind: Your computer has a lot of devices that you do not always use. These extra devices are loaded and initialized during every boot. When it does so, your computer's performance is slowed down.

Windows XP is now a lot more efficient and smarter during the boot-up cycle. In previous versions of Windows, the system would load one hardware device driver and then load another device driver in a series. The only problem with loading the hardware this way was that it could slow down the boot dramatically if one hardware device was taking a long time to initialize. One well-known culprit of this is the network card which pauses to wait to get an IP from a DHCP server.

Windows XP has a new way of initializing the hardware devices when the system boots up. Instead of loading the hardware device drivers in series, it now loads some of them in parallel. This allows the boot to be much faster. Although the hardware devices are loaded in parallel instead of series, the addition of more devices that the system has to load drivers for will probably still slow down the boot.

To disable hardware devices, you will want to use the Device Manager. Figure 8-4 shows the Device Manager and all of the different categories of devices. To get to the Device Manager, do the following:

1. Go to the Control Panel using the shortcut on the Start panel or menu if you are using the classic Windows interface.

2. Once you are in Control Panel, locate the System icon and run it. If you cannot find the System icon, most likely you are using the Control Panel Category View. If you are using the Category View, click the Performance and Maintenance icon and then you will see the System icon under the "or pick a Control Panel icon" heading.

3. Once the System Properties window has loaded, click the Hardware tab. Under the Device Manager section, click the button that says Device Manager.

4. Now that you are inside of the Device Manager, you can browse through your devices that are connected and currently running or disabled by browsing through the device type sections. To disable a device, right-click the device name, and then select Disable.

5. To re-enable a device, right-click the device name, and select Disable. This will remove the check from the menu and will re-enable the device.

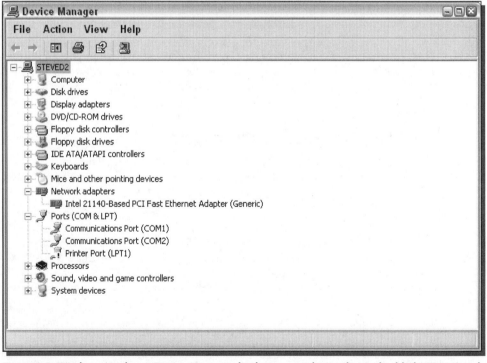

FIGURE 8-4: Windows Hardware Device Manager displaying one device that is disabled (COM1) and one device that has a problem (LPT1).

To quickly determine the status of a device, check out the icon next to its name. All devices that are disabled have a red X over the icon. All devices that have a question mark or an explanation point on them are not set up correctly or are having problems. All devices with none of the above additions to the icon are running—and doing so without any problems.

What hardware devices should I disable?

Each user uses (or doesn't use) devices differently, depending on the system setup. Nonetheless, some classes of devices are more commonly disabled than others. Knowing which ones will help you make a decision as to what devices you should disable. The following classes of devices are frequently disabled:

- *Network Adapters*: Especially on Notebook computers, there are often more than one network device. Disabling the network devices that you do not use will definitely save you some booting time.

- *Fire wire*: If you have 1394 connections, otherwise known as fire wire, you might consider disabling them. Unless you are using your fire wire port to connect your digital video recorder to your computer, or have other external fire wire devices, you have no need to have this device enabled.

- *Modems*: Do you have a broadband connection? If so, then consider disabling your modem. If you rarely use it, disable it. If you ever need to use it again, just re-enable it.

- *Multimedia devices*: Your computer has lots of multimedia devices. Take a look at the "Sound, video, and game controllers" section in Device Manager. You will find a lot of device drivers that are loaded during your boot. Some are used by all users, but others will find a few that they do not use. For example, I do not use my game port or my MIDI device, so I disabled both of those.

- *PCMCIA*: If you are a laptop user, consider disabling your PCMCIA card controller, located under "PCMCIA adapters." The PCMCIA (Personal Computer Memory Card International Association) slot is a special expansion slot that is rarely used today on laptops except for wireless and wired network cards and card reader attachments for compact flash and other solid state memory cards. Most laptops now have built-in network adapters and some even have built-in wireless adapters. If you do not use your PCMCIA adapter, it is yet another device that can be safely disabled.

Do not disable any hardware devices that are located under the *Disk Drives, Computer, Display Adapters, IDE Disk Controllers*, and the *System* sections (except for the system speaker) because these hardware devices are critical to the operation of your computer.

Removing extra fonts for speed

Windows XP has over 250 different font variations that it loads for use when the system boots up. Of these 250 variations, only a handful are used on a regular basis. Most likely, you really only use the core Windows fonts, such as Tahoma, Times New Roman, Arial, Verdana, Trebuchet, and

MS Sans Serif. All of the other fonts can be removed form the fonts folder. As you can imagine, loading over 250 fonts is something that will take the system more time to do. Users who have installed a fonts CD, which usually has hundreds of fonts, on their systems are increasing the amount of work their computer has to do during startup. Simply put, loading a lot of fonts will take more time, because the system has to load and index each font. Thankfully, there is a very simple answer to this: Just remove the fonts that you do not use from your font directory.

You can go about removing the unneeded fonts from your font directory in a number of different ways. The best way is to move the unused fonts to a separate folder on your system so that if you ever want to use one of those extra fonts again, you just have to copy it back to the fonts folder.

Caution

When you remove fonts from your computer, you will no longer be able to use them in any software application, including Microsoft Word and Excel.

Before you start removing fonts from your fonts folder, take at look at Table 8-1. These fonts are commonly used, for reasons that the table explains. Be careful not to remove any fonts on which the system normally depends.

Now that you know which fonts you should not remove, you also need to be aware of one more thing before starting your adventure in the fonts folder. Inside the fonts folder, there are several fonts with similar names. The fonts are broken up not only by font name but also by type style. For example, there is an Arial Bold, Arial Bold Italic, Arial Italic, etc. When sorting through the fonts to delete, you also can choose to delete only specific types of fonts.

Deleting fonts is fairly easy. But removing the fonts is a little more tricky because the fonts folder is not like a normal folder. In order to remove the fonts, you need to start off by creating a folder to put the old fonts in.

Table 8-1   Recommended Fonts to Keep

Font Name	Reason
Verdana	Often used on Web pages and applications
Arial	Often used within applications such as Outlook
Trebuchet	Used in the Windows interface on the Title Bar
Tahoma	Used in the Windows interface on the Menu Bar as well as in many applications and Web pages
Times New Roman	The default font for Web pages as well as applications such as Word
MS Sans Serif	Used in some applications and Web pages

1. Open up My Computer through the icon in your Start panel or from the icon on your Desktop. Navigate to the C: drive or whatever drive on which you have Windows installed.

2. Next, navigate to the Windows folder (or WINNT folder for some). If along the way you are prompted with a screen telling you that "this folder contains a file that keeps your system working properly; you should not modify its contents," ignore this message and click the text that says "show the contents of this folder."

3. Now that you are inside the Windows root folder, create a folder to store the fonts that you are going to remove from the fonts folder. Right-click the white space that lists the folder and files and select New and then select Folder. Call your folder Fonts Backup or something similar so that you will be able to identify that this is the place that your old fonts are.

4. Once you have created the new folder, open it.

5. Next, go back to the My Computer icon in your Start panel or Desktop and open another window. Navigate to the drive you have Windows installed on and then navigate to the Windows folder. Once you are inside the Windows folder, navigate to the Fonts folder.

6. Now that you have both the Fonts folder open and your backup folder open, arrange the two windows on your screen so that they look like the two windows in Figure 8-5.

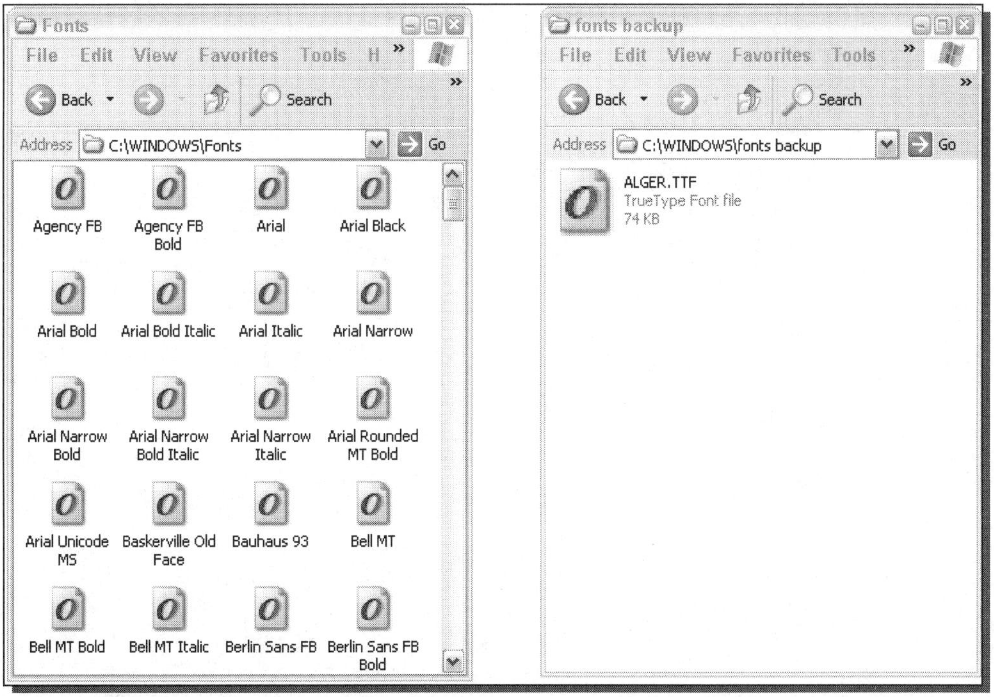

FIGURE 8-5: The Windows Fonts folder and a backup folder are arranged side by side on the screen.

7. Now that the two font folders are side by side, to remove a font from the system, all you have to do is click the icon in the Fonts folder that you do not want installed any more, and drag the icon over to the backup folder. This will automatically uninstall the font and will copy it to your backup folder.

In the event that you want to reinstall a font, all you have to do is drag the font file from the backup folder back to the Fonts folder. You will see an installation dialog box that will flash just for a second as it adds the font back to the library. Once you drag the file back to the Fonts folder, the file will still remain in the backup directory because it just copies it there. After you have confirmed that it was actually installed again, feel free to delete the font file from the backup folder.

Disabling unneeded services

A service is a software application that runs continuously in the background while your computer is on. The Windows operating system has numerous services that run in the background that provide basic functions to the system. Network connectivity, visual support, and external device connectivity such as printer services are all examples of the types of services that the Windows services provide. Each of the services running in the background take up system resources, such as memory and CPU time. Also, during the booting of the operating system, the service has to be loaded. On most computers, there are nearly 20 services that are loaded upon startup. Of these 20 services, only a handful are system-critical services. All of the others can be disabled. In order to disable a service, first you will need to know more about what the most common services do. Table 8-2 will help you understand what the most common services are, what they do, and if they can be disabled.

Table 8-2   Common Windows Services in Use

Service Name	Service Use
Automatic Updates	Used to download and then install updates automatically without the user going to Windows Update manually. This service is not system-critical and can be disabled, but unless you check for updates regularly, it is not recommended to disable this service
Background Intelligent Transfer Service	A service that transfers data in the background when the connection is not in use. One use of this service is to download updates automatically in the background. This service is not system-critical but can impair other services, such as automatic updates, if it is disabled
Com+ Event System	Basically controls the notification of certain system events, such as log on and log off. The system event notification is dependent on this service. This service is system-critical

Service Name	Service Use
Computer Browser	Keeps track of the other computers on your network running the Microsoft Client for networking. This is what provides the list of computers when you are browsing your workgroup computer in My Network Places. This service is not system-critical and can be disabled if you do not need the network browsing function
Cryptographic Services	Basically manages system security certificates as well as provides a database of signatures of key Windows files. This service is not system-critical but it is required to install many Microsoft programs that want to check system file signatures. It is not recommended to disable this service because doing so would not allow Windows Update to run and install new updates
DCOM Server Process Launcher	Basically is in charge of starting various other services. This service is required for RPC, which is required for over 39 other services to run. Because of that, it is not a good idea to disable this one
DHCP Client	Provides support for dynamic network configuration. This service is not system-critical but is needed for those that do not set their IP address manually
Distributed Link Tracking Client	Keeps track of links to files on a NTFS volume on your computer or across a network. This service is not system-critical and can be disabled.
DNS Client	Resolves domain names into IP addresses, as well as caches lookup results. This service is not system-critical but you will not be able to browse the Internet without it started
Error Reporting Service	Allows users to report failures of applications directly to Microsoft so that Microsoft may fix bugs in its software if it is the culprit. This service is not system-critical and can be safely disabled
Event Log	Allows event messages to be recorded to be viewed in Event Viewer. This service is system-critical and cannot be disabled
Fast User Switching Compatibility	Allows users to switch to other users on the same system without logging off. This service is not system-critical and can be safely disabled
Help and Support	Used for the Help and support center. This service is not system-critical and can be safely disabled

Continued

Table 8-2 *(continued)*

Service Name	Service Use
HTTP SSL	Allows the personal Web server built into Windows XP (IIS 6.0) to provide secure data transfers over HTTP. This service is rarely used because most people never even set up the personal Web server on Windows XP. This service is not system-critical and can be safely disabled
Indexing Service	Creates a searchable database of, the items on your hard drive. This service is not system-critical and can be disabled if you do not search your drive often or can wait a few extra minutes to find a file
IPSEC Services	Provides IP security for certain secure connections over IP. This service is not system-critical and can be safely disabled.
Logical Disk Manager	Detects and monitors new hard disk drives. This service is not system-critical but it is used when you are upgrading your hardware and installing additional storage devices or using USB storage devices. If you do not plan on using any of the items above, the service may be safely disabled
Machine Debug Manager	Provides support for program and script debugging. This service is not system-critical and can be safely disabled for most users.
Messenger	Allows users to send text popup messages to computers on the network. This service is abused by spammers to send you advertisements. It is highly recommended that you disable this service
Network Connections	Provides, support for network connectivity. This service is not system-critical but it is recommended that it is not disabled
Network Location Awareness (NLA)	Provides services to computers that share your Internet connection. If you do not use the Internet connection feature, then, you may safely disable this service because it is not a system-critical service
Plug and Play	Allows your computer to detect hardware. This service is system-critical and cannot be disabled
Portable Media Serial Number Service	Detects the serial number of an external media device. This service is not system-critical and can be safely disabled
Print Spooler	Provides services to print. This service is not system-critical but it is necessary to print from your computer
Protected Storage	Provides basic security over certain system files. This service is system-critical and should not be disabled

Service Name	Service Use
Remote Procedure Call (RPC)	Provides services for other services. This service is system-critical and cannot be disabled
Remote Registry (Not included in XP Home)	Allows the System Registry to be connected to remotely. This service is not system-critical and it is recommended that it be disabled
Secondary Logon	Allows programs, to be started under different accounts. This service is system-critical
Security Accounts Manager	A database of local account information. This service is system-critical and should not be disabled
Security Center	Monitors your system security settings to notify you if your settings are insecure. You should keep this service running unless you are confident about your computer's security. No other services depend on this service and it can be safely disabled given you have a good handle on your security
Server	Provides the ability to share files and your printer over your network. This service is not system-critical and can be safely disabled if you do not share files over a network
Shell Hardware Detection	Used to detect external storage devices automatically. If you do not use any external storage devices, such as external hard drives or memory cards, this service can be safely disabled
SSDP Discovery Service	Looks for Universal Plug and Play drives on your network. This service is not system-critical and can be safely disabled
System Event Notification	Tracks more system events. This service is system-critical and should not be disabled.
System Restore Service	Keeps track of changes made to your system to make restore points. This service is not system-critical but it is recommended that it is not disabled
Task Scheduler	Allows users, to schedule and configure tasks. This service is not system-critical and can be disabled if you do not need to schedule any tasks to run
TCP/IP NetBIOS Helper	Allows the NetBIOS network protocol to run over the TCP/IP Protocol. This service is not system-critical and can be disabled if you have no use for the NetBIOS protocol

Continued

Table 8-2 *(continued)*

Service Name	Service Use
Terminal Services	Allows users to connect to the computer with a remote desktop. This service is not system-critical but is used by the remote assistance Help feature. It can be safely disabled if you do not need the remote assistance feature
Themes	This is the service that gives Windows the new look. It allows visual styles to be applied over the normal gray Windows 2000 style windows. This service is not system-critical and can be disabled
WebClient	This service adds support for Web-based file management for technologies such as WebDav. Most users will never need to use this service. It is not system-critical and can be safely disabled
Windows Audio	Provides audio support for the operating system. This service is not system-critical and can be safely disabled if you would like to give up your sound
Windows Firewall / Internet Connection Sharing (ICS)	Protects your computer from intruders and malicious programs attacking your computer via your Internet connection. It also provides the ability to share your Internet connection among other computers on your local network. This service is not system-critical but I do not recommend that you disable it unless you have another personal firewall application installed on your computer
Windows Image Acquisition (WIA)	Used to acquire data from optical devices such as a scanner or a camera. This service is not system-critical and it can be safely disabled if you have no use for it
Windows Management Instrumentation	Provides system information to applications. This service is system-critical and should not be disabled
Windows Time	This service is in charge of synchronizing the Windows time. If you do not need to have your time synchronized, this service can be safely disabled
Wireless Zero Configuration	Configures wireless 802.11 devices. If you do not have any wireless hardware installed, you may safely disable this service
Workstation	Allows your computer to make connections to other computers and servers. This service is not system-critical but it is needed for any basic networking

Now that you know which services can be disabled and which services are important to your system, you can safely speed up your boot by disabling the extra services using the services management tool.

Tip

Before you begin changing your service setup, set a System Restore Point to easily restore your system to an earlier configuration. However, be careful when you restore from restore points. Any applications or files that were created after the system restore point will be deleted when reverting to an earlier restore point.

The Services utility is included in all versions of Windows XP and is hidden away. Do the following to disable a service using the Services utility:

1. Click the Start Menu and select Run. In the text box, type **services.msc** and click OK. This will start the Services utility, as shown in Figure 8-6.

2. Now that you are in the Services utility, you will see a list of a lot of services on your computer. First, you will need to stop the service that you want to disable. Right-click the service name and select Stop on the pop-up menu.

3. When the service is stopped, right-click the service again and select Properties. Located on the General tab, look for the Startup Type drop-down box. Click the arrow on the drop-down box and select Disabled.

4. Click the OK button and from now on, the system will not start the service any more during boot, speeding up your system start.

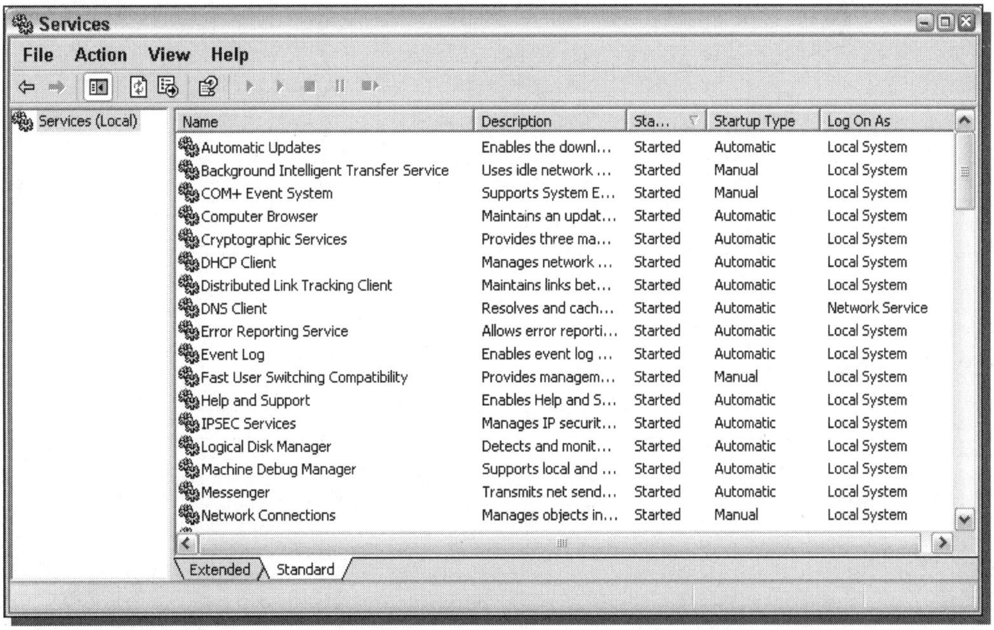

FIGURE 8-6: The Windows XP Services utility.

Bare-bones system service setup

To get the maximum amount of performance out of your system, you have the option of disabling all of the services on your computer that are not critical to the system. This would take away a lot of the nice features and conveniences of Windows, but you would have a much faster machine. The following is a list of system-critical services that should *not* be disabled. Feel free to disable all other services.

Bare Minimum Services:

- Com+ Event System
- Cryptographic Services
- DCOM Server Process Launcher
- DHCP Client
- DNS Client
- Event Log
- IPSEC Services
- Workstation
- Shell Hardware Detection
- System Event Notification
- Protected Storage
- Network Connections
- Plug + Play
- Print Spooler
- Remote Procedure Call
- Secondary Logon
- Security Accounts Manager

Recommended service setup

The bare-bones system service setup is a good setup for optimal performance. However, don't you want to have some of the conveniences of Windows XP? Check out the recommended services to disable shown in the following list. If you follow these recommendations, you will cut down on your boot time but you will also have the nice features and conveniences of Windows XP.

Disable the following services:

- Background Intelligent Transfer Service
- Distributed Link Tracking Client

- Error Reporting Service
- Fast User Switching Compatibility
- Help and Support
- Indexing Service
- Messenger
- Machine Debug Manager
- Network Location Awareness (NLA)
- Portable Media Serial Number Service
- Remote Registry (Only included with Windows XP Pro)
- SSDP Discovery Service
- Terminal Services
- Windows Image Acquisition (WIA)
- Wireless Zero Configuration (If you have a wireless network card, do not disable this one)
- Windows Time
- WebClient
- Task Scheduler

Optimizing the location of the boot files

The speed at which your files are read depends on where the files are located on your hard drive. Also, when a file is fragmented (which is when one file is scattered all over the disk), it takes more time to access that file than if all of the pieces of the files were side by side. Using tools that are available in Windows and other third-party utilities, you can defragment and place the Windows boot files on the disk where they will be accessed faster.

Windows XP has a new feature called the Prefetcher, which determines what files on the hard drive are used during the boot process and where they should be placed on the disk for optimal speed. Although this is not the only benefit that the Prefetcher provides, it makes optimizing the location of the boot files easy.

Using disk defragmenter

Windows XP includes a boot defragmenter, but it is a little tricky to get it to run. By default, it is run only in the background and cannot be started directly by a user. After your computer has been idle for some time, between 5 and 30 minutes, the system will read the Prefetcher's boot data and start the defrag. The system defrag is run in the background and is invisible to the user. Eventually, if you leave your computer on long enough, it will defragment the boot files.

Microsoft has a very talented team working for them and they even took into consideration that often your system boot changes. For example, you might install an updated device driver or add new hardware. To solve this problem, the system will re-defragment the boot files every three days.

Tip Windows keeps track of the last time it optimized the boot file so it can calculate how often it should run the boot defrag. If you are interested in finding out when the last time the boot defrag was run, open up regedit and navigate to: "HKEY_LOCAL_MACHINE\SOFTWARE\ Microsoft\Windows NT\CurrentVersion\Prefetcher" and then look for the key named "LastDisk LayoutTimeString".

An operating system that takes care of itself? Yes, Windows is getting smarter and smarter. However, there is still one problem: There is no possible way to directly initiate a boot defrag. The only way is to leave your computer on for a little while without using it at all. If you are impatient and do not want to wait, then I have a solution for you.

As I mentioned earlier, the system will only initiate the boot defrag when the system is idle. Typing in a command that will start the boot is not possible. However, you can tell your computer, even when it is not idle, to process the idle tasks. This will indirectly start the boot defrag. Although because the boot defrag is most likely not the only idle task waiting to be run, there will be other processes run as well, which can cause your computer to appear to be doing a lot of hard work as it completes all tasks. During this time, your computer should not be used for any intensive activities, such as playing games. If you try to use your computer while the idle tasks are being processed, you will notice slow performance until the tasks are completed.

Do the following to tell the system to start to process all idle tasks:

1. Click the Start Menu and select Run.

2. Type **Rundll32.exe advapi32.dll,ProcessIdleTasks** in the text box and select OK.

3. Your computer will now begin working on the tasks.

Performing these steps will allow your system to defrag the boot files. However, because the boot defrag is done every three days, processing the idle tasks more frequently than three-day periods will do nothing to help you boot because the boot defrag will not be on your idle tasks lists all the time.

Using other shareware boot defrag programs

The built-in boot defragmenter is pretty darn good. However, there are a few things that other, third-party programs, feel they do better. And in fact, there actually are a few applications, such as Diskkeeper and O&O Defrag, that actually do more in their boot defragmentation process.

During the boot-up process, there are a lot of different things going on at once. Among others, drivers are loaded, system files are loaded, settings are read from the system registry, the built-in boot defragmenter starts to lack in support when talking about the registry files, the file table records, and other system files. Just like any other system data files, the registry files can become fragmented with their daily use. In order to cut down on hard drive seek time for the registry and other system files, which can become quite large over time and more prone to fragmentation, it needs to be defragmented. This is where the third-party applications come in.

Boot time system defrag with Diskeeper

In order to defragment system files, and other files that are normally in use, the defragmentation must be done during the early stages of the system boot. This will allow the defrag program to have full access to all files so that it can place them together on the disk. One of the programs that allows this to be done is called Diskeeper, which is developed by Executive Software. A shareware copy of Diskeeper can be found on Executive Software's Web site, located at www.executive.com/downloads/menu.asp. If you have not already installed Diskeeper, please do so now before proceeding any further.

Do the following to run a boot time defrag:

1. Before you can run a boot time defrag, there needs to be continuous free space on your drive. To accomplish this, simply run a normal online defrag through the Diskeeper utility.

2. After you have completed the online defrag, click the Action menu bar item, expand Change Your Settings and select Boot-Time Defragmentation.

3. Once a new windows pops up, you will have the option to select the drive, as well as several other defrag options. Make sure that you check: Put all folders together on volume, Run the system CHKDSK utility, Defragment the paging file, and Defragment the MFT (Master File Table), as shown in Figure 8-7.

4. Once you have set the correct options and made sure that you selected On Next Manual Reboot, reboot your computer when you are ready for the defrag.

Boot time defrag with O&O Defrag

Just as with Diskeeper, with O&O Defrag there is a boot-time defragmentation option. This allows the system files that are in use to be defragmented, as well as other special files such as the master file table. O&O Defrag is developed by O&O Software and uses different defragmentation algorithms than the Diskeeper program. I have included a section on this program to give you a chance to try both programs and find the program that works better for your system. A shareware copy of O&O Defrag can be found on O&O Software's Web site, located at www.oo-software.com/en/download/.

Do the following to start a boot-time defrag in O&O Defrag:

1. Launch the O&O defrag application and select Add Job from the Jobs menu bar item.

2. Once you are in the Edit Job window, click the Volumes tab.

3. Next, click the drive letter of the drive you wish to defragment and the drive that your boot files are located on. Most likely this is your C: drive.

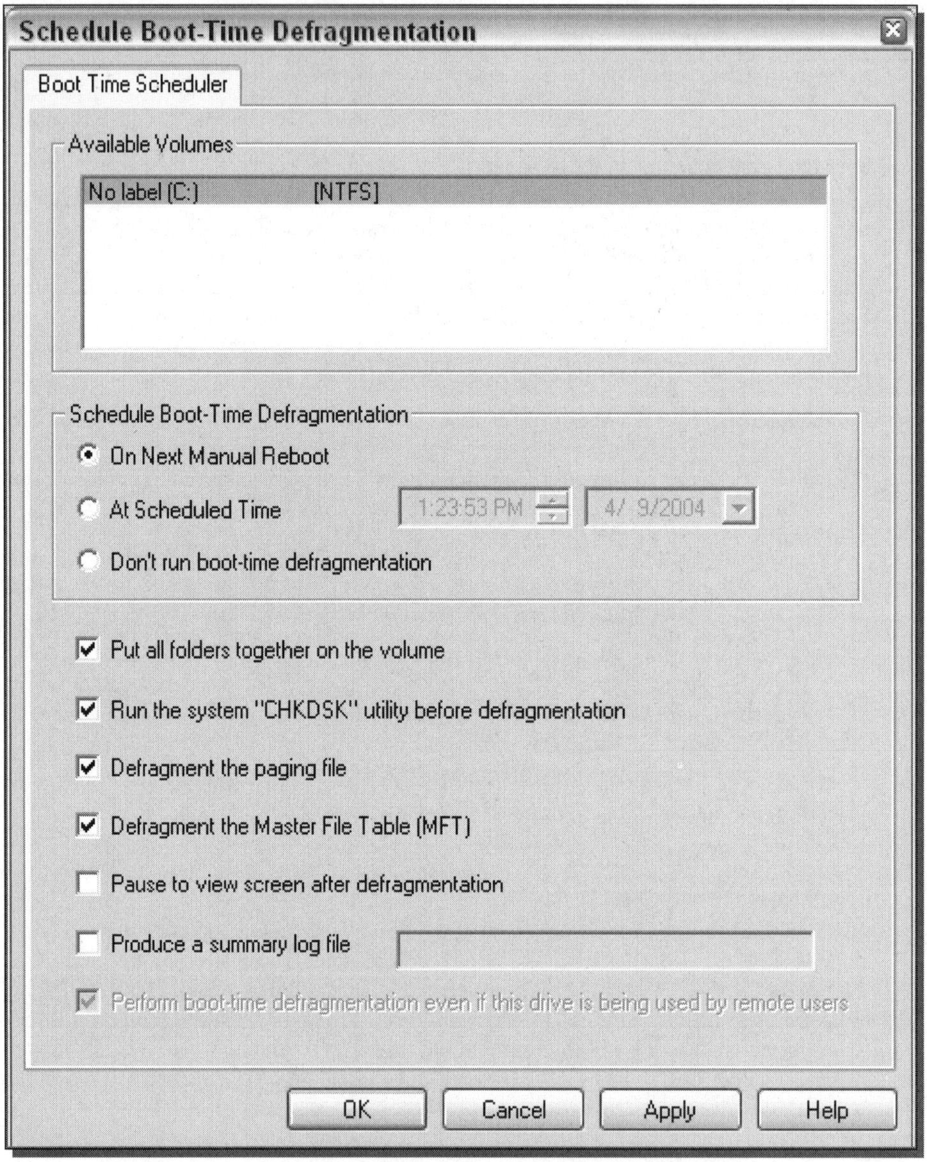

FIGURE 8-7: Diskeeper Boot-Time Defragmentation configuration window.

4. Select the Defragmentation Method for the Selected Volume you want to defragment. It is recommended that you select COMPLETE/Access for this defragmentation.

5. Once you have selected the method, make sure to check the box for Activate BootTime Defragmentation and then click the Set button.

6. Next, click the Time Plan tab and select when you would like the job to be run. You can also set up the job to be run on a weekly schedule by selecting Weekly in the Frequency drop-down box.

7. Click the OK button and you will see the job appear under the job list window. You are now finished setting up O&O defrag and your system will be defragmented at the time you scheduled the program to execute.

Summary

Throughout this chapter, you discovered many ways to lower the amount of time it takes your computer to boot up. First, you learned how to change some of the BIOS settings that can optimize your computer for maximum boot speed. Then, you discovered how you can remove your boot screen to shave off some more time. After that, you saw how you can disable other parts of Windows, such as hardware, fonts, and services, that you may never use, all of which take up time when your computer starts up. To wrap the chapter up, you found out how you can optimize the placement of the files used when your computer boots up, using the Prefetcher and two other disk defragment tools.

This chapter showed you how to speed up the first half of your computer's startup. The next chapter will pick up on the second half, the system logon. I will also show you some cool tips on how you can speed up.

Making Your Computer Load Faster

Ever wonder why it takes your computer so long to start up after you log on? After all, the system already loaded the majority of the operating system components. Does your computer take longer to load after you sign on than it used to take when you first brought it home? These are all questions that you will find the answers to in this chapter. You can make your system load faster by a number of methods. The last chapter touched on how to make the system boot faster. This chapter will concentrate on how to make the system load faster after the operating system has loaded and you are presented with the sign-on screen. But first, the system startup needs to be examined in more detail so that you will better understand what you will be doing.

After you turn on your computer, it goes through the boot-up process, which loads the main system components and drivers. Eventually, when those are finished loading, the Windows shell is started and you will be presented with the sign-on screen. Once the sign-on screen is displayed and you sign on, the system begins to load the rest of the Windows shell programs, such as Windows Explorer, which is the program behind the spiffy new Windows XP navigation and look. Once that is finished loading, the system moves on to starting up the applications in the startup folder as well as other sneaky registry startup programs. Once these applications are finished loading, your mouse will no longer display the hourglass, and you are set to do whatever you want with your computer.

This chapter will take you through the steps of speeding up all of the different parts of the system startup. First to be examined will be ways to speed up the logon process. Next to be discussed will be ways to get rid of all those extra applications that run at start that further slow down your computer. Additionally, interesting new features of Windows XP that are not turned on by default and will make your system even faster are explored. When you have finished reading this chapter and implementing the suggestions given, your system will have a much faster loading time and will be ready to use earlier than ever before.

in this chapter

- ☑ Setting Up Automatic Logon

- ☑ Removing a User's Password

- ☑ Cleaning Up Your Startup Programs

- ☑ Customizing Startup Programs for Different Users

- ☑ Removing Sneaky Programs from Startup

- ☑ Other Time-Saving Tips

Speeding Up the Logon

The system logon is the first half of the loading time. This process starts when you see the Windows Welcome screen, or the Windows 2000 style logon screen. After you type in your user information, your credentials are checked and then you are allowed access to the system. Although seemingly not much can be done to speed up this part of the system startup, in actuality a few hacks will change the way the logon is performed. By changing the way a logon is done, you can speed up your system logon by automating your system logon and removing unneeded steps.

Enabling automatic logon

Automatic logon is for you, if you primarily use just one user account on your computer and do not want to be forced to click the username and then enter your password each time you start your computer. Enabling automatic logon is a great technique that will save you time that is often wasted when your computer is waiting for you to key in your information. Even if you do not have a password assigned to your account, you are still required by the logon Welcome screen to click your name to sign in. And if you have the Welcome screen disabled, then you are still forced to click the OK button on the Windows 2000 style logon screen to get in. Having to do these tasks yourself is unnecessary and just a waste of time.

Caution

Automatic logon can be a great feature, but it can also create a security problem for your computer. If you use your computer for business, if you have data you prefer to keep safe from others, or both, I strongly recommend that you do not enable this feature. If you happen to step out of your office or if your laptop is stolen, you have left the door wide open to your computer. By enabling automatic logon, you are trading convenience for physical access security. However, you are not changing your network security so your data is still safe from network attackers. The risk of someone remotely connecting to your computer is the same as if you did not have automatic logon enabled.

Hacking your computer with a program called Tweak UI, which is an unsupported application written by Microsoft, allows users to enable the hidden automatic logon feature. Open up your Web browser and visit www.microsoft.com/windowsxp/pro/downloads/powertoys.asp to download a copy of Tweak UI. You will find the link to download the install file on the right side of the page. If you have a standard CPU, like the majority of us, make sure you download Tweak UI and not Tweak UI for Itanium-based systems. The Itanium version is for the new 64-bit CPU by Intel. If you are one of the rare users of that new CPU, however, download that version. Once you have the application installed, enabling automatic logon is really easy:

1. Start up Tweak UI by clicking the Start Menu and navigating to the PowerToys for Windows XP folder and then selecting Tweak UI.

2. Expand the Logon item and then click Autologon, as shown in Figure 9-1.

3. Then, check the Log on Automatically at System Startup box, as shown in Figure 9-1.

4. Type in the username that you want to use, if it is not already entered into the User Name field.

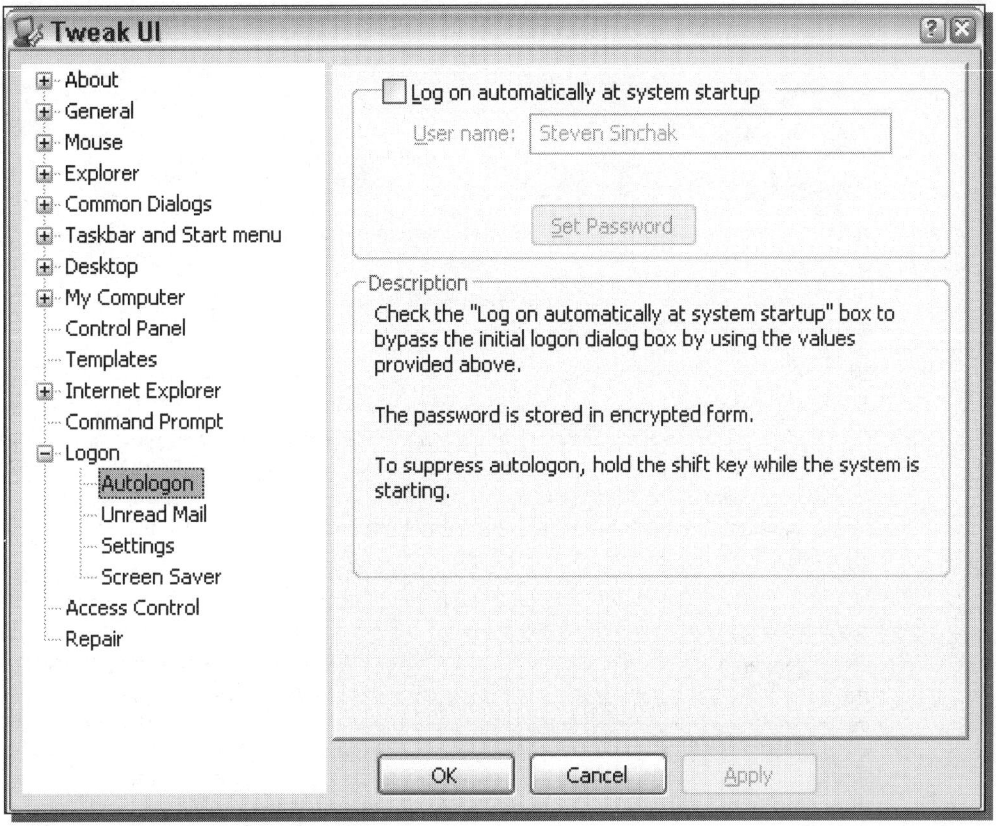

FIGURE **9-1: Tweak UI autologon feature properties.**

5. Click the Set Password button and type your password in both text boxes, as shown in Figure 9-2.

6. Once you have entered your password twice, click OK to save the password. Then click OK once more to save the autologon settings and close Tweak UI. Your system is now set up to log you on automatically.

Should you ever change your mind and wish to disable the automatic logon feature, just go into Tweak UI again and uncheck the Log on Automatically at System Startup box.

Removing user passwords

Some of you may have computer systems set up with multiple users. You might have a family computer for which each person has his or her own account for personal settings or for which you have separate accounts with different privilege levels. In some situations in which security is not a big concern, a requirement for each user to type in a password to access her account is

FIGURE 9-2: Setting a user autologon password with Tweak UI.

not necessary. In those cases, instead of clicking the user name and then typing in the password, the user would find it much easier to just click the name. An additional advantage of this simplification would be that, for those with a family computer, you would not have to worry about reminding everyone what their passwords were or needing to reset passwords when they were forgotten.

Before you begin removing the user passwords, a word of caution is in order about the possible dangers of removing user passwords. First, I strongly recommend that you leave a password on the Administrator account and any account that has administrative privileges. Additionally, before you start removing passwords, I recommend that you secure your system from external intruders on the Internet. If you do not have passwords on your user's accounts, it would be much easier to connect to your computer remotely. One simple solution is to turn on the built-in firewall and remove the Client for Microsoft Networks from your network adapter through which you get your Internet connection. Turning on the built-in firewall and removing the unneeded network protocol is really easy. If you need any help, refer to Chapter 12, which is all about protecting your computer from intruders.

Now that you know the consequences of removing the passwords and have secured your system, you are ready to get started. They can be removed in two ways. For those of you that are familiar with the Windows 2000 style computer management user snap-in control, I recommend you follow the second method. For everyone else, you will feel more comfortable using the first method.

New Windows XP user accounts method

Windows XP includes a new simple account management applet called User Accounts. This applet is a new approach to user management that replaces the Windows 2000 style user list with a nice-looking wizard approach. Follow these steps to remove passwords with the new management applet:

1. Launch the new applet by clicking the Start Menu and then selecting Run.

2. Key in **nusrmgr.cpl** and click the OK button. The applet will now launch.

FIGURE 9-3: User Accounts applet home screen.

3. Use your mouse to click the account from which you want to remove the password, as shown in Figure 9-3.

4. Next, click the text that says "Remove the password," as shown in Figure 9-4.

5. After clicking the text, you will be taken to a confirmation screen, where you will be required to type in the password of the user. Type in the password and then click the Remove Password button.

That's it! The password is now removed for the user that you selected. Repeat the previous steps for any other accounts for which you would like to remove the password.

If for any reason you change you mind and want to put a password back on a user's account, just go back into the User Accounts applet and click the user you would like to change. Then, instead of showing "Remove My Password," the applet will show, "Create a password." Click the Create text and enter the new password in the two text boxes and then click the Create Password button.

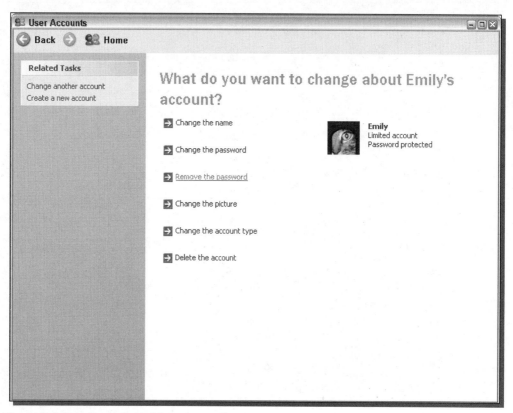

FIGURE 9-4: User Accounts applet user properties.

Local user and groups method

If you are like me, and like the Windows 2000 way of doing things, this section is for you. Windows XP was based off of code from Windows 2000. You could think of Windows XP as a revised version of Windows 2000. Although thousands of improvements have been made, some of the basic elements of Windows 2000 are still in place. However, they are not always easy to find, but they are still available if you know where they are. I have dug through the system files and have found the old MMC (Microsoft Management Console) applet that was used to manage local usernames and accounts. To start the old MMC applet and remove passwords, follow these steps:

The old Windows 2000 style user manager can only be found on computers running Windows XP Professional.

1. Click the Start Menu and select Run. Then type **lusrmgr.msc** in the text box and click OK.

2. This will start up the Local Users and Groups MMC applet. Click the Users folder to expand it to reveal the Users setup on your computer.

3. Next, right-click the name of the account you want to change and select Set Password, as shown in Figure 9-5.

4. A new window will pop up that informs you that you may lose some of the user's data if you change their password. According to the Microsoft Help file, you will only lose any files and e-mail that the user encrypted and any saved passwords for Web pages saved in Internet Explorer. Most personal use users never need to worry about this limitation, because they would not be encrypting anything. Although they might lose some saved passwords, unless they wrote them down somewhere, the loss would just be a minor inconvenience. If you have a user who is so concerned about his privacy that he encrypted his files, you should think twice about removing his password. Once you have decided if you still want to proceed, click the Proceed button and you will be shown the Set Password For Username window.

5. Leave both of the password boxes blank and click OK. That's it. You are now finished.

If you ever need to set a password again with this method, repeat the previous steps and type the password in the text boxes instead of leaving them blank.

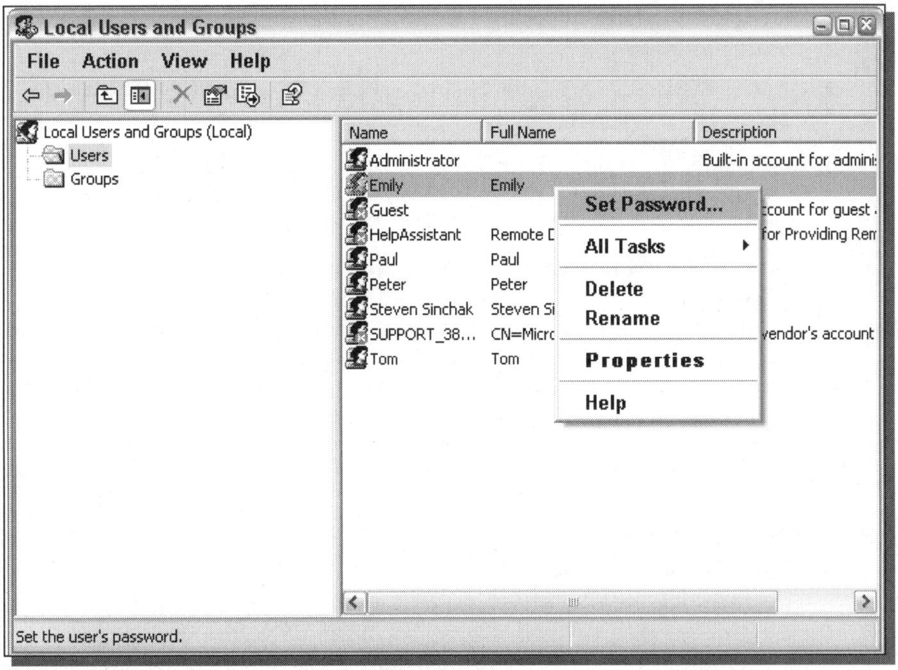

FIGURE 9-5: Local Users and Groups MMC applet.

Adjust the startup programs

After you sign on, the system finishes loading the system shell and then begins to load the startup programs that you have installed and also some that you have not. Often when you bring home a new computer it is filled with extra software that you do not need to be starting when your computer, starts up. One example of this kind of software is Windows Messenger, which was developed by Microsoft.

Every time I turn on my computer, Windows Messenger automatically loads and signs me on to the network. I love Windows Messenger, but I do not want it starting up every time I turn on my computer. It slows down my load and lets everyone know that I am on my computer, which makes avoiding certain people impossible. On top of loading Windows Messenger, and other visible programs such as antivirus software, a handful of other applications will start up automatically. This section will help you see what programs are starting up automatically and then will show you some great tricks to stop them all from starting up.

Identifying the auto startup programs

The first step in stopping the auto startup is identifying exactly what is starting up and what its purpose is. To do so, you will use a cool little program called the system configuration utility, which is built into Windows XP, and the Google search engine (www.google.com), which can look up what the entries are for. First, you will need to start up the system configuration utility and write down what programs are listed. To do so, follow these directions:

1. Start up the System Configuration Utility by clicking the Start Menu and selecting Run. Then key in **msconfig** and click OK.

2. Once the System Configuration Utility has loaded, click the Startup tab, as shown in Figure 9-6.

3. Now that the list of the active startup programs is visible, make a list of all of the items listed with the name as well as the file that is loaded, which is listed under the command column.

4. Once you have your list made, you can start researching which programs should be removed from the list and which programs should stay. Because almost every computer has different programs starting up after logon, I recommend that you browse the Web and look for a specific program and what will happen if it is removed from startup. One interesting site to visit is a database of common startup programs called AnswersThatWork. It is located at www.answersthatwork.com/Tasklist_pages/tasklist.htm. At that site, they can't present you with recommendations for each of the programs listed. If you can not find one of your programs listed on that site, just do a quick search on Google and most likely you will find several Web sites telling you what that program does and what removing it will do.

Removing programs from startup

The System Configuration Utility makes removal of items from the system startup very easy. Once you know the item that you want to remove, uncheck the check box next to the item, as shown in Figure 9-7.

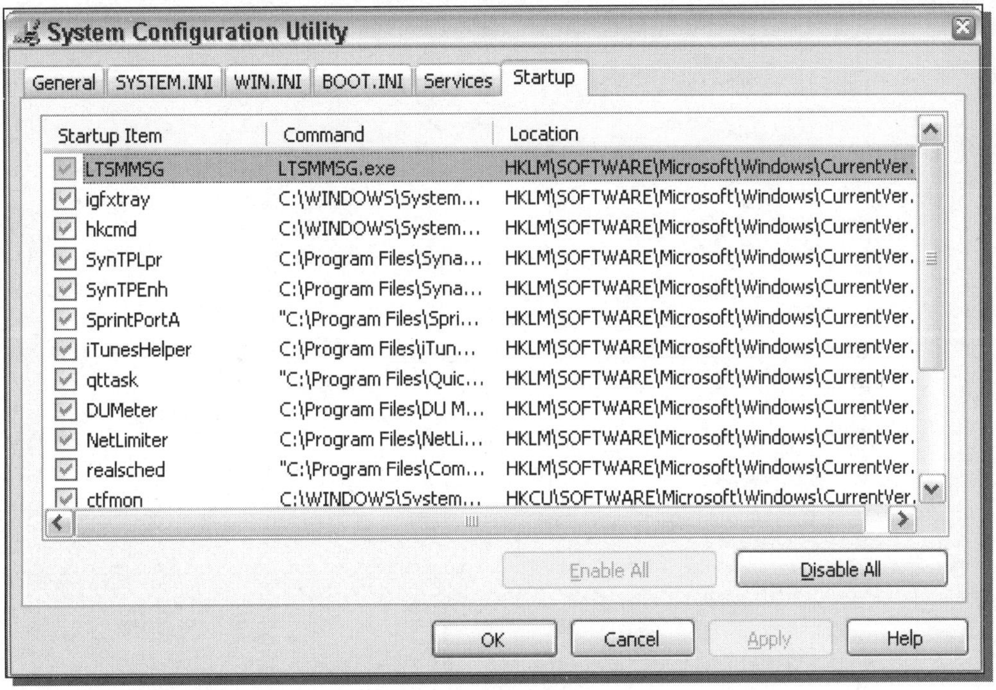

FIGURE 9-6: System Configuration Utility Startup programs tab.

Then, once you have unchecked all of the items that you no longer want to start at startup, click the OK button. This will cause a new window to pop up that asks if you would like to reboot now or later. Choose what is most convenient for you, as it has no effect on the changes you just made.

Once you reboot, the program should no longer be loaded. This procedure will work for the majority of the programs configured to start up automatically. You may notice, however, that a few sneaky applications refuse to go down without a fight. This next section will help you exterminate those.

Removing the sneaky programs

Some programs will just not go away. The software developers may be trying to make sure you use their application by making it difficult to tame or sometimes applications are just trying to make sure that other programs are not disabling them or taking over their turf.

Not uncommonly, competing software applications mess with each other. One example is what happened when I installed several media players on my PC. I installed the music programs Winamp, iTunes, RealPlayer, and Windows Media Player. The programs would fight for my music file associations (that is, what the file would be opened with). Every time I ran RealPlayer, it changed all of my music files over to be played in their player by default. The

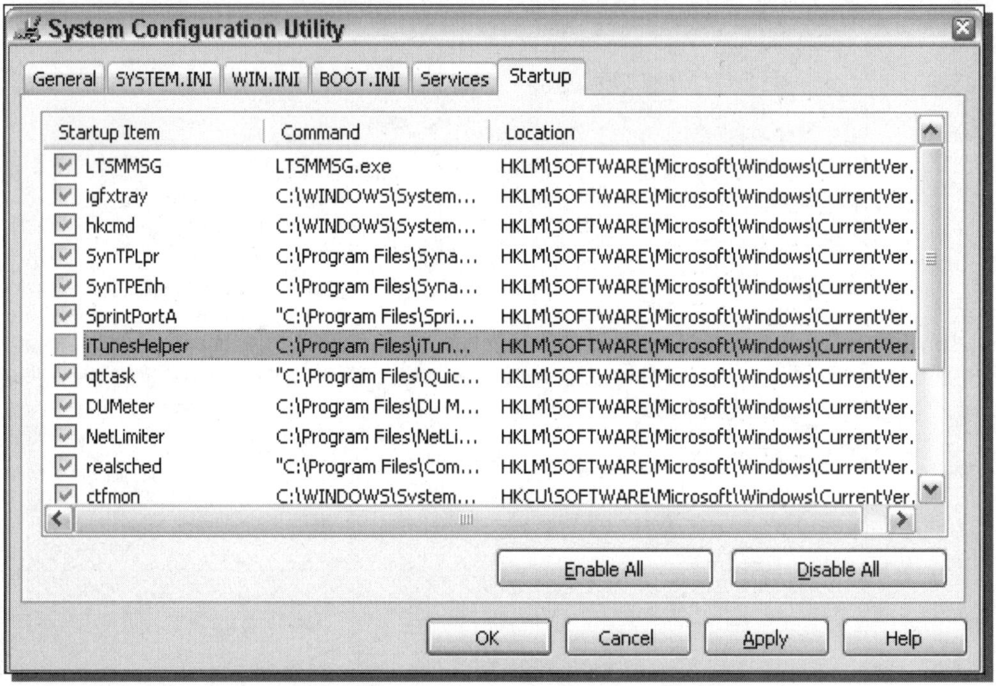

FIGURE 9-7: System Configuration Utility with an unchecked (disabled) startup item.

same thing happened when I tried to play my music files in other players. From this experience, I found that a not uncommon occurrence was for a media player application to install a program to be run at system startup that would check and take over (or preserve, as the developers call it) your file associations.

Only after I dug through the options and preferences of each of the applications and changed several options did I discover how to declare an end to the file association war. I could then proclaim Operation Music Freedom a success.

The only way to defeat these sneaky programs is to stop them from the inside. Disabling these programs from starting up is actually quite easy when you know where to look. In the paragraphs that follow, you will learn how to disable two of the most popular and most difficult applications from starting up automatically. Additionally, the methods that will be used can be applied to disable all other sneaky applications from starting up.

Taming RealPlayer

Real Networks, the developers of RealPlayer (previously known as RealOne), could have made it a little easier for users to disable some of the extra program features. RealPlayer is a good application, but it comes bundled with so much extra junk that knowing how to disable all of the extra features becomes a necessity.

Tip RealPlayer does not come preinstalled with Windows XP. If you did not download and install this application yourself, and it can not be found on the Start Menu, then you do not need to worry about taming RealPlayer.

One of the features of RealPlayer that I find most annoying is the Message Center application that automatically starts when you log on. When you least expect it, no matter what you are doing on your computer and after you have run the RealPlayer program, you will get a little pop-up message (see Figure 9-8) that alerts you to some random information or advertisement.

You can do two things to get RealPlayer under control. First, you will need to stop the scheduler from starting up every time you start Windows. You will recognize this application in the System Configuration Utility as `realsched.exe`. No matter how many times you uncheck this item in the System Configuration Utility, it will keep coming back. The only way to stop it is inside the RealPlayer application. Follow these steps to stop it for good:

1. Start the RealPlayer application by clicking the Start Menu and then selecting the RealPlayer player icon.

2. Once RealPlayer has loaded, click the Tools menu bar item and select Preferences.

3. This will load the program preferences. Expand Automatic Services and then select Automatic Updates.

4. Uncheck the Automatically Download and Install Important Updates check box, as shown in Figure 9-9.

5. Next, let's make sure that you will never again see a message from the so-called Message Center. To do so, select the Message Center entry listed under Automatic Services.

6. Hit the Select Message Topics button on the right side of the window.

7. When the Message Center window is displayed, uncheck Product News and Real Exclusives, located at the bottom of the screen, and click the Save Changes button.

8. Close the Message Center window so the Preferences window can be viewed again.

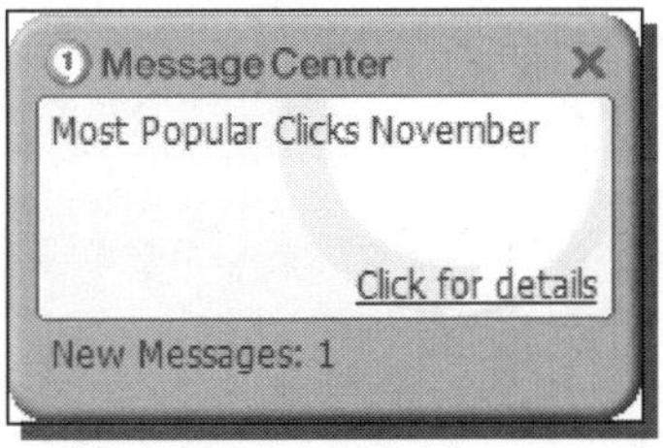

FIGURE **9-8:** RealPlayer Message Center alert.

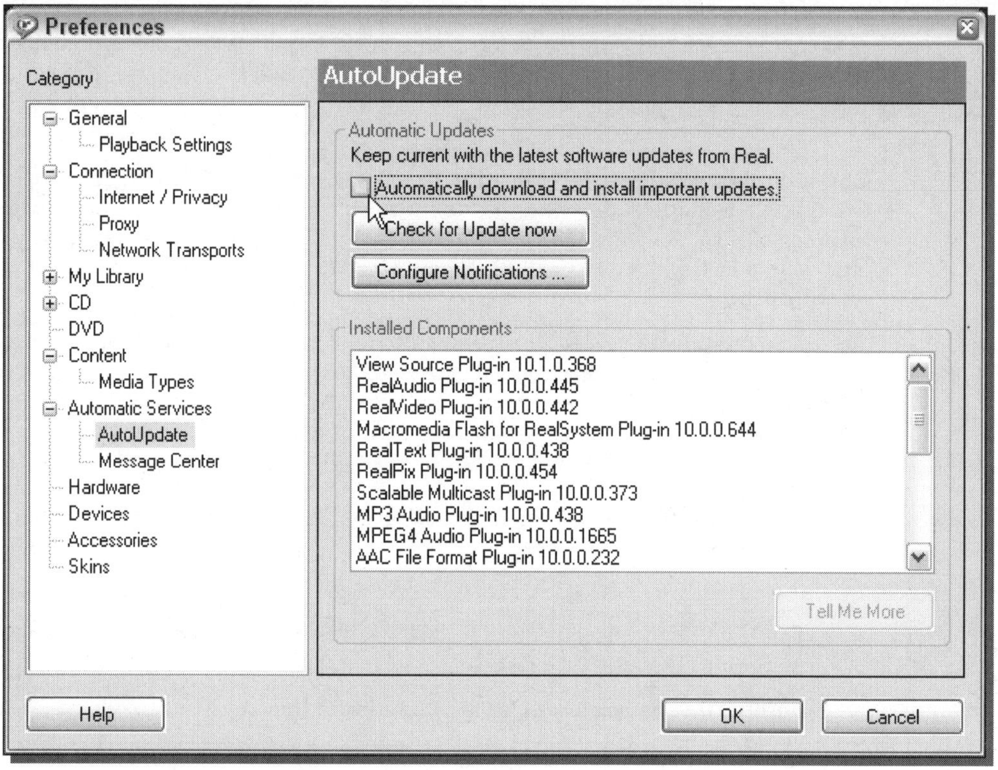

FIGURE 9-9: Disabling RealPlayer's automatic updates.

9. Once you are back to the Preferences window, click the Configure Message Center button.

10. Uncheck all of the boxes, as shown in Figure 9-10.

11. Click OK to close the Configure Message Center window.

12. A warning window will be displayed, informing you that you are disabling the Message Center. Click Yes to proceed.

13. Close the Message Center window again so that you can view the Preferences window.

14. Click OK to save your changes and close the Preferences window.

That's it. RealPlayer is now under your full control and will not be starting up automatically any more and will not be sending you advertisements.

Getting control of Windows Messenger

Windows Messenger is a great instant messaging program that I use frequently. The one problem with it is that it starts up automatically when you log on. Trying to stop this

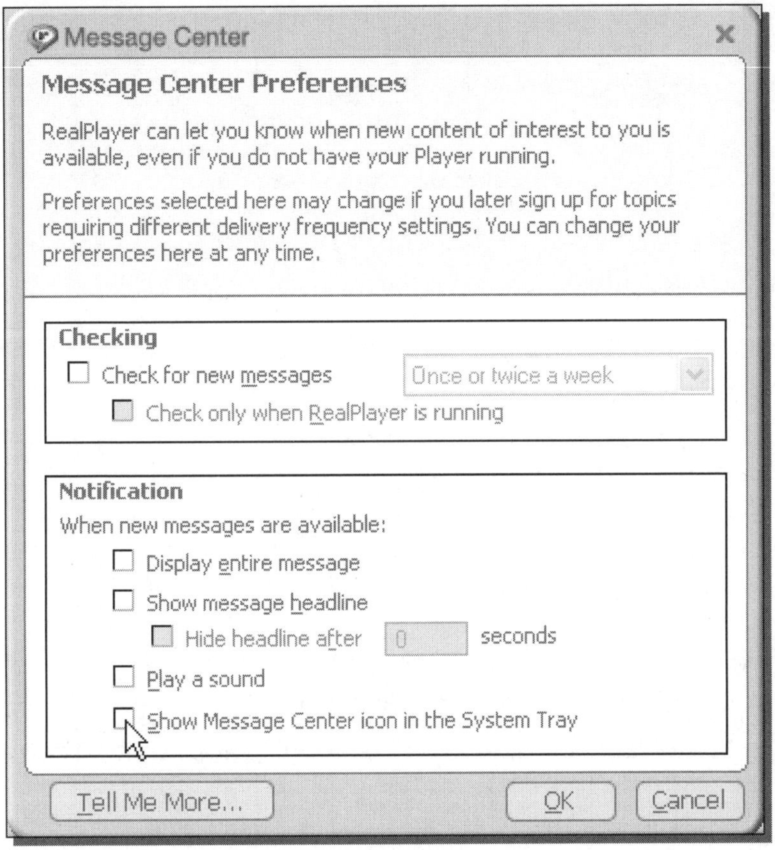

FIGURE 9-10: Disabling Message Center features.

behavior can be frustrating, because disabling the program with the system configuration utility is impossible. The only way to get control of Windows Messenger is from the inside, just as with RealPlayer. Although you have to go inside the program to change the settings, doing so with Windows Messenger is slightly easier than with RealPlayer because there is only one setting that has to be changed. In order to change that setting, follow these steps:

1. Open Windows Messenger by clicking its icon in the system tray or going to the Start Menu, expanding All Programs, and selecting Windows Messenger.

2. Once Windows Messenger is loaded, click the Tools menu bar item and select Options.

3. When the Options window is displayed, click the Preferences tab.

4. On the Preferences tab, you will find a check box that says "Run Windows Messenger When Windows Starts." Uncheck that check box, as shown in Figure 9-11.

FIGURE 9-11: Windows Messenger preferences.

5. After you have unchecked the box, click the OK button and exit the application. You are now finished. Windows Messenger will never be started automatically again.

As you can see, stopping sneaky programs from starting up automatically requires you to go into the programs options/preferences/settings. Once you are inside a program's settings, you have to uncheck any options of features that start up automatically. Most programs, such as Windows Messenger, are easy to disable from starting up automatically from within the preferences. However, other programs, such as RealPlayer, require a little more work, as you have to disable Automatic Updates and several Message Center features. The best way to stop other sneaky programs that keep starting up automatically after you try to remove them using the System Configuration Utility is to dig through the program's settings. Look in the program's Help file for information on how to disable automatic startup if you are stuck. If you cannot find any information, try searching on the Web for information or post a request for help on one of the various computer support Web sites, such as TweakXP.com's Support Forum, located at http://forum.tweakxp.com.

Customizing startup programs for different users

Windows handles the startup programs differently for each user. Certain programs may start up for one user but not for another. All of these settings are stored in the System Registry. With the help of the registry editing utility, regedit, you can manually change these entries.

But first, a word about the structure and where the startup programs are located in the registry. The registry stores startup information in two places for every user. It stores which programs will start for a specific user under the user's registry entry. It also stores a list of programs that will start automatically in the local machine entry. All of the programs listed in this entry will start automatically for all users on the computer.

Now that you know the two different types of startup items, user-specific and all user entries, you can begin hacking the registry to change the startup programs. First, you will find out how to modify the startup programs for all users, then you will learn how to modify the startup programs for individual users.

To modify all user's startup programs, you will need to start up the Registry Editor and follow these steps:

1. If you have not already done so, start up the Registry Editor by clicking the Start button and selecting Run. Then type **regedit** in the text box and click the OK button.

2. Once the Registry Editor is started, expand the entry labeled HKEY_LOCAL _MACHINE. Then scroll through the list and expand the entry labeled SOFTWARE. Scroll through the list again until you locate Microsoft and expand it. Then scroll through the list once again and expand Windows. Next, you will want to expand CurrentVersion. After you have gotten this far, you just have to expand Run and you will see a list of all of the startup programs, as shown in Figure 9-12.

Caution

Keep in mind that if you delete a program entry, there is no way to undo the action. I highly recommend that you create a restore point, as was reviewed in the introduction, so in case you accidentally remove a critical program, it can be easily undone.

3. If you want to remove a startup program, just right-click the name and select Delete.

4. If you want to add an additional startup program, right-click the white background on the right-hand side and select New and then select String Value. Type in a name for the entry and then press Enter. After you have the new entry named, right-click it again and select Modify. Then enter the path to the executable file in the value box and click the OK button.

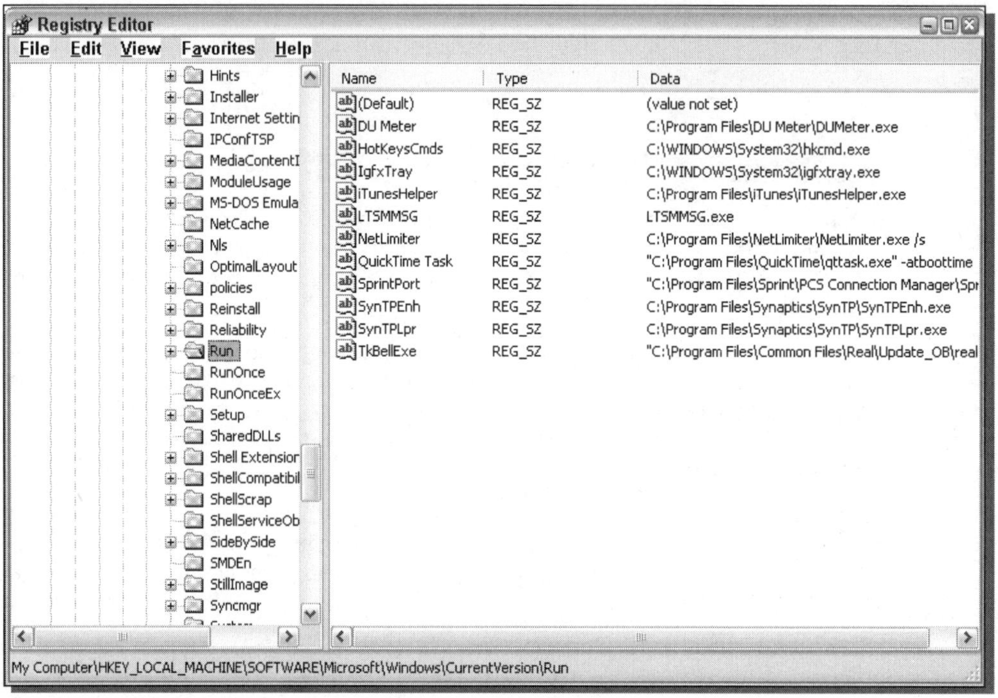

FIGURE 9-12: Registry Editor, showing all user startup programs.

That's it. You now know how to add and remove programs that will start up for all users on the computer. The steps for modifying the startup programs for specific individual users are very similar. The only difference is you have to go to a different place in the registry. Follow these steps to modify user-specific startup programs:

1. First, the easiest way to edit a specific user's startup programs is to log into their account.

2. Then, once you are logged into the user's account, you will want to start up Registry Editor again by clicking the Start button, selecting Run, and then typing **regedit** in the text box. Click the OK button.

3. After Registry Editor is open, you will want to navigate to the HKEY_CURRENT_USER entry and expand it. Then scroll through the list and expand Software. After expanding Software, scroll through the list again and select Microsoft. Then expand the Windows entry and then the CurrentVersion entry. After a little more scrolling, you will find the Run entry. This is where all of the startup information for a specific user is stored.

4. Add and remove string values from this section, as was indicated in step 4 of the previous list, to modify the startup programs.

Other Time-Saving Tips

The preceding paragraphs covered the largest factors in slow loading time, but a few other small tips can save you additional time. These tips, individually, do not save a lot of time, but when they are applied in combination, they can really add up. Additionally, if you are running Windows XP on a computer that is fairly old, these tips will help you significantly decrease your loading time even further.

Assigning alternative IP addresses

One of the most common network-related delays occurs in the last moments of the system startup. The majority of computer users use dynamic network card configuration. There is nothing wrong with this feature, but under certain configurations, the user can experience delays when getting an IP address.

Every time you turn on your computer, it has to set up the IP configuration. Often, this setup can result in your computer pausing for moments during the loading process. The delay is a result of your PC waiting for the DHCP server (a DHCP server dynamically assigns addresses to computers connected to a network), which is the provider of the network information, to respond. In other situations, a user can experience a delay when a DHCP server is not present on the network.

If you use a dialup connection to the Internet, your computer will rely on getting a dynamic IP address from your service provider when you connect. When you first turn on your computer, it will search for a DHCP server to get an address for the local networking components of the operating system. This is occurring when your computer is still in the early boot stages and is not connected to your dialup ISP (Internet Service Provider). Because you are not connected to a network that has a DHCP server, such as when you are dialed up to your Internet provider, your computer may experience a delay, as the computer is searching for a DHCP server when there really is none available.

Note This hack will only work for users that have network cards and modems installed. It does not apply to users that just have modem connections to the Internet.

One easy solution to this problem is to assign alternative information to your network card. This task is actually pretty easy, as it does not require any major tampering. Follow these steps to specify an alternative IP configuration for your computer:

1. First, get into Network Properties. This can be accomplished by going to the Control Panel through the Start Menu.

2. Once you are in the Control Panel, make sure that you are in the Classic View, as shown in Figure 9-13, and open Network Connections. If you are not in Classic View, just click the button on the left that states Switch to Classic View, as shown in Figure 9-14.

FIGURE 9-13: Control Panel Classic View, showing the Network Connections icon.

3. Now that you are in the Network Connections window, you will see a list of network adapters on your computer. Right-click the icon to which your network connection is hooked up and select Properties.

4. Doing so will launch a new window that lists the different protocols installed on the network card. Click the Internet Protocol (TCP/IP) to select it. Then click the Properties button.

5. Once the Internet Protocol (TCP/IP) Properties window is displayed, click the Alternative Configuration tab. This is where you will have to enter in your data.

6. First, you will have to click the User Configured radio button to allow the text boxes to be edited.

7. Next, type in an IP address for your computer that will be used for the sake of speed in the event that your computer cannot get a DHCP address because you are using a dialup Internet connection. I recommend you use **192.168.1.X**. Replace X with any unique number for each computer between 2 and 254. The exact IP address numbers that you choose do not matter. You just want to have a valid IP address filled in so that your

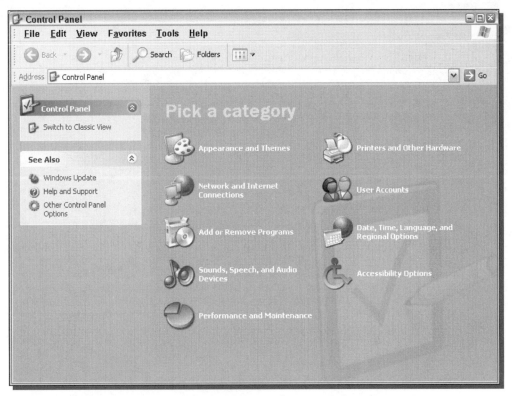

FIGURE 9-14: Control Panel Category view highlighting where to switch to classic view.

computer does not waste too much time looking for a DHCP address when there is no DHCP server giving out the address on your network.

8. Then, type in **255.255.255.0** as your Subnet Mask.

9. Your Default Gateway should be set to **192.168.1.1** because that is a valid gateway address. As I mentioned earlier, the exact numbers do not matter. We just want to have the computer assign some value instead of spending time searching when it will not find a DHCP server.

10. Then, enter in what your DNS servers should be. You can ask your ISP what they should be. But this information really isn't essential, as this configuration will almost never be used to connect to the Internet. It is just a default fallback in the rare case that you are having networking trouble. Feel free to leave these fields blank, as well as the WINS fields.

11. Click the OK button and then click the OK button for the network properties screen.

That's it; you are now finished.

Turning off the logon music

The music that Windows XP plays every time I log on is something that, frankly, I can do without. Hearing the tunes was really cool back when most people didn't have soundcards in their computers. But nowadays, everyone has a soundcard and the logon music is starting to get old. Additionally, having it play slows down your system's loading. Less is more, and when your computer has to load a 500KB media file to play, it slows things down. I would highly recommend you disable the logon music. To do so, follow these steps:

1. Go to the Control Panel and select the Sounds and Audio Devices icon from the classic Control Panel view.

2. Once the control has loaded, click the Sounds tab.

FIGURE 9-15: Sounds and Audio Devices Properties.

3. Locate the Program Events scrollbox. Look for Start Windows by scrolling through the list and click it to select it, as shown in Figure 9-15.

4. Then, locate the Sounds drop-down box and click the down arrow on the right to expand it. Scroll to the top of the list and select (None).

5. Click OK and you are finished.

That wasn't too bad. Plus, you just shaved another second or two off your loading time.

Summary

Throughout this chapter, you found out how to remove unnecessary steps from your startup procedure and method to cut the fat from the system load and make your computer load faster. You also learned how to automatically log users on and how to remove their passwords. Also touched on was the topic of removing startup programs as well as the sneaky programs that will further decrease loading time. Also discussed were other time-saving tips that offer even more ways to get that loading time down.

Ever wonder what the XP in Windows XP stands for? It stands for "experiences." This next chapter is completely dedicated to enhancing your experiences with Windows XP. It will concentrate on making the system more responsive. You will be working with making changes to the way the file system works, as well as changing settings for the user interface to improve your Windows eXPerience.

Making Your Computer More Responsive

N ow that the first two parts of the system startup are optimized, it is time to work on making your Windows experience better. This chapter will concentrate on different ways to make your computer more responsive and faster. First, it will talk about ways that the file system can run faster. This section will show you how to hack the System Registry and disable some extra features of the file system.

Once you have mastered the file system, the next section will show you how to make your menus pop up quicker, which will make your computer appear to be running significantly faster.

The next section will concentrate on all of the performance settings that are built into Windows XP. A handful of settings will, when disabled, provide you with a much faster experience. Although these options often take away visual effects and aspects of Windows XP, this section will help you find the right balance between the visual effects and a fast experience.

The last section of this chapter will show you how to remove one of the extra features built into Windows XP that does more harm than good, the indexing service. The service was designed to make it faster to search for files on your hard drive. This sounds great, but for users that rarely search their drive for files, this service becomes unnecessary and eats up a lot of system resources too.

Now that you know what this chapter will cover, you are ready to dive in.

Speeding up file browsing and access

You can speed up system access to a file and the system's browsing time through the files in several ways. So far, this book has already talked about defragmenting your drive, which will speed up accessing and browsing time. In addition, a few other things can be done to speed up how the file system works.

Making the file system run faster is easy. All you have to do is follow the next two sections, which will guide you through the steps of hacking the System Registry to change the file system settings. These settings will disable aspects of the file system that are not critical to the system and will help you with your system performance.

Before you go any further, be aware that the following speed tips for the file system will work only for the NTFS file system. If you do not know what file system your system is running on, you can go to My Computer and right-click your hard drive and select Properties. This will bring up the Local Disk (C:) Properties window, which will tell you the type of file system your hard drive is running. If your hard drive is running FAT32, these tips will not work for you.

In my opinion, NTFS is a far better file system. It has many advanced security features and also performs better on many machines. If you are still running FAT32, or for some odd reason your computer came preinstalled with FAT32, consider converting your hard disk to NTFS.

Tip Converting your drive to NTFS is a snap. Open up Command Prompt by clicking the Start button and selecting Run. Type **cmd** in the box and click OK to start up it up. Then at a prompt, type in **convert c: /fs:ntfs** and press Enter to start. If you want to convert a different drive letter, just replace the c: with the drive letter that you want. For example, if you want to convert your d drive, then you will have to type **convert d: /fs:ntfs**. The actual conversion process will take a little while, especially on large drives. Keep in mind that once you convert to NTFS, you cannot convert back to FAT32.

Now that the requirements are cleared up, you are all ready to get started.

Disabling the file access timestamp

Every time you access a file, or a program on the system accesses a file, the file system keeps track of when it was accessed. This feature can be useful if you are interested in finding out when a file was last read. Sometimes a program might find this information useful. For example, the Defragmenting application could use the access timestamps; it would be able to decide what the most frequently accessed files are and would then be able to put them on a fast part of the disk.

So, disabling the file access timestamp would obviously not be beneficial to the Defragmenting app. But the loss would not be a big one. Usually, when you defragment your drive, you will want the entire application files placed together on a disk for optimal speed. Defragmenting based solely on access timestamp will not give you a sizeable performance increase.

For systems that have many (several thousand) files and folders, disabling the access timestamp will give you a noticeable performance increase. Every time you open a file, the system has to write to the file and update its access timestamp. According to Microsoft, disabling the file access timestamp will help most systems with more than 70,000 folders. Nevertheless, based on my experiences and the experiences of others that have used this tip, it can still help users that have a fraction of that number.

The process for disabling the file access timestamp is quite easy. All that is required is one quick change in the System Registry. To do so, follow these steps:

1. Click the Start button and select Run. Then type **regedit** in the textbox and click OK.

2. This will start up the Registry Editor and will allow you to edit the file system settings. Once the Registry Editor has loaded, navigate to the file system settings by expanding HKEY_LOCAL_MACHINE, SYSTEM, CurrentControlSet, Control, and then FileSystem.

3. Depending on your system, you may see an entry called NtfsDisableLastAccessUpdate. If your system has this entry already listed, skip to the next step. If you do not see this entry, don't worry; just create it by right-clicking and selecting New and then DWORD Value, as shown in Figure 10-1. Key in **NtfsDisableLastAccessUpdate** for the name.

4. Now, modify the DWORD value. Right-click the name of the entry and select Modify. Then type a **1** in the box to disable the last access update feature.

5. Then click OK and restart your computer. The changes will be in effect.

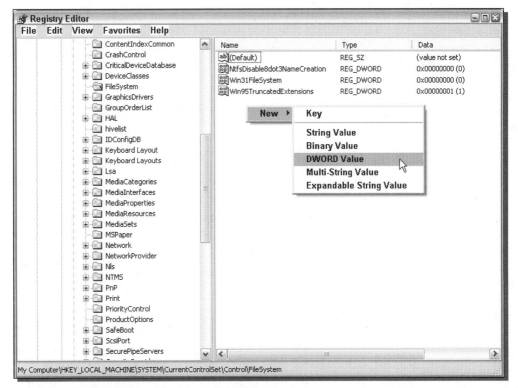

FIGURE **10-1: Registry Editor adding a new DWORD value.**

This setting will allow you to experience much faster file browsing. This hack is not without a price, as was mentioned at the beginning of this section. Disabling this feature may cause problems for certain applications, such as hard disk defragmenters and other programs. If you notice any strange behavior with your applications, try reverting to an earlier system restore point, or apply an undo script to the app.

The undo script is found in the Chapter 10 folder on the companion CD-ROM at the back of the book, called lastaccessupdate_undo.reg.

Disabling legacy filename creation

Backward compatibility allows users to upgrade to the latest version of Windows but still run many older programs that were designed for an earlier operating system. This feature is something that is very crucial to the success of Microsoft Windows. Without backward compatibility, users would be very reluctant to upgrade to the latest versions. Instead, they would be forced to wait until all of the applications that they use are rewritten to run on the new operating system.

Unfortunately, this backward compatibility is one of the reasons why Windows has become so large on the hard drive. Although it is getting packed with new features and technologies, the old features and technologies have to be included as well, even those that can slow the system down, for compatibility purposes. One example of the old features that can slow your system down is legacy filename support.

Over the years, the file system structure has changed dramatically. One of the first things that changed in the file system was the limited nature of the old MS-DOS 8.3 file system standard. The old file system would limit filenames to a maximum length of 8 characters plus a 3-character extension and also restricted what characters could be included in the name. This was something that needed to be changed to allow for greater user flexibility. Eventually, these limitations were expanded with the release of Windows 95, which bumped up the maximum filename limit to 255 characters, with a modified version of the FAT16 file system.

With the implementation of the new, longer filename support and the ability to have more characters in the filename came the added task of making sure that older applications that were written to run only with the 8.3 standard still worked on the new file system structure. This was accomplished by an extra entry in the file table. Now, for every file, there are two names saved. One is a real long filename and the other is a short 8-character version so that older programs will still be able to access the file.

The extra filename that has to be saved can cause decreased performance when you are working with the file system. Disabling this old feature can give you an extra boost that will make browsing through your files faster.

Keep in mind that disabling the old compatibility feature comes with one downside. Applications on your computer that depend on the old 8.3 standard to run will stop running and will give you errors when you try to run them. Although this technology is more than

10 years old, several popular applications, mentioned in the following paragraphs, still depend on the old standard. Unfortunately, in the software world, some companies don't bother fixing things if they aren't broken to increase the performance of the user's computers. For the most part, they do not have to worry about it because Microsoft supports the lazy programmers by leaving these old, inefficient features in the operating system.

Even though a few applications will have difficulties when this feature is disabled, the majority of users can still disable this feature and have no problems. Basically, you just have to watch out for problem applications. One type of program that has the most problems when the 8.3 standard is disabled are installer applications that many software developers use to get their programs up and running on your computer. For some reason, a few installers are still programmed using old 16-bit technology, which depends on the short filename compatibility feature to function.

Users frequently run into this error with Symantec's AntiVirus software. According to Symantec, users may receive an error stating "1639. Invalid command line argument" when they install certain versions of Symantec's software. For users of Symantec software who want to disable the old support for greater performance, the company recommends that they enable the 8.3-standard filename compatibility support when the software is being installed and then disable it once the software is installed. The software should then work fine.

That basic Symantec approach can be applied to any situations that you may run into when applications are being installed and errors received. Just enable the 8.3-standard filename compatibility support during the install, and then disable it once again after the install is complete.

That simple workaround will work for 95 percent of the problems that you will encounter when the 8.3 standard filename compatibility is disabled. The remaining few will encounter problems when the applications are running or trying to run. These applications are usually very old 16-bit applications. (Applications are now 32-bit and there are already 64-bit applications starting to pop up.) Either that, or the apps are just not programmed very well. If you have an old application that refuses to run when the compatibility feature is disabled, consider upgrading to a new version of the application to see if that will help. If it still does not work, then you will be in the position of having to keep the legacy support enabled.

Now that you are aware of the possible problems that can be caused by disabling the legacy filename standard, and also know what to do if you experience any, you are ready to disable the feature. Disabling the legacy support is not as easy as clicking a button, but is not very difficult either. Follow these steps to disable/enable this feature:

1. Click the Start Menu and select Run, then type **regedit** in the box and click OK. This will start up the Registry Editor.

2. Once the Registry Editor has loaded, navigate to the file system settings by expanding HKEY_LOCAL_MACHINE, SYSTEM, CurrentControlSet, Control, and then FileSystem.

3. Look for the key that is named NtfsDisable8dot3NameCreation and right-click it and select Modify, as shown in Figure 10-2.

4. In the Edit DWORD Value box, type in a **1** and click the OK button.

5. Then, restart your computer and you are done!

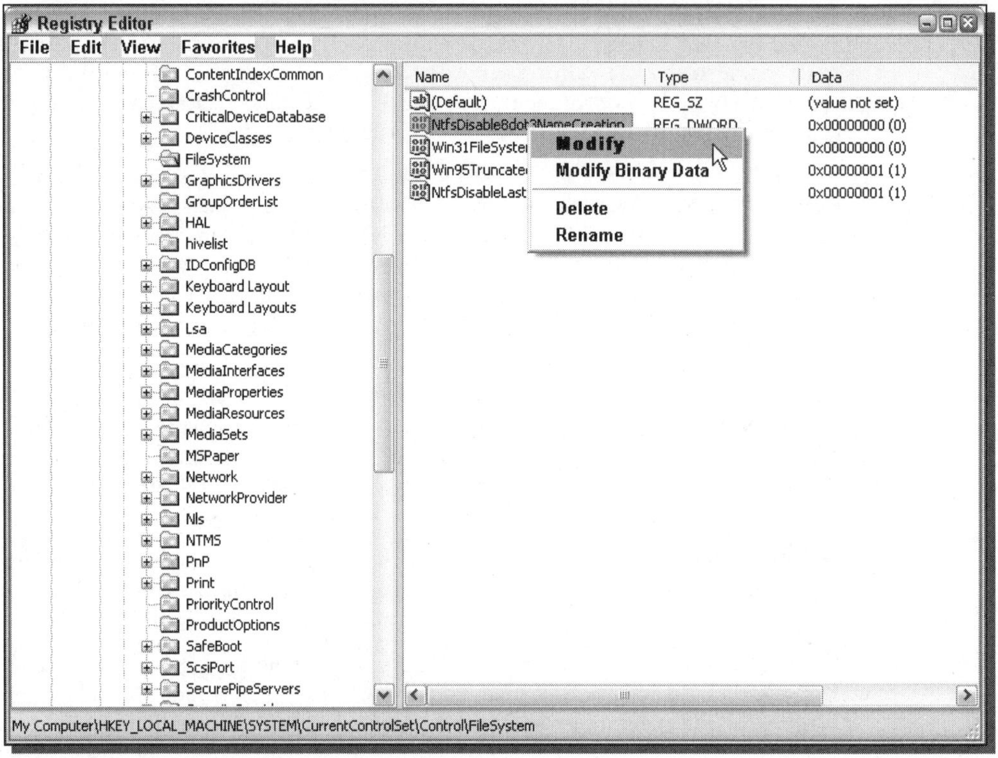

FIGURE 10-2: Changing NTFS 8.3 compatibility with regedit.

Once your computer restarts, the new settings will be in effect. If you ever experience any of the aforementioned problems with older applications and installers, the first thing you should do is re-enable the compatibility feature to see if it is the culprit.

On the CD To make this easier for you to do, I have included a registry file on the companion CD in the Chapter 10 folder so that you can just import the registry file into the registry instead of repeating all of the preceding steps to enable and disable the feature.

Speeding Up the User Interface

Various features built into Windows XP slow down the performance of the system. The new look and effects degrade overall system performance. If you have a very fast computer, leaving these features enabled will not slow down your computer very much, but you will still notice a difference if you have some of them disabled.

On top of taming some of the new features, you can also fine-tune some of the other settings, such as menu delay, to make your computer more responsive by eliminating unnecessary delays.

The following paragraphs show you how to do this—so dig in!

Reducing the menu delay

Whenever you move your mouse over an item that expands in the Start Menu, you have to wait for the system to expand that menu and show you the submenu. By default, your system is configured to wait 400 milliseconds before it automatically expands any submenu. Navigating through the Start Menu is when you will notice this delay the most.

Using the system Registry Editor, you can hack the System Registry to modify the amount of time that the computer waits before it automatically expands a submenu.

The best value for the menu delay is different for every person. You might like the submenu to show up instantly, although others might like it to appear after the mouse hovers over the item for a little while, or vice versa. The best way to fine-tune this setting is by testing it a few times with different values. If you want the submenu to show up instantly, then set the delay to 0. This may have a bad effect for some that do not have very fast computers, as just dragging your mouse over the Start Menu will cause your computer to open up every submenu over which the mouse is dragged. Doing so will cause your computer to do a lot of work, and if your computer's hardware is slow, then everything on your computer will slow down as a result when the menus are expanding. If you have a fast computer, then your computer will have no problem keeping up. I prefer to set my menu delay to 100 milliseconds because this does not open up any menu that the mouse moves over but still gives a very fast response.

Now that you know a little about what the best values for the delay are, follow these steps to change the menu delay on your computer:

1. Start up the Registry Editor by clicking the Start Menu and selecting Run. Then type **regedit** in the box and click OK.

2. Once the Registry Editor has opened, navigate to HKEY_CURRENT_USER, Control Panel, and then Desktop.

3. Look for the MenuShowDelay entry and right-click it and select Modify, as shown in Figure 10-3.

4. Enter the new value in the box and click OK.

5. Close the Registry Editor and restart your computer to see the new changes.

On the CD In the Chapter 10 folder, you will find an undo script to reset the menu delay back to the default value of 400ms.

You may have to repeat the preceding directions a few times so that you get the menu delay just the way you like it.

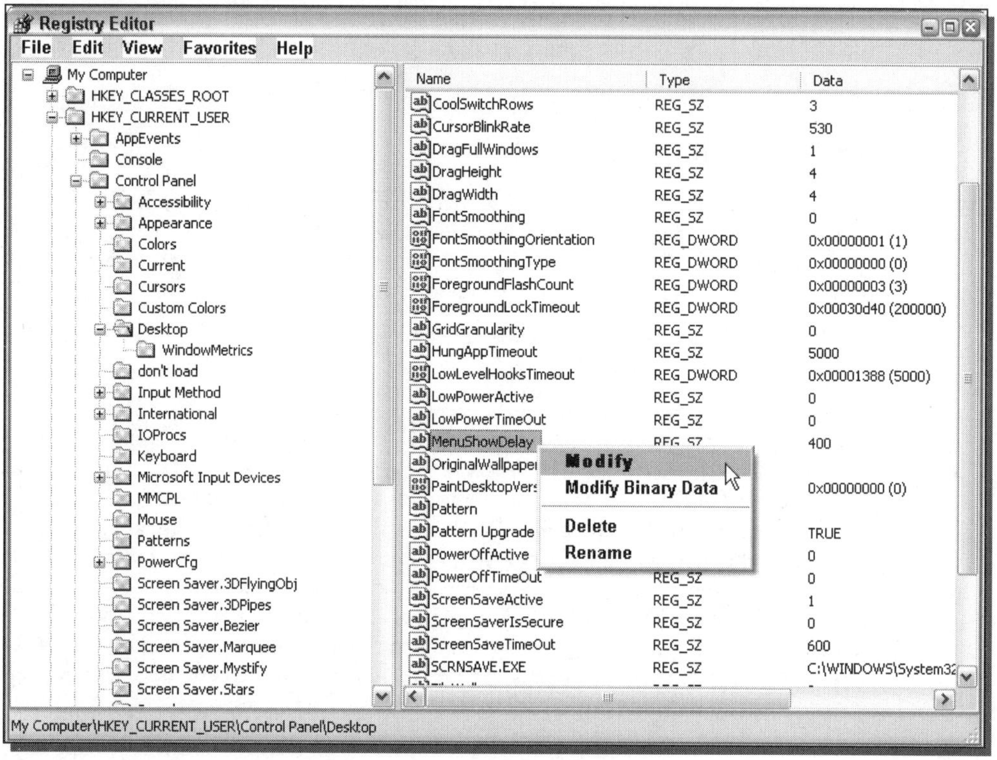

FIGURE 10-3: Registry Editor showing how to edit MenuShowDelay.

If you ever have problems after changing your menu delay, such as the submenus never showing up, then go back into the System Registry and make sure that you did not type in a large value by accident. Remember that the default value is 400 milliseconds, in case you want to revert to the default.

Working with the performance options

All of the new visual effects that Windows XP includes can be customized so that you can turn off the ones you don't need or like. This capability allows you to find a balance between performance and appearance.

Some of the visual effects are very taxing on systems that are not very powerful. This section will help you identify the graphical effects that are slowing down your system and will show you how to manage them.

Hidden away under System Properties is a Settings panel that allows you to enable and disable each effect or feature. Follow these steps to get to the Settings screen:

1. Right-click the My Computer icon in the Start Menu or on the desktop and select Properties.

2. Then, click the Advanced tab and click Settings under the Performance section.

3. This will launch the Performance Options screen, as shown in Figure 10-4. Click the Visual Effects tab, if the tab is not already displayed.

4. Now that you have the Visual Effects settings screen on your screen, you will notice four different settings: Let Windows Choose What's Best for My Computer, Adjust for Best Appearance, Adjust for Best Performance, and Custom. The Let Windows Choose What's Best for My Computer setting does not seem to work very well, because I have not seen Windows choose to disable anything on any computer, even on some very old machines. The Adjust for Best Appearance setting enables all options, whereas the Adjust for Best Performance setting disables all options. The Custom setting is the best setting to use on your computer. Click the Custom radio button to enable this setting.

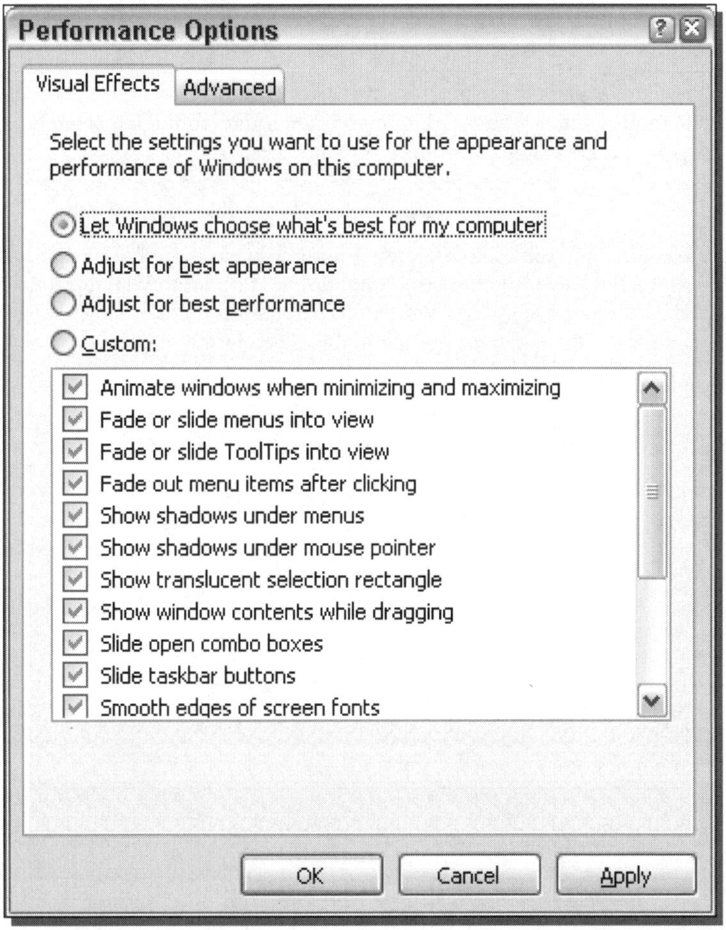

FIGURE 10-4: Performance options.

5. Now you will be able to manually check and uncheck the various boxes listed below for each of the different effects. Refer to the following list for recommendations on each of the effects. Once you are finished, click the OK buttons and you are set.

The following is a list of different effects, along with my recommendations on what to do for the best balance between appearance and performance.

- *Animate windows when minimizing and maximizing*: This effect will animate the title bar along with the border by enlarging and shrinking instead of instantly changing the size of the active window. This effect is not very heavy on the system. When the effect is disabled, no change can be detected in the system, such as the amount of memory used and the CPU usage. You would think that the CPU usage would decrease, but compared to when the effect is disabled, the usage of the CPU to minimize and maximize a window is the same. Even though there is no performance change in the numbers, your system will appear to be running faster because the windows will instantly resize and be displayed. Because of that, I recommend that you disable this effect.

- *Fade or slide menus into view*: This effect allows the menus that pop up throughout the system to fade in. You will experience this when you navigate through a menu bar or when you right-click something. This effect does not affect the performance of the system except for when the effect is called on. Some users that have older computers and slower video cards can experience better performance with this effect off.

- *Fade or slide ToolTips into view*: This effect will allow the yellow ToolTips in various parts of the system to slowly fade in when either an event occurs or you hold your mouse over an object. This effect has no effect on the system performance of most users, but once again, those with older systems should disable this effect for better performance.

- *Fade out menu items after clicking*: This effect will fade the submenus in the Start Menu out after you click an item within the menu. This effect, just like the other fade effects, is slower on older systems and should be disabled for best performance.

- *Show shadows under menus*: This effect will display a light shadow when pop-up menus are displayed, giving more of a 3D appearance to the flat interface, as shown in Figure 10-5. My analysis of the system data when the effect is enabled and disabled resulted in such a small difference that this effect does not matter if it is or isn't on for the average user. Also, just like the fade effects, this is something that users of older machines can disable to get better performance.

- *Show shadows under mouse pointer*: This effect allows the mouse to have that semi-3D effect. However, it is not applied to the mouse when the mouse is over certain applications, such as Microsoft Word. The shadow under the mouse seems to have no influence on the system performance for the average computer. However, just as with the shadow and fade problems mentioned earlier, older machines may have problems with this effect too.

- *Show translucent selection rectangle*: When this effect is enabled, you will see a nice-looking blue border with a semi-transparent blue interior when you drag the mouse to select items, instead of the old dotted line box as we have all seen in older versions of Windows. Figure 10-6 shows the two different types of selection rectangles. On older machines, I have seen this effect working very slowly and often interfering with the mouse's selection

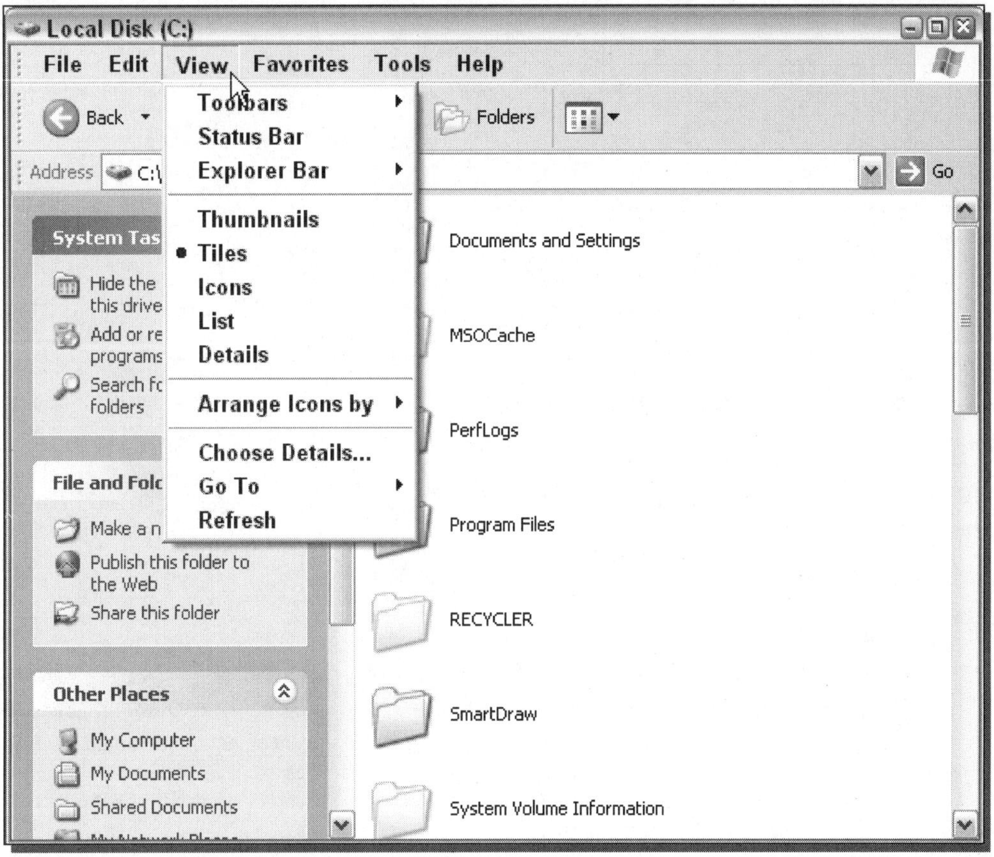

FIGURE **10-5: Shadows under menus.**

of items because it seems to use up a lot of the CPU. On the average computer, this effect presents no problems at all. If you have a slow machine, then disable this effect, but if you have an average machine, then keep it enabled and enjoy the nicer look.

- *Show window contents while dragging*: This effect will not slow down the average computer but will cause some problems for users of older machines. On my older desktop that runs Windows XP, I have disabled this effect, and the system is now much more responsive.

- *Slide open combo boxes*: This effect has no effect on performance at all. I do not see why anyone would want to disable this effect, but if you are the type of person that cannot wait an extra 50 milliseconds to view the contents of the combo box, then knock yourself out disabling this one.

- *Slide taskbar buttons*: This feature has very little effect on system performance, but it may affect system responsiveness on older machines when the machine is doing a lot of work. You will notice this when you are doing something in the background and you can slowly

FIGURE 10-6: Left: Normal selection rectangle; right: translucent selection rectangle.

see the taskbar items for open programs resizing. If you ever have that experience, go ahead and disable this effect.

- *Smooth edges of screen fonts*: This feature seems to depend more on your video card than your system. Use of any type of font smoothing will require it to do more work. On older machines, I would disable this effect. Also, if you have a cathode ray tube type monitor, you will not benefit all that much by having this enabled. The font smoothing effects, especially ClearType, work best on TFT (Thin Film Transistor, also known as Active Matrix)–based flat panel monitors.

- *Smooth-scroll list boxes*: This effect has no effect on performance based on my tests. You would have to be crazy to disable this effect, because it is just so cool.

- *Use background image for each folder type*: This effect has a small effect on the performance of browsing through folders. On faster computers you won't notice anything, but on the average and older computers, this is something that you can live without. On top of that, some of the background images are so light that they do not show up on some monitors, such as my old laptop's LCD panel that does not have good contrast with light colors. My advice is to get rid of them.

- *Use common tasks in folders*: This feature is nice–looking and makes Windows Explorer look different but it really is not very useful. It was born in Windows 98 SE and now has completely evolved into some massive navigation aid. I never find myself using the items on this menu. When you go to My Computer, it gives you the option to View System Information, Add or Remove Programs, or Change a Setting under the System Tasks block. It never seems to cross my mind to get to these features this way. Unless you are a beginner computer user, then go ahead and disable this feature. It will speed up your browsing through folders and will also allow you to view more files at once on your screen.

■ *Use drop shadows for icon labels on the desktop*: I have noticed that some older computers with bad video cards can benefit from this feature being disabled. Personally, this feature is a nice addition to Windows XP and I would always leave it enabled. However, if you don't like the look, disable it and you will see a small benefit.

■ *Use visual styles on windows and buttons*: This effect is what makes Windows XP look so different from older versions of Windows. If you disable this effect, the whole new interface of Windows XP will be gone. If you do not like the new look and are one of the people that feel the interface was made for a child, disable this feature and you will see a big performance increase. But beware, the system will look like Windows 2000, as Figure 10-7 shows. The amount of free RAM will increase by a megabyte or two and the system will be much more responsive.

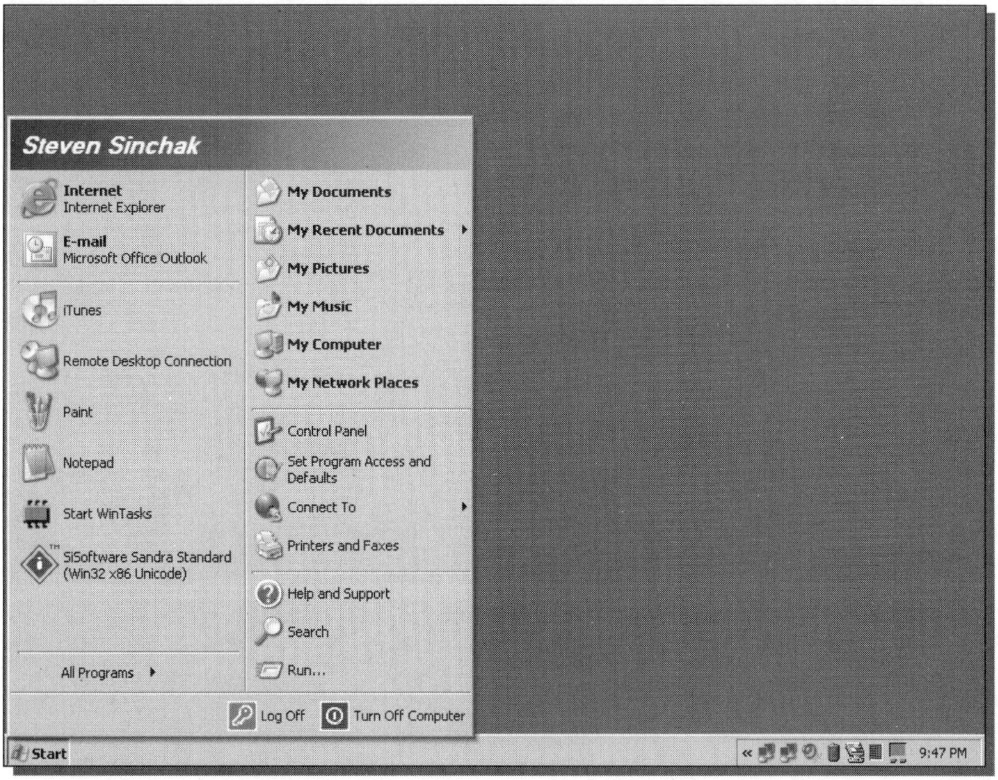

FIGURE 10-7: Windows XP naked.

Disable Indexing Service

The Windows Indexing Service is a service that is designed to index all of the files on your computer into a database. Your computer can then search through all of your files faster. The idea behind the service is great; it will drastically cut down on the amount of time that is needed to search your hard drive. Although this is a great benefit, you have to consider the downside of this feature. In order to create a database of files, the service has to continuously monitor the files on your computer and import basic file details into its database when new files are found. The monitoring is not always done in real time, but at times you will notice it running. The most common symptom of this service working is when you are reading something on your computer and all of a sudden your hard drive starts making a lot of noise as if it is working really hard. That is because it is working hard to update the Indexing Service's database.

Just like any other service that starts up when the system does, the Indexing Service takes up memory—quite a bit of memory compared to other services. In fact, the service takes up exactly 4364KB of memory when the service first starts up on your computer. Eventually, about 30 seconds after the service has started, the amount of memory used decreases to 306KB. This

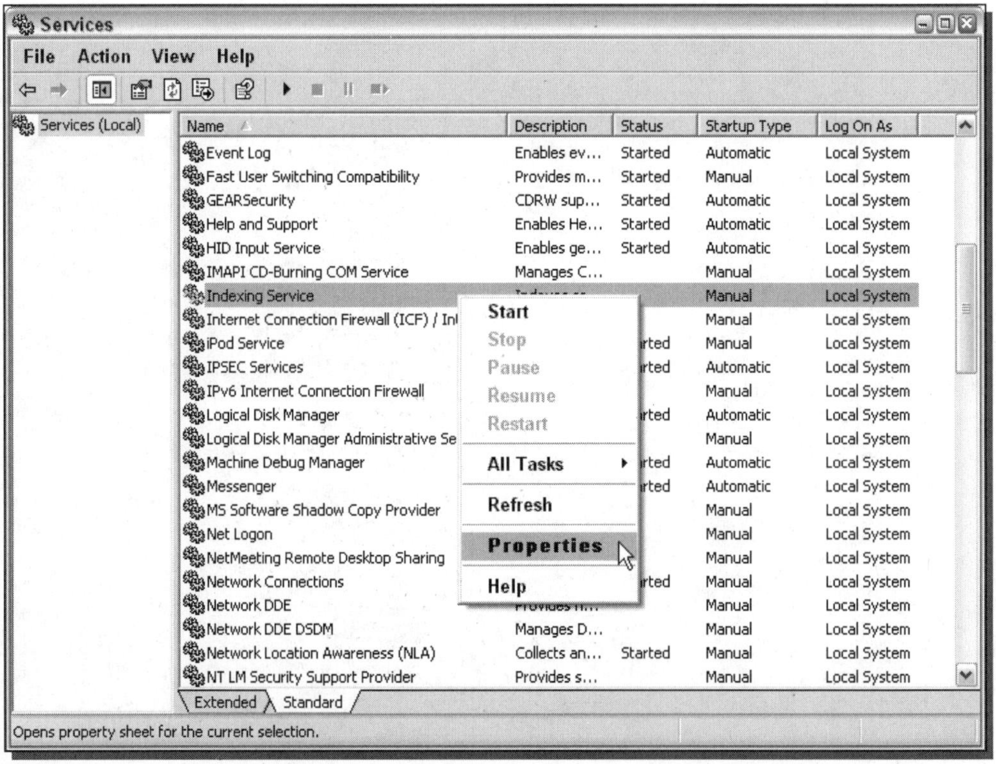

FIGURE 10-8: Indexing Service Properties.

looks good, but after you use your computer for a little while, the memory usage will start to creep up again. On average, the service takes up about 1316KB of memory.

When the service is idle on your computer, it is just taking up memory. Also, it is running at the lowest CPU priority, so you can be sure that it won't interfere with other applications very much at all.

Personally, I rarely use the Search feature of Windows XP and would much rather disable the Indexing Service and take the performance hit the one time every few months that I actually do need to search for a file. In return, I get more free memory space that can be used for more useful services and applications. Follow these steps if you rarely search for files and would like some more free memory:

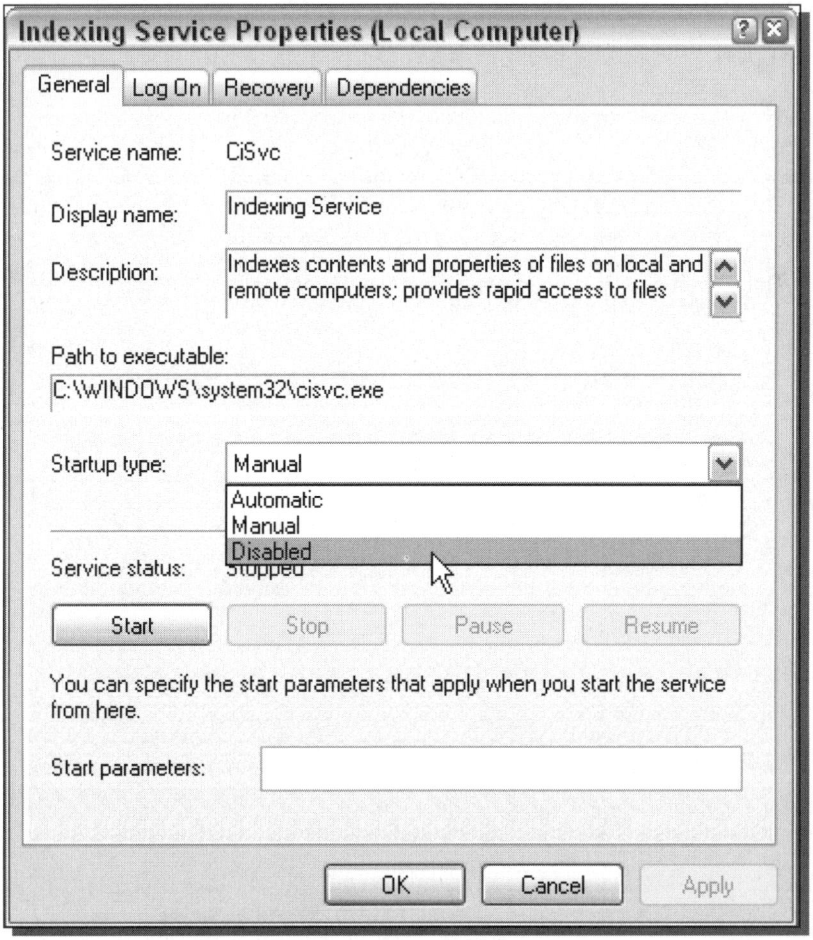

FIGURE 10-9: Setting the Indexing Service to Disabled.

1. Click the Start Menu and select Run. Then key in **services.msc** in the box and click OK.

2. This will start up the Services snap-in control, where you can manage all of the services on the system. Look for the Indexing Service on the list, right-click it, and select Properties, as shown in Figure 10-8.

3. Once you see Indexing Service Properties, click the Stop button, if the service is already running. Then, click the Startup Type drop-down box and select Disabled, as shown in Figure 10-9.

4. Click the OK button and you are finished!

Now you don't have to worry about the Indexing Service using any more of your memory.

Summary

The things you have done to your computer in this chapter may make seemingly minor changes to the performance of your computer, but these hacks do work and you will benefit from them. Tweaking the file system settings, removing unneeded delays, fine-tuning the visual settings, and getting rid of seldom-used or never-used services are all valuable skills to have when you are trying to make your computer run at top performance.

Speeding Up Your Computer

T he last three chapters have all been about speeding up your computer. Chapter 8 discussed speeding up the boot; Chapter 9 examined speeding up the startup; and Chapter 10 explored hacks that will make your computer more responsive. Now, Chapter 11 will show you several cool hacks and tips that will speed up your computer even further by increasing the performance of your applications.

To do so, you will be working with the many different parts of the operating system that affect the speed of your applications. The amount of memory the system has, how the system is using that memory, the location of the files on the hard disk, and system performance-enhancing features are all factors that influence the performance of your applications.

This chapter will guide you through the steps of optimizing all of these factors so that your system will be running in top shape.

Working with the Windows Prefetcher

What is the Prefetcher? It is a very nifty component of Windows XP that can seemingly read your mind and will start loading your program seconds before you actually start it to boost the startup of the application.

Although the Prefetcher keeps track of the applications that you run, creates optimized copies of them, and stores them in a special cache on your computer, this special cache is simply a location on your hard disk that has no, or very few, file fragments and stores application setting files. The next time you start your program, Windows will load it out of the Prefetcher cache, which is what causes the application to start up quicker.

If you really want to investigate this matter further, take a look at the Prefetcher cache. It is located in the Windows directory inside the Prefetcher folder. You will notice that the cache does not have an exact copy of each application because the files are a fraction of the size of the actual application executable file. Rather, it just has fragments of applications that are used to boost the performance of the startup.

The Windows Prefetcher is the same Prefetcher that was discussed previously in Chapter 8 with the boot defrag. The Prefetcher constantly monitors what applications you are running, even during parts of the bootup. That information is then passed on to help the disk defragmenter optimize the boot files.

The Prefetcher is a very complex component. The majority of the settings can be changed by hacking the registry; however, due to a lack of documentation on these settings, changing them without any guidance would be very risky. Thankfully, a few tips have surfaced in the vast documentation buried at Microsoft's site and revealed in Microsoft's applications.

The paragraphs that follow will explore some of these.

Hacking the registry to optimize the Prefetcher

Located inside the System Registry are the settings for the Prefetcher component of Windows XP. Several different settings can be changed, such as the mode that the Prefetcher is running in, the number of items that are tracked by the Prefetcher, and where the Prefetcher cache is located. Several more can be manipulated, as shown in Figure 11-1.

Almost all of these settings are not published in documentation available to the public. The only setting that Microsoft has said anything about is the EnablePrefetcher setting. Some users of Windows XP were having trouble with the Prefetcher, which caused problems with certain

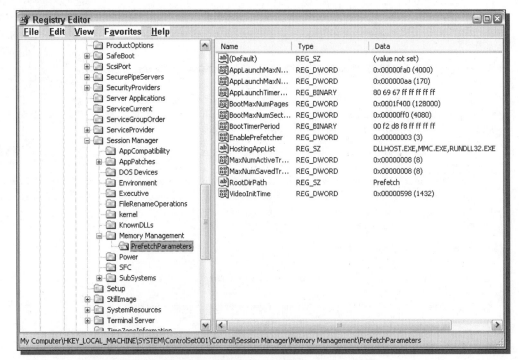

FIGURE 11-1: Registry Editor displaying the Prefetcher settings.

unknown applications, so Microsoft released information on how to disable the Prefetcher. Also, around the same time, information became available on how to disable or enable certain parts of the Prefetcher.

The Prefetcher can be either disabled or set to optimize the boot only, to optimize applications only, or to optimize both applications and the boot. By default, the Prefetcher is set to optimize both. This default mode sounds like it is the best one for all users, but some people have discovered better performance by experimenting with the different modes. To change the modes of the Prefetcher, follow these steps:

1. Start the Registry Editor by clicking the Start Menu and then selecting Run. In the text box, type **regedit**, then click the OK button.

2. This will load the Registry Editor. Once it has loaded, expand HKEY_LOCAL _MACHINE.

3. Expand SYSTEM.

4. Expand ControlSet001.

5. Expand Control next.

6. Now you will see Session Manager. Expand that as well.

7. Because you will be changing the setting for memory, expand Memory Management.

8. Finally, open PrefetchParameters and you will see all of the Prefetcher settings.

9. Locate the EnablePrefetcher doubleword value and right-click it and select Modify, as shown in Figure 11-2.

10. Once the Edit DWORD Value box is shown, update the number with the corresponding number. Which number you use depends on how you want the Prefetcher to act. Refer to Table 11-1 for all of the options and their meanings for this value.

11. Click the OK button after you have updated the value and restart your computer.

Experiment with these different settings on your computer to see which ones work best for you. I highly recommend that you do not disable your boot prefetch, as the prefetch information used by this mode is also used in other parts of the operating system to improve speed. For example, it is used by the boot defrag, which is discussed in Chapter 8.

Feel free to experiment with other settings, such as AppLaunchMaxNumPages, AppLaunchMaxNumSections, BootMaxNumPages, and BootMaxNumSections. I would leave all of the other settings alone because they are all in hexadecimal format, which can be difficult to work with. But make sure that before you do any tampering, you use system restore to create a restore point so that any problems that you may cause can be easily undone.

Accelerate specific applications with prefetch

How the prefetch system operates is often mysterious. Much about the technology is undocumented, so the general public does not know much about it. Sometimes the only way we find out about features of the operating system is when Microsoft uses them. One example of this

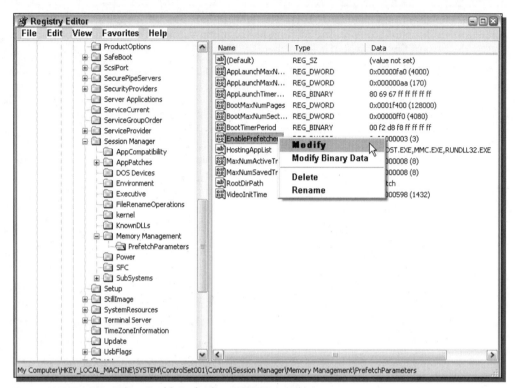

FIGURE **11-2:** Registry Editor EnablePrefetcher DWORD options.

is with the release of Windows Media Player 9.0. On top of all of the new multimedia technologies that this release brought to Windows was an insight into the unknown world of the Prefetcher. Hidden away in the shortcut to the application in the Start Menu was an application flag that appears to be an option flag for the Windows Prefetcher system.

What does the shortcut look like? `C:\Program Files\Windows Media Player\ wmplayer.exe" /prefetch:1`.

Table 11-1	EnablePrefetcher Options
Value	**Meaning**
0	Prefetching Disable
1	Application prefetch only
2	Boot prefetch only
3	Prefetch both (Default value)

The /prefetch:1 flag does not appear in any documentation released by Microsoft. The only way to investigate what this flag does is to experiment.

Because I am a very curious person, I tried to apply this flag to all of the popular programs that I use. When doing so, I noticed an increase in loading time during the second application launch, even after a reboot. It is clear that this flag positively affects the loading time of an application. How it does this is unknown, and will remain unknown unless Microsoft decides to share with us the inner workings of the Prefetcher.

During my experimentation, I have found that this option flag does not work on all applications. The applications that it does not work on tend to be programs that get the option flag confused with a file that you want it to open. For example, when you type **mspaint /prefetch:1** at the command prompt, Microsoft Paint will open, giving you an error that it can't load the prefetch bitmap file because it thinks you are trying to send it a bitmap file to open. You will experience this problem with other applications as well, but the vast majority of programs work well with the flag.

I recommend that you play around with this flag and see if it helps your applications. If you are unclear how to add the flag, follow these steps:

1. Locate the shortcut file that you are interested in modifying to use the prefetch flag.

2. Right-click the Shortcut file and select Properties.

3. Click at the end of the text in the Target textbox and type in **/prefetch:1** or any variation of this that you would like to try, such as **/prefetch:22**. If your shortcut has quotes around the path to the program, place the option flag on the outside of the quotes, as shown in Figure 11-3.

4. Click OK and that's it.

Unfortunately, no list is available of what programs will work with this and what programs will not. If you load a program after modifying a shortcut and you get an error, just remove the option flag that you added and you will be back to normal.

How much improvement in loading time you observe will vary, depending on the speed of your computer, how your PC is configured, and the like, but it's definitely worth a try.

Using the Intel Application Accelerator

The Intel Application Accelerator is a great program, released by Intel, that will boost the performance of a user's system by optimizing the flow of information between the CPU and the storage devices. This improvement is accomplished by replacing the storage drivers that come with Windows XP with drivers that are optimized for their motherboards. According to Intel, the Application Accelerator will eliminate the data storage system bottleneck on the motherboard, which will allow the CPU to be more efficient and will speed up various aspects of the system.

On top of the bottleneck solution, which improves system performance, the Application Accelerator claims to increase application and even game performance because it will increase

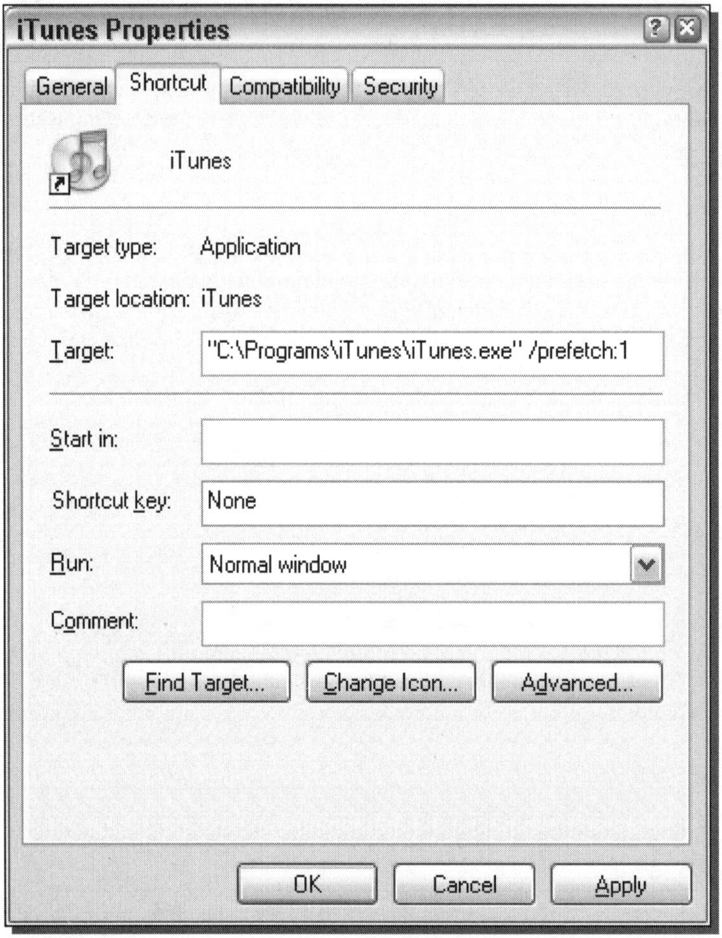

FIGURE **11-3:** Shortcut properties with prefetch option added.

the speed of disk inputs and outputs. In other words, the applications and games can read and write data faster.

Additionally, the Application Accelerator is optimized for the Intel Pentium 4 processor, and it therefore uses new high-speed Pentium 4 extensions to accomplish the high speeds. On top of this, the Application Accelerator also promises to decrease your boot time. This seems to be a by-product of the elimination of the bottleneck and faster disk reads.

But that's not all. The Intel application acceleration also includes 48-bit logical block addressing. That means that you can use hard disks larger than 137GB. In addition, the Application Accelerator will automatically detect and optimize the transfer modes of your storage devices as high as possible to ensure that your hardware is running at top speed.

The Intel Application Accelerator seems almost too good to be true. Did I mention that this utility is free too? Intel has made some very bold claims about their application. Are these claims true? Find out by reading the next section.

How well does the Intel Application Accelerator work?

The Intel Application Accelerator works surprisingly well. I never thought that a software program could improve the performance of a computer so much. According to Intel performance benchmarks, users of the Application Accelerator will significantly increase the speed of their computer. Intel tested the application accelerator by running the popular benchmark program Winbench99 on a machine with a 2.0 GHz P4 CPU. The score of the machine after installing the Intel Application Accelerator was 34 percent faster than when the Application Accelerator was not installed. Additionally, the boot time of the same computer was 58 percent faster after the program was installed.

The Application Accelerator program actually works as promised. Searching the Web, you will find hundreds of success stories for users that have installed the Application Accelerator with very good results. Users have reported their applications starting up twice as fast as before, and having many seconds shaved off of their boot time.

What are the system requirements?

Unfortunately, the Intel Application Accelerator will only run on certain systems, and your system must meet the strict requirements for it to run without causing problems. After all, the reason why it works so well is because it can optimize the storage driver to work at peak performance for a specific motherboard.

Basically, your PC must meet the following three different qualifications:

1. Your PC must be running an Intel CPU: the Pentium II, III, IIII, as well as the Celeron-based processors and Xeon series of processors. Sorry, AMD users.

2. You must have the Intel Chipset Installation Utility installed, if your chipset requires it. Visit www.intel.com/support/chipsets/inf/inf.htm to view a table of motherboard chipsets that need to be installed. It your motherboard requires it to be installed for the system to correctly identify your chipset, visit http://downloadfinder.intel .com/scripts-df/Product_Filter.asp?ProductID=816 to download a copy.

3. The last qualification to use the Intel Application Accelerator is that you must have a supported motherboard chipset. Refer to Table 11-2 to see what chipsets are supported.

Tip

If you do not know what kind of chipset your motherboard has, Intel has a free utility that will detect your chipset and display the model number for you. Visit www.intel.com/support/ chipsets/inf/chipsetid.htm to download a copy of this utility.

If your chipset is not listed, then check the Intel Application Accelerator Web site, which is located at www.intel.com/support/chipsets/IAA/.

Table 11-2   Intel Application Accelerator Compatibility

Chipset	Support
440	Not Supported
810	Supported
810E	Supported
810E2	Supported
810L	Supported
815	Supported
815E	Supported
815EM	Not Supported
815EP	Supported
815G	Supported
815EG	Supported
815P	Supported
820	Supported
820E	Supported
840	Supported
845	Supported
845E	Supported
845G	Supported
845GE	Supported
845GL	Supported
845GV	Supported
845PE	Supported
848P	Not Supported
850	Supported
850E	Supported
852GM	Not Supported
852GME	Not Supported
855GM	Not Supported
855GME	Not Supported

Chipset	Support
855MP	Not Supported
860	Supported
865G	Not Supported
865P	Not Supported
865PE	Not Supported
875P	Not Supported

Also, if your chipset is not currently supported, there is always the chance that someday Intel might add support.

Caution

If your chipset is listed on Table 11-2 as not supported and is also listed on the Intel Web page as not supported, installing the Application Accelerator on your computer will result in big problems. Doing so will screw up your computer so much that it will not boot.

Additionally, Intel Application Accelerator has been confirmed by Intel to work with Windows XP SP1 Home/Pro. Windows XP SP2 Home/Pro has not yet been officially confirmed to work on supported Intel hardware but it is still worth giving it a try. Just make sure that you are using system restore to make backups so that you can easily revert to your previous settings.

How to install Intel Application Accelerator

Installing the Intel Application Accelerator is very simple. This cool application will be running on your computer in no time if you just do the following:

1. Visit `http://downloadfinder.intel.com/scripts-df/Product_Filter .asp?ProductID=663` to download a copy of the Application Accelerator.

2. Then once you have the file downloaded, install the application by following the onscreen directions.

3. After the install is completed, reboot, and the Application Accelerator will be installed and running.

If you have a laptop that has a supported chipset, you should be aware that in the recent version of the Intel Application Accelerator, version 2.3, support for mobile devices was removed. You will have to install version 2.2.2 instead.

Fine-Tuning the Windows Paging File

The Windows paging file, also known as the swap file and virtual memory, is very important to the operation of the operating system. Providing a critical memory feature by allowing the operating system to use more random access memory (RAM) than the computer actually has allows users to use more robust programs without having to upgrade their memory.

The paging file can be thought of as a large file on the hard disk that is a collection of system memory used by open applications and operating system components. As more and more applications are started, the amount of free space in the system memory, the RAM, decreases and can eventually be completely used up. When a user starts a program and the RAM used is full, the operating system still loads an application into memory. Before it can do that, it must first make room, and so it pushes a page of low-priority memory out of the RAM and into the paging file.

The exact method that the system uses to decide what programs will stay in the physical RAM and what programs will go is unknown. However, there are several paging file hacks that will help you optimize your computer's use of the paging file. With the help of hacks to the System Registry, you can prevent certain files from being pushed into the paging as well as completely disabling the paging file.

This next section will guide you through the steps of optimizing the paging file for your computer.

Disabling the paging file

Users of computers with a large amount of RAM have the ability to stop the operating system from pushing any data out into the paging file. This will allow for the faster memory management and memory access that is physically possible for your RAM. Reading and writing directly to the RAM is always significantly faster than having to use the page file. Reading and writing to the paging file requires multiple steps and that takes time. Moreover, reading from the hard drive is nowhere as fast as reading from the RAM.

If your system has a large amount of RAM, over 1 gigabytes, then you can consider disabling the paging file. If you have less than 1 gigabyte of RAM, do not even consider disabling the paging file or else you will be running into problems.

What can happen if you disable your paging file? If you have enough RAM, then nothing. But if you do not have enough RAM, then if you run a large program such as Photoshop and are working on a large image, you will run into "out of memory" errors and the application will crash, causing you to lose all of your work. This is a pretty extreme example, but it *can* happen.

Basically, stick to the 1 gigabyte minimum and you will have no problems. But be aware that if you ever choose to run some memory-intensive applications, such as rendering a two-hour 3D movie, you could run out of memory easily.

So, now that I have warned you, you are ready to follow these steps to disable the paging file:

1. Enter System Properties, either by right-clicking the My Computer icon on the desktop and selecting Properties or by doing the same to the My Computer icon in the Start Menu.

2. Once the System Properties window has loaded, click the Advanced tab and then click the Settings button under Performance, as shown in Figure 11-4.

3. Once you are in the performance options, click the Advanced tab again.

4. Click the Change button that is located under the Virtual Memory section.

5. This will load the Virtual Memory screen. Locate and select the No Paging File radio button, as shown in Figure 11-5, under the Paging File Size for Selected Drive section.

6. Click the Set button and then click OK three times and you are finished. After you reboot, your page file will be disabled.

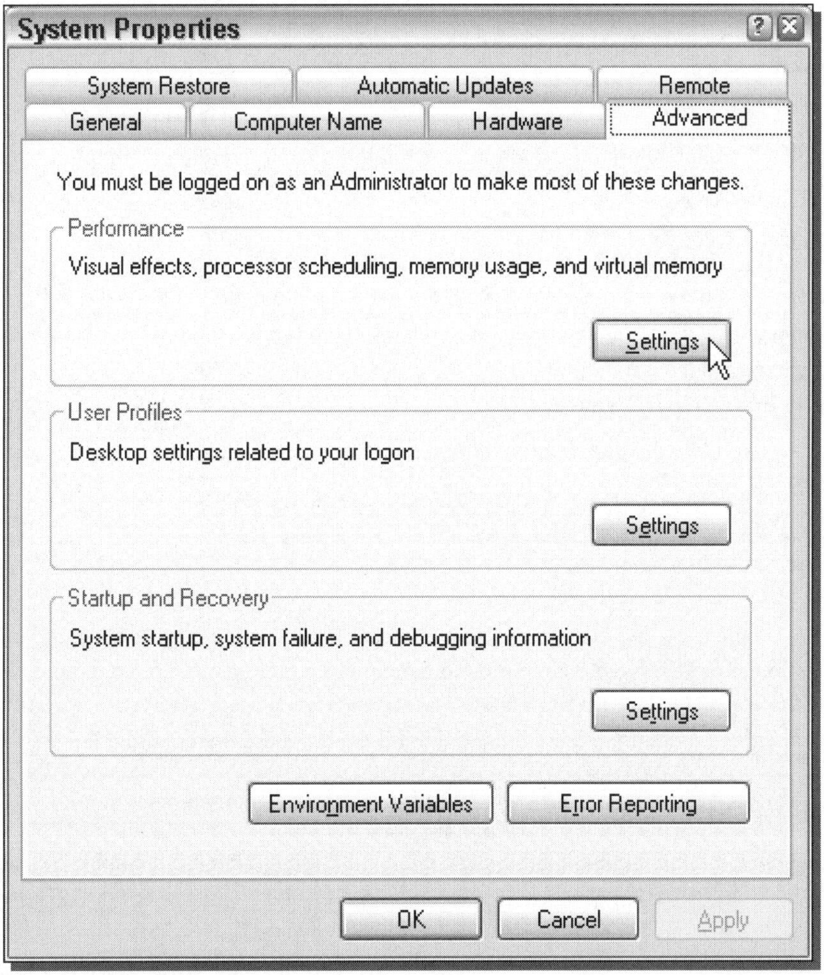

FIGURE **11-4: System Properties Advanced Settings.**

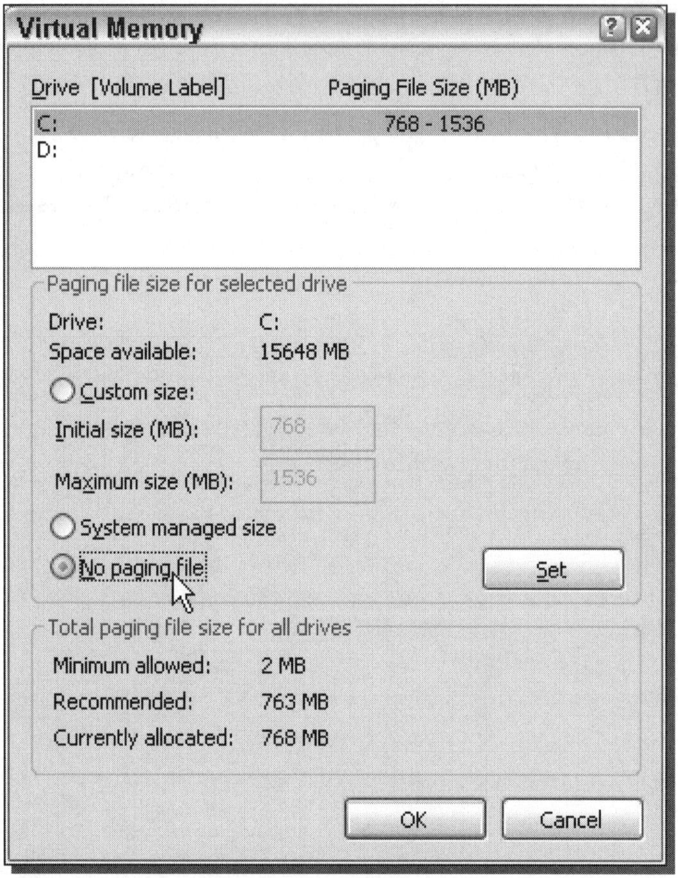

FIGURE 11-5: Virtual Memory No Paging File option.

Feel free to delete the `pagefile.sys` file from your hard drive after you reboot to claim some extra few hundred megabytes of free space.

If you do not have enough RAM to disable the paging file completely, follow the directions in the next section to adjust the size of the paging file for best performance.

Adjusting the size of the paging file

The size of the page file can automatically be set by the system or it can be set by the user. In some situations, having the page file managed by the system is a good idea, but in others, it is better to manage the paging file yourself.

The biggest argument for setting the paging file size and limit manually is to eliminate the growing on the page file when it is set by the system. When the system is managing the size of the paging file, it will monitor the size of the file and will then automatically make it larger when it is needed. This causes two problems. First of all, it causes a noticeable delay for all applications running on your computer because the computer has to expand the paging file and this is a hard disk–intensive operation. Secondly, allowing the system to grow and shrink the paging file causes fragmentation errors.

For the sake of having enough speed, your page file should not have any file fragments. In the next section on defragmenting, you will learn exactly how to do this. But before the defragmentation can be successful, the page file needs to have a constant size. If the page file will be growing frequently, and because the defrag utility has no clue by how much, it cannot put the file in a place on the hard disk so that it will never get fragmented, as is the case when you set the page file manually to Constant Size.

Setting the paging file to a constant size does have some disadvantages. For example, the lost disk space taken up by the paging file can be as high as 1 gigabyte. Additionally, when you set the maximum paging file size manually, you are setting a limit that your computer can never go above. Should you run some extremely memory-intensive application and your limit is too low, your paging file will fill up and you will be out of luck.

The previous example is why setting the correct paging file size is so important. A real easy way to calculate the maximum size of your page file will be to take the recommended size of the page file from the Virtual Memory Settings window, as shown in Figure 11-6, and multiply it by 2.5. If you are having problems finding where your computer states the recommended size, perform the following steps for changing the paging file to a constant size, because this value is on the same screen as that on which you will be working.

Now that you are ready to optimize the paging file to a constant size, follow these steps:

1. Get inside the System Properties again. Do so by right-clicking one of the My Computer icons that is either in the Start Menu or the desktop and selecting Properties.

2. Next, click the Advanced tab and click the Settings button under the Performance section.

3. On the Performance Options window, click the Advanced tab and then click the Change button under the Virtual Memory section.

4. This will bring up all of the page file settings. Once this information is shown, you will want to modify the custom values so that the initial and maximum sizes are the same. Enter in the value that you calculated in these two boxes, as shown in Figure 11-7. If you have not yet calculated what your size should be, you will find the recommended size on the bottom of this window, as was shown in Figure 11-5.

5. Click the Set button and then click OK three times to close all of the windows and save your settings.

Once you restart, you will be using the new constant size paging file. You are now ready to run your defragmenter to defragment the paging file to ensure optimal performance.

Be aware: The method that I use to calculate the size of the constant paging file is a very conservative approach. I figure it would be better to be safe than sorry. The method of calculating the size is an effective one. However, if you feel the need for more free disk space, feel free to

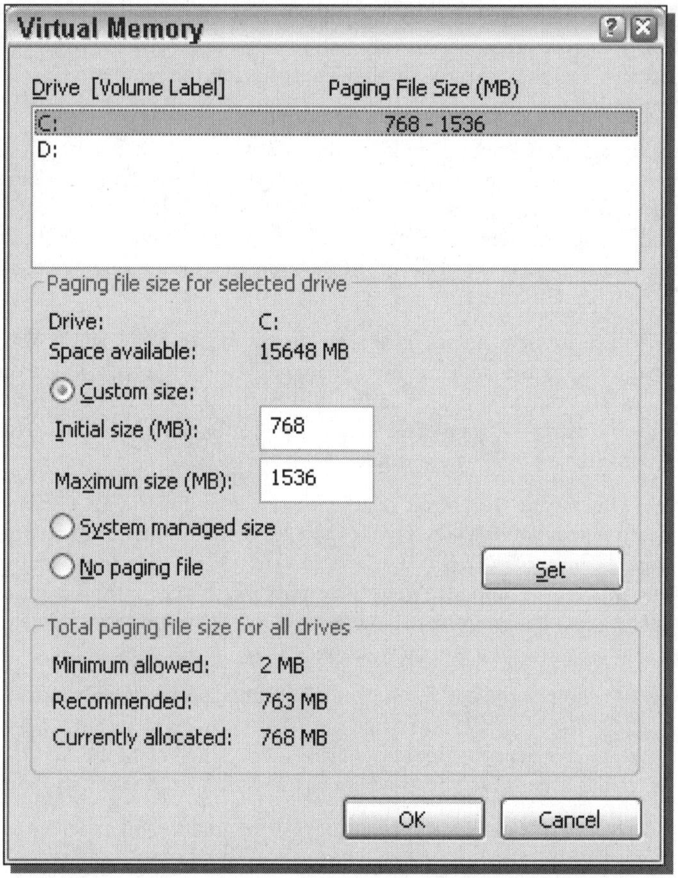

Virtual Memory   [?][X]

Drive [Volume Label]   Paging File Size (MB)

C: 768 - 1536
D:

Paging file size for selected drive

Drive: C:
Space available: 15648 MB

⦿ Custom size:

Initial size (MB):   768

Maximum size (MB):   1536

◯ System managed size

◯ No paging file   Set

Total paging file size for all drives

Minimum allowed: 2 MB
Recommended: 763 MB
Currently allocated: 768 MB

OK   Cancel

FIGURE 11-6: Virtual Memory settings, showing the recommended Paging File Size.

play around with the calculation, such as only multiplying the recommended amount by 2 or maybe even 1.5. Although if you do that, keep in mind that you will be increasing your chances of maxing out your paging file.

Changing the location of the paging file

The paging file can be placed all over your machine. If you really wanted to, your PC could move it to one of those keychain USB thumb drives that use a compact flash card. Although this would be insane because compact flash cards are extremely slow compared to hard drives, it is possible.

If you have multiple hard drives in your system, and I am not talking about multiple partitions on the same drive, you may see a performance increase if you move your paging file off the main system drive.

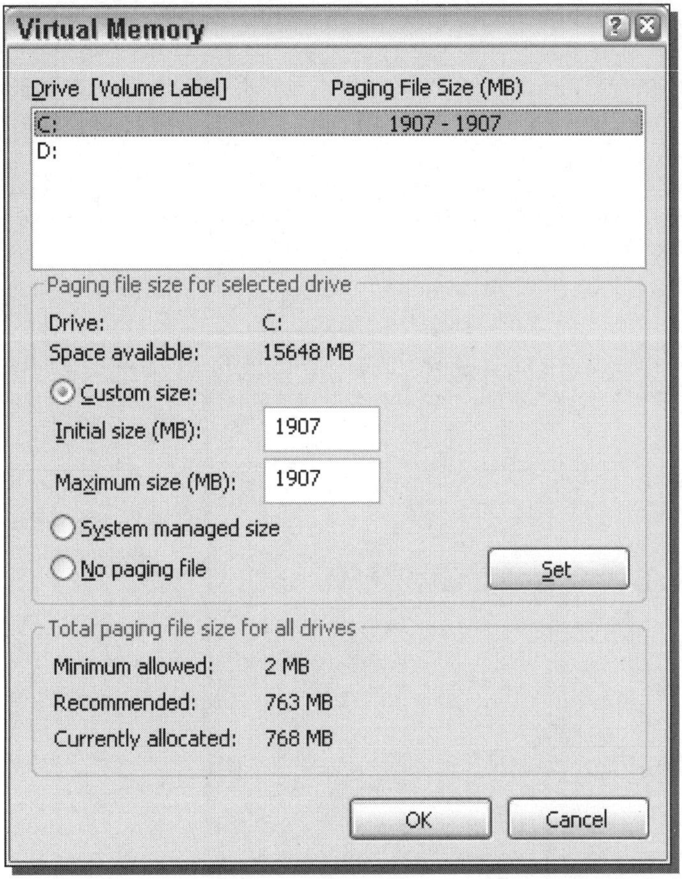

Virtual Memory

Drive [Volume Label]   Paging File Size (MB)
C: 1907 - 1907
D:

Paging file size for selected drive
Drive: C:
Space available: 15648 MB
⦿ Custom size:
Initial size (MB):   1907
Maximum size (MB):   1907
○ System managed size
○ No paging file   [Set]

Total paging file size for all drives
Minimum allowed: 2 MB
Recommended: 763 MB
Currently allocated: 768 MB

[OK]   [Cancel]

FIGURE 11-7: Virtual Memory settings, showing a constant paging file setup.

Moving the paging file off your main drive will allow it to be accessed faster in situations in which your primary hard drive is busy. Also, often when users add hard drives to their computers, they were purchased after their computer was made and usually are faster because hard drives, just like everything else in the computer, get faster as time passes. Moving your paging file to the faster hard drive will also help performance.

Changing the location of the paging file is very easy. Just follow these steps and you will have it done in no time:

1. Once again, you will want to get back to the Virtual Memory settings. If you can get there on your own, feel free to skip to step 4. For those of you that would like directions one more time, follow this and the next two steps. Right-click the My Computer icon located on the desktop in the Start Menu and select Properties.

2. Then click the Advanced tab and click the Settings button under the Performance section.

3. Next, click the Advanced tab and then click the Change button under the Virtual Memory section.

4. Now that you have the Virtual Memory settings displayed, you will want to select the drive on which your current paging file is located from the list of drives, as shown in Figure 11-8.

5. Before you make any changes, write down what the initial and maximum size text boxes contain, if your page file is set to the custom setting. Then, click the No Paging File option and click the Set button.

6. Select the hard drive on which you want your new paging file to be placed from the list of drives (see Figure 11-8) by clicking it.

7. When the new hard drive is highlighted, click the Custom Size radio box and enter in the number that you wrote down before. If you are not using the Custom Size mode,

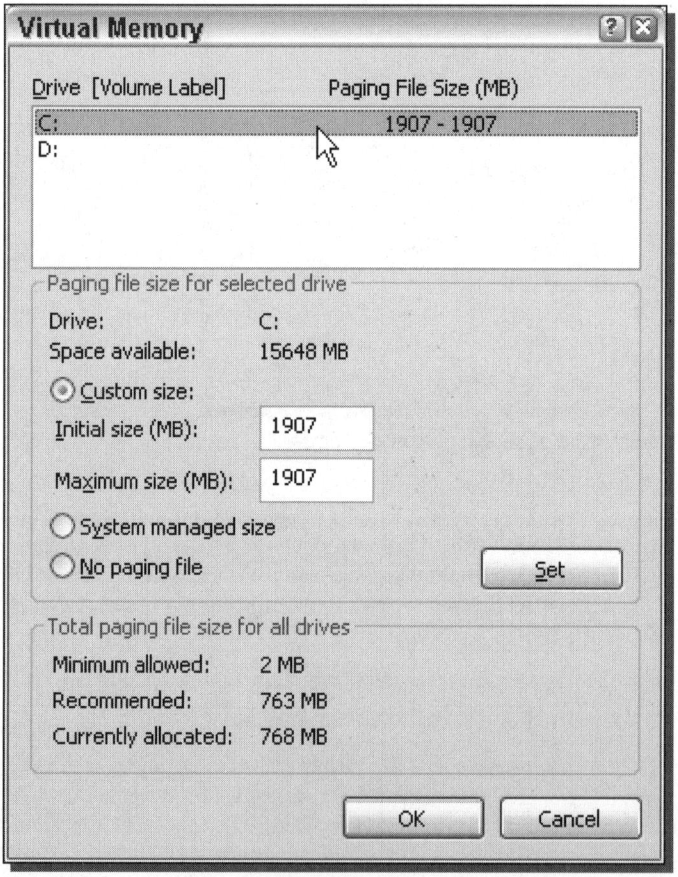

FIGURE 11-8: Virtual Memory Drive setting.

then click the System Managed Size mode but reconsider what was talked about in the last section, because it will really help your performance.

8. Click the Set button and then click OK three times to close all of the settings windows, and you are finished.

After a reboot, your system will be using the paging file on the new hard drive. Feel free to delete `pagefile.sys` from your old hard drive location because it is no longer needed there.

Defragmenting Your Drive

Fragmentation is everything when it comes to maintaining your hard drive. Over time, as your hard drive fills up and you install and uninstall programs and games, the files on your hard drive can become fragmented, as Windows has to find open spots on your hard drive to place the file. Often the file is broken up into thousands of little pieces and scattered all over the hard drive. This cannot cause any significant problems for your computer, but it can cause a noticeable performance slowdown, which can be easily cured by running a software program known as a defragmenter.

Defragmenters do a very simple task of just moving the bits of the files around on the hard drives so that they are all placed together. This arrangement allows the hard drive to load a file faster because the head, which is the arm that reads the data off the plates inside the drive, does not have to scatter all over the place to read the data.

In Chapter 8, I discussed using several utilities to defragment the boot files. The same utilities can be used to defragment the whole drive as well as the special files. This next section will concentrate on two of those special files because defragmenting the whole drive is done at the same time.

Defragmenting the Windows paging file

The Windows paging file can be quite large, as you know from the previous sections. Once you have created a constant size paging file, or if you just want to defragment the paging file, you can defragment the file during the next system boot. Windows will not allow any program to move the paging file around on the hard drive when the operating system is in use. The main reason why Windows does not allow this is because other programs are running in the background as well as operating system services that will depend on the paging file. This is why the defragmentation can only be done during the boot, because very few files are in use then.

The built-in Windows XP defragmenter does not defragment the paging file during a normal defrag. Microsoft has a workaround for this limitation. It tells users to do a normal defrag first, then after the free space is consolidated, to delete the paging file by disabling it and then re-creating it right after a fresh defrag. Doing so will cause the operating system to create one big, continuous file on the hard drive.

There is nothing wrong with Microsoft's approach, since it will accomplish the task, but there is an easier way to do this. I recommend that, if you have not already done so, you download the disk defragmenter utility called Diskeeper, by Executive Software (www.executive.com), which was discussed in Chapter 8. All you have to do in order to defragment the paging file is to run a boot defrag. By default, the option to defragment the paging file is already set. If you do not remember how to do a boot defrag, go back to Chapter 8 and review the step-by-step instructions in the section *Boot time system defrag with Diskeeper*.

Defragmenting the NTFS master file table

The master file table, or MFT, is very important to the operation of the file system on your computer. Think of it as a phone directory of all the files on your computer. It is a big database of every file on your computer and it is stored on the hard drive. As the number of files and directories on your computer increase, so does the master file table. Over time, the master file table can also become fragmented. Because the master file table is so important to computer operations, it is used any time you want data from the hard drive. Defragmenting it will help your performance.

The built-in defragmenter will not defragment the MFT. Microsoft recommends that you adjust the amount of space that is reserved for the MFT, then back up your drive, and then do a full reformat and then restore your whole drive. This seems like way too much effort expended to me. Once again, Diskeeper by Executive Software comes to the rescue. Also, by default, when you perform a boot defrag, the option to defragment the master file table is already selected.

Using the Diskeeper method, instead of the Microsoft method, will save you hours of time wasted backing up and restoring your drive.

Adjusting Your Application Priorities

Ever since the introduction of the multitasking processor, operating systems have been able to handle running multiple programs at once using the new task switching and segmentation features provided by the CPU. These new technologies are what made it possible for an operating system like the Windows series to be made. Even though PCs nowadays are able to multitask, they really only can do one thing at a time. In order for the operating system to support running hundreds of applications at once, it has to slice up all of the available processing time and give each application a turn.

Operating systems use a variety of techniques to determine which application will get the next available slot to use the CPU. One of the factors that determines this for Windows XP is the priority level at which the application is running.

Every application that runs on your computer has a priority level attached to its runtime record. By default, the operating system starts each application at normal priority, which is right in the middle of the priority spectrum. Applications can run and be assigned six different priority levels ranked highest to lowest: real time, high, above normal, normal, below normal, and low. Because the CPU can only do one thing at a time, the different priority levels allow the operating system to decide which application will get the next CPU burst. If an application is running at high or above normal priority level, it will get more CPU time than an application running at normal.

As you can see, the priority you give an application can impact how fast the program runs.

Using Task Manager to adjust priorities

The Windows Task Manager is something that we all have experience with when we have problems with a frozen program. The Task Manager is actually a very useful utility, as was discussed in Chapter 7. Another use of the Task Manager is to change the priority at which an application is running while it is running. The Task Manager makes it possible to dynamically change the priority of application. This capability can be very useful when you have a lot of programs running on your computer.

Setting any application to real time can be dangerous, because doing so will allow the application to hog all of the CPU time and will make exiting a program that is running at this high priority impossible, if for some reason it crashes. Because the program is hogging all of the CPU time, it takes a very long time to just load the Task Manager to end the application.

If you have a program that is doing a lot of CPU-intensive operations, such as rendering a video clip or a game, you can adjust the priority of the application by following these steps:

1. Load the Task Manager by clicking the Start Menu and selecting Run. Then type **taskmgr.exe** in the text box and click the OK button.

2. Once Task Manager loads, click the Processes tab.

3. Right-click the name of the process for which you would like to adjust the priority, select Set Priority, and then select the level, as shown in Figure 11-9.

4. After you click the priority level, your change is complete.

If your computer has multiple processors or supports hyperthreading, then you will notice an extra option when you right-click a process called Set Affinity. This option will allow you to specify on which CPU the application will run (or which virtual CPU, in the case of hyperthreading users).

Using the Task Manager to change the priority levels is great. However, there is one downside. When an application on which you have altered its priority level is closed, the priority level it was running at will be lost. The next time the program is started up, it will be running back at the default level. This can be a real annoyance for some users; however, there is a great trick to fix this problem, which will be shown in the next section.

Starting applications with a user set priority

Using a wonderful command built into Windows XP allows you to start any program and specify what priority it should be run at. This cool utility is called the Start command. Using the Start command with priority flags, followed by the executable, will allow any program to start at the priority level at which you want it to start.

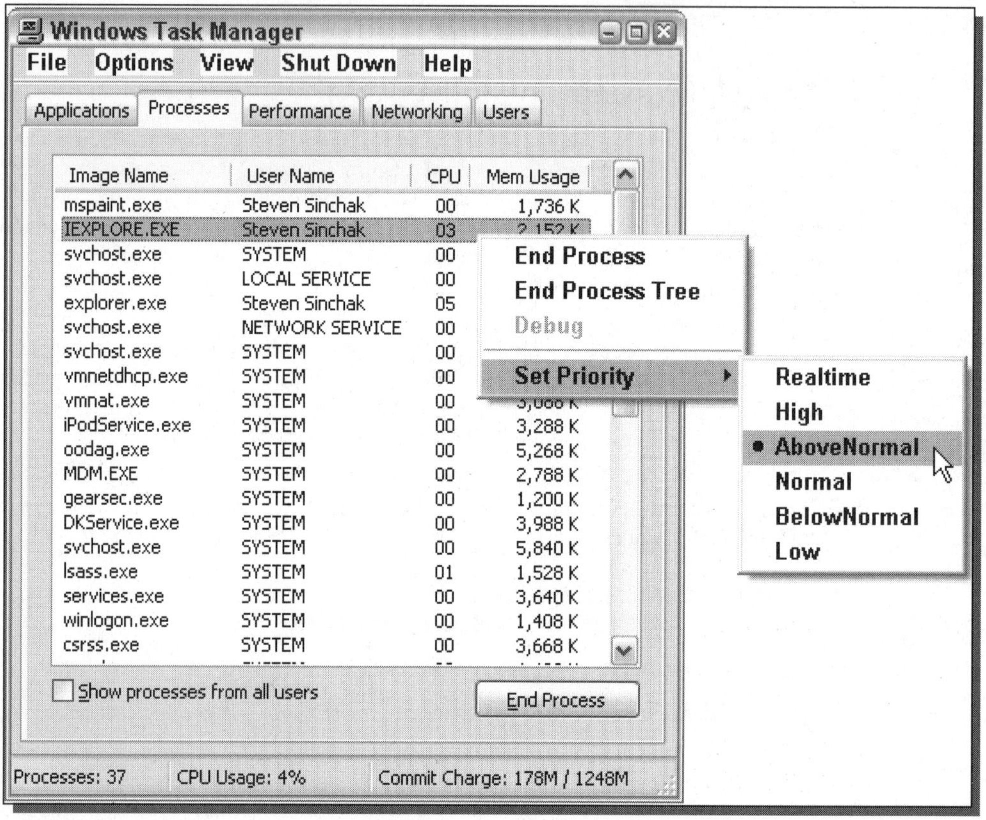

FIGURE 11-9: Task Manager adjusting application priorities.

For the sake of demonstrating how to use the command, assume that the calculator is set at high CPU priority. Follow these steps to set the command:

1. First, open Notepad so that you can type in the command so that it can be turned into a batch script file. This can be done by starting Notepad from the Accessories item in the Start Menu's All Program entry.

2. Once Notepad is open, key in **start /high calc.exe**. If you want to start the calculator at a different priority, you can replace **/high** with **/low, /normal, /realtime/, /abovenormal,** and **/belownormal.**

3. Once you have the priority level keyed in, click the File menu bar item in Notepad and select Save As. Change the file Save As Type to All Files and type **launchcalc.bat** in the filename box. You can call the file anything you want, but make sure that it has the .bat file extension so that Windows knows to execute the commands in the file.

4. Then specify a location on your hard drive to save it, such as your Desktop, and click the Save button. You are now finished and may exit Notepad.

Now that you have the batch command file created, just double-click the file to launch the calculator application at the high-priority level.

The same technique can be applied to any program on your computer. Instead of typing **calc.exe** at the end of the command, type the name of the executable of the program that you want to start. Additionally, this command can be used on nonexecutable files such as documents.

For example, you can type in **start /high mydocument.doc** and it will start Microsoft Word in high priority with your document opened.

Using WinTasks to profile your priorities

Another great utility, made by LIUtilities, is called WinTasks Pro. This utility is like the Windows Task Manager, but on steroids. It offers tons of new features that the Windows Task Manager does not have, such as the ability to see individual CPU and memory graphs for each application, scripting capabilities that allow the user to set up triggers based on CPU and memory activity for each application, and most importantly, the ability to have preset profiles for application priority levels. Also, on top of these features, it has built-in information about quite a few commonly known processes to help users figure out each process that is listed because they are often not easily identified by the process name.

The ability to have a profile for your open application priority levels enables you to automatically change the priority of several applications at the click of one button.

WinTasks 4 professional can be downloaded from www.liutilities.com/support/ downloads/. Download a copy now and install it if you would like to follow along with these steps, which will guide you through creating a profile of your priorities:

1. Start WinTasks by clicking the Start button, expanding All Programs, and selecting Start WinTasks from the WinTasks folder.

2. When WinTasks is loaded, you will see a list of all of the different processes running on your computer. You can adjust the priority at which each process is running by right-clicking the process and then selecting either Increase or Decrease Priority. Go ahead and change the priorities of all of the applications that you have running to what you would like them to be.

3. When you are satisfied with all of your priority changes and are ready to create a profile of them, click the little key icons in the Presets toolbar, as shown in Figure 11-10.

4. Type in a name to save the state of all of the priorities, as in the Save Preset window, and press OK.

5. Next to the key icon that you pressed, you will notice the name showing up in the button to the right of it. Every time you press this button, it will reset all of the priorities to what you changed them to for this preset.

6. Repeat the previous steps, changing the priority levels for each application to a different value, and then click a different key icon to save the new preset again.

Now that you have multiple presets of application priority levels, you can easily switch between them by clicking the buttons.

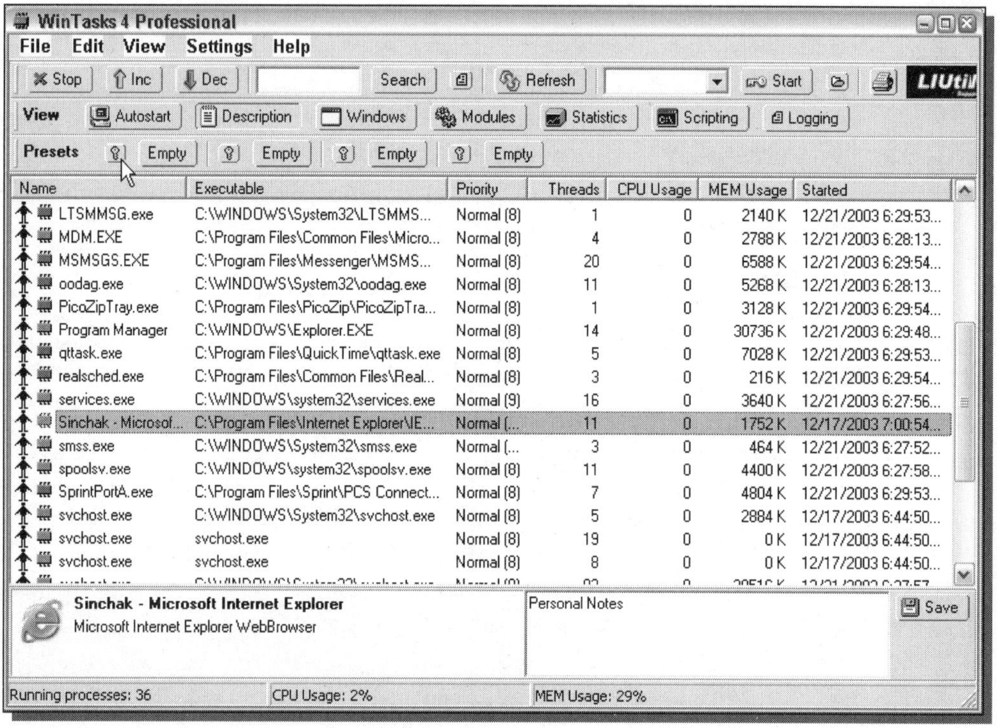

FIGURE 11-10: WinTasks Professional Presets save icon.

The capability to create separate presets of priority levels for different applications allows you to optimize certain programs, depending on what you are doing. For example, you can create a profile for your processes when you want to play a game. To do that, you could decrease the priority of many of the system processes and applications running in the background so that a game running at normal or higher priority will have more CPU time.

Lower the priorities of all of the other background applications, such as your instant messaging programs and other programs that run in the background. This will allow your game to run faster, because these other background applications will have a lower priority.

Speeding Up Your Network

The speed of your network connection does not just depend on the speed of your hardware. Windows is an operating system that is designed to work on a variety of different hardware and network setups. Because of the abstract nature of the operating system, it cannot be optimized for user-specific hardware setups.

Depending on the type of network connection you have, you might be able to tweak your connection so that the speed of your Internet, as well as your local area network, will be faster.

By hacking the System Registry and editing the TCP/IP parameters, you can fine-tune the values to take advantage of the more reliable, faster Internet connections, such as DSL and cable.

These next sections will guide you through the steps of increasing both the speed of your local area network and your Internet connection.

Increasing network browsing speed

Does your computer slow down when you browse your local area network and connect to other computers that are sharing data? One of the most common causes of this slowdown is a feature of Windows Explorer that looks for scheduled tasks on remote computers. This effort can take some time on some computers and can really slow down your browsing. The window with which you are browsing the network may appear to freeze momentarily, as the system is waiting for a response from the remote computer.

Although this problem is a complex one, the solution is very simple. Instead of having to wait for the remote scheduled tasks, which is useless information to anyone who is not a system administrator remotely configuring scheduled tasks, you can disable this feature.

In order to do this, you will have to hack the System Registry and delete a reference to a key so that this feature will not be loaded. To do this, follow these steps:

1. Open up the Registry Editor by clicking the Start Menu and selecting Run. Then type **regedit** in the text box and click the OK button.

2. Once the Registry Editor has loaded, expand the HKEY_LOCAL_MACHINE key.

3. Next, expand Software and then Microsoft.

4. Locate Windows and expand that as well.

5. You will want to be editing the main system files, so expand CurrentVersion.

6. Because this feature is a feature of the Windows component known as Explorer, expand the Explorer key.

7. Next, you will want to modify the remote computer settings, so expand the RemoteComputer key and then expand the NameSpace key to show all of the features that are enabled when you browse to a remote computer.

8. In the NameSpace folder you will find two entries. One is "{2227A280-3AEA-1069-A2DE-08002B30309D}" which tells Explorer to show printers shared on the remote machine. The other, "{D6277990-4C6A-11CF-8D87-00AA0060F5BF}," tells Explorer to show remote scheduled tasks. This is the one that you should delete. This can be done by right-clicking the name of the key and selecting Delete.

Tip

If you have no use for viewing remote shared printers and are really only interested in shared files, consider deleting the printers key, "{2227A280-3AEA-1069-A2DE-08002B30309D}", as well. This will also boost your browsing speed.

Once you have deleted the key, you just need to restart and the changes will be in effect. Now your network computer browsing will be without needless delays.

 An undo file for this hack can be found on the companion CD in the Chapter 11 folder called `remote_tasks_undo.reg`.

Disabling unneeded protocols

With every computer comes programs installed that you do not need. As with extra programs taking up space, extra protocols are just wasting your network connection and can actually slow it down. How is this possible? By default, a few different protocols are installed on your computer to allow for maximum compatibility with other computers on a network; these protocols each require bandwidth to operate. Most users will not use too many protocols, and their computers will use up a portion of their connection as they respond and transmit information for these protocols.

Additionally, with extra protocols installed on your network adapter connected to the Internet, you increase your risk of security-related problems. One of the most common risks for broadband users is that they have the Client for Microsoft Networks networking protocol enabled on their connection. This protocol allows everyone in their neighborhood to connect to the users' computers and view any files that they may be sharing. This fact alone should be a good enough reason for you to turn off the extra protocols. But with them disabled, you will also save a little bandwidth as well.

Viewing protocols on your network adapters

Viewing the protocols installed and active on your various network adapters is easy. Just follow these quick steps and you will be viewing them in no time:

1. Right-click the My Network Places icon on the desktop or in the Start Menu and select Properties. If the My Network Places icon is not in either of those locations, then go to the Control Panel and click the Network Connections icon that is shown under the Classic view.

2. Next, right-click the network adapter with which you want to view the network protocols and select Properties.

3. This will bring up a list of the protocols installed as well as active on your adapter, as Figure 11-11 shows. The protocols that are installed but not active are indicated by the absence of a check in the checkbox.

Disabling a specific protocol

Now that you have the list of installed and active protocols on your screen, you are ready to disable a protocol. To do so, just click the check box to remove the check. Then click the OK button and the protocol is no longer active on the network adapter.

I highly recommend that you disable all protocols except for the TCP/IP protocol (also referred to as the Internet Protocol). Doing so will optimize your adapter for speed and security.

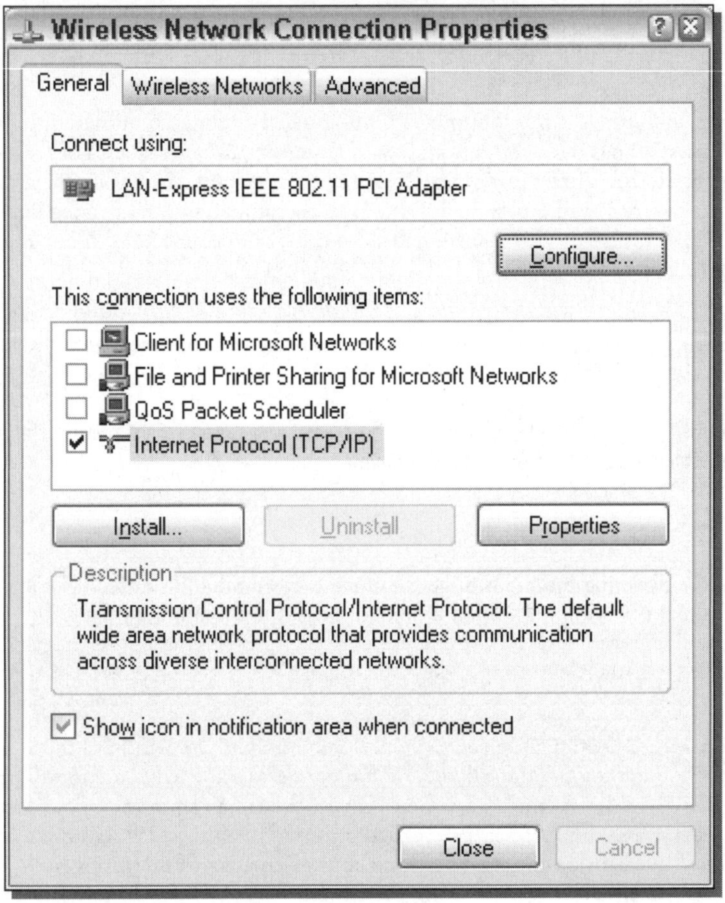

FIGURE **11-11: Network adapter protocol list.**

Be aware that if you remove the Client for Microsoft Networks protocol and the file-sharing protocol, you will no longer be able to share your files. Additionally, you will no longer be able to connect to remote computers to view their shared files.

Also keep in mind that if you have multiple adapters in your machines, such as a wireless adapter, a wired network adapter, and a dialup modem, you will have to repeat the preceding instructions for each adapter.

Tweaking your Internet connection for speed

Almost every computer user has different Internet connection conditions. Some users have very high-speed connections, while others have slow connections. Some users have high-speed connections using cable-based technologies, while others have high-speed connection through DSL-based technologies. On top of these differences, some are located farther away from their local network switching station than others and have a higher latency (delay) on their connections because of the distance the data has to travel. All of these different connection conditions make every user unique.

The TCP/IP protocol settings can be optimized for best speed under each of these situations. By default, Windows XP has these settings set in a "one size fits all" approach. As I mentioned earlier, Windows has to be abstract in certain areas because of its broad user base. Because of this approach, many users can fine-tune their settings to be optimal for their connection conditions. Doing so will optimize the data transferred so your network connection will be more efficient, leading to high speeds.

With a little help from some fine online tools and software programs, you can test your Internet connection and decide what needs fine-tuning. The process of tweaking your Internet connection is not always easy, but it is doable.

 Caution Before going any further, you are strongly advised to create a system restore point, so that if things go wrong, which is not very likely, you will have a backup.

The next step in the tweaking process is to get all of the software that is needed. The main software program that you will use is called CableNut, which is developed by CableNut Software and is available for free at www.cablenut.com. CableNut is a great program that allows users to edit their Internet settings easily. Visit their Web page and download and install the latest copy.

The type of Internet connection that you have determines what you will have to do next. Because the settings are the same for all 56K dialup connections, I have included a settings file in the Chapter 11 folder on the companion CD-ROM, made from the calculator at www.j79zlr.com/cablenutXP2k.php called 56K_Cablenut.ccs. If you have a 56K dialup connection, you can skip the next section about calculating the settings for CableNut and jump to the next section using the file from the CD-ROM. Skip to the next section, *Using CableNut to adjust settings*, to find out how to apply the settings file to your computer.

Calculating settings for CableNut

Once you have downloaded CableNut, you are ready to start getting information to use with the program. The first value that you will need to calculate is the latency of your connection when it is active. To do this, you will use the trace route command built into Windows XP. Follow these steps to get the latency value to use for your connection:

1. First, open up a Command Prompt window. This can be done by clicking the Start Menu and selecting Run. Then type **cmd** in the text box and click the OK button.

2. Once Command Prompt is loaded, you are ready for the next part. Because you will need to test your connection when it is active, you will need to find something large to download that will run the duration of the test, which will be approximately 30 seconds. I

recommend that you head over to www.microsoft.com/downloads and find some huge file, such as the .NET SDK framework, which is over 100,000 KBs. For the test, you want a file big enough so it will be downloading throughout the whole test. Those of you on a dialup connection can pick a much smaller file than those on a high-speed connection.

3. Once you have your download test file picked out, start the download and switch back to the Command Prompt window. In that window, type **tracert www.tweakxp .com**. During the test, you will see many times displayed in milliseconds. After the test finishes, pick the highest time, as shown in Figure 11-12. This is the number that you will use as your latency. Also, feel free to cancel the download after the test is finished.

Now that you have the latency value calculated, you are ready to enter this information into a great online CableNut settings calculator written by Joe Zeiler, who is one of the talented moderators at the TweakXP.com support forums. Open up your Web browser and visit www.j79zlr.com/cablenutXP2k.php (the URL is case-sensitive!), then follow these steps to get the values to enter into CableNut:

1. Once you have opened up the site, the first part of using the settings calculator is to select your connection type from the drop-down box.

2. Next, you will have to do a little research and find out exactly what your upload and download speeds should be for your Internet connection. I had to contact Comcast, my ISP, to find out the exact values, because the values are not always advertised. Once, you get those values, make sure that they are in kilobits per second and not kilobytes per second (KB = kilobytes; Kb = kilobits), then enter them in the corresponding text boxes on the Web page.

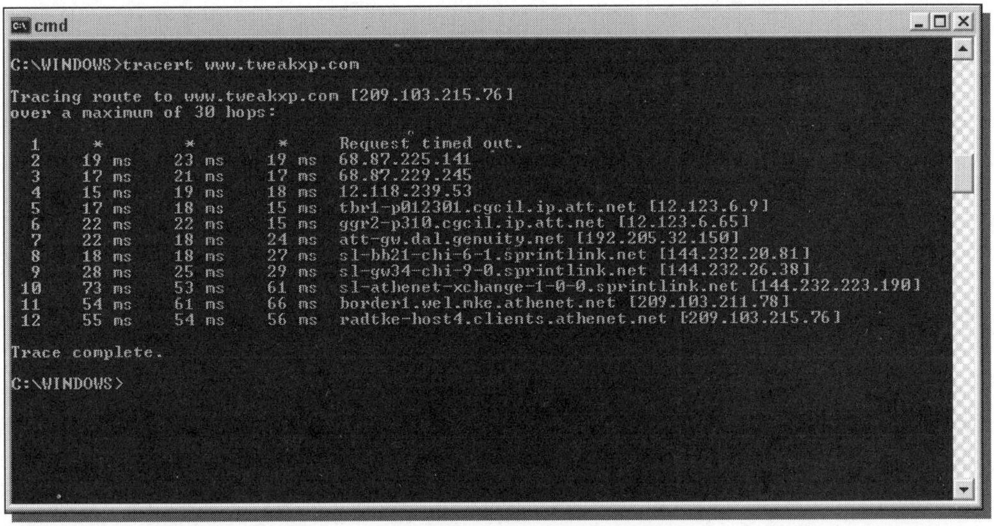

```
cmd                                                                        _ □ ×

C:\WINDOWS>tracert www.tweakxp.com

Tracing route to www.tweakxp.com [209.103.215.76]
over a maximum of 30 hops:

  1     *         *         *      Request timed out.
  2    19 ms     23 ms     19 ms   68.87.225.141
  3    17 ms     21 ms     17 ms   68.87.229.245
  4    15 ms     19 ms     18 ms   12.118.239.53
  5    17 ms     18 ms     15 ms   tbr1-p012301.cgcil.ip.att.net [12.123.6.9]
  6    22 ms     22 ms     15 ms   ggr2-p310.cgcil.ip.att.net [12.123.6.65]
  7    22 ms     18 ms     24 ms   att-gw.dal.genuity.net [192.205.32.150]
  8    18 ms     18 ms     27 ms   sl-bb21-chi-6-1.sprintlink.net [144.232.20.81]
  9    28 ms     25 ms     29 ms   sl-gw34-chi-9-0.sprintlink.net [144.232.26.38]
 10    73 ms     53 ms     61 ms   sl-athenet-xchange-1-0-0.sprintlink.net [144.232.223.190]
 11    54 ms     61 ms     66 ms   border1.wel.mke.athenet.net [209.103.211.78]
 12    55 ms     54 ms     56 ms   radtke-host4.clients.athenet.net [209.103.215.76]

Trace complete.

C:\WINDOWS>
```

FIGURE 11-12: Windows Trace route program displaying latency values.

3. Enter the latency value that you calculated earlier into the latency text box on the Web page and then click the Calculate button.

4. After you hit the Compute Settings button, scroll down and you will see the values that were calculated. Now, you are almost done. Continue scrolling down until you see a button labeled CCS File Generator under the Cablenut setting files section. Click that button and a new window will pop up with some text in it. Make sure that you have any pop-up blockers disabled when you are using the calculator.

5. Use the mouse and select all of the text and numbers that are displayed in the pop-up window. Right-click the mouse and select copy to copy all of the text on the page to the clipboard.

6. Now open up Notepad from the Accessories folder. In the blank Notepad window, paste the contents of the clipboard by right-clicking the white background and selecting Paste.

7. Once Notepad is displaying the information that you copied from the pop-up window, all that is left is to save the file in the CableNut format. To do this, click the File menu bar item and select Save As. Then in the Save As Type drop-down box, select All Files. Key in **myCableNutSettings.ccs** in the file name text box. Specify the Save location, such as the desktop, and click the Save button.

You are now finished with the calculations that will optimize your Internet connection. That wasn't too hard now, was it?

Using CableNut to adjust settings

Now that you have created your CableNut settings file, or will be using the 56K settings file, you are ready to start using CableNut. Follow these steps to import the new optimized settings into your system:

1. Start up the CableNut application by opening the Start Menu and browsing to the CableNut folder and selecting the adjuster application.

2. When CableNut has loaded, click the File menu bar item and select Open Custom Settings File. Navigate to where you saved your settings file, or if you are a 56K user, use the file that is on the companion CD, called 56K_CableNut.ccs, and then click the Open button.

3. Now you will see the information boxes for all of the different parameters filled with your connection-specific information, as shown in Figure 11-13. The last step is to click the Save to Registry button and you are finished. After you click the Save button, reboot, and your new settings will be in effect.

Caution

According to www.j79zlr.com/cablenutXP2k.php, some of the CableNut settings can cause problems for a small amount of DSL customers. If you are experiencing network problems after optimizing your connection, use System Restore to revert to your last restore point. You may try the settings again, but blank out the MaxNormLookupMemory, MaxFreeTcbs, MaxHashTableSize, and FastSendDatagramThreshhold fields before applying. If you continue to

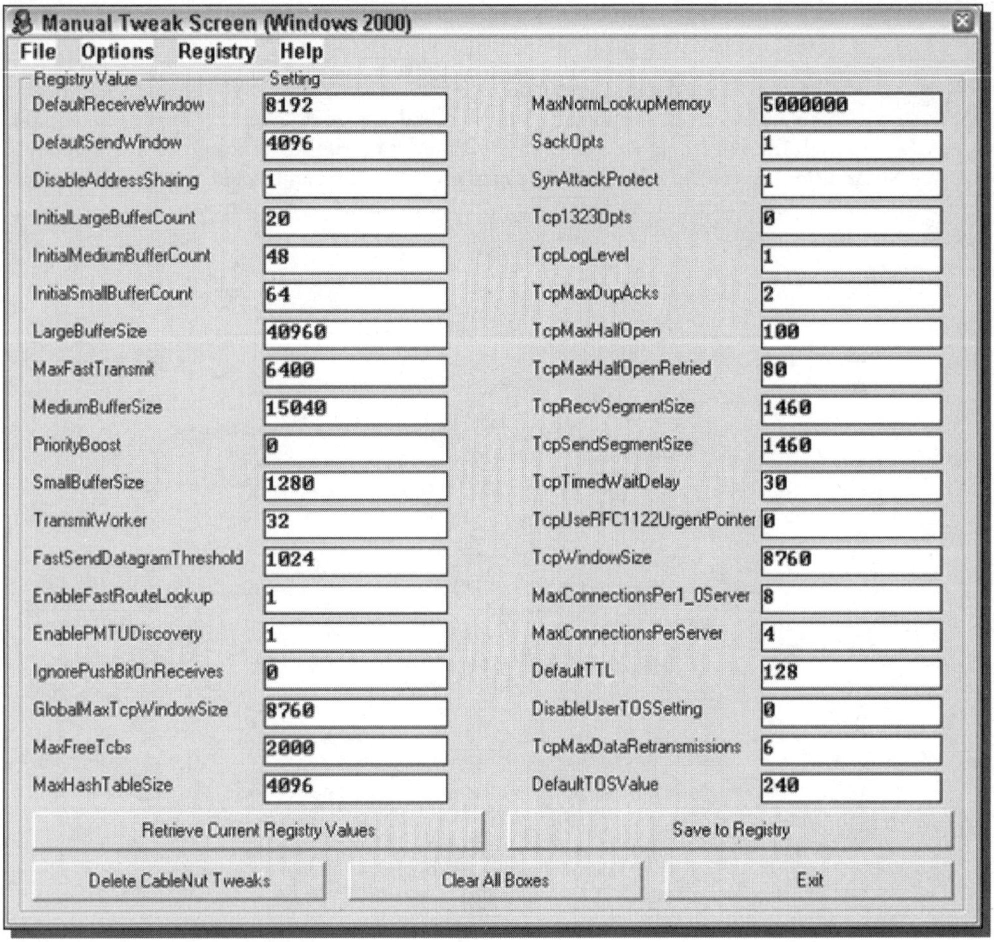

Manual Tweak Screen (Windows 2000)

File   Options   Registry   Help

Registry Value	Setting		
DefaultReceiveWindow	8192	MaxNormLookupMemory	5000000
DefaultSendWindow	4096	SackOpts	1
DisableAddressSharing	1	SynAttackProtect	1
InitialLargeBufferCount	20	Tcp1323Opts	0
InitialMediumBufferCount	48	TcpLogLevel	1
InitialSmallBufferCount	64	TcpMaxDupAcks	2
LargeBufferSize	40960	TcpMaxHalfOpen	100
MaxFastTransmit	6400	TcpMaxHalfOpenRetried	80
MediumBufferSize	15040	TcpRecvSegmentSize	1460
PriorityBoost	0	TcpSendSegmentSize	1460
SmallBufferSize	1280	TcpTimedWaitDelay	30
TransmitWorker	32	TcpUseRFC1122UrgentPointer	0
FastSendDatagramThreshold	1024	TcpWindowSize	8760
EnableFastRouteLookup	1	MaxConnectionsPer1_0Server	8
EnablePMTUDiscovery	1	MaxConnectionsPerServer	4
IgnorePushBitOnReceives	0	DefaultTTL	128
GlobalMaxTcpWindowSize	8760	DisableUserTOSSetting	0
MaxFreeTcbs	2000	TcpMaxDataRetransmissions	6
MaxHashTableSize	4096	DefaultTOSValue	240

Retrieve Current Registry Values   Save to Registry

Delete CableNut Tweaks   Clear All Boxes   Exit

FIGURE 11-13: CableNut settings.

have problems, or if you have problems with the directions and still want to optimize your connection, a great forum to get help on this topic is at www.broadbandnuts.com, or feel free to visit the TweakXP.com support forum at www.tweakxp.com/forum/.

Summary

This chapter focused on speeding up loading time and speeding up your network. Now you know how to optimize your applications and some of the operating system settings, such as the paging file and your application priorities. You also know how to defragment not only the files on your hard drive but also the paging file and the Windows master file table. On top of finding out about all sorts of intriguing performance hacks and tips, you also learned the steps to correctly optimize your Internet connection.

You are now finished with the second part of *Hacking Windows XP*. The next part of this book is completely dedicated to making Windows XP a more secure operating system and protecting yourself from the other type of hacker, the kind that tries to break into your computer. Additionally, the next chapters will touch on the popular and troublesome topic of Spyware and will even touch on hacking Windows XP to maintain your privacy.

Securing Your System

Protecting Your Computer from Intruders

Computer security is one of the most important issues in the computer world. With the number of viruses and other malicious software that prey on exploits in the Windows operating system increasing, you need to take preventative measures to make sure that your computer does not become infected.

The days of only having to worry about e-mail attachments and documents on a floppy disk are over. Nowadays, viruses or worms actively seek out computers to infect without the computer user even doing anything.

Once a virus or worm has gained entry to a system, the invaded computer can turn into a virus distribution center. Often, the computer sends copies of the virus to all of the people in its address book. Even worse, the infected computer may begin to scan a block of IP addresses (that is, computer addresses) to try to find more machines that it can infect. If your computer is not protecting its connection to the Web, it is at increased risk of becoming infected.

So how do you protect your Internet connection? That topic is what this whole chapter is about. You will learn how to test your computer and see how vulnerable it actually is. Then, you'll find out how you can use firewalls to build a "brick wall" around your computer. You'll also learn how to turn off some unnecessary services to lower the risk of infection even further. Additionally, you'll discover how you can secure wireless network connections, as they are growing so much in popularity.

Once you have your computer locked down from the outside, some connections to your computer may still be open, which you do not want to close down. Remote connections need to have certain ports open on your computer so that you can connect remotely to your computer. Additionally, if you want to share files with other computers on your local network, then you will want to leave the Client for Microsoft Networks unblocked. However, when you have openings in your computer's security, you leave yourself vulnerable, allowing users to get in. To help combat that vulnerability, you'll learn about ways to use the various user accounts settings to assign complex passwords and permissions to users.

How Vulnerable Is Your System?

Our computers are a vault of important information. You could have sensitive data on your computer that you do not want the whole world to see. Data such as family photos, personal documents, and financial information can be found on almost everyone's computer. If a virus or an attacker connected to your computer remotely and gained access, that intruder could wipe out years of work and memories as well as steal sensitive personal information. This section will show you how to test your computer and find out how vulnerable it really is. To do this, you'll be using a nifty online utility to test your Internet security. Then, proper security update procedures will be examined, so you can see if you are really doing what you should to ensure a secure PC.

Testing your Internet security

Ports are the gateways inside your computer. When a computer program wants to communicate with a remote computer, it makes a connection to the remote computer with a port, with which it can then talk to the computer. Each computer has thousands of ports—65,535 to be exact. The different ports of a computer can be thought of as a bunch of different mailboxes. When a program wants to send data to a remote computer, it sends it to a specific port (mailbox) number. Then, provided that a program is on the remote computer that is set up to receive data at a particular port (mailbox), the remote computer can then work with the data that it was sent.

Theoretically, nothing is wrong with this scenario. In the real world, however, programs don't always work this way. Programs are not perfect, nor are they always efficient. Sometimes, they are sent data that they are not programmed to receive, which causes all kinds of program errors, including errors that can allow a remote attacker to connect and run commands on your computer. The technical name for data sent to a program that results in problems is *exploit*.

Because of errors in programs and the exploitation of the errors, you need to protect your computer. Even though you may have all the latest security patches installed, your computer will not be protected forever. It is just a matter of time before someone figures out a new exploit and it starts to spread. Only after the fact is the patch usually developed and distributed.

So how do you protect yourself from future attacks? It is actually a very simple concept. There are a lot of open ports (mailboxes) on your computer that just don't really need to be open to the outside world. Why not close all ports except for one or two you absolutely need so that exploits can no longer get through because they never have a chance to connect to your computer? How do you close ports and protect your computer? Use a firewall, as shown in the *Firewalls* section found in the second half of this chapter.

To give you an idea of how open your computer really is to the outside world, I recommend that you use one of the various online security screening tests that attempt to probe your computer to find weaknesses. The following is a list of sites that I feel do a good job of letting you know how open your computer really is:

- *Symantec Security Check*: http://security.symantec.com

- *Sygate Online Services*: http://scan.sygate.com/

- *Gibson Research Shields Up*: www.grc.com
- *DSL Reports*: www.dslreports.com/scan

Visit a few of these sites and follow their directions to scan your computer. You will be presented with a report that shows you the open doors that they found.

Updating your computer

Because programs are not perfect, they require updating. Windows XP is a great operating system; however, no operating system is perfect. In order to keep your machine secure and free of the latest exploits, you must update your computer regularly. Visiting the Windows Update Web site (www.WindowsUpdate.com) once every few months is not going to result in a secure, up-to-date computer. Microsoft releases security updates monthly and emergency security updates whenever they are needed. The only way to stay on top of these updates is to check Windows Update daily, subscribe to the *Microsoft Security Newsletter*, or enable automatic updates.

Windows Update

Microsoft's Windows Update Web site offers an easy way to view all of the updates that are available for your computer. Microsoft releases both critical and features updates that update various software apps and add interesting new features to Windows XP. For example, critical updates fix major security concerns, such as the widespread exploit for Windows XP known as the W32.Blaster.Worm worm. This worm spread to other computers by using a vulnerability in a component of Windows known as RPC (remote procedure call). To fix the security hole, Microsoft released a critical patch that fixed the security hole. Feature updates update bugs and add new features to common Windows applications such as Windows Movie Maker. Using the Windows Update Web site is very easy too. Just key in **www.WindowsUpdate.com** in your Web browser Address window, click Go, and you will be there in no time.

Security Newsletter

The *Microsoft Security Newsletter* is a great way to keep informed about all of the latest security patches that Microsoft releases. Receive an e-mail in your inbox every time Microsoft releases a critical security patch. If you are a home user, visit www.microsoft.com/security/security_bulletins/alerts2.asp for more information on the newsletter. On that page, Microsoft also offers a more technical version of the *Microsoft Security Newsletter* that will not only notify you of a critical security patch, but will also explain the full vulnerability. If you are an IT professional and want to know exactly what the patch is for, the technical version is for you.

Microsoft TechNet also offers a monthly newsletter that offers security news and advice. This is another great newsletter to subscribe to. It was primarily intended for IT professionals, but home users may also find it useful if they are interested in a more technical approach. Visit www.microsoft.com/technet/security/secnews/newsletter.htm for a copy of the latest newsletter, as well as information on how to subscribe.

Automatic Updates

Windows XP has a great Automatic Updates service. With the release of Service Pack 2, that service is now even better. With the ability to set a specific time every day to check and install new updates, you now can schedule a time for your computer to automatically check for and apply updates so that you will not have to visit the Windows Update Web site manually.

Turning on Automatic Updates is a great way to make sure your computer is up-to-date. However, it is a good idea to visit the Windows Update Web site every few months to make sure that Automatic Updates is still working. If it is, then you should not see any critical updates available when you visit the Web site.

Working with the Automatic Update settings is not a difficult task. Just right-click the My Computer icon located in the Start panel or on your desktop and select Properties. Then, click the Automatic Updates tab and specify the setting that you want, and click OK to save your changes. Figure 12-1 is a shot of the Automatic Updates screen, with the automatic download and install feature enabled. I selected 12:00 p.m. so my computer will automatically install new updates when I am at lunch and not using my computer. Also, this is a time when it is pretty much guaranteed that my computer will be on.

As you can see from Figure 12-1, there also are settings to automatically download patches that then prompt you to confirm the install as well as a feature that will just notify you of new patches. Unlike the technical security newsletter that was mentioned earlier, the notification of new updates will just give you the basic information instead of all of the technical reasons for the update.

Users also have the ability to turn off Automatic Updates by selecting the last option on the Automatic Update tab. You would have to be crazy to do this unless you plan on checking the Windows update Web sites daily or subscribing to the *Microsoft Security Newsletter*. The Automatic Updates service does not consume a lot of system resources. The resources that it does consume are well worth it because of the invaluable service that Automatic Updates provides.

Firewalls

You now know that your computer is vulnerable to viruses and attackers from the Internet. You also know that one way to help fight those attackers is to block access to your computer on all of the different ports, which can be gateways into your computer. How exactly to block all the ports? Use a firewall. A firewall is a special application that acts like a brick wall that is protecting all of the ports on your computer.

When a remote computer attempts to access a computer on which a firewall has been installed, which is blocking the port on which the remote machine is trying to connect, it will not be able to connect and the data that was sent will be ignored and discarded. Depending on the way the firewall is configured, when data is sent to a blocked port on your computer, the firewall will either respond to where the data was sent from with a message that the port is closed or it will do nothing, giving your computer a stealth presence. Most firewall applications are set up by default to run in a stealth mode, which will provide the maximum amount of protection. Any remote computer trying to connect or send data to your computer with a firewall installed

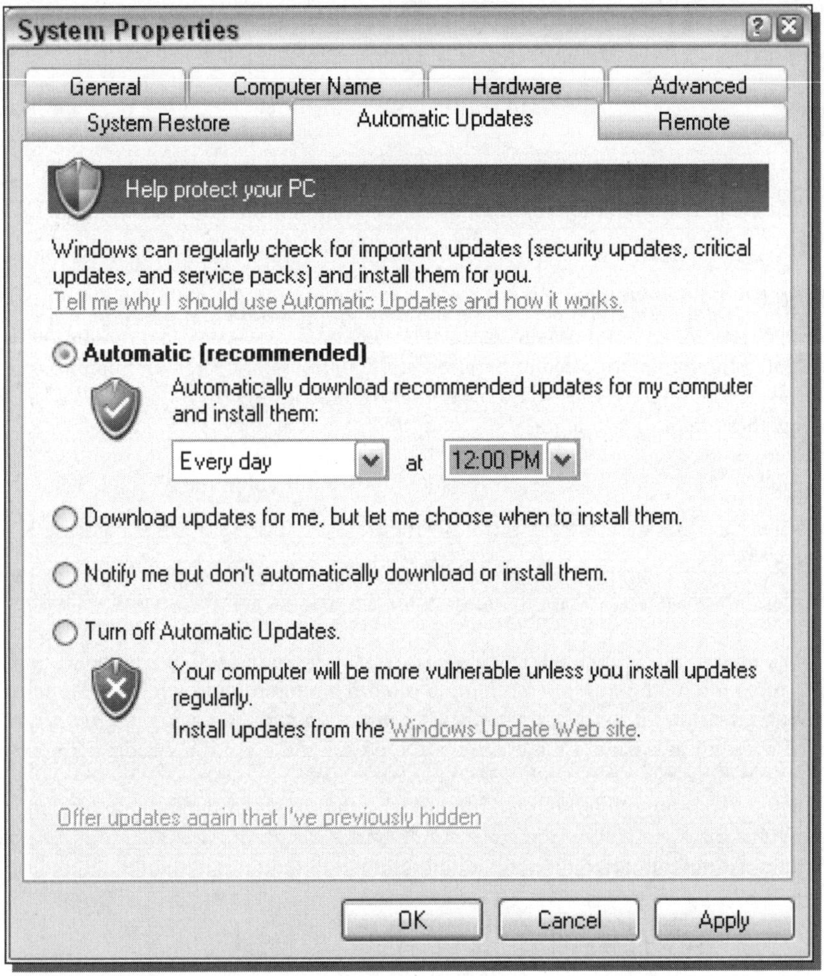

FIGURE 12-1: Windows XP Service Pack 2 Automatic Updates settings.

running in stealth mode will think that your computer has gone offline because it is not getting any response.

Firewalls can be a very powerful security device. Windows XP benefits greatly from a firewall because it can lower, if not completely eliminate, the chance that your computer will be compromised. This next section will show you how to use the new and improved firewall of Service Pack 2 as well as two popular third-party firewall utilities.

Using the Windows firewall

Windows XP has included a firewall—specifically, Internet Connection Firewall (IFC) software—since the product was first shipped. Although the firewall has not been turned on by default, it has always been there. The original firewall was a basic one-way firewall that would block incoming traffic from the Web. One feature allowed users to open up ports so that they could still use remote applications. This way, a user could protect all of the ports on the computer except one or two that they had set to remain open so that they could use a program such as remote desktop to connect to their computer from a different location.

The new version of the firewall included as part of Service Pack 2 has a bunch of new features that makes use of a firewall even easier while the protection it provides your computer remains the same.

Enabling the Windows firewall

The new Windows firewall is usually disabled by default on any computers running Windows XP, including those that upgraded to Service Pack 2, unless your computer manufacturer has turned this feature on for you. If you want to use the built-in firewall to protect your computer, just follow these steps to enable it:

1. Click the Start button and select Run. Key in **firewall.cpl** in the box and click OK.

2. When the Windows Firewall settings window loads, just select On and click OK to save your changes.

3. Click OK once more to save the settings for the adapter, and the firewall will be activated.

Now that you have the firewall set up, try using all of your common Internet applications. If you find that some of them do not work, then you can configure the firewall to allow them to pass through the firewall so that they can still be useful. Instant messaging programs can have problems with firewalls when a remote user attempts to send you a file. Sending files often requires the remote computer that is sending you the file to be able to connect to your computer. Because your firewall is designed to block all connections by default, you will have to configure it so that it will let certain applications work through the firewall. How to do so is described in the next section.

Configuring the Windows firewall

Configuring the firewall to allow certain programs to work through it is not always the best thing to do, because it will expose your computer more to the outside world and increase your risk of getting infected with something. However, in the short term or for an application that you must use, you can make it work through the firewall. In the original version of the firewall, the only possibility was to specify a port number to open. Now, it is much easier to make an application work though the firewall. Instead of typing in a port number, users can just select the program on their computer that they want to have accessed through the firewall. This capability makes the firewall configuration much more user-friendly. Additionally, in Service Pack 2, Microsoft left in the old way to open up the firewall manually by entering in a port number, so that users still have total control if they really want it. The end result of these two methods is the same; the only difference is the ease of use for less experienced Windows XP users.

Using the new feature to open up holes in the firewall is pretty cool. Follow these steps to open up the firewall for a specific application:

1. Open up Network Connections again by clicking the Start Menu and selecting Run. Then, type **firewall.cpl** in the box and click OK.

2. When the Windows Firewall settings window loads, click the Exceptions tab.

3. You will see a list of all of the different exceptions that are currently enabled, as signified by the check in the box. By default, a few applications will be enabled. I recommend that you uncheck all of the entries unless you use them. If not, then you are just taking an unnecessary risk by leaving those doors open.

4. If you want to add an application to the exception list so that it will be able to accept connections and data from the outside world, such as an Instant Message program that wants to receive files from other users, just click the Add Program button.

5. Select the name of the program from the list or click the Browse button on the Add a Program window to select the executable of the application that you want to open to the world.

6. When you are finished selecting the program that you want to be able to access through the firewall, click OK and it will appear on the list, as shown in Figure 12-2.

7. Now that the program is on the list, just check the box next to the name to open up the firewall for the application.

8. Click OK to activate your new firewall settings.

Windows Firewall also includes settings on how you want your computer to respond when several different standard Internet messages are sent to it. For example, one setting you can specify is the ping command, which is a network command used to estimate turnaround time between sending data to a computer and receiving a response. All of these settings are found on the Advanced tab by clicking the Settings button under the ICMP section. The screen is pretty straightforward. If you want your computer to have a stealth presence on the Web, as I mentioned earlier, you should uncheck all of the entries listed on the ICMP tab.

Using ZoneAlarm personal

Several different software companies have released their own firewalls and protection utilities. One of the oldest and most popular programs is called ZoneAlarm, by Zone Labs. ZoneAlarm comes in two different flavors: a pro version, which is a two-way firewall plus a boatload of other features, and a free version that is just the basic two-way firewall. ZoneAlarm is a different type of firewall than the firewall that is included with Windows XP and Windows XP Service Pack 2. ZoneAlarm includes a special two-way firewall that not only blocks traffic that remote users are sending to your computer but also blocks traffic that your programs are trying to send out.

Now, why would you want to block traffic that your computer is sending? Sometimes, people are concerned about their personal privacy and do not want their computer applications phoning home to the developer's Web site sending usage data, checking for updates, or validating licenses. Additionally, it is nice to be able to control what applications have access to the Internet. If you let someone use your computer and they accidentally fell for some trick and

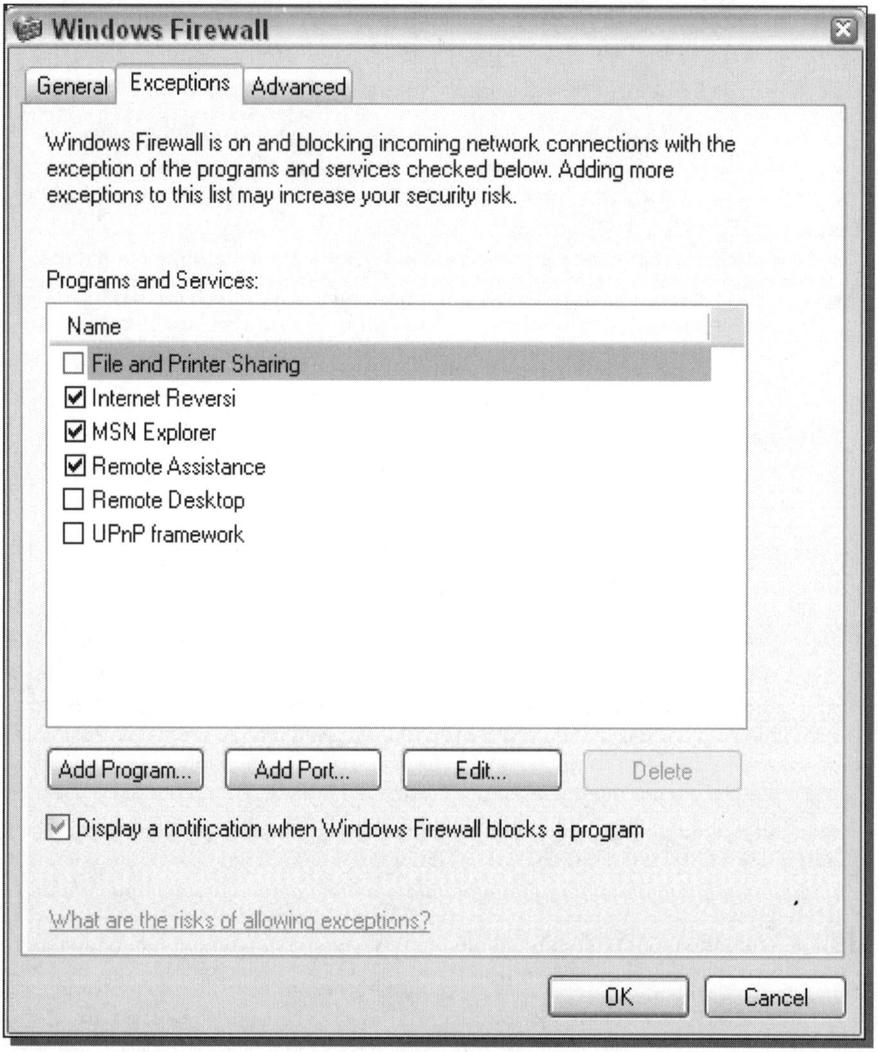

FIGURE 12-2: Adding an application to the firewall Exceptions list.

installed software that turns out to be a Trojan (a program that allows others to mess with your computer), the Trojan will not be able to phone home to its creators, alerting them that your computer is now compromised.

Two-way firewalls, such as ZoneAlarm, will render such applications useless because they are contained in an isolated box and are not able to access the Internet.

ZoneAlarm is a great application to play around with and see which of your applications are trying to send data out to the Web. Follow these steps to get ZoneAlarm up and running on your computer:

1. Visit ZoneAlarm's Web site at www.zonealarm.com and download a copy. The free version is a little hard to find. Your best bet is to look for "ZoneAlarm (free)" under Direct Links, found on the mid-right side of the page.

2. Once you have ZoneAlarm installed and have followed the Getting Started wizard to get your computer's policy configured, you are ready to start up ZoneAlarm.

3. By default, certain applications, such as Internet Explorer, will always have access to the Web. However, the first time you run a program that requires access to the Internet, such as Windows Messenger, you will be prompted with a message from ZoneAlarm, asking if you really want it to have access, as shown in Figure 12-3.

4. Click Yes on the pop-up window to allow Windows Messenger to connect to the Internet. If you see a request such as the one shown in Figure 12-3 and do not know what the program is, click No and do a search on the Web to try to find out what that program does. If your search on the Web reveals that it could be spyware or adware, read Chapter 13 to find out how to remove it.

ZoneAlarm Alert

New Program

Do you want to allow Windows Messenger to access the Internet?

Technical Information

Destination IP: 63.240.76.4:DNS
Application: msmsgs.exe
Version: 4.7.3000

More Information Available

This is the program's first attempt to access the Internet.

AlertAdvisor   [More Info]

☐ Remember this answer the next time I use this program.

[Yes]   [No]

FIGURE **12-3:** ZoneAlarm prompting about an Internet access request.

5. If you want to fine-tune your application blocking settings, select Program Control from the left menu and then click the Program Wizard button, as shown in Figure 12-4.

6. Then, select the Advanced setting and click Next. You will be shown a list of programs that will be exempt from the firewall, to which you can add entries. This list is similar to the exception list for the built-in Windows firewall.

7. Once you are finished, click Finish, and you are done.

ZoneAlarm is a great application. It adds a valuable two-way firewall to Windows, which can be very useful. I recommend that you give it a try and see how you like it. Just remember to disable the built-in Windows firewall when you are using ZoneAlarm to make sure there are no conflicts.

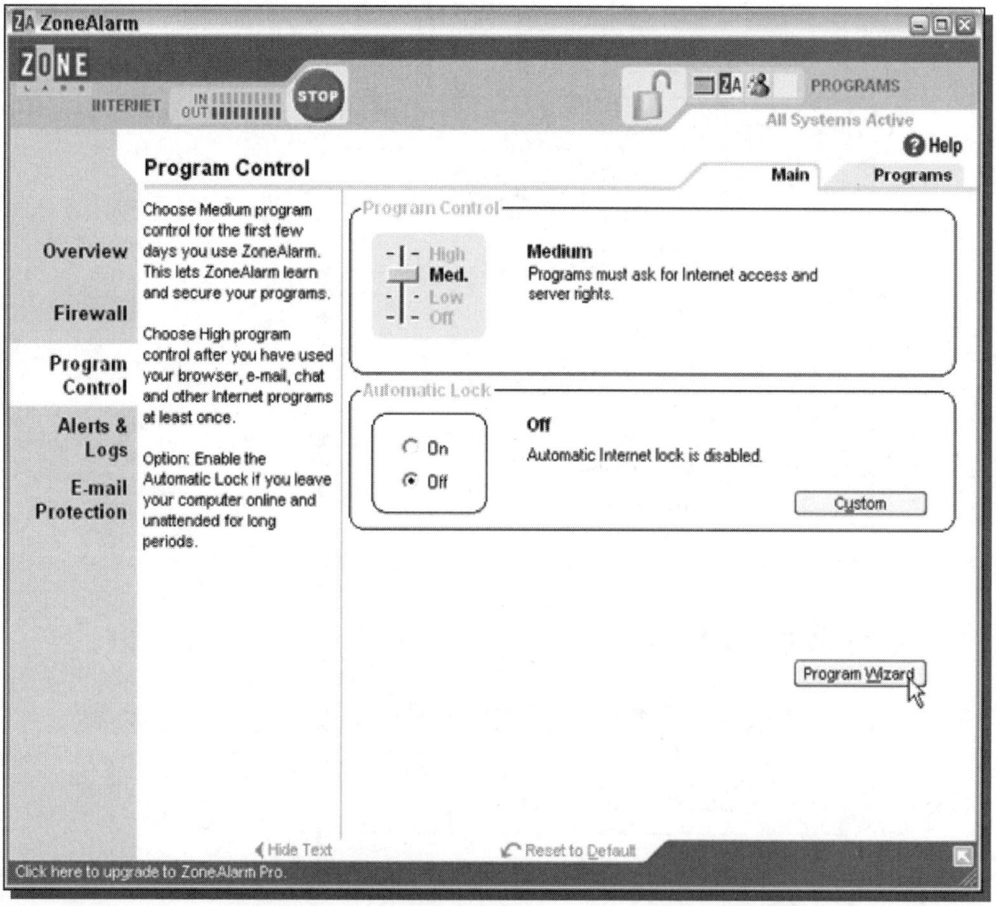

FIGURE 12-4: Configuring ZoneAlarm's Program Control.

Using Sygate Personal Firewall

Sygate is another company that makes a great personal firewall. Just like ZoneAlarm, Sygate Personal Firewall includes a two-way firewall that audits your incoming as well as outgoing traffic. ZoneAlarm and Sygate are very similar products. The only real difference is the user interface of the firewall. I personally like the way Sygate Personal Firewall displays the incoming and outgoing connections better than ZoneAlarm. Figure 12-5 shows the nice list interface of all of the connections that have been granted as well as all of the connections that have been blocked.

The Sygate user's interface is also different and a little easier to use than ZoneAlarm's, yet it offers a lot more power on the main screen. The interface shows detailed graphs and also the icons of the open programs, as shown in Figure 12-6. You can simply right-click the icon and select Block or Allow to set a program to a specific access setting.

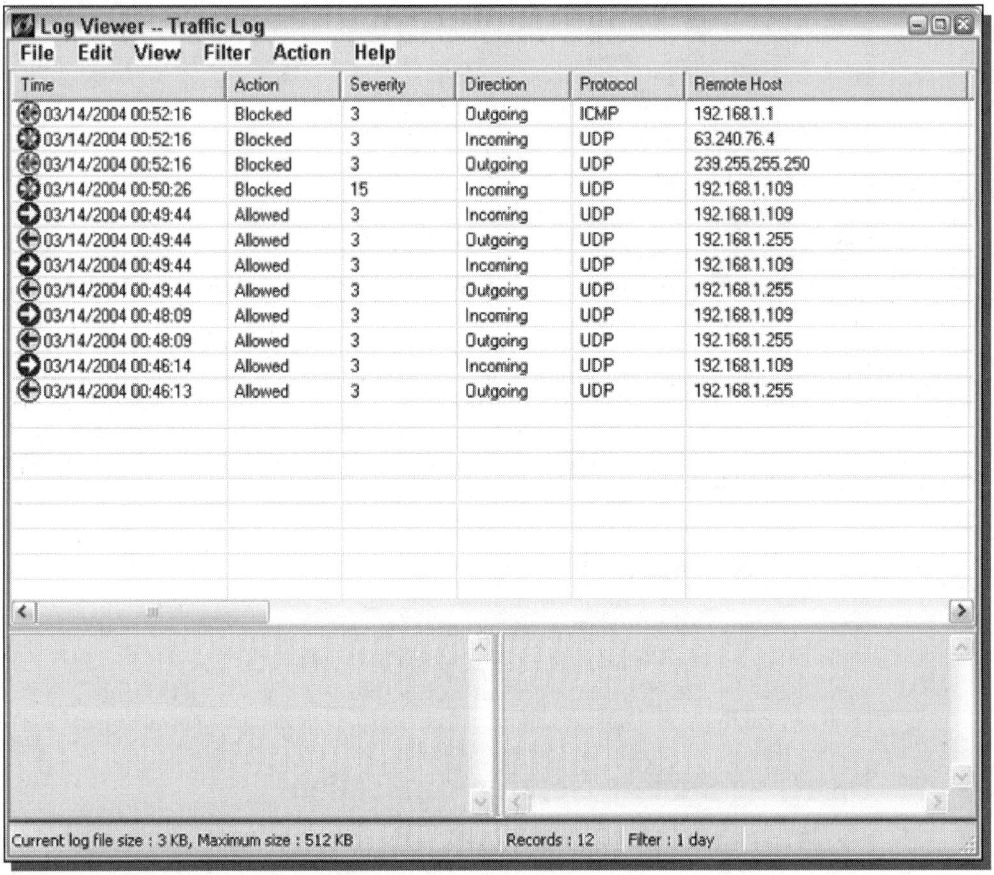
Log Viewer -- Traffic Log
File Edit View Filter Action Help
Time Action Severity Direction Protocol Remote Host
03/14/2004 00:52:16 Blocked 3 Outgoing ICMP 192.168.1.1
03/14/2004 00:52:16 Blocked 3 Incoming UDP 63.240.76.4
03/14/2004 00:52:16 Blocked 3 Outgoing UDP 239.255.255.250
03/14/2004 00:50:26 Blocked 15 Incoming UDP 192.168.1.109
03/14/2004 00:49:44 Allowed 3 Incoming UDP 192.168.1.109
03/14/2004 00:49:44 Allowed 3 Outgoing UDP 192.168.1.255
03/14/2004 00:49:44 Allowed 3 Incoming UDP 192.168.1.109
03/14/2004 00:49:44 Allowed 3 Outgoing UDP 192.168.1.255
03/14/2004 00:48:09 Allowed 3 Incoming UDP 192.168.1.109
03/14/2004 00:48:09 Allowed 3 Outgoing UDP 192.168.1.255
03/14/2004 00:46:14 Allowed 3 Incoming UDP 192.168.1.109
03/14/2004 00:46:13 Allowed 3 Outgoing UDP 192.168.1.255
Current log file size : 3 KB, Maximum size : 512 KB
Records : 12
Filter : 1 day

FIGURE 12-5: Sygate Personal Firewall with connections log.

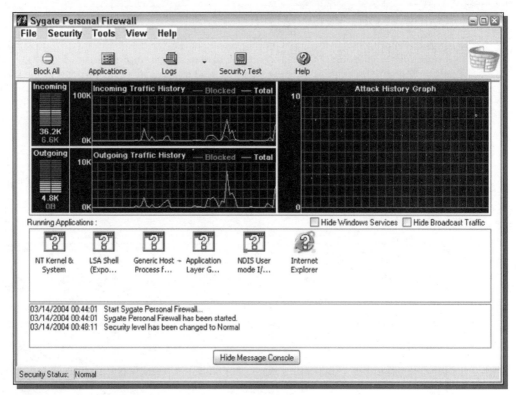

FIGURE **12-6:** The main Sygate Personal Firewall interface.

The operation of Sygate Personal Firewall is similar to that of ZoneAlarm. When a program attempts to access the Internet, it is caught, and the user is prompted to confirm if he or she wants the program to access the Internet or not. It all comes down to personal preference. If you like the cleaner and more accessible interface of Sygate personal firewall, visit Sygate's Web site at http://smb.sygate.com/products/spf_standard.htm and download a free copy.

Disabling Unneeded Services

Windows XP includes a lot of extra services and features that most users just do not use and have no reason to have running. In Part II of this book, you learned how you can disable unneeded services to increase the performance of your computer. Now, I am going to show you some services that you should disable that will make your computer more secure.

Disabling Remote Desktop connection

The Remote Desktop feature of Windows XP is a great way to be able to access your computer when you are away from the office or home. However, if you have poor computer security, the Remote Desktop also is a great way for anyone to be able to access and control your whole computer. Remote Desktop is a very risky application to leave exposed to the world. Its security relies solely on your account password, which for most users is easy to guess.

If you do not use Remote Desktop, then it would be a good idea to disable the feature. Doing so is a snap. Just follow these steps to turn it off:

1. Right-click the My Computer icon on the desktop or in the Start Menu and select Properties.

2. Click the Remote tab to expose the remote access settings.

3. Next, uncheck the box under Remote Assistance, as shown in Figure 12-7.

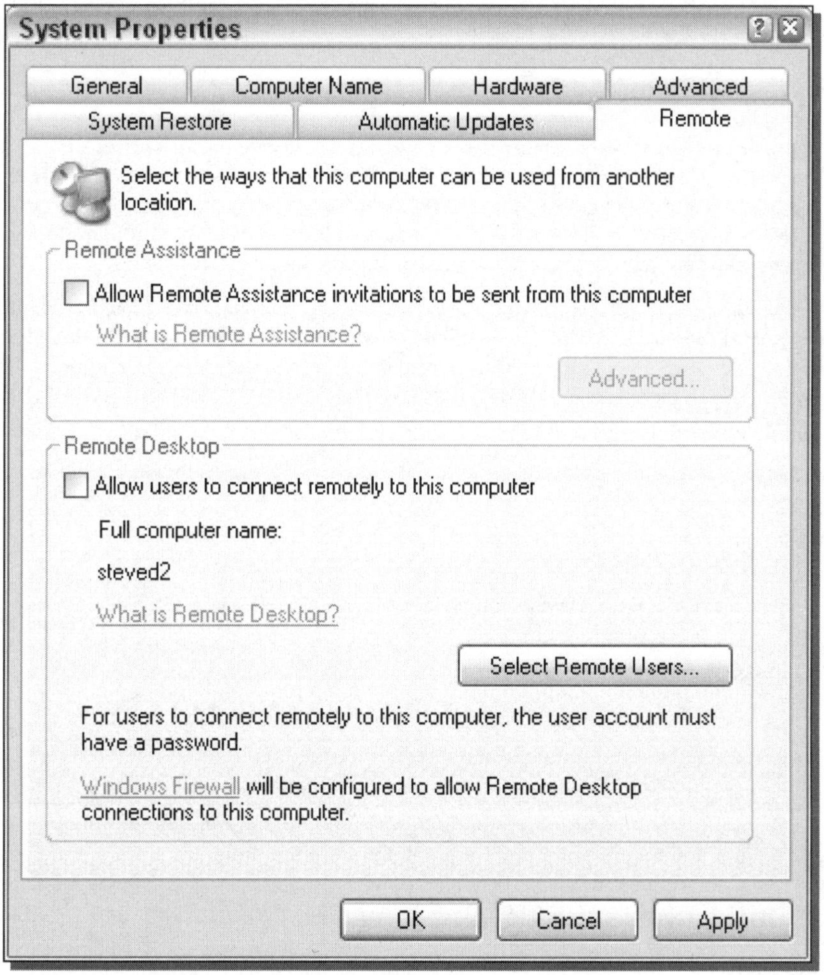

FIGURE 12-7: Remote Assistance & Desktop connections disabled.

4. Uncheck the box under Remote Desktop as well.

5. Click OK to save your changes.

When Remote Desktop connections are disabled, you have one less thing to worry about—namely, someone having the ability to break into your computer.

Disabling Messenger Service

Microsoft has included a service in the last few versions of Windows that allows system administrators to send pop-up messages to all computers on a local network. This service can be an invaluable resource for administrators who want to get the word out about some upcoming server maintenance. For example, end users would see a message pop up on their screens that notifies them that the workgroup file server will be inaccessible for the next hour while routine maintenance is performed.

This is a great service—when it is used correctly. Unfortunately, the Messenger Service has been abused. Just because any user *can* send messages to the entire workgroup doesn't mean that she or he *should*. This capability is sometimes not a good thing. Users that are part of large local area network, such as just about every Internet user, can send out a mass message to all users in the same subnet. As you can imagine, some users that know how to use the service have started to abuse it by sending spam to all the users in their same subnet. Nowadays, you may get spam not only in your inbox but also in a pop-up window that could appear at any time.

The Messenger Service, just like any other service or program that is accessible to the outside world, increases your security risk. Although there is currently not an exploit for the Messenger Service that allows remote users to execute commands on your computer, who knows what the future will hold? To be safe, it is best to just disable this service. You will also be cutting down on a new type of spam.

Disabling the Messenger Service can be done by using the Service Manager. Follow these steps to get started:

1. Click the Start button and select Run.

2. Key in **services.msc** in the box and click OK.

3. The Services Manager will load. Scroll though the list and right-click Messenger and select Properties.

4. Change the Startup Type to Disabled, as shown in Figure 12-8.

5. Click the Stop button and then click OK to save your changes.

Now the Messenger Service is one less thing to worry about. You can kiss the annoying pop-up text ads goodbye and also reduce your risk for an attack in the future.

Disabling Universal Plug and Play

Universal Plug and Play (UPnP) is kind of like an expanded version of the old Plug and Play hardware support. Many years ago, when you would buy a new soundcard, you would have to

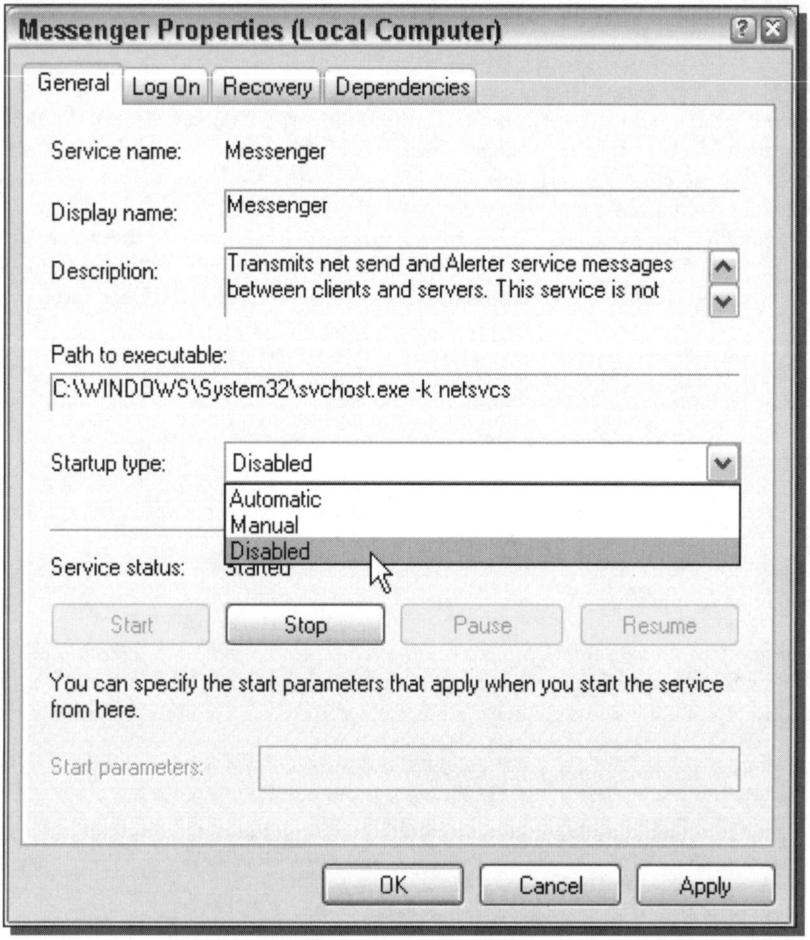

FIGURE 12-8: Disabling the Messenger Service.

manually set up all of the configuration data, such as the interrupt and address that it was going to run at. Then Plug and Play technology came around and automated that whole process so that the user did not have to worry about managing interrupt and address numbers any more. Now there is Universal Plug and Play, which expands the easy install concepts of the original Plug and Play to a whole new class of devices. Universal Plug and Play can not only detect local devices such as hardware (the original version), but it can also detect external hardware such as printers across the network or other PCs' shared drives.

Universal Plug and Play, theoretically, is a great idea. It gives you the ability to easily add and control devices such as a printer across your local network, an MP3 player, a television, lighting devices, and so on. Universal Plug and Play can be thought of as a way to make all of the different electronic devices in your home, or local network, work together. However, there are very few devices, other than remote printers and file shares, that take advantage of the new protocol. Universal Plug and Play will play a big role in our computing lives in the future, but not yet.

Universal Plug and Play also presents a security risk for your computer. It continuously scans your local network, which could be a network that is open to the world, for new devices and negotiates new connections. Just as with the Messenger Service, with Universal Plug and Play the surface exposure of your computer is increased, which increases the risk that your computer could become attacked and infected. Unlike with the Messenger Service, with Universal Plug and Play a flaw has been found in the service and has already been exploited. Microsoft was forced to release a critical security patch to fix Universal Plug and Play so that users' computers would no longer be vulnerable (this patch can be found on the Windows Update Web site mentioned earlier).

Because there are almost no devices that use Universal Plug and Play currently available on the market, and it also presents a security risk, it is a good idea to just disable the new protocol for now because 99.9 percent of you have absolutely no use for it. Disabling UPnP is not a hard task. Just follow these steps to disable the service with a nifty utility, called UnPlug n' Pray, by Gibson Research:

1. Visit www.grc.com/unpnp/unpnp.htm and download a copy of UnPlug n' Pray.

2. Start up the utility and click Disable UPnP, as shown in Figure 12-9.

3. Click the Exit button, and you are done.

Using the utility by Gibson Research is much easier than going back to the Service Manager and disabling the service. Moreover, if you ever find that you need to use Universal Plug and Play, you can just run the utility again and click Enable UPnP and the service will be restored.

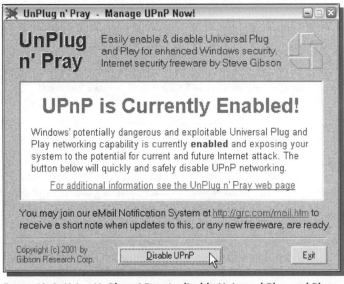

FIGURE 12-9: Using UnPlug n' Pray to disable Universal Plug and Play for users who do not need it.

Disabling Remote Registry Access

As already mentioned, the System Registry is one of the most important parts of the operating system. It's where all of the system settings and configuration data is stored. If you do not know what you are doing and you just start editing entries found in the System Registry, you can render your computer useless. So, protecting your computer's registry is very important.

Included with Windows XP Professional (not Windows XP Home) is a service that allows users with administrative privileges to connect your computer's registry and edit it. Having this service enabled and running is just way too big a security risk. The vast majority of computer users have little or no use for this service. Why would you even want to give anyone a chance at trying to break into one of the most critical parts of the operating system?

Disabling this service is a snap. Just follow these steps:

1. Click the Start button and select Run.

2. Key in **services.msc** in the box and click OK to launch the services manager.

3. Scroll through the list and right-click and select Properties on the Remote Registry entry.

4. Set the Startup Type as Disable and click the Stop button.

5. Click OK to close and save your changes.

Now you have knocked off yet another unneeded service from your computer.

Disable DCOM support

The Distributed Component Object Model, or DCOM, is yet another feature that was built into Windows that has caused a great deal of problems. Sure, it provides an acceptable programming interface for programmers who are trying to write network apps, but there are better ways to do that than to use a DCOM.

DCOM has presented quite a few problems in terms of security. Exploits have been discovered for it that have allowed an Internet worm to spread to hundreds of thousands of Windows machines worldwide. Additionally, a very small number of applications actually use DCOM. In all of my computing experience, I have only seen one application that used DCOM, and that was an inventory and store management software suite. Home and professional PC users probably will never even use an application that uses DCOM.

So why is it on your computer? DCOM was one of Microsoft's attempts to please software developers. However, this attempt has clearly failed, and yet they still include it. The only thing that it has given to operating systems such as Windows XP is headlines in the newspapers about how some worm exploited it and has now infected thousands of PCs.

Disabling the Distributed Component Object Model is a good idea for most computing users. That is, it is for everybody except the rare few who actually have an application that the developers wrote using DCOM. To shut down DCOM and increase the security of your computer, follow these steps:

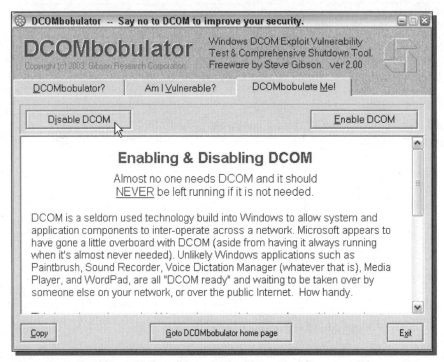

FIGURE 12-10: Disabling Distributed Component Object Model support with DCOMbobulator.

1. Gibson Research has come up with another cool utility to take care of Windows security shortcomings. This one is called DCOMbobulator and will help you disable DCOM on your computer. Visit www.grc.com/dcom/ and download a copy.

2. Start up DCOMbobulator and click the tab labeled DCOMbobulator Me!

3. Click the Disable DCOM button, as shown in Figure 12-10.

4. Click the Exit button and you are finished.

If you find that you are forced to use a program that needs DCOM, just run the utility again and click the Enable DCOM button on the DCOMbobulator Me! tab.

Wireless Networks

Wireless networks are growing in popularity because of the ease of installation and the terrific benefits that they offer. Nothing beats the ability to take your laptop and not have to worry about plugging into the network to do your work. The added freedom of a wireless network is very pleasing. Nevertheless, many people do not realize how insecure most wireless networks actually are. To fully understand this, you must realize how exactly a wireless network works.

Basically, wireless connections are made up of a base station and a client adapter. The wireless base station broadcasts all of the data to the clients in a circle around the base station, as do the client's adapters. This creates a large area over which information is broadcast. If you care about the security of your computer and personal information such as credit card numbers, you must configure your wireless base station to encrypt the data that it sends. Otherwise, just about anyone can connect to your wireless network and gain access behind your firewall to all of your unprotected computers. Additionally, users can sniff the wireless traffic and see exactly what you are sending back and forth.

It really is amazing how many people leave encryption turned off on their wireless base stations. I was always surprised when I took the train into Chicago and worked on my laptop on board. Every now and then, I would notice my laptop connecting to various wireless access points for a few seconds as the train was moving past them. Securing your wireless base station/access point is very important.

Using WEP for secure communication

Wired Equivalent Privacy, or WEP, is the first security standard for wireless networks. The basic concept for WEP security is to encrypt the data that is sent back and forth between the access point and the client adapter. This is done using various degrees of encryption strength. A special key, known as the encryption key, is used by computers to connect to a WEP-protected wireless network. This allows the client computer's adapter to be able to decrypt and also send encrypted messages in the same language as the base station.

This standard sounds like a great way to secure a wireless network. However, it presents some flaws. The largest one is that the whole system relies on just one key. If someone's laptop is stolen that is part of a corporate network, the encryption key must be changed for the base station and for all of the other computers using the wireless connection. This change is necessary because the current encryption key could be easily extracted from the system settings. Additionally, someone can potentially derive the encryption key by carefully analyzing the data they intercepted.

If you have a wireless base station, I highly recommend that you enable WEP to protect your home. Setting up WEP is different on every set of hardware, but the following are the basics:

1. Connect to your base station setting remotely using your Web browser. This address and port number varies, but usually is http://192.168.1.1 or http://192.168.2.1. Often, the port number is changed to 8080 so people don't think you have a Web server running. In that case, try http://192.168.1.1:8080 or http://192.168.2.1:8080.

2. Once you connect, you usually are asked for a password. For all Linksys hardware, the Username field is left blank and the password is admin. Other hardware manufacturers use some sort of a variation of the above. It also would be a good idea to change the password to something other than admin when you are working in the administration settings.

3. Locate the WEP settings and specify the encryption strength in bits. Then, come up with an encryption key and type that in. Write down your encryption key and strength for use in step 5.

4. Save your changes. You can now close the Web administration site.

5. The last part of setting up WEP is configuring the client computers that will connect to the base station. Once again, this information varies, depending on your wireless card. Consult the manual for your card to find out how to set up your card to use WEP.

Setting up WEP will greatly increase the security of your wireless network. Even though there are some flaws, it is much better than using no protection at all. It has the same effect as a car alarm. If a burglar has to choose between a car that clearly has an alarm or one that doesn't, which one will they choose to break into?

Using WPA for a more secure wireless connection

Wi-Fi Protected Access, or WPA, is a new, improved security standard for wireless connections. WPA has addressed the weaknesses of WEP; it was developed to create a viable alternative to WEP that is more secure than that standard. The fundamentals are the same between the standards, but WPA has improved some of the various mechanisms that plagued WEP. For example, encryption keys are now dynamic and change often automatically. Additionally, the complexity of the encryption key has also been increased to help fight off users who try to derive a key from data that they capture. One of the largest improvements in WPA is the addition of authentication to the wireless connection. Now, users have to have the right encryption settings, as well as a valid username and password, to gain access to the network.

This new standard is just starting to gain momentum. Microsoft has released a special patch for Windows XP that adds this new standard to Windows. However, installing the patch will not allow you to use this new standard. Just as with WEP, WPA is programmed into the firmware of the hardware components. In order to use WPA, you must have hardware that specifically supports it. Currently, only a few companies offer base stations and wireless adapters that support this new method of security. However, that will change in time.

The next time you are considering purchasing a wireless base station and adapter, do some research and pick one that supports WPA to ensure that your wireless communications will not be decrypted and your privacy is secure.

Controlling access to your computer

So far, you have spent a lot of time locking down your computer. You have closed down ports and have removed unused services from your computer. The next step to secure your computer is to reinforce the main entry point, the logon. No matter what you do to secure your computer, it all comes down to your security at the user level. If you have no password on your account and have a computer that is not protected by a firewall and other devices, then you are at huge risk of being attacked.

Managing user accounts is very important with Windows XP because the accounts are the keys into the system. This next section will show you some good secure practices, as well as some tips that will help make your box even more secure.

Managing user accounts

Windows XP includes the same old account manager found in Windows 2000. This easy-to-use and straightforward interface can be found in the Local User and Group Management interface. There are various "good" security practices that you can follow to make your computer practically invincible to many attackers.

Assign a password and rename the guest account

Windows XP includes a guest account that is disabled by default. However, at some time, this account may be enabled by an application. If you have Windows XP Professional, I recommend that you disable this account using the old Windows 2000 Local User and Group application. Just in case it becomes enabled again, I recommend that you rename the guest account and also assign it a password. Follow these steps to disable the guest account:

1. Click the Start button and select Run.

2. Key in **lusrmgr.msc** and click OK.

3. The Local User and Group application will launch. Right-click the Guest username and select Set Password.

4. You will be prompted with a warning screen. Just click Proceed.

5. Type a complex password in both boxes and click OK.

6. The password has now been set. Next, rename the account by right-clicking it and selecting Rename.

7. Type in a new name, such as **Disabled,** and click Enter to save the changes.

The vulnerable guest account is now less of a problem.

Clearing the last user logged on

If you are using the classic logon screen, every time a user logs into your computer, their username is stored, and that name is displayed the next time the classic logon screen is displayed. This can be a nice feature, but it also can be a feature that causes a security problem. Knowing a user's username is half the battle of breaking into a computer. If you have sensitive information on your computer, I suggest that you follow these instructions to hide the last user logged on:

1. Start up the Registry Editor again by clicking the Start Menu and selecting Run. Then type **regedit** in the box and click OK.

2. Navigate through HKEY_LOCAL_MACHINE, SOFTWARE, Microsoft, Windows, CurrentVersion, policies, and system. Locate the dontdisplaylastusername entry.

3. Right-click the entry and select Modify. Then type in a **1** to activate the feature. Click OK, and you are finished.

If you ever want to reverse this hack, just repeat the instructions above and replace the **1** with a **0** for the value of dontdisplaylastusername.

Disable and rename the Administrator account

The Administrator account is the most important account on the computer. Users should not be using the computer under the Administrator account. That just is not a good security practice for anyone that is running Windows XP Professional and has sensitive data on their computer. I like to disable my Administrator account and rename it, so that anyone trying to get in with that account and at that privilege level will not be able to. To disable the account, perform the following steps:

1. Click the Start button and select Run.

2. Key in **lusrmgr.msc** and click OK.

FIGURE 12-11: Disabling an account with the local user and group administrator.

3. When you have the Local User and Group application on your screen, just right-click the Administrator entry and select Rename. Give your administrator account a new name, such as **admin123**.

4. Next, disable the account by right-clicking the entry and selecting Properties.

5. Check the Account Is Disabled box, as shown in Figure 12-11.

6. Click OK to save your changes.

Make sure every account on your computer has a complex password

All of the accounts on your computer should have a complex password associated with them if your computer is ever exposed to the Internet. Passwords such as easy-to-remember words and key combinations like "asdf" just do not cut it. A complex password is a password that is at least seven characters long and consists of uppercase and lowercase letters as well as numbers or other symbols. Ftm3D8& is an example of a complex password. Something like that is impossible to guess and will take quite some time for a brute-force technique to crack.

Using complex passwords on all of your accounts might not be easy at first, but after a while they will grow on you and you will have no problem remembering them.

Summary

This chapter has shown you how to test to see how vulnerable your computer is to attacks and how to protect it by using firewalls and lowering your computer's exposure to the world by disabling unneeded services. You have learned how to secure your wireless networks and how to strengthen your account security.

The next chapter will show you how to protect your computer from spam, spyware, and adware. Additionally, it will show you some great utilities that will help you detect and clean your system, as well as some cool tricks to eliminate spam.

Fighting Spam, Spyware, and Viruses

This chapter will show you how to defend your computer against the major menaces of operating a computer: spam, spyware, adware, and viruses. Viruses have been around for a very long time; spam just keeps getting worse and worse; and now there is a new computer menace that is infecting millions of computers, known as spyware and adware. Spyware is the name for applications that are secretly installed on your computer and record your personal activities or do other tasks with your computer of which you would probably not approve if you knew about them. Adware is very similar to Spyware, but can be a little worse. Instead of just spying on your activities, it uses its monitoring data to display relevant advertisements on your computer.

All of these computer menaces can be eradicated (or at least severely limited) by tweaking some of the settings of Windows XP and using various protection and defense apps. This chapter will show you how you can make Windows XP defend against some of the most popular types of viruses and spyware. It will also present some great utilities that you can use to battle spam and remove spyware and viruses from your computer.

Eliminating Spam

Spam is everywhere these days. Recently, I have been forced to change all of the e-mail addresses that I had used for years because I just started to get way too much spam. If you are tired of receiving messages from advertisers about debt consolidation, male sexual enhancements, and messages from the president of Congo asking you to help him launder $40,000,000 by giving him your bank account number, then this section is for you. When you are finished reading it, you will know how to stop spam from starting in the first place and how to filter the spam you already get.

Stopping spam in the first place

Users can do a lot of things when browsing the Internet to make sure that they do not end up receiving spam. But before anyone can prevent the actual receipt of spam, he or she needs to be aware of why spam is received in the first place. So, why is that annoying spam sent?

To start off, the most common reason why users receive spam is because they submit their e-mail address to a Web site or company that starts sending them advertisements or sells their e-mail address. Usually, most Web sites notify you when they intend to sell your e-mail address, if they plan on doing so. This notification is commonly hidden away in the terms of service agreement or privacy policy—so much so that 99 percent of Web visitors check the agreement box but never actually take a look at the information.

This is by far the number one reason why users receive spam. They sign up for some service that promises them some great free offer, such as free movie tickets, and then they end up receiving tons of spam because they didn't realize that they gave the Web site permission to sell their e-mail address to thousands of other companies. If they would have taken the time to read the terms of service agreement and the privacy policy, they would have found out that by using the so-called free service, they give the Web site permission to do whatever they want with your personal information.

Paying attention to the details is very important when you're using the Web. With the absence of useful laws that actually make a difference on certain Internet subjects such as spam, some companies take advantage of users. If you are considering signing up for a site and cannot find their terms of service or privacy policy, do not use their service. That lack of information should be a huge warning sign.

Another common reason why users end up with inboxes packed with spam is because they inadvertently sign up for various newsletters. I shop online a lot and end up creating many different accounts at different stores so that I can purchase items. During the signup process, you are almost always asked if you would like to sign up for their deal-of-the-week newsletter or some other kind of promotional material. They want you to give them permission to send you more advertisements so that, it is hoped, you will buy from them again. You may think that this is nice, but when you have accounts at 25 different online stores, you could be getting a lot of messages that are just advertisements. When you are creating accounts at online shops or other Web sites, make sure that you uncheck all of the newsletter links, unless you really want to get one. These options are usually placed on the Web page in a location that you may overlook. The check boxes are checked on purpose so that those people that miss them automatically end up on the advertisement mailing list. Keep an eye out for these boxes and you will be able to cut down on spam.

If you follow the two tips just mentioned you will dramatically cut down on the amount of spam you receive. Another way to fight spam is to create separate e-mail accounts. There are several different Web sites on the Web from which you can get free e-mail. Create separate accounts on these free sites or request more mailboxes from your Internet Service Provider. Then, use each mailbox for a different purpose. I like to have one mailbox that is just for my personal mail from my family and friends. I never give away that address on any Web site and even tell my family and friends never to submit that address to any Web site on my behalf. I have been doing that for the last two years and still to this day have not received any spam to that account. I highly suggest that you create an e-mail that you will use for personal mail only and never give that address to any Web site.

I also have a separate account that I use for all of my online purchases. This way, if I ever start to get too many weekly newsletters and some unethical store sells my information, I can just close the e-mail account and start up a new one with a different name. Additionally, I have a separate e-mail address (my junk mail address) that I give to any Web site that requests an e-mail to sign up for something. This way, I can still get the confirmation message that a lot of sites require you to do something with to verify your e-mail address and not have to worry about the site sending me tons of junk that will fill up my personal inbox. You should defiantly create a separate junk e-mail address so that you can give that address out to Web sites instead of using your personal address.

Using filtering software

I have shown you how to lower your chances of receiving spam from sites on the Web. However, what if you already receive a lot of spam? If you fit into that category, you have two choices. You can either create a new e-mail address or start using the tips that I have given you previously, or you can try some filtering software. There are thousands of different anti-spam software apps on the Web. Everyone is trying to cash in on spam. Because of the mass amounts of spam apps, it is a little difficult to find the best programs. No spam filtering app is 100 percent accurate. If they are anything close to 90 percent, that is great.

I am not going to show you how to use all of the different spam filters; instead, I am going to give you a list of the best anti-spam apps (Table 13-1) so you can try out a few to find the program that works best for you.

Blocking external links in HTML mail

Every time you receive an e-mail, and your e-mail client supports graphical HTML-based e-mail messages the possibility exists that the sender could be tracking you if you read the message. This can be done by using a hidden image link in the message that points to a Web server where a special tracking program resides. This may not sound like a big deal, but when you take into consideration that spammers use this type of technology, it is a whole new game.

Spammers can use this type of technology to weed out e-mail addresses from their database that are no longer in use. When you open up spam, it can send a signal home to a spammer's Web server, alerting them that your e-mail address is active and that you read your e-mail. If you could prevent that signal from being sent to the spammer's servers, then you could make your e-mail address appear to be inactive and could be removed from their database.

Thankfully, Microsoft automatically blocks all external image links in HTML messages in Outlook 2003. Additionally, with the release of Windows XP Service Pack 2, Outlook Express also gains this feature. If you have not already upgraded to Service Pack 2, and use Outlook Express as your e-mail program, you should definitely upgrade. Your computer will not only be more secure, but you will also be protected against some spammers as well.

Table 13-1 Anti-Spam Apps

Application Name	Description
McAfee SpamKiller	SpamKiller is a good app that filters messages based on its database, which is automatically updated once a day. Aside from the standard filtering features that all anti-spam apps have, SpamKiller has a quarantine area for your spam and also allows you to report spam senders to McAfee to help them keep an up-to-date database. It supports Web-based e-mail accounts such as MSN and Hotmail, as well as POP3- and IMAPI-based e-mail accounts. SpamKiller costs around $40. Visit www.McAfee.com for more information
SAproxy Pro	SAproxy Pro is another good program that uses the same database as McAfee Spamkiller (the open source spam assassin database). It includes all of the basic features of spam filters, as well as the effective Bayesian learning engine that allows the program to get smarter at catching spam based on what it observes you classifying as spam. Currently, SAproxy Pro only supports POP3-based e-mail accounts and sells for $30. Visit www.statalabs.com for more information
K9	K9 is another popular spam filtering app that allows you to filter your incoming mail from a constantly updated database as well as "statistical analysis". It supports only POP3-based e-mail accounts, but is available for free. Visit www.keir.net/k9.html to download a copy and for more info
Cloudmark SpamNet	SpamNet filters incoming mail based on its own database of spam that is updated from its 800,000+ subscriber base. This app works only with Microsoft Outlook and Outlook Express. It installs a special toolbar in these applications that allows you to manage your spam. Unlike other commercial spam programs, SpamNet works on a subscription basis of $4 a month. SpamNet supports any e-mail accounts that you can use with Outlook and Outlook Express, including Hotmail and MSN e-mail accounts. Visit www.cloudmark.com/products/spamnet/ for more information
Spam Inspector	Spam Inspector filters all of the incoming mail using its own database that is updated by its users daily. Also gives users the ability to make messages bounce so it appears that your e-mail address no longer exists. Recently introduced fraud protection that automatically flags fraudulent scams that you may also receive. Spam Inspector currently supports Outlook, Outlook Express, Eudora, and Incredimail and sells for $20. Visit www.giantcompany.com to download a trial and for more information

If you are using Outlook Express, this blocking of external image links in HTML messages can be turned on by working with the Security tab of the Options window, located under the Tools menu bar item. If you are using a different e-mail program, I recommend that you read through the Help files or contact the developer of your program to find out how to disable HTML images and other external content.

Outlook and Outlook Express also provide a safe sender list that allows you to enable this feature for only certain senders, such as messages from your bank or newsletters that you have signed up for. Just right-click a message and add the sender to your safe list to enable images and other external content for a specific sender.

Defending Spyware and Adware

Spyware is becoming the largest menace of computers in the last year. Hidden away within free applications, these programs can spy on your computer activities and report home various information about your computer habits. Adware is another menace that is closely related to spyware. Just like Spyware, it can be secretly installed on your computer and will monitor what you do. Then, when the time is right, some Adware apps will display relevant advertisements. Did you ever visit eBay.com and then notice an advertisement for Ubid.com, one of eBay's competitors, pop up on your screen? If so, then you are infected with a bad case of adware.

How does your computer get infected? There can be a number of reasons why, but the most common reason is that you visit a Web site and are prompted to click Yes on some pop-up box to allow an application to install that you think is a game or some cool browser utility such as a search toolbar. Often, these utilities are spyware themselves and are also bundled with other spyware and adware. Unfortunately, users never seem to read the terms of service agreements that are presented when they are installing these free apps on their computers and pass right over the notices that this software will display ads and will monitor your browsing habits.

These next few sections will show you how to detect and remove spyware and adware from your computer, as well as what to look out for to protect your computer from getting infected in the first place. Additionally, you will learn how to use some of the new features of Windows XP Service Pack 2 to protect your computer from getting infected if you accidentally try to install spyware or adware.

Detecting and removing spyware

There are a bunch of free apps on the Web that will help you scan your computer for adware and spyware. There are two programs I recommend that you use to scan your computer. Each of these programs has its own database of adware and spyware that is updated frequently. To make sure that no spyware and adware goes undetected, it is a good idea to scan your computer with both programs. The first app is called Ad-aware, which is published by Lavasoft. This is a great program that has a basic version available for free when used for personal use. The second app is called Spybot S&D, which is developed by Patrick M. Kolla and is also free.

Using these two apps to detect and remove spyware and adware from your computer will not only rid your computer of those annoying programs, but will also speed up your computer and free up disk space. Follow these steps to get started using Ad-aware:

1. Visit www.lavasoft.de and download a copy of the basic version of Ad-aware that is free when used on personal computers.

2. Once you have Ad-aware installed on your computer, start it up by clicking the Ad-aware icon on your desktop.

3. When Ad-aware is loaded, the first thing you should do is update the data files. This can be done by clicking the globe icon, as shown in Figure 13-1.

4. Then, on the Webupdate screen, click the Connect button. It will tell you if a new update is available. If one is, just click OK and it will be downloaded and installed.

5. Now that Ad-aware is updated, you are ready to scan your computer. Just click the Start button in the lower-right corner of the window.

6. Select Perform Smart System-Scan on the Next screen and click Next. The scan will begin.

7. Once the scan has finished, you will hear a sound. Click the Next button again to view the results.

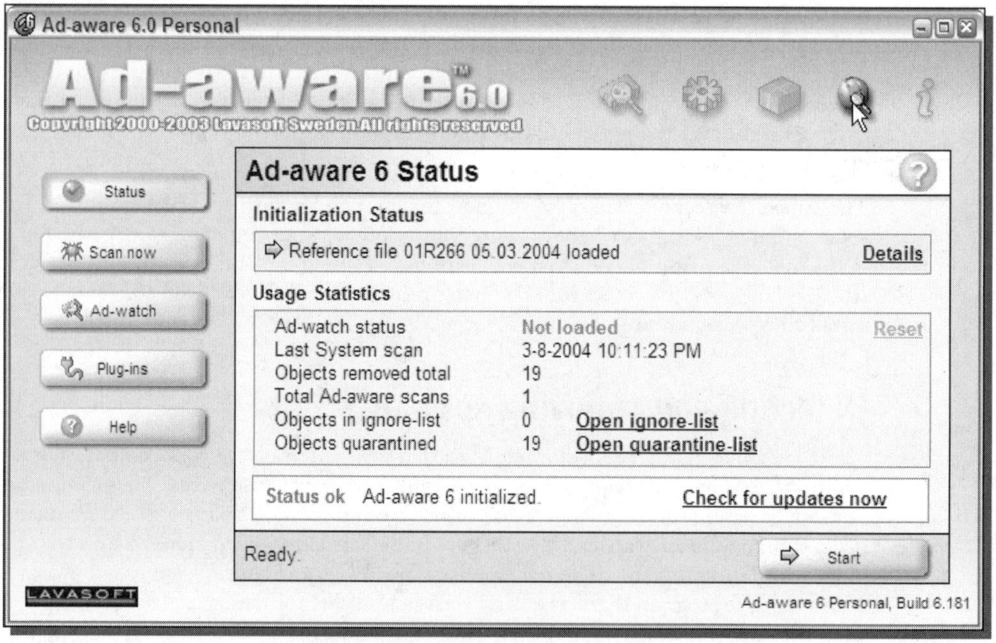

FIGURE 13-1: Checking for updated data files for Ad-aware.

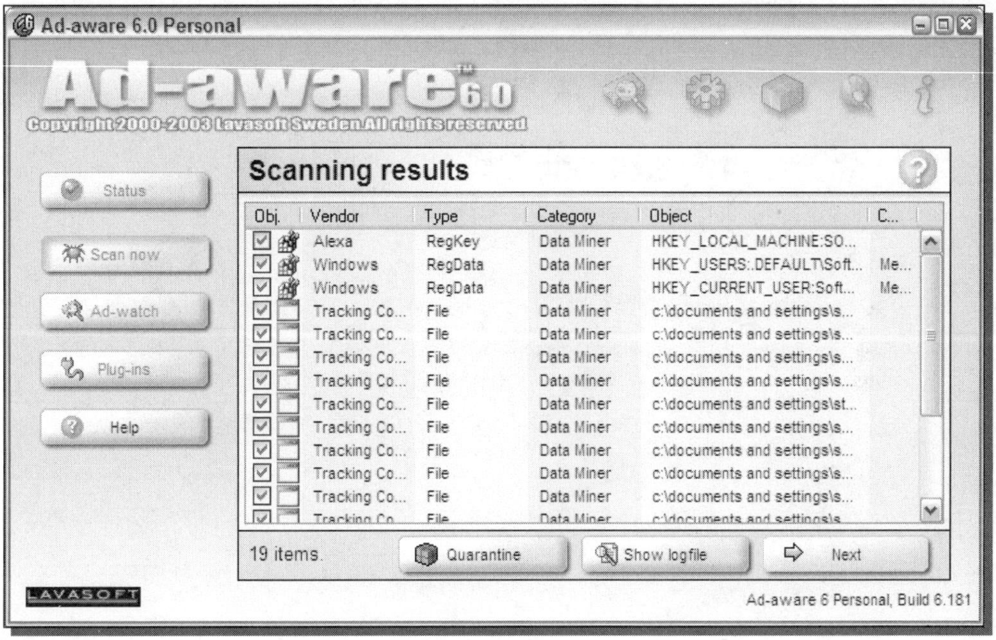

FIGURE **13-2: Browsing the results of the Ad-aware scan.**

8. The Scanning Results screen will be shown, which lists any instances of spyware and adware on your computer, as shown in Figure 13-2. Scroll through the list and uncheck any objects that you do not want to remove. Then, click the Next button again.

9. You will be asked to confirm that you want to delete the items on the list. Click OK to continue removing the files and registry entries associated with spyware and adware.

The files will be quarantined as a backup just in case you experience any problems with the operating system after you remove the files and registry entries. You are now finished with using Ad-aware and can close the application.

You are now ready to get Spybot Search & Destroy installed and set up on your computer so that you can ensure that you have removed all spyware and adware from your computer. To do that, just follow these steps:

1. Visit Spybot's Web site at www.spybot.info and download a copy of Spybot Search & Destroy.

2. Once Spybot S&D is installed on your computer, start it up by expanding the Spybot Search & Destroy folder and selecting Spybot S&D (easy mode). The first time it is run, you will have to select the language that you want to use and will be shown a few legal disclaimer screens.

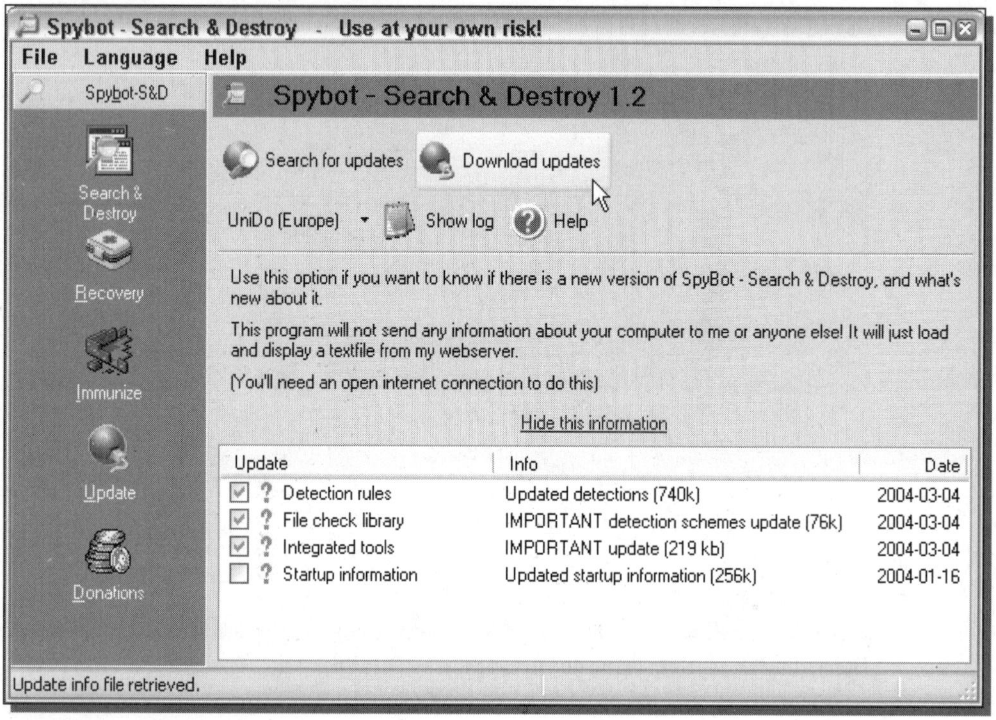

FIGURE 13-3: Updating Spybot Search & Destroy.

3. When Spybot loads, you will want to update its data files as well. This can be done by clicking the Search For Updates screen located in the middle of the screen.

4. Check all of the updates that are shown on the screen and click the Download Updates button, as shown in Figure 13-3.

5. Once Spybot has finished downloading and installing the updates, it will restart itself. When that happens, you are ready to begin scanning your computer. To begin scanning, just click the Check for Problems button.

6. Once scanning has finished, you will be presented with the Results screen. Click the Fix Selected Problems button, as shown in Figure 13-4, to remove all of the selected search results.

7. When all of the entries in the search box have check marks, Spybot is finished cleaning your system. You may now close Spybot.

Your computer has now been scanned and cleaned with two great spyware cleaning software apps. As you can see, Spybot picked up on some things that Ad-aware missed. Using both of these programs together will allow you very good detection and removal of spyware on your computer.

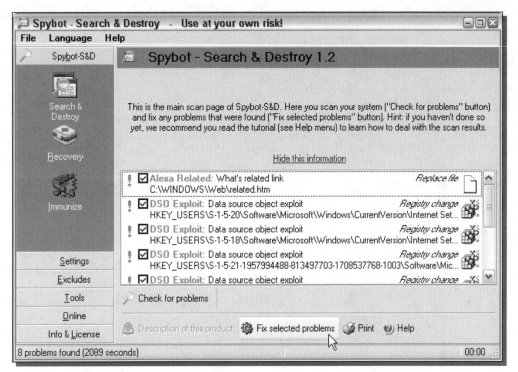

FIGURE **13-4: Using Spybot Search & Destroy to remove spyware & adware found during a system scan.**

Locking down Internet Explorer

Now that you have removed all of the spyware and adware on your computer, let's turn off certain features of Internet Explorer so that you will be less likely to accidentally install more spyware. To get started, change the ActiveX install settings to prevent any new ActiveX apps to be installed. Follow these steps to change this setting:

1. Open up a copy of Internet Explorer.

2. Click the Tools menu bar item and select Internet Options.

3. Click the Custom Level button on the Security tab.

4. Locate Download Signed ActiveX Control at the top of the list and select Disable.

5. Click OK and click Yes on the confirmation screen.

6. Select OK once more to close Internet Options.

A change in this setting can prevent you from installing new ActiveX controls from all Web sites, good and bad. If you ever run into some problem with a Web site not loading correctly, just re-enable this setting and try the site again.

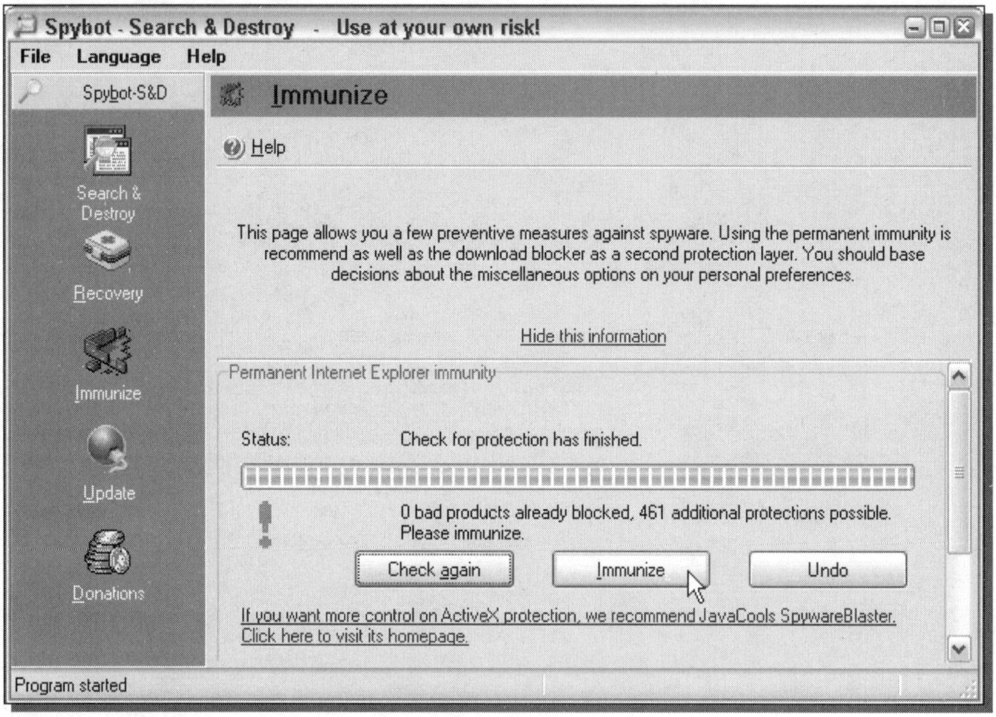

FIGURE 13-5: Immunizing your computer from common spyware apps.

Immunizing your computer

Spybot Search & Destroy does a lot more than just scanning your computer and removing spyware and adware. It also offers the ability to immunize your computer against some of the most common types of spyware. This feature provides a great added level of protection that can only help in your battles with spyware. To use this feature, follow these steps:

1. Start up Spybot by expanding the Spybot Search & Destroy folder and selecting Spybot S&D (easy mode).

2. Once Spybot S&D is loaded, click the Immunize button on the left of the window.

3. Then, just click the Immunize button, as shown in Figure 13-5, and you are now protected.

Defending against Viruses

Windows XP Service Pack 2 has many new features that make Windows XP the most secure Microsoft operating system to date. One of the new features, called execution protection, takes advantage of a new hardware protection found in the latest CPUs of modern computers.

One of the most common types of computer break-ins and virus exploits has to do with buffer overflows. These occur when data is being sent to a buffer faster than the CPU can process it. When the buffer becomes filled, the system can become unstable and sometimes can execute code that was placed in the buffer. This is how many types of viruses spread. They take advantage of an unchecked buffer and can get the CPU to execute their malicious code. One easy solution to solve this problem is to include a feature in the CPU that will disable executing of data in all buffers. By doing this, a virus might be able to get its code into the buffer, but because of limitations of the CPU, the code would never be executed, rendering the virus useless and unable to spread.

The new CPU level security can be found on the AMD Athlon 64 processor and new versions of the Intel Pentium 4 Prescott. If you have one of these chips with the execution protection feature, this feature is enabled by the operating system. However, having this feature enabled for all programs may cause some application errors because some need to be able to execute data in their buffers. To allow for this, Microsoft has created an exception list for such programs. You are advised to make sure every once in a while that no application has automatically added itself to the exception list. You really need to make sure that only the applications that truly need to be there *are* there. To do this, follow these steps:

1. Right-click the My Computer icon located on the desktop or Start Menu and select Properties.

2. When System Properties loads, click the Advanced tab.

3. Then, click the Settings button under the Performance section.

4. Next, click the Data Execution Prevention tab and make sure that Help Protect All Programs Except: is selected.

5. Then, review the list and remove any apps except for the ones that you are 100 percent positive should be there.

6. Click OK to save your changes.

7. Select OK once more to close System Properties.

Use an antivirus program

If you still are not running an antivirus program, then you really should reconsider your decision. Viruses, especially in e-mail attachments, are very prevalent these days. I highly recommend that you install an antivirus program on your computer if you do not have any protection currently installed. Additionally, if your current virus definitions subscription has expired and you no longer can download updates to the data files, your antivirus program is almost completely useless. You must always be running up-to-date antivirus data files so that your computer is always protected from the latest viruses.

If you do not want to spend $40 or more on getting some antivirus software, you can avail yourself of the many free antivirus applications. My favorite free antivirus app is called AVG by GriSoft. AVG is a very good antivirus program that is free for home use. Follow these steps to get AVG up and running on your computer:

1. Visit GriSoft's Web site at `www.grisoft.com/us/us_dwnl_free.php`.

2. Scroll the bottom of the page and click the Download AVG Free Edition button. Be sure to enter a valid e-mail address on the form after the License Agreement page, because they will send you a serial number that you will need to use when installing AVG.

3. Once you have downloaded and installed AVG, make sure to update the virus definitions with the Update Wizard that is shown the first time you run AVG.

4. When you get your virus definitions updated, you are advised to do a full system scan by clicking the Run Complete Test button.

Summary

Now your computer has been cleaned and protected from spyware, spam, adware, and viruses. The tools and techniques discussed in this chapter will help you maintain a computer that is free of all computer menaces. Make sure you scan your computer using the spyware and adware tools at least once a month, as well as with your antivirus application. Also, take care that you read the fine print when you sign up for things on the Internet to make sure you know what a company will do with your personal information. Create two or more e-mail accounts so you do not have to give out your personal e-mail account to Web sites. Doing so will greatly reduce the amount of spam that you receive with your personal messages.

The next chapter will shift over to protecting your privacy further. Internet Explorer and Windows Explorer both keep track of a lot of the things that you do on your computer. Events such as opening a file and visiting a Web page are all logged in various parts of Windows XP. Chapter 14 will show you how to clean all of the various user histories of Windows XP and how you can turn off certain features. It also will show you how to use some nifty apps that will make maintaining your computer privacy very easy.

Protecting Your Privacy

Windows XP keeps track of activities that you do on your computer. It records the Web sites that you visit, the addresses that you type in, the applications that you launch, and even the files that you open. Why does it do this? The majority of the information is used to tailor your computer experience and power features such as the frequently run programs or recently run documents lists. These features can be very useful and save you time. Other activities, such as typing in addresses for Web sites, are also logged. This information is used to save you time when you are typing in addresses at a later time. As you type in part of the address, possible suggestions based on your history will appear. However, this is not always the best. This information, combined with the useless browser history, will allow anyone to see what you browse on the Web.

Because of the vast amounts of information that Windows XP records, your privacy can become at stake when others are using your computer. This chapter will show you how to clean all of the recorded data from your computer. Additionally, you will learn to protect your privacy further by taking advantage of some interesting features of XP.

Internet Explorer

Internet Explorer is one of the most difficult parts of Windows to clean because it stores its data all over your drive, which makes clearing the data a little more tricky because you can't just clear one folder. Basically, four different parts of Internet Explorer need to be cleaned to ensure that you maintain your privacy: clearing recent addresses, removing history files, erasing temporary Web files, and removing cookies. The first part of this section will show you exactly how to clean those parts.

The second part of this chapter will show you how you can protect your privacy further by using a great utility and disabling some extra unnecessary features.

Removing address bar suggestions

Windows XP, like other versions of Windows, includes a feature called AutoComplete that is always activated for the address box. This can be a convenient feature because it can help you when typing in an address by presenting you with various suggestions. The suggestions are based upon your address box history. As you can see, because of this feature, your privacy can be at risk. When I start typing **www.Twea** in my address bar, it automatically suggests www.tweakxp.com, because I have visited that site. Anyone who uses my computer and starts typing addresses in manually can see sites that I have visited. If they just type in **www.c** or **www.t,** they will be presented with a small list of all the sites that I have visited that have URLs that start with c or t.

How do you stop the suggestions? You have to go after the source. Unfortunately, this effort can be a little tricky. The file that stores this information is called the URL cache and is named index.dat. This file resides in your Cookies directory within Documents and Settings. To remove information that Windows records, you just have to delete the file. However, deleting this file is not as easy as deleting normal files. The URL cache file is always in use when the operating system is running. And because it is impossible to delete files that are in use, the only way to delete this file is to delete the file in Safe mode or when the system is loading. One solution to this dilemma is to use a nifty utility called Dr. Delete, which will help you schedule the file to be deleted the next time that your computer restarts. Follow these steps to delete the index.dat file with Dr. Delete:

1. Visit Dr. Delete's Web site, located at www.docsdownloads.com/dr-delete.htm, and download a copy of Dr. Delete.

2. Once you have downloaded a copy of Dr. Delete and have it running, click the Browse button to specify the file that you want to delete.

3. Navigate to the C:\Document and Settings folder.

4. Then expand the folder that is named after your User Name.

5. Expand the Cookies folder and then select the index.dat file.

6. Click Open when you have the file selected.

7. Once you see the path of the file in the text box, click the Delete! button, as shown in Figure 14-1.

8. Click Yes on the confirmation screen.

9. You will be shown a message that says that the file will be deleted after the next reboot. Reboot your computer now to delete the file.

Once your computer reboots, the file will be deleted and the URL cache will be cleared.

Clearing visited Web sites history

Internet Explorer, by default, is configured to record all of the Web sites that you visit for a 30-day period. If you are concerned about your privacy, your browsing history should be cleaned frequently and history settings configured best for privacy. Doing so will ensure that any user of your computer will not be able to easily see what you have been doing. Keep in mind, however, that if you get rid of the browser history, you will eliminate the ability to use the history to go back to Web sites for which you might have forgotten the URL.

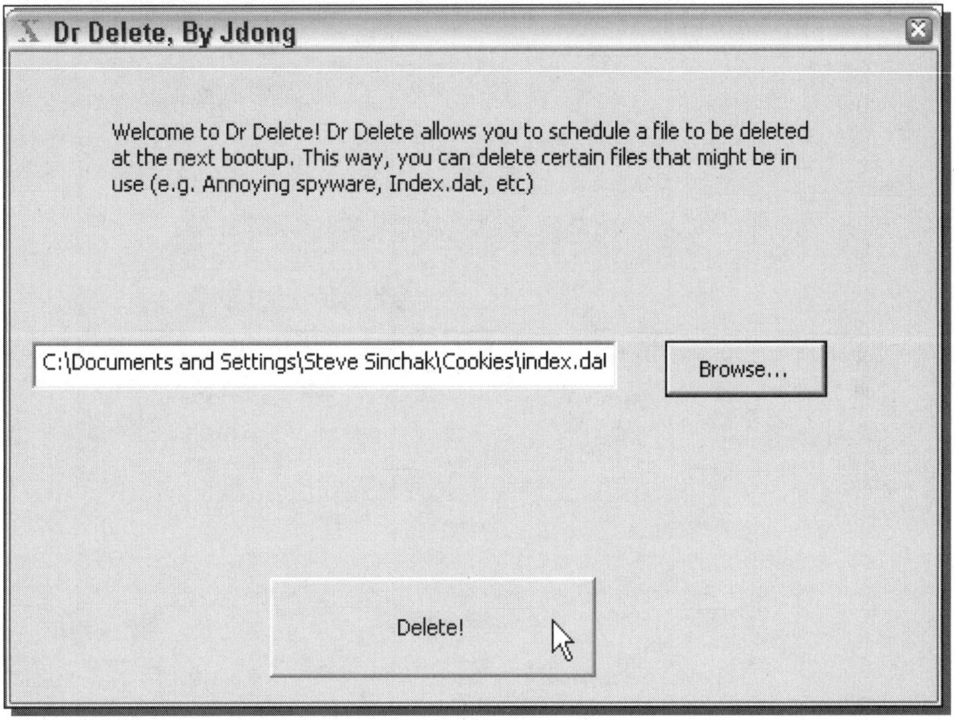

X Dr Delete, By Jdong

Welcome to Dr Delete! Dr Delete allows you to schedule a file to be deleted at the next bootup. This way, you can delete certain files that might be in use (e.g. Annoying spyware, Index.dat, etc)

C:\Documents and Settings\Steve Sinchak\Cookies\index.dat   Browse...

Delete!

FIGURE 14-1: Using Dr. Delete to delete the URL cache file.

That use is really the only reason I can think of that makes the browser history useful. If you can live without that convenience, then follow these steps to clear your history from your PC:

1. Open up a copy of Internet Explorer by using either the icon on the desktop or on the Start panel.

2. Once Internet Explorer is open, click the Tools menu bar item and select Internet Options.

3. Then, just click the Clear History button, as shown in Figure 14-2.

4. Your history will now be cleared. Because you still have Internet Options open on your screen, adjust the amount of days that your browsing history is stored.

5. As mentioned earlier, the default setting for this value is normally 30 days. Highlight the number in the days to keep pages in history box and type in **0** to maximize your privacy.

6. Then, click OK to save your changes and exit the Internet Options screen.

After you have cleared your browser history and modified the history setting, your privacy will be much easier to protect.

Figure 14-2: Clearing the browser history.

Clearing temporary Internet files and cookies

Every time you visit a Web site, the files for the Web page, such as the HTML and the images, are downloaded and stored in a temporary directory known as Temporary Internet Files. Over time, this directory can become full of images and HTML from various Web sites that you have visited. This directory can end up taking up a lot of space on your hard drive. Additionally, a user can browse your Temporary Internet Files directory and find out exactly what site you have been visiting just as if they were looking at your browser history. If you are concerned about your privacy, or just concerned about disk space, then clearing the Temporary Internet Files is a must.

Cookies are another item that is created on your computer when you visit a Web site. Contrary to popular belief, cookies are really not that bad. Most Web sites use them to save user data to a browser. One example of this is site preferences or automatic logon when you visit a Web site. The Webmaster of the Web site can detect if their Web site has already given you a cookie that has your user ID stored in it. If it finds one, then it knows exactly who you are and logs you on automatically. Advertisers also use cookies to store personal data. Instead of showing you the same advertisement 50 times, they use cookies to keep track of how many times an advertisement is displayed on your screen.

A common myth about cookies is that they allow Web sites to track other sites you visit. That is just not true. The only cost of having cookies on your computer is a privacy concern for local users. Any user that has physical access to your computer can browse to the directory that the cookies are stored and view what Web sites you visit because the cookies are named after the Web site that instructed your browser to put them on your computer.

Clearing the Temporary Internet Files and removing the cookies is a very simple task. Just follow these steps to clear these files:

1. Open up another copy of Internet Explorer.

2. Click Tools and then select Internet Options.

3. Under the Temporary Internet Files section, click the Delete Files button.

4. You will be prompted to confirm if you would also like offline files to be deleted. For maximum privacy, check the box and Click OK.

5. Once the files are erased, you will be shown the Internet Options screen again. Taking care of the cookies for your privacy is just as easy. Just click the Delete Cookies button.

6. Click OK on the confirmation screen.

7. Select OK once more to close Internet Options and you are done.

Now users will no longer be able to see what Web sites you visit from the cookies and Temporary Internet Files that are stored on your computer. Additionally, you will have freed up some disk space by deleting these files.

Adjusting your cookie security policy

As mentioned, cookies are not as bad a thing as some people in the computing world would like you to believe. Instead, the only real risk they present is a loss of some privacy, as mentioned earlier. If you allow your browser to be instructed to create cookies on your computer, then over time your PC would have quite a collection of them. Anyone who used your computer would then know what sites you visited, if they knew where the cookie files were located.

The latest version of Internet Explorer includes many new enhancements. One of the enhancements includes a new way of accepting cookies. Now, you have the ability to specify if you would like your browser to block all cookies or just certain types. To be able to use this new feature, you will have to understand what the two different types of cookies are: first- and third-party cookies. First-party cookies are placed on your computer by the current site that you are visiting. Third-party cookies are placed on your computer by remote sites such as advertisement servers.

If you do not want your computer to accept third-party cookies so that marketing companies cannot identify what ads they have shown you, or if you just want to adjust your cookie acceptance settings, then follow these steps:

1. Open up a copy of Internet Explorer.

2. Click the Tools menu bar item and select Internet Options.

3. When Internet Options loads, click the Privacy tab.

4. You will see the up-and-down slider that allows you to select different levels of cookie security. I recommend that you bypass this and just click the Advanced button instead.

5. Once you click the Advanced button and see the Advanced Privacy Settings window, check the box that says Override Automatic Cookie Handling.

6. Your settings for first- and third-party cookies will now be available for adjustment, as shown in Figure 14-3. I recommend that you always accept first-party cookies. You can decide if you want to block or select the prompt to accept third-party cookies. Prompt will pop up a dialog box notifying you that a cookies request has been received.

7. Once you are finished with your settings, click the OK button to save your changes and return to Internet Options.

8. Click OK once more to close Internet Options.

FIGURE 14-3: Adjusting the cookie privacy settings.

Now that you have set the cookie privacy setting manually, you can eliminate cookies from being stored on your hard drive in the first place. Doing so will allow you to protect your privacy and still be able to use Web sites that need cookies.

Saying no to encrypted Web pages

If you manage your finances or shop online, then you have probably had experience with using secure Web connections, otherwise known as SSL. These secure connections encrypt the data that is transferred from a Web server to your computer. Once the data gets to your computer, your browser has a special key that decrypts the information and displays it on your computer. During this process, when the file is decrypted, it is saved in the Temporary Internet Files directory so that the browser can display it.

This default appears to be harmless because the Web page is only saved on your computer. If no one has remote access to your computer, the data would be safe, right? Not necessarily, because your data is now vulnerable to anyone who has physical local access to your computer. If that person is clever and lucky enough, he or she can sort through your Temporary Internet Files directory to find confidential information, such as your online banking information. All of this information is saved by default on your hard drive for anyone to look at. They do not even need to know your password or even log into your account on the bank's Web site, because a snapshot of the Web page is stored locally on your computer.

What can you do to protect your computer from this vulnerability besides setting up better computer security such as complex passwords? There is a cool feature of Internet Explorer that you just have to turn on that will eliminate the problem completely. Simply called Do Not Save Encrypted Pages to Disk, this feature, when enabled, will solve your problems. To enable it, follow these steps:

1. Open up a copy of Internet Explorer.
2. Click Tools and select Internet Options.
3. Then, select the Advanced tab.
4. Scroll down through the list toward the bottom of the window until you see the Security section, as shown in Figure 14-4.
5. Locate Do Not Save Encrypted Pages to Disk, and check the box to the left of it.
6. Click OK to save and activate your changes.

Now you will no longer have to worry about pages that were encrypted being saved to your drive for anyone who has access to your computer to see.

Disabling AutoComplete

You already know about AutoComplete from the address bar. We have taken care of that privacy problem by clearing the file that stored the information, as was shown in the section about removing the address bar suggestions. However, that is not the only situation where AutoComplete attempts to provide assistance. Another situation where AutoComplete tries to

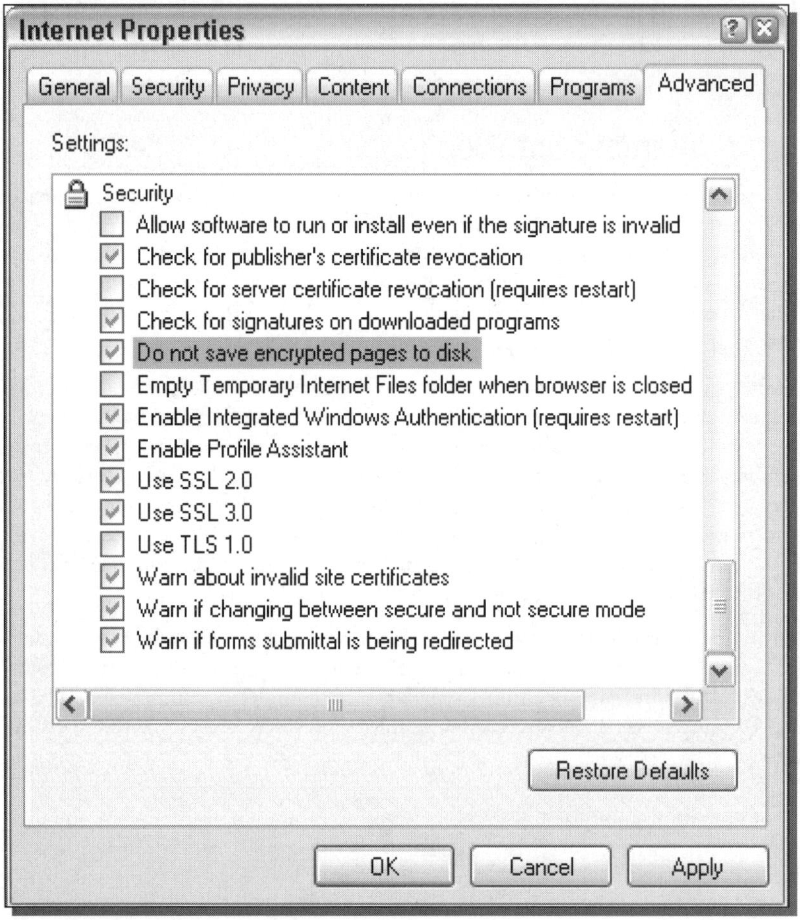

FIGURE: **14-4: Changing IE's security settings.**

give a helping hand is when you are filling in text boxes on Web pages. AutoComplete in this situation works exactly the same as AutoComplete with the address bar. As you begin to fill in the text box, several suggestions will appear, based on information that you have already typed in.

To get an idea how this works in action, visit a search site such as Google (www.google.com) and start to type in words for which you want to search. When you do so, words similar to the ones you have typed in the box on other visits to the site will appear. This capability allows anyone that uses your computer to be able to see what other users of the computer have searched for on the site, even if the browser history was cleared.

Clearly, having this feature enabled would be a big concern if you were concerned about your privacy. Disabling the AutoComplete feature is not very difficult and will completely take care of this privacy concern. Follow these steps to put an end to AutoComplete:

Internet Properties

General | Security | Privacy | Content | Connections | Programs | Advanced

Content Advisor

Ratings help you control the Internet content that can be viewed on this computer.

Enable...   Settings...

Certificates

Use certificates to positively identify yourself, certification authorities, and publishers.

Clear SSL State   Certificates...   Publishers...

Personal information

AutoComplete stores previous entries and suggests matches for you.

AutoComplete...

Microsoft Profile Assistant stores your personal information.

My Profile...

OK   Cancel   Apply

FIGURE **14-5: Adjusting the AutoComplete settings by entering AutoComplete settings.**

1. Open up an instance of Internet Explorer.

2. Click Tools and select Internet Options.

3. Select the Content tab and click the AutoComplete button, as shown in Figure 14-5.

4. Once the AutoComplete Settings window has loaded, just uncheck all of the boxes that are listed under Use AutoComplete For. This will disable this privacy concern completely.

5. Although you have the AutoComplete window open, you can also click the two clear buttons at the bottom of the window to clear any data that is in the file stores for this data.

6. When you are finished, just click the OK button to save your changes.

7. Select OK once more to close Internet Options and activate your changes.

AutoComplete is now a thing of the past. You will not have to worry about people using your computer being automatically shown all of the things that you type into your address and text boxes.

Clearing Temporary Internet Files automatically

Earlier, you learned how to clear your Temporary Internet Files so they will not be a privacy concern. Over time, your Temporary Internet Files folder will fill up again and once again become a privacy concern. One easy way to fix this is to use an interesting hidden feature of Internet Explorer that will automatically delete these files every time you close Internet Explorer. This way, you will not have to worry about clearing all of the files every time you use IE. Follow these steps to activate this great feature:

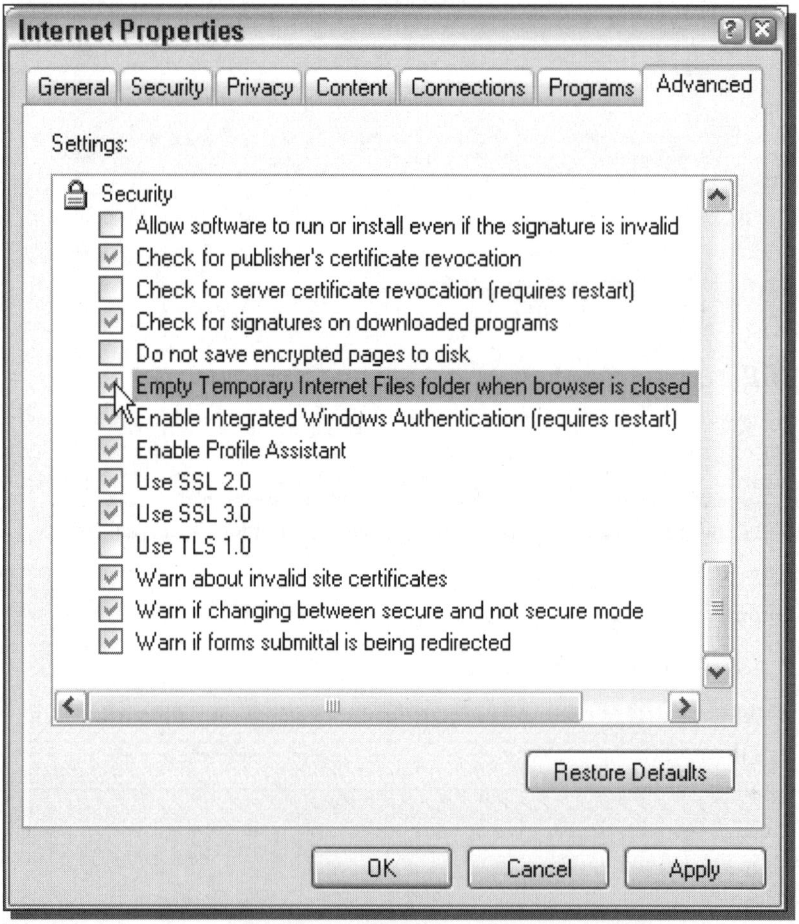

FIGURE 14-6: Setting up IE to automatically clear the Temporary Internet Files.

1. Open up a copy of Internet Explorer.

2. Click the Tools menu bar item and then select Internet Options.

3. Select the Advanced tab and scroll down to the bottom of the screen.

4. Locate and check Empty Temporary Internet Files Folder When Browser Is Closed, as shown in Figure 14-6.

5. Click OK to close Internet Options and activate your changes.

Enabling Automatic Empty is a great way to easily maintain a clean PC. Keep in mind that this will only delete your Temporary Internet Files and not your cookies. You will still have to delete the cookies using the method mentioned previously in this chapter.

Windows Interface

Once you have Internet Explorer under control, you can move on to cleaning the rest of the Windows interface. Just like Internet Explorer, Windows Explorer keeps track of the applications that you run and files that you open. It does this so it can tailor your computer to your personal use with features such as the frequently run programs list on the Start panel. Features like this are designed to speed up the use of your computer. However, the side effect of the convenience is a loss of privacy. These next few sections will show you how to recover your privacy, albeit at the expense of convenience.

Clearing Frequently Run Programs list

One of the great new features of Windows XP can also be a pain when you are concerned about your privacy. Being able to select the program that you use frequently directly on the Start panel instead of navigating through the entire Start Menu can save you some time. However, over time, this list can become cluttered with programs that you do not want. Additionally, anyone who uses your computer can easily see what programs you use.

If you are concerned about your privacy or just want to clear the list and start fresh, follow these steps :

1. Right-click the Start button and select Properties.

2. Click the Customize button next to Start Menu.

3. Under the Programs section, click the Clear List button, as shown in Figure 14-7.

4. Once you click the button, nothing seems to have happened. Don't worry; it has cleared your list so you do not need to keep clicking the button. Click OK when you are finished to close the Customize Start Menu window.

5. Then, click OK once more to close Taskbar and Start Menu Properties.

FIGURE **14-7: Clearing the program list on the Start panel.**

The program list is now clear and you can start from fresh building your list of frequently run programs.

Clearing the recently opened document list

Windows XP monitors all of the files that you open on your computer so it can construct the recently opened document list. This is designed to allow you to easily open up files that you have been working on. All types of documents are listed in this list. Every time you open up a Word document or a digital image, an entry is created within the list. Although this feature exists, I never find myself using it and the only value that it adds to my computer is a privacy concern.

Clearing the recently opened document list every once in a while is a good idea, so your documents are kept confidential and your privacy high. Clearing the list is very easy. Just follow these steps:

FIGURE **14-8: Clearing the recently opened document list.**

1. Right-click the Start button and select Properties.

2. Then click the Customize button next to the Start Menu radio button.

3. Once the Customize Start Menu window appears, click the Advanced tab.

4. Under the Recent Documents section, click the Clear List button, as shown in Figure 14-8.

5. Once you have cleared the list, click the OK button to close the Customize Start Menu window.

6. Then, click OK once more to close Taskbar and Start Menu Properties.

Removing temporary files from your hard drive

Over time, your hard drive can become cluttered with temporary files left behind from applications and the operating system. These files not only take up space, but they can be tracks of activity on your computer. Removing the temporary files is a great way to clean up any garbage information that was left behind; you'll then increase your privacy and also free up some disk space.

Windows has advanced greatly over the course of its existence. Back in the early versions of Windows, there was just one temp folder that all temp files were located in. With Windows XP, there are temp folders all over the place. To remove the files, you could go to all of the different folders and manually erase the files. This would work, but there is a better way.

To clear my temporary files from my hard drive, I like to use a program called TempCleaner. TempCleaner is a free application, written by Paul Wesson, that will automatically detect your temporary directory and delete all the files. With TempCleaner, you do not have to worry about where to navigate on your hard drive to delete the files. Instead, just execute the program. To get started using TempCleaner to clean your hard drive of temporary files, follow these directions:

1. Visit TempCleaner's Web site, located at www.ipaw.net/product_tempcleaner.php and download a copy.

2. Expand the archive and run the installer.

3. Once the installer has finished, just start up TempCleaner by clicking the Start Menu, expanding All Programs, and expanding the TempCleaner folder.

4. TempCleaner has a very simple interface. When it is running, you will just see a simple window that says Cleaning Up Your Temp Folder, as shown in Figure 14-9.

5. Once TempCleaner has finished, the screen will disappear. If you would like TempCleaner to remove files from other folders, such as the temp folder used by certain applications, this can be done within TempCleaner's options. The TempCleaner Options screen can be viewed by using the TempCleaner Options shortcut in the TempCleaner Start Menu folder.

6. Once the TempCleaner Options screen is loaded, just click the Folder button next to Add Folder and select the folder in which you want the files to be deleted. Click OK when you are finished.

7. Click OK and the TempCleaner Options window will close.

The next time you run TempCleaner, the folder(s) that you added will also be cleaned on top of the Windows temp folders. If you like to keep your computer clear of temp files for

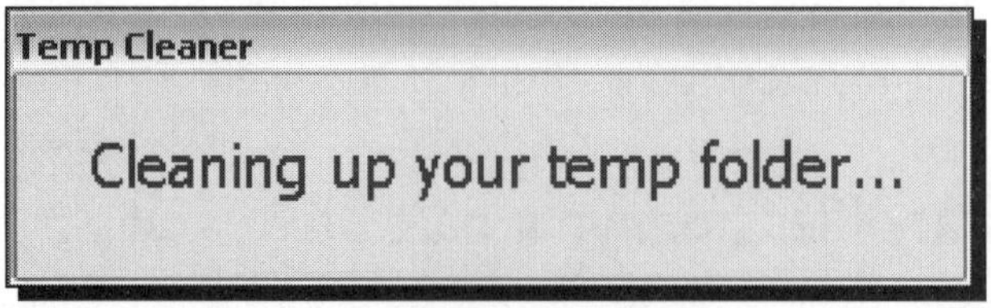

FIGURE 14-9: TempCleaner removing temp files.

maximum privacy and disk space, add the TempCleaner shortcut to your startup folder in the Start Menu so that it is run every time you turn your computer on.

Removing saved passwords

When you visit a Web site that requires authentication or attempt to connect to remote computers, you are given the option to save your password so that the next time you visit the page or attempt to access a remote resource, you do not have to reenter your password. This feature can be a huge convenience, especially if you access a particular Web site or resource frequently. The downside to this convenience is the potential for horrible security and privacy problems. Essentially, you are taking the password off all of the sites and resources for which you saved a password. Anyone who has physical access to your computer can get in using your username and password, even if they do not know your password.

Removing your saved passwords from your computer is a very good idea, because doing so will protect your accounts and also increase your accounts privacy. Removing the password is a little tricky in Window XP because there is no easy way to access a list of all the accounts that have passwords stored for them within Control Panel or any other user interface element. Fortunately, there is a great hack that will do just that.

Hidden away in the keymgr.dll system file is an interface for viewing stored usernames and passwords. To use this interface, follow these steps:

1. Click the Start Menu and select Run.

2. Type in **rundll32.exe keymgr.dll,KRShowKeyMgr.**

3. The Stored User Names and Passwords window will load, showing you a list of all of the accounts that are saved on your computer, as shown in Figure 14-10.

4. To remove a saved password, select the account on the list and click the Remove button.

5. Click OK on the Confirm screen and the account will be removed from the list, erasing your stored password.

6. Repeat the previous steps for any other accounts that you want to remove.

7. When you are finished, just click Close.

You can also use the Stored User Names and Passwords window to add more usernames and passwords to your computer. If you have a Web site or resource and you do not care about your privacy, such as some news Web site, and you are running Windows XP Professional, then just click the Add button when the Stored User Names and Passwords window is loaded.

Setting file and folder permissions

Windows XP Professional boxes running the NTFS file system have the capability to set individual file permissions on both files and folders. File and folder permissions allow you to

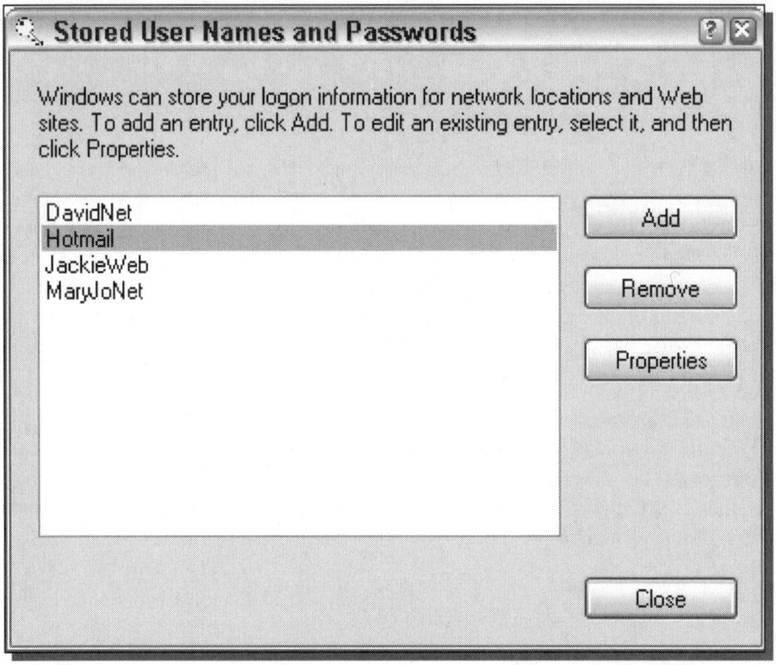

Stored User Names and Passwords

Windows can store your logon information for network locations and Web sites. To add an entry, click Add. To edit an existing entry, select it, and then click Properties.

DavidNet
Hotmail
JackieWeb
MaryJoNet

Add

Remove

Properties

Close

FIGURE 14-10: The Stored User Names and Passwords administration screen.

specify exactly who will be able to read, write, execute, and even list or access a folder. So, file and folder permissions can be a very powerful tool to protect your data from others' eyes.

Tip   If your file system is FAT32, then you will not be able to set permissions. Fortunately, an easy way exists for you to convert your FAT32 file system to NTFS. Do a search in the Windows Help and Support Center for Convert to NTFS and you will be shown directions on how you can go about converting your drive's file system.

Setting the permissions on with a lot of control requires you to disable simple file sharing and security. To do so, follow these steps:

1. Open up any folder on your computer and expand the Tools menu and select Folder Options.

2. Click the View tab and scroll to the bottom of the Advanced Settings box.

3. Uncheck the Use Simple File Sharing option at the bottom of the list.

4. Click OK, and you are finished restoring full control over your file permissions.

Now that you have disabled simple file sharing, you can proceed and easily configure the permissions on any file or folder that you desire. Setting the permissions is very easy once you do it a few times. Follow these directions to set the permissions to maximize your privacy:

1. Right-click any file or folder for which you want to modify permissions and select Properties.

2. Then, click the Security tab. (When simple file sharing was enabled, this tab did not exist.)

3. First, remove all users from the group or username list to whom you do not want to give access. It is a good idea to remove the Everyone group because this does include everyone that can access your computer. However, make sure that you do not accidentally remove your username from the list. Also watch out for the SYSTEM account. This is one account that the operating system uses to access files. Removing it may cause unexpected results. But, fortunately, if the system actually does need it, you can always add it again if you remove it and it causes problems.

Tip If you are having difficulties removing users from the username list, this could be because the user is inherited from a parent folder. Permissions are passed down to all subfolders and files. If you want a user to have access to a folder but not its subfolders, then you will have to click the Advanced button on the security tab of the Properties window. Once the Advanced Security Settings window loads, uncheck the option that says Inherit from Parent the Permission Entries that Apply to Child Objects. A Security notification box will pop up. Click the Remove button to remove all of the inherited permissions so that you can have full control of the folder.

4. Now that you have the list of users and groups taken care of, set the specific permissions that the user has on the file or folder. Select the name of the user that you want to modify, then check the corresponding boxes in the Permissions For list for the activities that you want them to be able to do, as shown in Figure 4-11.

5. When you have finished setting the permissions for all of the users, click OK to exit the Permissions screen.

Once you have set the permissions for all of sensitive directories, you will have greatly increased your security and privacy. Also keep in mind that file permissions are inherited. Every folder within a folder inherits the permissions of the parent folder unless they are specifically removed. Therefore, if you set the file permissions for a folder, all of the subfolders and files will be automatically set with the same permissions. File and folder permissions can be very useful. If you have a program on your computer that you do not want anyone else running, simply set the permissions on that folder so that only you can read and execute.

Encrypting Files

Another cool feature of Windows XP Professional's NTFS file system is its ability to encrypt files. Permissions on files and folders work well to protect them when the operating system is running. However, if special software and hardware are used, the raw data can be accessed on the hard drive. With the absence of the operating system running to protect its data, anyone can very easily lift the data off the drive no matter what permissions were set on the file. Such software and hardware is usually expensive and primarily used by data recovery companies and law enforcement agencies.

To protect your computer's files and folders from conventional recovery methods, you can encrypt the files. Doing so will scramble and encode the data within the files so that the only

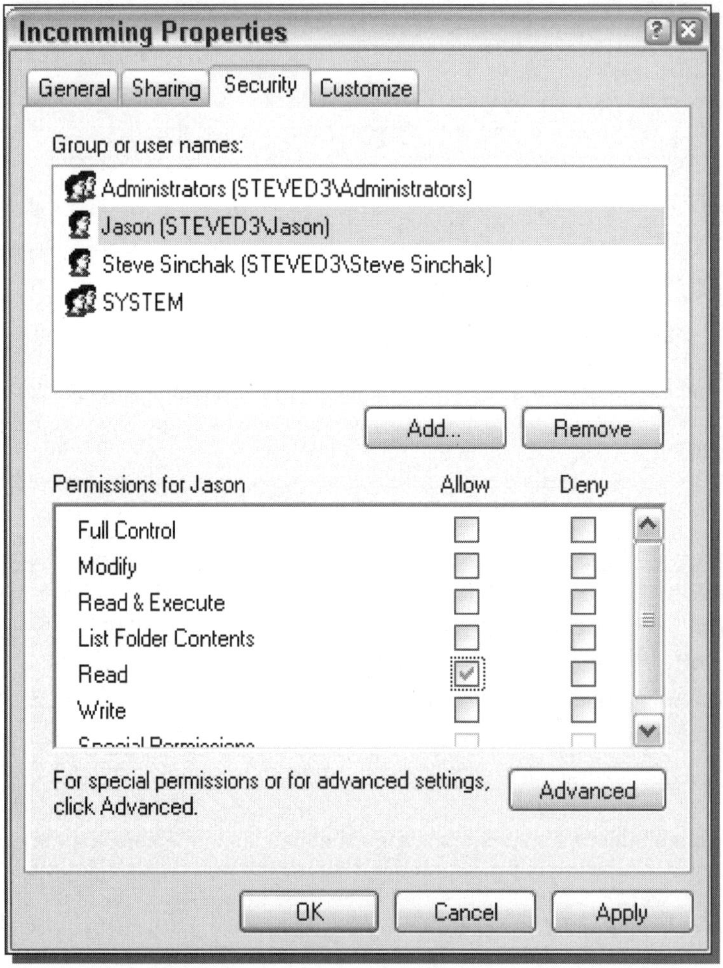

FIGURE **14-11: Adjusting the permissions for Jason. Jason now only has permission to read files in the incoming folder.**

data lifted off the hard drive with recovery tools when the operating system is not running will be scrambled garbage.

Encrypting files is not just for personal use. If you work for a company that has very sensitive information on their computers and laptops, you would be wise to encrypt the folders and files that contain important and confidential data. If you do so, the confidential information is a lot less likely to get out in the open should the hardware ever be stolen.

Before I go any further, I should mention that encrypting files is not always 100 percent secure. All files that are encrypted can eventually be cracked. It is only a matter of time before a high-speed computer that is trying every possible encryption key finds the correct key. Nevertheless, there are millions, if not billions, of possible keys. As you can imagine, even with the fastest computers in the world, cracking the key will take some time (several, if not hundreds of years). But there always is the chance that someone could randomly pick the correct key, although the odds of that happening are about equal to winning the lottery twice in your lifetime.

Now that you know about how encrypting files can help your privacy and security, get started encrypting files. Encrypting a file is as simple as changing a file attribute. Follow these steps to tell Windows to encrypt a file:

1. Right-click a file or folder and select Properties.

2. Then, click the Advanced button next to Attributes.

3. The Advanced Attribute window will load. Check the box to enable encryption, as shown in Figure 4-12.

4. Click OK to return to save your change.

5. Select OK once more to close the Properties window and activate encryption.

Once all of your sensitive files are encrypted, your privacy and security are greatly increased. Setting your file permissions and enabling encryption is the perfect combination for protecting your sensitive files.

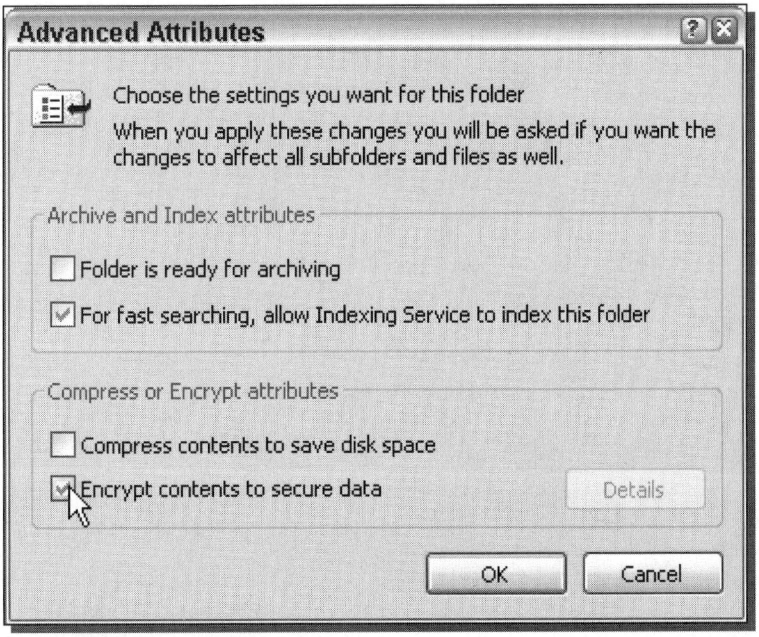

FIGURE 14-12: Enabling encryption.

Summary

Throughout this chapter, you found out how to increase your privacy with Internet Explorer. Because Internet Explorer records so many pieces of your browsing experience, that information can leave yourself open to huge threats to your privacy. To fight that, you need to remove histories of sites browsed and addresses entered, as shown earlier in the chapter. Then, you learned how to delete cookies, as well as how to set up Internet Explorer to clean itself.

The second part of the chapter addressed the privacy concerns of the Windows interface. Just like Internet Explorer, Windows records many of our computer activities. Clearing those records has become an essential part of protecting your privacy. First, you found out how to clean up Windows. Then, you learned about ways to protect your privacy further with the help of permissions and encryption. If you follow all of the tips outlined in this chapter, you will have no problem creating a secure system.

You have now finished *Hacking Windows XP.* You were shown how to customize everything that can be customized in Windows XP in Part I. Now you know how to make your computer look and feel completely different. In Part II, you were shown how to speed up all the different stages of Windows XP. From the boot up to the speed of your applications, you were given tips to optimize the performance of your computer. Part III shifted into the hot topic of securing Windows XP. You learned how to protect your computer from attackers, defend against spyware, adware, and viruses, and protect your privacy. Now that you are done with this last chapter, you have finished the most complete guide ever written to fully optimize and improve your Windows XP experience.

What's on the CD-ROM

This appendix provides you with information on the contents of the CD that accompanies this book. For the latest and greatest information, please refer to the ReadMe file located at the root of the CD. Here is what you will find:

- System requirements
- Using the CD with Windows XP
- What's on the CD
- Troubleshooting

System Requirements

Make sure that your computer meets the minimum system requirements listed in this section. If your computer doesn't match up to most of these requirements, you may have a problem using the contents of the CD.

- A PC running Windows XP Professional or Windows XP Home edition.
- At least 128 MB of total RAM installed on your computer; for best performance, we recommend at least 256 MB.
- An Ethernet network interface card (NIC) or modem with a speed of at least 28,800 bps.
- A CD-ROM drive.

Using the CD with Windows XP

To install the items from the CD to your hard drive, follow these steps:

1. Insert the CD into your computer's CD-ROM drive.

2. The CD-ROM interface will appear. The interface provides a simple point-and-click way to explore the contents of the CD.

If the CD-ROM interface does not appear, follow these steps to access the CD:

1. Click the Start button on the left end of the taskbar and then choose Run from the menu that pops up.

2. In the dialog box that appears, type *d:*\setup.exe. (If your CD-ROM drive is not drive d, fill in the appropriate letter in place of *d*.) This brings up the CD Interface described in the preceding set of steps.

What's on the CD

The following sections provide a summary of the software and other materials you'll find on the CD.

Author-created materials

All author-created material from the book, including registry files, are organized on the CD in chapter folders.

Applications

The following applications are on the CD:

AVG Anti-Virus, from Grisoft USA

Freeware version for Windows XP.
Description: AVG Anti-Virus is a great AV application that will protect your computer from viruses for free. Chapter 13 will show you how to get this application up and running on your box. For more information, check out www.grisoft.com/us/us_dwnl_free.php.

Bitstrip

Freeware version for Windows XP.
Description: Bitstrip is a cool app that will allow you to convert an animated GIF image file into a framed bitmap file that you can use to change the internet explorer animated logo as shown in chapter 6. For more information, visit
www.virtualplastic.net/redllar/bitstrip.html.

O&O Defrag Professional, from O&O Software

Shareware version for Windows XP.
Description: O&O defrag is a great file system defragmentation utility that will help you optimize the location of the files on your hard drive including optimization of the boot files as is discussed in chapter 8. For more information, visit www.oo-software.com.

PCMark04, from Futuremark Corporation

Free feature-limited version for Windows XP.
Description: PCMark 04 is one of the most popular benchmarking programs for the PC. It will run various tests on your computer simulating everyday activities and will then assign an overall score that you can compare to other computers on the web. Chapter 7 will help you get PCMark 04 running on your computer. For more information, visit www.futuremark.com.

Sandra Standard, from SiSoftware

Free feature-limited version for Windows XP.
Description: Sandra Standard is a benchmarking and information suite. It provides several different benchmarking tests as well as boatloads of system stats. Chapter 7 will show you how to use Sandra Standard. Visit www.sisoftware.co.uk for more information.

Spybot Search & Destroy

Freeware version for Windows XP.
Description: Spybot S & D is one of the most popular applications for detecting and removing spyware from your computer. Chapter 13 will show you how you can use this great app to remove spyware from your computer. For more information, visit www.safer-networking.org.

Style Builder, from TGT Software

30-day trial version for Windows XP.
Description: Style builder is used to create visual styles for use with Windows XP's built-in visual style engine. Directions on its use can be found in Chapter 4. For more information, visit www.tgtsoft.com/prod_sxp.php.

Style XP, from TGT Software

30-day trial version for Windows XP.
Description: Style XP provides an easy way to use visual styles without having to patch Windows XP's visual style engine. Directions on its use can be found in Chapter 4. For more information, check out www.tgtsoft.com/prod_sb.php.

WinTasks 4 Professional, from Uniblue Systems Ltd.

Trial version for Windows XP.
Description: WinTasks 4 Professional is a task manager on steroids. It provides normal running process information as well as the ability to increase and decrease performance, profiles, priorities, and respond to system events. Chapter 11 shows how to use WinTasks. For more information, visit www.liutilities.com/products/wintaskspro/.

Bonus Applications

The following bonus applications provided by Joel Diamond and Howard Sobel of the Windows Users Group Network (www.WUGNET.com) are on the CD in the bonus folder. These bonus applications will help you get even more out of Windows XP by providing you with useful tools to hack your computer and add cool new features and effects that will make

Title	Filename
3DNA Screensaver	3DNA.exe
3DNA Screensaver software provided courtesy of 3DNA.™	
AccountLogon Password Manager	Account_Logon.exe
AccountLogon Password Manager software provided courtesy of Rhodes Software Pty Ltd.	
Advanced System Optimizer	AdvancedSystemOptimizer.exe
AlphaXP Transparency Effects	AlphaXP.exe
AlphaXP Transparency Effects software provided courtesy of ZeroHero Software.	
AutoFTP Manager	AutoFTP.exe
AutoPilot XP	AutopilotXP.exe
AutoPilot XP software provided courtesy of Sunbelt Software.	
BoostXP	BoosterXP.exe
Cache Boost Pro	CacheBoostPro.exe
CompreXX	Comprexx.exe
CompreXX software provided courtesy of MimarSinan International.	
CyberScrub ES Pro	CyberScrubPro.exe
CyberScrub software provided courtesy of CyberScrub LLC. CyberScrub is a registered trademark of CyberScrub LLC. All rights reserved.	
Digital Media Converter	DigitalMediaConvertor.exe
DiskTriage Free Space Manager	DiskTriage.exe
DiskTriage Free Space Manager software provided courtesy of TimeAcct Information Systems.	
Downshift Download Manager	Downshift.exe
Downshift software provided courtesy of Rose City Software.	
ExplorerPlus	ExplorerPlus.exe
ExplorerPlus software provided courtesy of Novatix™ Corporation.	
Fantasy Moon 3D Screensaver	FantasyMoon3D.exe
Fantasy Moon 3D Screensaver software provided courtesy of 3PlaneSoft.	
FeedDemon RSS Reader	FeedDemon.exe
FeedDemon RSS Reader software provided courtesy of Bradbury Software, LLC.	
FolderMatch	FolderMatch.zip
FolderMatch software provided courtesy of Salty Brine Software.	

Title	Filename
FTP Voyager	FTPVoyager.exe
FTP Voyager software provided courtesy of Rhino Software, Inc.	
Galleon 3D Screensaver	Galleon.exe
Galleon Screensaver software provided courtesy of 3PlaneSoft.	
GhostSurf Pro Privacy Protector	GhostSurfPro.exe
MoveMe File Transfer Wizard	MoveMe.exe
MoveMe File Transfer Wizard software provided courtesy of Spearit Software, Inc.	
Multi Desktop 2003	MultiDesktop2003.exe
Multi Desktop 2003 software provided courtesy of Gamers Tower, Inc.	
Nautilus 3D Screensaver	Nautilus.exe
Nautilus 3D Screensaver software provided courtesy of 3PlaneSoft.	
Open+	OpenPlus.exe
Open+ software provided courtesy of Capio Corporation.	
PC Booster	PCBooster.exe
PC Booster software provided courtesy of inKline Global, Inc.	
Registry Compactor	RegComp.exe
Registry Compactor software provided courtesy of Rose City Software.	
Registry First Aid	RegistryFirstAid.exe
Registry First Aid software provided courtesy of Rose City Software.	
Registry Mechanic	RegistryMechanic.exe
Registry Mechanic software provided courtesy of GuideWorks Pty Ltd.	
SOS Data Protection Recovery	SOS_Data_Protection_Recovery.zip
SOS Data Protection Recovery software provided courtesy of DataTex Engineering.	
SnagIT Screen Capture	SnagIT.exe
Spirit of Fire 3D Screensaver	SpiritofFire3D.exe
Spirit of Fire 3D Screensaver software provided courtesy of 3PlaneSoft.	
Sticky Notes	StickyNotes.exe
System Mechanic	SystemMechanic.exe
System Mechanic software provided courtesy of iolo technologies, LLC.	

Continued

Title	Filename
System Sentry	SystemSentry.exe
System Sentry software provided courtesy of Easy Desk Software, Inc.	
Tuneup Utilities 2004	Tuneup_Utilities.exe
TweakMaster Pro	TweakmasterPro.exe
TweakMaster Pro software provided courtesy of Rose City Software.	
Watermill 3D Screensaver	Watermill3D.exe
Watermill 3D Screensaver software provided courtesy of 3PlaneSoft.	
WinGuide Tweak Manager	WinGuideTweakManager.exe
Your Uninstaller 2004 Pro	YourUninstaller2004Pro.exe
Your Uninstaller 2004 Pro software provided courtesy of URSoft, Inc.	

XP look and act better. Howard and Joel worked very hard to get the permissions together for distributing this software last minute. Without them, the bonus applications would not exist. Thanks guys!

Shareware programs are fully functional, trial versions of copyrighted programs. If you like particular programs, register with their authors for a nominal fee and receive licenses, enhanced versions, and technical support. *Freeware programs* are copyrighted games, applications, and utilities that are free for personal use. Unlike shareware, these programs do not require a fee or provide technical support. *GNU software* is governed by its own license, which is included inside the folder of the GNU product. See the GNU license for more details.

Trial, demo, or evaluation versions are usually limited either by time or functionality (such as being unable to save projects). Some trial versions are very sensitive to system date changes. If you alter your computer's date, the programs will "time out" and will no longer be functional.

eBook version of Hacking Windows XP

The complete text of this book is on the CD in Adobe's Portable Document Format (PDF). You can read and search through the file with the Adobe Acrobat Reader (also included on the CD).

Troubleshooting

If you have difficulty installing or using any of the materials on the companion CD, try the following solutions:

- **Turn off any anti-virus software that you may have running.** Installers sometimes mimic virus activity and can make your computer incorrectly believe that it is being infected by a virus. (Be sure to turn the anti-virus software back on later.)

- **Close all running programs.** The more programs you're running, the less memory is available to other programs. Installers also typically update files and programs; if you keep other programs running, installation may not work properly.

- **Reference the ReadMe:** Please refer to the ReadMe file located at the root of the CD-ROM for the latest product information at the time of publication.

If you still have trouble with the CD, please call the Wiley Customer Care phone number: (800) 762-2974. Outside the United States, call 1 (317) 572-3994. You can also contact Wiley Customer Service on the web at www.wiley.com/techsupport. Wiley will provide technical support only for installation and other general quality control items; for technical support on the applications themselves, consult the program's vendor or author.

Index

Wiley Publishing, Inc.
End-User License Agreement

READ THIS. You should carefully read these terms and conditions before opening the software packet(s) included with this book "Book". This is a license agreement "Agreement" between you and Wiley Publishing, Inc. "WPI". By opening the accompanying software packet(s), you acknowledge that you have read and accept the following terms and conditions. If you do not agree and do not want to be bound by such terms and conditions, promptly return the Book and the unopened software packet(s) to the place you obtained them for a full refund.

1. License Grant. WPI grants to you (either an individual or entity) a nonexclusive license to use one copy of the enclosed software program(s) (collectively, the "Software") solely for your own personal or business purposes on a single computer (whether a standard computer or a workstation component of a multi-user network). The Software is in use on a computer when it is loaded into temporary memory (RAM) or installed into permanent memory (hard disk, CD-ROM, or other storage device). WPI reserves all rights not expressly granted herein.

2. Ownership. WPI is the owner of all right, title, and interest, including copyright, in and to the compilation of the Software recorded on the disk(s) or CD-ROM "Software Media". Copyright to the individual programs recorded on the Software Media is owned by the author or other authorized copyright owner of each program. Ownership of the Software and all proprietary rights relating thereto remain with WPI and its licensers.

3. Restrictions on Use and Transfer.

    (a) You may only (i) make one copy of the Software for backup or archival purposes, or (ii) transfer the Software to a single hard disk, provided that you keep the original for backup or archival purposes. You may not (i) rent or lease the Software, (ii) copy or reproduce the Software through a LAN or other network system or through any computer subscriber system or bulletin-board system, or (iii) modify, adapt, or create derivative works based on the Software.

    (b) You may not reverse engineer, decompile, or disassemble the Software. You may transfer the Software and user documentation on a permanent basis, provided that the transferee agrees to accept the terms and conditions of this Agreement and you retain no copies. If the Software is an update or has been updated, any transfer must include the most recent update and all prior versions.

4. Restrictions on Use of Individual Programs. You must follow the individual requirements and restrictions detailed for each individual program in the About the CD-ROM appendix of this Book. These limitations are also contained in the individual license agreements recorded on the Software Media. These limitations may include a requirement that after using the program for a specified period of time, the user must pay a registration fee or discontinue use. By opening the Software packet(s), you will be agreeing to abide by the licenses and restrictions for these individual programs that are detailed in the About the CD-ROM appendix and on the Software Media. None of the material on this Software Media or listed in this Book may ever be redistributed, in original or modified form, for commercial purposes.

5. Limited Warranty.

    (a) WPI warrants that the Software and Software Media are free from defects in materials and workmanship under normal use for a period of sixty (60) days from the date of purchase of this Book. If WPI receives notification within the warranty period of defects in materials or workmanship, WPI will replace the defective Software Media.

(b) WPI AND THE AUTHOR(S) OF THE BOOK DISCLAIM ALL OTHER WAR-RANTIES, EXPRESS OR IMPLIED, INCLUDING WITHOUT LIMITATION IMPLIED WARRANTIES OF MERCHANTABILITY AND FITNESS FOR A PARTICULAR PURPOSE, WITH RESPECT TO THE SOFTWARE, THE PROGRAMS, THE SOURCE CODE CONTAINED THEREIN, AND/OR THE TECHNIQUES DESCRIBED IN THIS BOOK. WPI DOES NOT WARRANT THAT THE FUNCTIONS CONTAINED IN THE SOFTWARE WILL MEET YOUR REQUIREMENTS OR THAT THE OPERATION OF THE SOFTWARE WILL BE ERROR FREE.

(c) This limited warranty gives you specific legal rights, and you may have other rights that vary from jurisdiction to jurisdiction.

6. Remedies.

(a) WPI's entire liability and your exclusive remedy for defects in materials and workmanship shall be limited to replacement of the Software Media, which may be returned to WPI with a copy of your receipt at the following address: Software Media Fulfillment Department, Attn.: Hacking Windows® XP, Wiley Publishing, Inc., 10475 Crosspoint Blvd., Indianapolis, IN 46256, or call 1-800-762-2974. Please allow four to six weeks for delivery. This Limited Warranty is void if failure of the Software Media has resulted from accident, abuse, or misapplication. Any replacement Software Media will be warranted for the remainder of the original warranty period or thirty (30) days, whichever is longer.

(b) In no event shall WPI or the author be liable for any damages whatsoever (including without limitation damages for loss of business profits, business interruption, loss of business information, or any other pecuniary loss) arising from the use of or inability to use the Book or the Software, even if WPI has been advised of the possibility of such damages.

(c) Because some jurisdictions do not allow the exclusion or limitation of liability for consequential or incidental damages, the above limitation or exclusion may not apply to you.

7. U.S. Government Restricted Rights. Use, duplication, or disclosure of the Software for or on behalf of the United States of America, its agencies and/or instrumentalities "U.S. Government" is subject to restrictions as stated in paragraph (c)(1)(ii) of the Rights in Technical Data and Computer Software clause of DFARS 252.227-7013, or subparagraphs (c) (1) and (2) of the Commercial Computer Software - Restricted Rights clause at FAR 52.227-19, and in similar clauses in the NASA FAR supplement, as applicable.

8. General. This Agreement constitutes the entire understanding of the parties and revokes and supersedes all prior agreements, oral or written, between them and may not be modified or amended except in a writing signed by both parties hereto that specifically refers to this Agreement. This Agreement shall take precedence over any other documents that may be in conflict herewith. If any one or more provisions contained in this Agreement are held by any court or tribunal to be invalid, illegal, or otherwise unenforceable, each and every other provision shall remain in full force and effect.